The Book of Dembitz (Dębica, Poland)

Translation of *Sefer Dembitz*

Original Yizkor Book:

Edited by: D. Leibl

Published by Association of Former Residents of Debica

Published in Tel Aviv, 1960 (Hebrew and Yiddish, 204 pages)

Published by JewishGen

**An Affiliate of the Museum of Jewish Heritage - A Living Memorial to the Holocaust
New York**

The Book of Dembitz (Dębica, Poland)
Translation of *Sefer Dembitz*

Copyright © 2016 by JewishGen, Inc.
All rights reserved.
First Printing: March 2016, Adar 1 5776
Second Printing: March 2019, Adar II 5779

Translation Project Coordinators: Marc Seidenfeld and Aviva Weintraub
Translator: Jerrold Landau
Layout: Alan Roth
Image Editor: Jan R. Fine and Larry Gaum
Cover Design: Nili Goldman
Map of Poland: Jan R. Fine
Indexing: Debbie Terman

Published by JewishGen, Inc.
An Affiliate of the Museum of Jewish Heritage
A Living Memorial to the Holocaust
36 Battery Place, New York, NY 10280

"JewishGen, Inc. is not responsible for inaccuracies or omissions in the original work and makes no representations regarding the accuracy of this translation. Digital images of the original book's contents can be seen online at the New York Public Library Web site."

The mission of the JewishGen organization is to produce a translation of the original work and we cannot verify the accuracy of statements or alter facts cited.

Printed in the United States of America by Lightning Source, Inc.

Library of Congress Control Number (LCCN): 2015944047
ISBN: 978-1-939561-35-0 (hard cover: 406 pages, alk. paper)

Front Cover photograph: Courtesy of Dr. Shosh Millet

JewishGen and the Yizkor-Books-in-Print Project

This book has been published by the **Yizkor-Books-in-Print Project,** as part of the **Yizkor Book Project** of **JewishGen, Inc**.

JewishGen, Inc. is a non-profit organization founded in 1987 as a resource for Jewish genealogy. Its website [www.jewishgen.org] serves as an international clearinghouse and resource center to assist individuals who are researching the history of their Jewish families and the places where they lived. JewishGen provides databases, facilitates discussion groups, and coordinates projects relating to Jewish genealogy and the history of the Jewish people. In 2003, JewishGen became an affiliate of the **Museum of Jewish Heritage - A Living Memorial to the Holocaust** in New York.

The **JewishGen Yizkor Book Project** was organized to make more widely known the existence of Yizkor (Memorial) Books written by survivors and former residents of various Jewish communities throughout the world. Later, volunteers connected to the different destroyed communities began cooperating to have these books translated from the original language—usually Hebrew or Yiddish—into English, thus enabling a wider audience to have access to the valuable information contained within them. As each chapter of these books was translated, it was posted on the JewishGen website and made available to the general public.

The **Yizkor-Books-in-Print Project** began in 2011 as an initiative to print and publish Yizkor Books that had been fully translated, so that hard copies would be available for purchase by the descendants of these communities and also by scholars, universities, synagogues, libraries, and museums.

These Yizkor books have been produced almost entirely through the volunteer effort of researchers from around the world, assisted by donations from private individuals. The books are printed and sold at near cost, so as to make them as affordable as possible. Our goal is to make this important genre of Jewish literature and history available in English in book form, so that people can have the personal histories of their ancestral towns on their bookshelves for themselves and for their children and grandchildren.

A list of all published translated Yizkor Books in the project with prices and ordering information can be found at:
http://www.jewishgen.org/Yizkor/ybip.html

Lance Ackerfeld, Yizkor Book Project Manager

Joel Alpert, Yizkor-Book-in-Print Project Coordinator

JewishGen
Yizkor Book Project

This book is presented by the
Yizkor Books in Print Project
Project Coordinator: Joel Alpert

Part of the
Yizkor Books Project of JewishGen, Inc.
Project Manager: Lance Ackerfeld

These books have been produced solely through volunteer effort
of individuals from around the world. The books are printed and
sold at near cost, so as to make them as affordable as possible.

Our goal is to make this history and important genre of Jewish
literature available in English in book form so that people can have
the near-personal histories of their ancestral towns on their bookshelves for themselves and for their children and grandchildren.

Any donations to the Yizkor Books Project are appreciated.

Please send donations to:
Yizkor Book Project
JewishGen
36 Battery Place
New York, NY 10280

JewishGen, Inc. is an affiliate of the
Museum of Jewish Heritage
A Living Memorial to the Holocaust

Title Page of Original Yizkor Book

סֵפֶר דֶמְבִּיץ

הוצאת ארגון יוצאי דמביץ בישראל

תש״ך   ●   תל־אביב   ●   1960

Translation of the Title Page of Original Yizkor Book

The Book of Dembitz

Published by Association of Former Residents of Debica

Published in Tel Aviv, 1960

Acknowledgements

Special thanks to the National Yiddish Book Center in Amherst, Massachusetts and the New York Public Library for supplying the high resolution images used in this book.

Our sincere appreciation to Mayer Goldman and Menachem Ofer, of the Dembica Landmanshaft in Israel, for permission to put this material on the JewishGen web site and publish this translation.

Special acknowledgement to Jerrold Landau for his superb English translation and thorough foot notes.

Thanks to Dr. Shosh Millet for the image used on the front cover and for the story behind that photograph.

BALTIC SEA

LITHUANIA

RUSSIA

Vilnius

POLAND

BELARUS

GERMANY

Poznan

Warsaw

Lodz

Dembitz

Prague

CZECH REPUBLIC

Krakow

UKRAINE

SLOVAKIA

250 miles

0

0   250 Km   500 Km

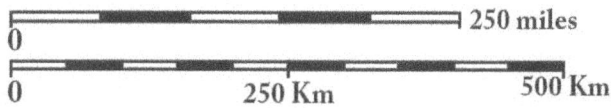

POLAND - Current Borders

Map of Dembitz in Current Borders of Poland

Created by Jan R. Fine

Geopolitical Information:

Alternate names for the town are: Dębica [Polish], Dembitz [Yiddish, German], Debitsa, Dembica, Dembits, Dembitsa, Dembiza

Region: Krakow

Dembitz is located at 50°03' North Latitude and 21°25' East Longitude.

	Town	District	Province	Country
Before WWI (c. 1900):	Dębica	Ropczyce	Galicia	Austrian Empire
Between the wars (c. 1930):	Dębica	Ropczyce	Kraków	Poland
After WWII (c. 1950):	Dębica			Poland
Today (c. 2000):	Dębica			Poland

Nearby Jewish Communities:

Pilzno 8 miles SW
Ropczyce 9 miles E
Przecław 11 miles NNE
Wielopole Skrzyńskie 11 miles SE
Brzostek 12 miles S
Radomyśl Wielki 12 miles NNW
Sędziszów Małopolski 13 miles E
Jodłowa 14 miles SSW
Rzochów 14 miles NNE
Mielec 16 miles N
Kołaczyce 16 miles S
Radgoszcz 17 miles NW
Ryglice 17 miles SW
Frysztak 17 miles SSE
Wampierzów 18 miles NNW
Tuchów 19 miles WSW
Tarnów 19 miles W
Zgłobień 19 miles E
Czudec 20 miles ESE
Kolbuszowa 21 miles NE
Dąbrowa Tarnowska 21 miles WNW
Jasło 21 miles S
Strzyżów 21 miles SE

Biecz 23 miles SSW
Widełka 23 miles ENE
Borowa 23 miles N
Szczucin 23 miles NW
Sadkowa-Góra 23 miles N
Żabno 24 miles WNW
Rzepiennik Strzyżewski 24 miles SW
Gromnik 24 miles SW
Niebylec 25 miles ESE
Radłów 25 miles W
Jedlicze 25 miles SSE
Głogów Małopolski 25 miles ENE
Rzeszów 26 miles E
Wojnicz 27 miles WSW
Połaniec 27 miles NNW
Ciężkowice 27 miles SW
Majdan Królewski 27 miles NNE
Tyczyn 28 miles ESE
Gorlice 29 miles SSW
Osiek Jasielski 29 miles S
Pacanów 29 miles NNW
Korczyna 29 miles SE
Raniżów 29 miles ENE
Zakliczyn 30 miles WSW

Dembitz Yizkor Book Summary

This translated edition of the Dembitz Yizkor Book is nearly 300 pages long. It contains information on the town's institutions, organizations, buildings, and families as recounted by survivors and prewar emigrants in addition to first-hand reports of survivors of the massacre and of Jews who joined the partisans, family histories of extended families of the town and all the photographs and illustrations from the original Yizkor Book.

Records of the earliest history show Jews living in Dębica as early as 1673 (scientifically confirmed). The date of 1471 cited by Nathan M. Gelber has not been confirmed by any historical sources available. Local tradition had it that the Jews were allowed to settle in Dębica after being banished from the nearby town of Pilzno. At the beginning of the twentieth century there were about 2200 Jews or about 55% of the population. This vibrant small Jewish community was best known for two independent Jewish communities with two separate rabbinates and communal institutions (for Old Dębica and New Dębica), excellent kosher meat and the famous Horowitz rabbinical family. While about several hundreds emigrated to Palestine and the USA, settling primarily in Tel Aviv and New York City, by the late 1930s there were approximately 3300 still living in Dębica. The Jews were primarily in the following occupations: lawyers, doctors, teachers, bakers, butchers, tailors, shoemakers and merchants of various trades. When the Nazi forces occupied Dębica in 1939 through to 1944, the Jews were imprisoned in the local ghetto to perform forced labor in Pustków near Dębica and were finally sent to the Bełżec death camp. About 500 Jews from Dębica were shot in the nearby forest at the Wolica neighborhood. Approximately a total of 13,000 Jews from the Dębica county were murdered in the Holocaust, including about 3000 Jews from the city of Dębica. A few survivors escaped, survived the camps and were hidden by Poles (to cite the famous story of 13 members of the Reich family rescued by Dr. Aleksander Mikołajków), as many of 50-100 survived the war. Their stories are presented in this volume as well as the dynamic story of Dębica when it was a living part of world Jewry prior to 1939 as recalled by prewar emigrants who contributed to the Yizkor project. Today there are some descendants of Dębica community living around the world today, especially in Tel Aviv and its neighborhoods in Israel. Read the details in the survivor's own words as they remember and bring to life the once vibrant Jewish community of Dębica. Today there are no Jews living in Dębica, Poland.

Ireneusz Socha (Dębica, Poland)
www.dembitzer.pl
May 2, 2015

SKETCH OF DEMBIZA TOWN

1:500

PILZNO →

WISTOKA

GORA

← ROPCZYCE

INDEX

1. MEMORIAL
2. GIRLS SEMINARY
3. BURIAL RUINS
4. ABATTOR FOR FOWLS
5. BEIT MIDRASH
6. SYNAGOGUE
7. BEIT MIDRASH LECHASIDIM
8. RABBI'S SYNAGOGUE
9. RABBI'S RESIDENCE
10. ABATTOR & POWER STN.
11. HIGH SCHOOL
12. AGRICULTURAL COOP
13. CINEMA
14. MARKET
15. GHETTO
16. POOR HOUSE
17. RAILWAY STATION
18. BARRACKS
19. GESTAPO HOUSE
20. MUNICIPALITY
21. OLD SYNAGOGUE
22. COURT
23. CHURCH
24. ELEMENTARY SCHOOL
25. SLAUGHTER HOUSE
26. JEWISH SCHOOL
27. CATHOLIC BOARDING
28. SCOUTS CLUB
29. ORPHANAGE
30. CASTLE MARKET
31. GENTIL'S CEMETERY
33. JEWISH CEMETERY

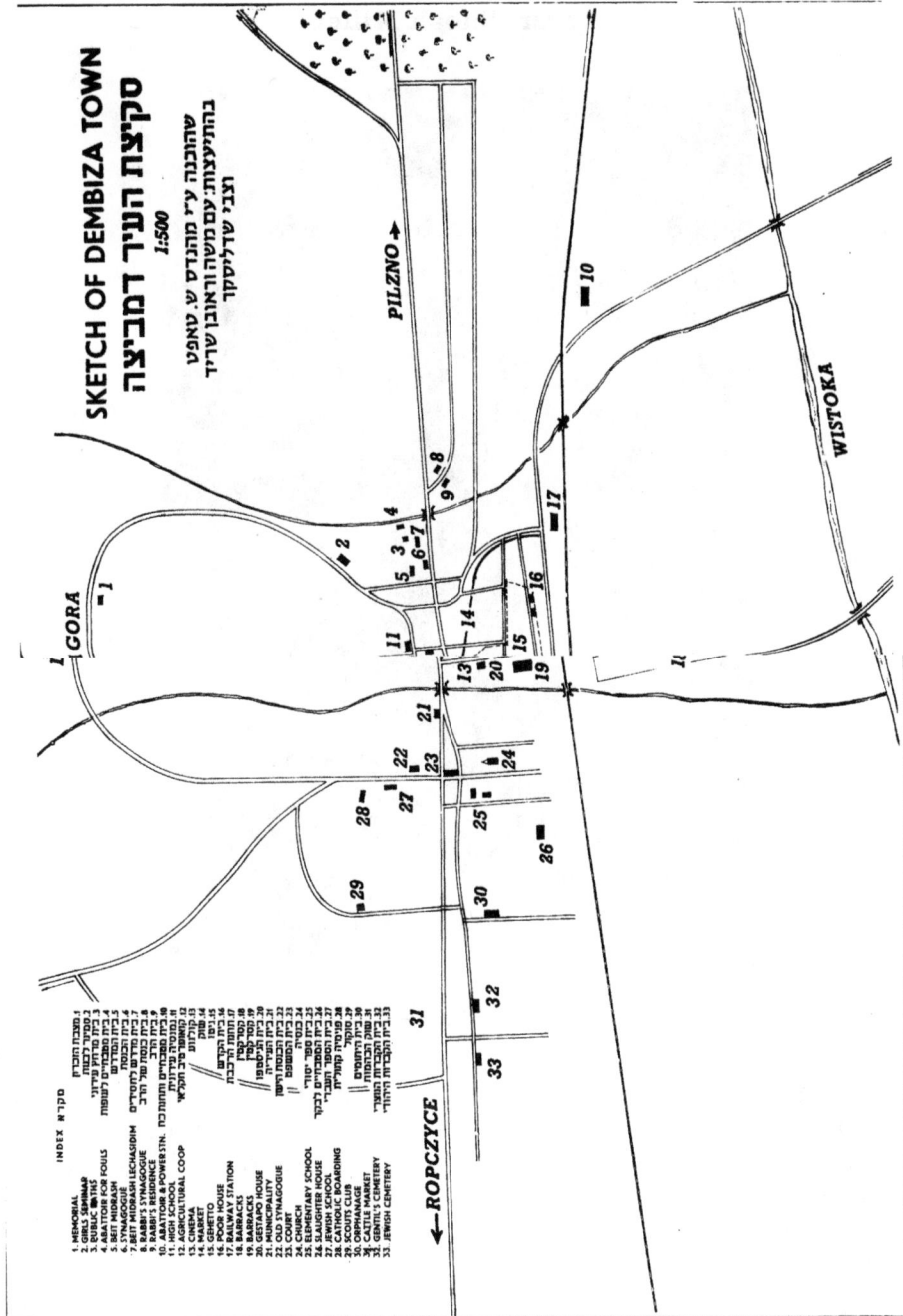

Map of Dembitz

Story Behind the Front Cover Image

By Dr. Shosh Millet

Shedlisker Family, Dembitz, Poland

All through my childhood I would look at the picture of my paternal grandmother Hannahle-Hannah Shedlisker, the mother of Reuven Sarid-Shedlisker. It was a black and white framed photo, quite large, of a woman wearing a blouse decorated in white. The picture hung on the wall above my parents' bed in their bedroom. The picture accompanied us in all the houses in which we lived.

Ten years ago we arrived at my aunt's house just before she died. My aunt was Rivka Sarid, married to my father's brother, Moshe. Here was the same picture of Grandma Hannahle hanging on the wall. My aunt told me, just before she passed away, that Grandma Hannahle had saved her, gave her a coat, married her off and sent her to *Eretz-Israel*.

Grandma's picture was taken from a larger family photo taken in 1935 just before the young couple left for Eretz Israel. In the picture Grandma is in the center, Moshe and Rivka-the couple making Aliyah, and the four brothers who remained in Dembitz in the big house. It was a business selling construction material and iron. The oldest was Avraham and Belka and Tunka were the sisters; little Reuven is on the left. My father was 15 at the time. These were happy times for a loving family- always hugging and kissing.

Belka was murdered in a mass grave while Avraham and Tunka disappeared in Auschwitz. My father, Reuven, was the only one who survived. He spent two and a half years in Auschwitz and was transferred in 1945 to Mauthausen. The Americans liberated him and the other survivors in May 1945.

My father describes in his testimony: "In the last days I lay on the upper bunk of the shack after I returned from the building where the dead bodies lay. My friends threw liquids at me. When the Americans arrived my friends carried me across the fence so I would feel the fresh air of freedom. Slowly, my eyes opened...The Jewish American doctor took me and gave me some Sulfa. It was decided to take me to the house of an Austrian couple in the village. He threatened them to force them to look after me. A few days later I felt that I could stand on my own two feet and I decided to return to the camp. On the way I went to a photo shop and had my picture taken. This is the picture of liberation from Mauthausen".

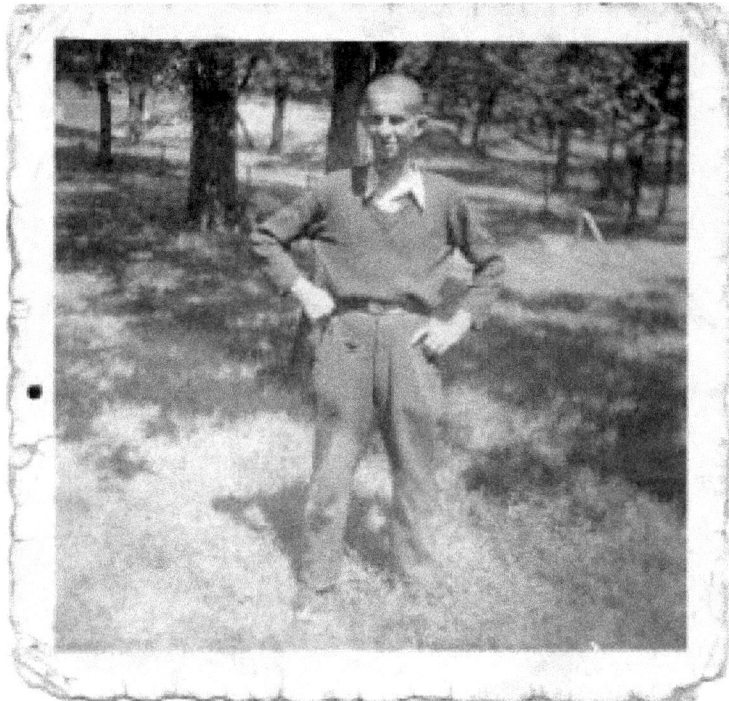

Reuven Shedlisker shortly after his liberation from Mauthausen

Days passed and my father wandered to Italy. He was in a refugee camp and he sent the picture from Mauthausen to his brother Moshe in *Eretz-Israel*. On the picture he wrote:"Your brother is alive, Mauthausen, May 1945". The picture came in an envelope with the inscription that the postal sack had survived an explosion.

My father arrived in Eretz Israel on a ship of newcomers. He met the family with great excitement and group hugs. He fought in the War of Independence and the Sinai Campaign. He was elected Chairman of the Association of Former Residents of Dembitz and lectured, all his life, to the soldiers of the IDF about his life. He suffered a heart attack at one of the lectures and did not survive. This happened in 1988. We sat Shiva during the week of Yom Hashoah (Holocaust Remembrance Day).

In 2007 I joined a group on a trip to Poland. I arrived in the village of Dembitz. My life had been filled with stories and memoirs of it.

In the village, near the family home, I showed the group my grandmother Hannahle's letters in Yiddish. She had special stationary with a Polish logo "Hannah Shedlisker, Business selling construction material and iron". Grandmother was a feminist. She used to collect donations for brides in a black handkerchief so no one would see how much others gave.

She died in 1936.

We arrived in the Dembitz cemetery ...35 descendants of the village.

We were circulating among the graves and the headstones when suddenly a shout was heard: "Shoshy, Shoshy, come quickly"... I ran towards the shouter.

I did not know what was waiting for me...I saw the grave...Hannah Shedlisker, daughter of Yaakov. Another shout from the right..."Look Shoshy... this is the date", "What date?"

"Today is 24 Av, 71 years since your grandmother's death". I am very excited. How did this happen? I had just finished telling the group about it and I managed to reach her grave on the anniversary of her death. We lit memorial candles and a prayer was said. No doubt the Almighty was with us. The tears fell by themselves...

Who found the grave? Moshe Levi, the grandson of Yochanan Zumer who had officiated at my father Reuven's Bar Mitzvah. My father had been orphaned at the age of six. We came around a full circle, here in Dembitz.

Shosh Millet (middle) finds her grandmother's grave in Dembitz with second cousins Shmuel Shedlisker (left) and Israel Shedlisker Sarid (right)

The miracles continued. I visited Mauthausen in 2008 and on a wall in the museum I saw a large picture showing the Allied forces liberating the inmates. My father can be seen in it, lying on a stretcher and carried by his friends.

In 2011 I received from the Nazi archives all documents about my father Reuven Shedlisker.

The pictures, the stories I heard all my life, the testimonial diary and the videos filled my family with pride in amazing survival and goodness that has no parallel.

Notes to the Reader:

Within the text the reader will note "{34}" standing ahead of a paragraph. This indicates that the material translated below was on page 34 of the original book. However, when a paragraph was split between two pages in the original book, the marker is placed in this book after the end of the paragraph for ease of reading.

Also please note that all references within the text of the book to page numbers, refer to the page numbers of the original Yizkor Book.

The original book can be seen online at the NY Public Library site:
http://yizkor.nypl.org/index.php?id=2099

A list of this book and all books available in the Yizkor-Book-In-Print Project along with prices is available at:
http://www.jewishgen.org/Yizkor/ybip.html

Holocaust Righteous Gentiles Recognized by Debica

By Jacek Dymitrowski

English Translation by Ireneusz Socha

Jacek Dymitrowski's address

Aleksander and Leokadia Mikolajkow settled in Debica as a married couple in 1930. They had acquired the ownership of the house at 248, Kosciuszki Street. It was in there where their two sons – Leszek and Andrzej – were born. Both had been professionally engaged in the health care. He was a social insurance doctor; and she was a hygienist working for children and youth. Apart from the professional duties they were active in the Polish Red Cross. They did carry on like that until the outbreak of the WW2. The cruel wartime was to bring an eternal glory to them.

As soon as the German occupants had entered Debica, they immediately began to persecute both the Jews and the Polish intelligentsia. After a ghetto had been established in 1941, doctor Aleksander Mikolajkow employed a young boy named Efraim Reich as an office assistant and a messenger. As a result the boy was able to keep away – for some time at least – from imprisonment in the Debica ghetto. In July 1942, when the Germans began the first ghetto liquidation action, the doctor and his wife took Efraim's entire family in – upon his request.

That was contrary to the then occupation law. The Poles who kept Jews in hiding and the hidden Jews – as well as their entire families – were all subject to the death penalty on the Generalgouvernement territory. Despite the clear evidence, there are some people today defying the fact that 1/3 of all persons recognized as Righteous Among the Nations are Poles, and claiming that Poles could have saved much more Jews. I can answer the claims by reminding of the German regulation that provided that anyone who would hide Jews in the occupied Poland was subject to the death penalty – while, let us say, in the occupied France that was a fine totaling one-day salary. It is really hard for a normal individual to convert human life to a relatively small amount of money. Please bear in mind that the German occupants had encouraged Poles to denounce their Jewish neighbors by offering a high compensation, e.g. a one-kilo bag of sugar or a bottle of vodka, in exchange for a human life. Subsequently, there in fact were some mean individuals who out of greed, jealousy, envy or an ordinary human wickedness would denounce Jews and Poles to the Gestapo. The people, called "szmalcownicy", were later uncovered by proper units of the Home Army and judged severely by the Polish Underground State's tribunal that not infrequently would adjudicate the death penalty.

After the first liquidation action, the Germans posted up announcements saying, "Those who do not turn in the hidden Jews will be shot dead". Consequently, the Reichs had decided they would not endanger the Mikolajkows' lives and would go back to the ghetto immediately. But Dr. Mikolajkow said, "I am always willing to risk my life to save respectable and innocent people", and continued to keep them hidden for the next few days. After a few days, when the things had calmed down a little in the ghetto, the Reichs went back to it. In the meantime, Ms. Leokadia would bring some food to the Jews in the ghetto despite the fact that any Christian caught near the ghetto fence would also be shot dead.

The Jewish family was re-evacuated in November 1942, when the Germans began to prepare themselves to the second liquidation action. The Reichs had found a shelter in the Mikolajkow house again. After a few days they had returned to the ghetto once more. Happily, they were not to stay there long. Thanks to the nature of his profession and his interpersonal contacts, Dr. Mikolajkow had learned that yet another liquidation action was due towards the year's end. So it had to be the final evacuation. In a few days, the 13 members of the Reich family sneaked across the ghetto fence to the Mikolajkow house. Since that time, between December 1942 and the end of August 1944, the Reichs' shelter would in turn be an attic, a garage, a cellar and the attic again. Without access to light, running water and fresh air, they would stay hidden in complete darkness – sometimes up to the neck in rainwater that flooded the garage – under the immediate and permanent threat of uncovering, until the Red Army liberated Debica. To make things even more dreadful, all that time the Gestapo had its headquarters in a building next to the Mikolajkow house. After nine months, the Gestapo commandeered the doctor's garage to use it for their needs and consequently they did not give him much room for maneuver in his fugitive relocation efforts.

Evidently, Aleksander and Leokadia Mikolajkow were not able to bear the cost of supporting a group as large as that all by themselves. Nevertheless, they had never taken or demanded any money from the fugitives. Everything the Mikolajkows were doing for them, they were doing out of the goodness of their hearts. Happily, the Mikolajkows' efforts had been secretly supported by activists of the county branch of the nationwide charity organization called Central Welfare Council – headed by Princess Helena Jablonowska and Mr. Franciszek Sadowski – the principal of the local high school.

Moreover, Aleksander and Leokadia Mikolajkow were regularly helping the Jewish children who had survived the liquidation actions and were placing them in Polish orphanages. They were also engaged in some underground activity. When the Red Army was liberating Debica, the Home Army was in the middle of its nationwide military action called "The Storm". The height of the action's progress in our region was a battle the Home Army soldiers fought with the Germans in the Kaluzowka clearing. During the battle the Mikolajkows had been medically supporting the area.

It may be deemed a historical paradox that on the very same day that the 13 members of the Reich family were saved, their benefactor was killed. Aleksander Mikolajkow's body was allegedly found by his son Leszek first and then by his wife Leokadia. It still cannot be resolved today, who had fired the bullet that actually hit him: a Soviet or a German soldier? Anyway, please bear in mind that it was a time when everyone was shooting at everything that moved. Dr. Mikolajkow was buried in the Old Cemetery in Debica. An inscription on his tombstone says, "He lived and died serving his neighbors". Yet the most beautiful epitaph was written and published in the New York Post by the saved young Efraim Reich in 1960, "I remember the anniversary of his death every year. I believe in life after death, and I believe that Dr. Mikolajkow is one of the greats there. If there are still people like him around, the world will have to become a better place at last."

After his death, the widow had to obtain a livelihood all by herself and her life was full of humbling experiences. Actually, she had suffered the worst humiliation of all when the government of the United States turned her visa application down despite a special invitation sent in by the New York Jews. In the meantime, the same government would keenly welcome some ex-Nazi experts. Upon several petitions, when Ms. Mikolajkow had finally been allowed to the U.S., the ultimate tribute was paid to the great woman. The Jews had stopped the traffic to greet her, then they put her into a limo and pulled it by tow ropes along the main street by hand among the cheering crowds. Israel had also remembered the heroic couple. The Israeli parliament had awarded the state's supreme decoration for non-Jews, that is the "Righteous Among the Nations" medal, to her and her husband posthumously. Two trees had been planted in their honor around the Yad Vashem Institute site.

The young Efraim Reich had undergone a spiritual metamorphosis in the occupation hell. A happy-go-lucky young man had turned into a man of immense faith. He had become a rabbi in New York and then he left for Israel where he lives and teaches to this day.

On January 31, 2006, at its 35th session, the City Council of Debica did approve the petition submitted by the Society of Friends of the Debica Region and it gave the name of Aleksander and Leokadia Mikolajkow to the square located between Kazimierz Wielki Square, Rzeszowska Street, Gawrzylowski Brook (earlier known as Debica Brook) and Solidarity Square. This is a great news that will help rescue the eminent individuals from oblivion among Debica residents today. It is all the more so since the historic building, that once was the scene of the events described above, has recently been designated for demolition. It must be added that the building is located in the immediate neighborhood of the aforementioned square. One must certainly recognize the road communication needs of our fellow residents but nevertheless one must also bear in mind that it was just the communication needs that once persuaded the authorities of the city of Krakow to demolish the old city walls. Not infrequently, the present day descendants of the councilmen kick themselves when foreign tourists (Poles are not as naïve as this) happen to ask, "What's the name of the invaders who have wreaked such havoc in the cultural heritage of the city?".

Perhaps a cheaper way (note that one has to provide substitute accommodation for all of the current residents) would be to move the building and lay it on new foundations 5-6 meters away? That manner of operation would help save the nearly 100-year-old building that surely may not be considered an outstanding architectural relic but admittedly is one of the town's existing monuments of the tragic history of the 20th century. Some proper promotional activities may make the house known globally as a symbol of our town as well as of its residents' dedication. It is already the most recognizable Debica building among visitors from the U.S. and Israel.

However, if Debica residents – by the agency of their City Council representatives – choose to demolish the house anyway, one should place a memorial plaque with a proper description of the dramatic events in there.

Memory of the likes of Aleksander and Leokadia Mikolajkow should be retained for ever. Thanks to people like them we may still pass the tale of goodness and humanity on to next generations. And we are thankful to them for this.

The author is a historian and the president of the TPZD.

The article was published in the Obserwator Lokalny Weekly No. 6 (287) in Debica, Poland on February 11, 2006

Reprinted here with permission of Jacek Dymitrowski.

Table of Contents

Translated by Jerrold Landau

The Book of Dembitz

{Page 4}

This book was published through the efforts of the organization of Dembitz emigres in Israel, which was founded in 5711 (1950-1951). The members are: Ruchama Bornstein, Yehuda Gruenspan, Fruma Grosman (Salomon), Pinchas Sommer, Aka (Rivka) Zilbershatz, Asher Salomon, Yitzchak Freiman, Rivka Shenker, Matilda Siedlisker, Reuven Siedlisker, Chaim Shneps – organized by Daniel Leibel.

"The Book of Dembitz" attempts to portray the city as it was without any ideological censorship. It does not claim to exhaust the task, it is sufficient if it succeeds in establishing a memorial for our birthplace and for the Jewish life that was cut off by the enemy.

The essays and lists are in Hebrew or Yiddish, in whichever language they were originally written, with the exception of the chapter on the history of the community at the beginning, and the chapter on the Holocaust at the end, which appear both in Hebrew and Yiddish.

Published by "Achdut" company, Tel Aviv.

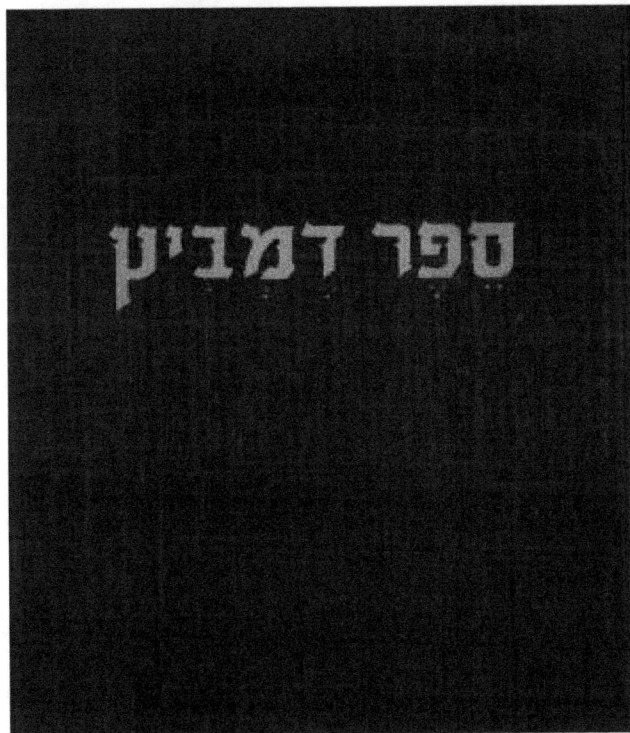

סֵפֶר דֶמְבִּיץ

הוצאת ארגון יוצאי דמביץ בישראל
תש״ד • תל־אביב • 1960

Preface
by Daniel Leibel

Translated by Jerrold Landau

A community such as Dembitz, which was small in population and far removed from the centers of activity and influence of the country, never had the ability to produce its own independent history. It always lived its life without fanfare. Its voice was never heard when earth shattering decisions were to be made. However, Heaven forbid that we should say that it was separate from the Jewish people and the lot of the rest of the nation. Whatever was the lot of the Jews of the country at large was the lot also of the Jews of Dembitz, what exalted them exalted her, and what lowered them lowered her as well. At one point or another, whatever befell the Jews of the neighboring areas, be it for good or for bad, also came upon Dembitz.

A community such as this, which only had small villages in its immediate vicinity, villages which only had very few Jewish families amongst great numbers of gentiles, always looked toward the larger communities that were farther afield – from their came forth Torah, from their came good tidings, and also, Heaven forbid, bad tidings.

When a large community is beset with difficulties, whether due to natural causes or to decrees of the gentile government, – the leaders would gather together to figure out means to overcome the problems. Wise men and men of action would take counsel together to figure out methods of salvation expert and experienced emissaries [1] would be sent to the government to negotiate in favor of the persecuted Jews, and to attempt to soften the evil decree through bribery, or simply to make their protests known. If the problem was too difficult for a single community to handle, emissaries would be dispatched to other communities, both near and far, to enlist their help in overcoming the problems, whether through influence of through monetary assistance.

A small community could not function in such a manner, since its connection with the larger cities and governing authorities would be more tenuous. Its own resources would be very limited, it was far away from the centers of activity, and it had to deal with difficulties, both large and small, on its own. These difficulties would often result in oppression, plunder, and murder.

Who can describe all of the woe of such an isolated community throughout the centuries, from the darkness of the middle ages which lasted for the Jews until the end of the 18th century – and who can describe all the strength and splendor of such a community as it stood up as a lamb among wolves, whose honor is in its inner life: to the outside word they were despised, suspect, and persecuted, but to themselves they were proud in their isolation, full with the meaning of "You have chosen us"[2]; clad in humility toward the outside world and the physical strength that comes from it, yet full of pride in the inner chambers of the heart with the noble legacy of Abraham, Isaac, and Jacob which brings with it the gifts of intellectual understanding and a merciful heart, love of Torah, family purity [3], and many other fine traits which our brethren the Jewish people have in contradistinction to the nations of the world, amongst whom they find themselves dispersed.

These Jews did not write down their chronicles, and if one from among them decided to write down the events of his time, the people who came after him did not have the wherewithal to preserve the documents, due to the manifold evil decrees, persecutions, and fires. The also did not preserve their record ledgers, which were written for the purposes of the Poretz [4], the king, or the church. These record ledgers were for the most part written in Latin, which was referred to as "Galachit" [5], or in the local vernacular, which they generally could not read very well. In any case, the chronicles of the Jewish people would have been of little interest to those who forced them to keep these record books.

Thus, the history of hundreds of small Jewish communities throughout the centuries is lost without a trace, unless an event took place which was of such significance that it was recorded in the ledgers of the large communities, or in the ledgers of the "Vaad Arba Aratzot"[6]. Even of those records only a small portion survived.

The luck of our community Dembitz was both good and bad. The good luck was that no earth shattering events took place that would have required the assistance of the larger communities of Poland. The bad luck was that is that no written records, whether from secular or Jewish communal sources, were preserved at all until the end of the 17th century. Therefore we, who come to preserve a monument to the life of the community that was cut off by the enemy, are only able to include the history of our town with the history of all of the rest of the Jews of Poland, in all its regions. Whatever befell Jacob befell Joseph [7], and whatever events, whether for life or for death, that befell Krakow, to the west of Dembitz, Lublin to the north, Przemysl and Lwow to the east, also befell Dembitz, the younger sister that was on the Wisloka River. Woe unto us, whose knowledge of the history of the destruction of the community is far greater than our knowledge of the history of the community in its growth and glory. G-d forbid that our dearth of knowledge of the beginnings of the community, and our minimal knowledge of other periods of its history should prevent us from salvaging what we can of the history of our life. A very important overview of the history of the community of Dembitz is presented here. It is a first class research essay, the fruit of the pen of the eminent historian of Galician Jewry, Dr. N. M. Gelber. We owe to him a great debt of gratitude. Oh how wonderful it would be if we could write a great book on the Jews of Poland, in all its detail and minutiae, and if we could uncover further archives and concealed books that would shed light on our community. We could then shed further light onto the history of this community, which even though little is known of its beginnings, was certainly blessed with the crown of a good name amongst Jewish Poland. May its memory last forever.

Daniel Leibel

{Page 6}

The Synagogue in the New Town after the Destruction.

{Page 8}

{Page 9}
Dr. N. M. Gelber

The History of the Jews of Dembitz

Translated by Jerrold Landau

There was already a settlement in Dembitz from the first half of the 14th century. The Church of Dembitz is mentioned three times between the years 1326 and 1328 in the account books of tithes and the letters of St. Peter that are kept in the Vatican archives in Rome. The area is described in those books as a settlement surrounded by forests – Decanatus de silvis sede Dambitia [8]. It is evident that in those days the area had a very sparse population.

It was in the year 1358, more than 600 years ago, that King Kazimierz the Great granted to a man by the name of Sziontoslaw, the owner of the area, the rights to establish a city on his estate in accordance with the German statute that was in force in the city of Sroda [9] that was in western Poland (prawo sredzkie). Sziontoslaw was appointed as mayor (advocatus, wojt) of the city, and was given the authority of justice over the population. Seven advisors (lawnicy) were appointed to help him. At that time Dembitz was given the right to hold a weekly market day, which took place on Wednesdays. This is a definite sign of the beginnings of civic life.

Apparently the initial development of the city was very slow, since after less than 14 years, on June 10 1372, Sziontoslaw passed over the leadership of the city to a man by the name of Mikolai, who was previously the mayor of the village of Lipin. He was commissioned to establish the city according to the statute of Magdeburg [10], which was more lenient. Thus Dembitz gained an equal footing with the rest of the cities of Lesser Poland [11]. At this occasion, Sziontoslaw promised to give fields to all the residents without having to pay for seven years. He also freed them from civic service, and from the duty to raise horses for the service of the King, his entourage, and for the needs of the officials who traveled on government business.

Apparently at that time the city began to become firmly established. It became worthwhile to buy the position of mayor for a sum of money, as is testified to by a deed from the year 1441, where Jan Mapodgarodza was required to pay the former mayor Pioter Makonari 300 Grivna [12] to obtain the position of mayor of Dembitz. At that time the surrounding villages of Nagawczywa, Pustinya, Kodokow (Globokowa), Stasiowa and Gumniska were affiliated with Dembitz.

The city expanded further in those years, and its economic connections widened. In 1446, Tomasz Wielski requested from King Wladislaw the Third, the Varnai, an additional privilege: the right to hold special fairs in additional to the weekly fair. The representative of the King, the Kasztlan of Krakow [13] Jan Meziezow, issued a special permit that permitted Dembitz to arrange two additional annual fairs in which merchants from other cities would participate. This was in addition to the regular weekly fair which took place on Saturday in which the local store owners and stall owners participated.

An additional benefit came to the residents of the city in 1470 when the master of the city, Lord Jadwiga issued a proclamation "for eternity" which required his heirs to refrain from drafting and coercing the residents of the city into public service and duty (panszczyzna).

The family which owned the city in the 14th and 15th century was appointed by the Gryfici brigade, which participated in the battle of Grunwald against the Knights of the Cross on July 15, 1410. One member of this family, Mikulai of Dembitz participated that year in the Battle of Koronowa, in which the German Knights of the Cross were inflicted a decisive defeat. Several members of that family rose to important positions in the State, including Zbigniew Kavniezionski, Mikulai Liatuzynski, Stauslaw Langsalza, and others.

Mention is made of Jews in Dembitz for the first time in an agreement which was signed between the Priest Pioter and the master of the city Jan Podgrodzki in 1471, which required all residents of the area, with the exception of the Jews and non-Catholics to pay a tithe to the church. The fact that the master of the city insisted on this indicates that there already were Jews, most probably very few, among the residents of Dembitz before the end of the 15th century. However, apparently all the Jews let the city in the difficult times that came upon the city after that time, since from 1471 to 1690, a period of over than 200 years, no mention is made of any Jews with reference to Dembitz.

At the beginning of the 16th century, Dembitz suffered very greatly from the Tatar invasion, in particular in the year 1502, which brought great destruction in its wake. In addition, a large fire broke out in Dembitz in 1504 which practically destroyed the entire city. The residents were unable to fulfill their financial dues to the city and the state, and this forced the masters of the city, Jan Podgrodzki and Katrina Meliatuszin to release them from all payments for 14 years. In a sitting of the Sejm [14] that took place in Piotrikow in February 1504, the King Alexander freed the residents of Dembitz from all taxes and farming dues for one year, and from all rental payments for six years. On July 26, 1505, the urban residents of Dembitz were again freed from all taxes (ab omnibus ex-actionibus) for four years.

From its beginnings until the 18th century, Dembitz was primarily an agricultural town. Nearly all of the urban residents had control of plots of land that were owned by the masters of the area. After some time, particularly in the latter half of the 17th century, the local artisans began to organize into guilds (cechy). In a privately owned city such as Dembitz, these guilds required only a permit from the masters of the area. If, however, the particular guild took upon itself to meet the standards of a guild of a national city, it would be exempted from any permit. [15]

These heads of these guilds were chosen by the members. These guilds maintained strict disciplines with respect to professional, ecclesiastical, and social affairs. These disciplines were written down in charters which were burnt in the fire of 1660, and they were re-chartered again in the years that followed.

{Page 10}

The shoemaker's guild was re-chartered by the master of the city on November 18th, 1660, the butcher's guild in 1690, and the weaver's guild in 1691. It is very interesting to note that the in the charter of the butcher's guild at that time, the fees that the Jews had to pay for slaughter of each animal (according to the Jews laws of ritual slaughter) were specified. The Jews were forbidden to organize a union for the purpose of ritual slaughter, and they were also forbidden from importing their meat from any other locality. Since these charters were authorized by the masters of the area, they did have the force of law, and were therefore incumbent upon the Jews as well. The importance of these facts is that the mention of Jews and Jewish ritual slaughter helps to establish the earliest definitive date of the establishment of a Jewish community in Dembitz.

The charter of the weaver's guild included an invitation by the masters of the city for members from Germany and Silesia to help develop that trade in the city. The weavers trade had existed in the city for many years by that time. This guild existed until the beginning of the 19th century, but it disbanded with the economic decline of the city at that time.

In 1655, the Swedish army invaded the city and destroyed a significant portion of it. In 1660 another great fire broke out, which left many residents homeless.

This fire caused an important change in the history of the city. Those residents whose residences were destroyed by the fire began to set up houses in the southern portion of the city near the Church of St. Barbara. This area was described in documents prior to 1655 as being outside the city (extra oppidi). This new area was now known as oppidum Nova Debica, and from then on the city was divided into two portions: the old city, and the new city.

At that time a debate broke out between the church and the master of the city Kazimierz Glinski, who accepted loans from the Canonicus Mikulai

Meludzki in order to set up the plots of land in the new city, but did not fulfill his obligations. The priest, who was not sympathetic to the populace, wished to gain control of the land and the houses. In 1701 a compromise was worked out, and the plots of land in the new city were exempted from the church tax (koscielne), and remained under the control of the master of the city. The hospital that was next door to the Church of St. Barbara also remained under the control of the master of the city.

Just as the internal dispute was being forgotten, the Swedes invaded Dembitz for a second and third time in 1702 and 1705. Under the command of the Swedish General Steimbok, they ignited and burnt the monastery and the estates of the Priest Mikulai Meludzki, and the houses of the masters of the city Winiarski and Glinski.

We will now begin to tell the story of the establishment of a permanent Jewish settlement in Dembitz.

Due to the lack of evidence and documentation, it is hard to establish exactly when the era of Jewish settlement began. As mentioned earlier, from a document signed in the year 1471, it is possible to conjecture that individual Jews resided in Dembitz already in the 15th century. A more or less organized Jewish community did not exist until the latter half of the 16th century. Since Dembitz is located in the district of Sandomierz, we can conjecture the Jewish settlement date of Dembitz from the settlement dates of other cities in the district. The oldest Jewish community in the Sandomierz area was in the city of Sandomierz itself (1367), and the next community was Tarnow (1445). Other communities in the district were founded between 1501-1581. It would make sense to conjecture that an established Jewish community was founded in this time frame as well, even though the first document that provides concrete evidence as to the existence of an organized Jewish community was from the 17th century. This document was the aforementioned charter of the butcher's guild of 1690, which specified the regulations on Jewish slaughter.

Until the end of the 17th century, the Jews in Dembitz were concentrated in the old city. After the fire of 1660, when the settlement of the new city began, the Jews also began to settle there. They founded their own community with their own synagogue and Parnas [16], who was called Senior Synagogae novi oppidi Dembica (the head of the Jewish community of the new city of Dembitz). The two communities of Dembitz were organized along the same lines as all other Jewish communities in Poland, who were headed by Parnasses and trustees. The head of the community in the new city in 1712 was Reb Levi the son of Yitzchak, who was called Lewek Isakowicz in Polish. The head of the community in the old city at that time was Reb Hershel (Herszko).

These two names were recorded in a document that was unique to that time period.

The expanding Jewish community in the new city began to arouse suspicion and ill-will in church circles at that time, in particular due to the controversy between the Priest Meludzki and the master of the city Glinski. Since the masters of the city permitted the Jews to settle in the new city, and, as has been mentioned, the church disputed the masters' ownership of the land there, the Priest Meludzki found a pretext to exert pressure upon the owner of the land by bringing up the issue of the expanding number of Jews to the church authorities.

The Cardinal of Krakow, Prince Kazimierz Lubienski ordered an inquiry into the status of the Jewish communities of the old and the new city, and sent a special delegation there to carry out this investigation. They were to inquire into the legal status of the new city in particular, where, according to the complaint, the community was founded and established in contravention to the laws of the state and the synod, and also in contravention to the decision of the supreme court. The delegation decided that the synagogue (house of study?) in the new city should be dismantled, and that it should not be rebuilt in the future.

The Jews of Dembitz did not accept this decree. In the presence of the head of the community Reb Levi the son of Yitzchak, the community issued testimony under oath to the Cardinal of Krakow that the house under discussion is not a synagogue at all. Rather they claimed that this house was set up with the knowledge of the Episcopate of Krakow as a private house for the communal offices and for study (i.e. as a study hall), without any opposition from the local Catholics and the local church – in a separate area from the residential area of the Catholics, outside the old city, and with letters of permission from the kings and the masters of the city. The large community which settled in the area was separate from the residential areas of the Catholics, and should be tolerated since, just as in the old city, the community paid all customary taxes and fees to the church and the priests. Therefore, they feel justified in requesting that their synagogue can also be housed in that building.

{Page 11}

Reb Hershel, the head of the community of the old city, was also present at the meeting, and requested permission to maintain his community separate from the community of the new city.

The matter was brought again before the committee, which included the nobleman Jan Nowakowski, and Dr. Albert Olszowski. After much deliberation, the committee decided against the request of the Jews. They decided that the Jews of the old city and the new city were required to gather in one building, and if they would not abide by this decision, they would be required to pay a fine of 50 talents [17] to help rebuild the monastery that was destroyed by the Swedish invasion.

The committee also noted that the Jewish population was increasing and the Catholic population was decreasing, and that the Jews were taking over all property and business that should have been in the hands of the Christians. Therefore, the committee decreed that the Jews must close their houses and not appear in the streets during the times of church processions, that they must not pour drinks on Sundays [18], and that they must not employ Christian maids in their homes. All of this was under the penalty of severe fines.

Apparently, however, the study hall (Beis Medrash) was not destroyed.

Until 1730, the community of Dembitz was affiliated with the district of Rzeszow. From the documents that describe the head tax paid by the Jews of that district at that time, it can be established that Dembitz was considered part of that district, and paid its taxes along with that district. Dembitz paid 500 gold coins toward the general sum of 10,930 gold coins that was imposed on Rzeszow and area.

A change occurred in this matter in 1730. That year, the community of Rzeszow and its environs, along with Jaroslaw, and for a time also Dowromil split off from the Przemysl district. The community of Dembitz seized that opportunity to split off from Rzeszow, and began to pay its taxes independently. This split took place with the assistance of the master of the city, and was to a large part precipitated by the embezzlement and extortion of tax funds by the heads of the community of Rzeszow. In the head tax accounts of 1734, the community of Rzeszow and its environs (z partykularzami) is registered for the sum of 7,500 gold coins, and the Jews of Dembitz are registered separately for the sum of 500 gold coins. This is the same sum that Dembitz had originally paid on its own. In 1736 and 1737, Rzeszow is registered for 7,560 gold coins, and Dembitz separately for 500 gold coins. This split did not last for long, for in 1738 Dembitz again is registered together with Rzeszow for a total sum of 8,034 gold coins, of which Dembitz was responsible for 500 gold coins. However, this arrangement also was not long lived. In the following year, 1739, Dembitz appears again as an independent community and not as a dependency of Rzeszow. In that year, Rzeszow was required to pay 8,164 gold coins, and Dembitz 500 gold coins.

From 1739 and onward Dembitz is registered as an independent community. In 1753, Dembitz paid a head tax of 500 gold coins, and the Jews of Rzeszow 7,693 gold coins. In 1756 Dembitz does not appear on the list, and Rzeszow appears alone registered for a sum of 6,753 gold coins. From the registers of the community of Rzeszow of that year, it is possible to verify that Dembitz was again included in the district of Rzeszow.

In the latter half of the 18th century Dembitz was affiliated for administrative purposes with the area of Pilzno, which was included in the district of Sandomierz. In the first Polish census, which took place in the year 1764, after the disbanding of the Council of the Four Lands, Dembitz is listed as having 911 Jews. In reality there were many more Jews, since a large number of Jews avoided the enumeration, due to a fear of harm to either themselves or the community. The census of the Jewish community was carried out by a census committee consisting of the Rabbi, a monthly Parnas [19] and the sexton. The committee would go from house to house enumerating all Jewish individuals, even those who were not present in their homes at the time. The Jews of the outlying villages were required to present themselves in the cities to register the number of people in their households. The lists were signed by all the members of the committee. In national cities they were signed by the Starosta [20], and in private cities such as Dembitz, they were signed by the masters of the city. Then the lists were brought by the officials to the capital of the district, where they were required to take an oath as to their accuracy. The oath ceremony for the Jewish census committees took place in a synagogue. In some cases the lists were written in Hebrew and then translated into Polish afterward, since the Jewish officials often did not know how to write in the Polish language.

Of the 911 Jews who were enumerated in Dembitz, 573 resided in the city and 338 resided in the outlying villages that were affiliated with Dembitz. In the city of Dembitz, 135 heads of families were registered (33% [21]). Of this, only 33 worked for a living at a trade: 1 retailer, 3 hat makers, 1 rope maker, 7 tailors, 1 goldsmith, 5 bakers, 7 butchers, 1 engraver, 1 barber, 1 musician, 4 teachers, and 1 cantor.

Only 24.4% of the families had a head of the household who was employed, 1 retailer – 0.7%; 25 laborers – 18.5%; 7 in independent trades – 5.2%. (These numbers are from the book "Yidn in Amoiken Poiln in Licht Fun Tzipern" by Dr. Rafael Mahler [22].)

We can also learn about the professions of the Jews of Dembitz from the head tax registry of 1764, in which is listed: 1 grain dealer, 1 cantor, 4 teachers, 1 musician, 1 rope maker, 7 tailors (of which only one retained an apprentice), 3 hat makers, 1 smith, 7 butchers, 5 bakers, 1 engraver, 1 medic.

Without doubt, the number of employed and professionals was significantly higher. However, the enumerators intentionally did not list such occupations as merchants, store owners, middlemen, glass blowers, etc., due to "the fear of the evil eye". [23] The registries certainly do not give an accurate picture of the total number of Jews in the city. The complete numbers were not registered, due to fear of persecution and oppression, and it is impossible for us at this point to paint an accurate picture. The Jews of Dembitz, having learned from experience of previous years, attempted as much as possible to keep the authorities from knowing the complete and accurate account of their numbers and professional activities.

In 1773, an event took place which shook the community to its foundations: on April 12, the Jewess Sofia, Yaakov Meirek (Meir) and his wife Rachel, and one other girl who was the daughter of the owner of the tavern of Nagawczywa, all together converted to Christianity at the Catholic church under the supervision of the priest Mikolai Wieczchovski. The owner of the tavern of Nagawczywa himself remained Jewish. His daughter took the name Antonina-Francesca-Teresa. The patrons [24] of the baptism were: the Canonicus, Prince Antony Mikolai Rodziwil, the noblewoman Teresa Stoyowska, Judge Josef Jordon Stiowski, and Francesca Wlodok, the wife of Horaunt Wlodok.

{Page 12}
One can only imagine the dismay of the Jews of Dembitz at that time.

A recognizable improvement in the development of the city took place in the 1730s, due to the efforts of the master of the city Frantisek Biolinski and his wife Dorota Henrietta, who granted the residents various benefits and incentives in order to encourage them to build houses in the empty plots of land that were given to them.

In 1768, the ownership of Dembitz was passed to Prince Mikolai Rodziwil. In a special oath taking ceremony that took place in the house of the owner of the city, the mayor, his advisors, the noblemen of the area and the mayors of the neighboring towns were gathered together and took an oath to fulfill their duties in good faith. In that year the city suffered from the traversal of the Russian army, which passed through Poland in order to support the Pact of the Nobles (the Confederation) that was set up in Radom in opposition to the Pact of the Patriots that was set up in the city of Bar [25]. Several of the noblemen from the area of Dembitz and the surrounding towns were party to the Pact of the Patriots. The war between the two sides continued until 1772, and fierce battles were fought in the vicinity of Dembitz, in particular in a valley that was known as Za Okopem – "The Rear of the Ramparts".

The war between the two sides ended with the first partition of Poland.

Poland was divided amongst the three neighboring powers: Russia, Austria, and Germany. The section of Poland that was given to Austria, which included Dembitz and its environs, was known from then on as Galicia [26]. On December 29, 1773, the residents of the city gathered for the oath of allegiance to the Empress Maria Teresa, which took place in the presence of the Austrian governors, the heads of the city, a representative of the new city, and the secretary of the city. From this time on the Jews of Dembitz shared the same lot as the Jews in all of Galicia. At first the city was part of the district of Myslenice [27], later part of the district of Rzeszow [28], and finally part of the district of Tarnow. The Jews of Dembitz, along with all the Jews of Galicia, benefited from a general improvement in the economic status of the country. However, they also suffered from many machinations[29] of the Austrian regime, who spared no effort to "civilize" them, and to make them into enlightened citizens of the Hapsburg monarchy.

In 1785, the national organization of Jewish communities, which was established by a decree of Maria Teresa in 1776, was disbanded. A national organization was never re-established after that time. The local communal functionaries did retain their positions, however. With the exception of the communities of Lwow and Brody, which had seven Parnasim at their helm, all the rest of the communities, Dembitz included, had only three Parnasim each. The job of the Parnasim was to represent the community before the governing authorities, to look after communal matters in conjunction with the Rabbi, to maintain the birth, marriage, and death registries, and to collect the communal tax and the "Jewish tax". These Parnasim were affiliated with the local government, who looked upon them only as a means of enacting their will upon the community. Aside from these Parnasim, the community also chose synagogue trustees, charity trustees, assessors, and bookkeepers. The community of Dembitz did not have a Rabbi, but rather a teacher who served as a judge of Jewish law who drew a salary of 20 Florin, and a cantor who drew a salary of 15 Florin. The burden of taxation upon the Jews was very heavy: a personal tax (Toleranzsteuer) upon each individual, income and property taxes that depended upon one's income, a candle tax [30], a marriage tax, a title tax (i.e. if one bore a special title such as "Moreinu" – our teacher). All this in addition to the communal tax (Krowka) that was also controlled by the governing authorities.

From time to time new taxes were imposed, such as the lodging tax (Quartiersteuer), in lieu of providing lodging for army captains, the field tax (Rustikalsteuer) in addition to the house tax, the consumption tax, and income tax. The taxation burden increased greatly, and after the upgrading that took place in 1789, the government taxes upon the Jews were raised even further.

The marriage tax in particular caused much suffering for the Jews. An event took place in Dembitz with regard to this tax which preoccupied the government for several years, and served as a precedent for the future.

In October 1778, a Jew from Tarnow named Zindel was to marry a girl from Dembitz by the name of Chana. The bride paid the sum of 20 Florin for the marriage tax, and the groom died shortly before the wedding. The bride asked the government to return the money she paid, or to hold it on account for her until she would eventually marry. After much deliberation, the authorities in Vienna decided to give her the option of having the money returned, or having it kept on account for her until she would eventually marry.

At that time, there were many "makers of plans" [31] among the Jews of Galicia, who would propose all sorts of economic and financial ideas to the government. The aim of these plan makers was to gain an opportunity to go to Vienna on the pretext of presenting their plans to the officers of the central government. One of these "plan makers", Reb Moshe Wien lived in Dembitz at the time. In 1878 he proposed to the Vienna government that the government should set up a monopoly for the candle wax trade. This proposal would have wreaked havoc on a significant number of Jewish businessmen and merchants. To their good fortune, this proposal was rejected by the government.

Dembitz had its share of informers who would report unregistered marriages to the government, and would then request payment from the government for this information [32]. These informers were persecuted by the community, and they would then turn to the government and request that they be permitted to flee to Vienna to escape their persecutors. On one occasion, a Jew by the name of Yisrael Kissel was permitted to leave for Vienna. When he arrived, he request financial support from the government in compensation for the persecution he suffered on account of the duty he performed for the government.

In 1787 a decree was issued that the Jews of Galicia were required to take on German family names, starting from January 1789. From that time on the surname "Dembitzer" became very well known in Galicia itself, and also in the lands that Dembitz natives immigrated to. (It is quite probable that the ancestors of the famous supreme court judge of the U.S.A., Louis Brandeis-Dembitz, originally had their roots in Dembitz, and from there settled in Bohemia, from where one of them eventually immigrated to America.) The German names were intended by the government to promote the process of Germanization and assimilation of the Jews of Galicia. For the same reason, communities and businesses were required to keep their ledgers and accounts in German only. They were forbidden to use Hebrew or Yiddish for this purpose, and they were even forbidden to use the Hebrew alphabet.

In an effort to promote these plans, in 1787 the government authorities in Galicia set up 51 German schools for the Jews of Galicia, according to the counsel of the Maskil Hertz Homburg. One such German-Jewish school was set up in Dembitz. Meir Kuch was appointed as teacher, and he was given an annual salary of 200 Florin, which was 10 times the salary of the Rabbi of the city.

{Page 13}

We do not know if this school continued functioning all the way until 1806, when this entire school system was disbanded. There is no hint of this fact in the archives that we have available.

In 1785, when thousands of Jewish families were left without livelihood due to the behavior of the Jewish technocrats, Kaiser Josef II issued a decree on August 16, 1785 that Jews should immediately begin to settle in agricultural settlements. Dembitz was required to provide 8 families toward the quota of 1400 Jewish families required. They would receive 4 plots of land, 4 cow sheds and huts, horses, oxen and cows. In investigations that were conducted in 1796 and 1804, it was found that in contradistinction to the rest of the communities of Galicia, not one family from Dembitz had actually taken up settlement. The community was again requested to provide 8 families, but once again, the community did not respond to the request. We do not know the reasons why.

In 1790, the nobleman Tyowski was arrested for illegally leasing a portion of his estate to a Jew from Dembitz. The governing authorities of the Tarnow region fined the nobleman 100 Florin for breaking the law (gestzwidrige Judenpacht). The Jew was sentenced to a flogging of 10 lashes with a staff. The nobleman petitioned his punishment, and it was reduced to 50 Florin. However, the punishment of the Jew was not reduced.

On March 18, 1788, the Vienna government decreed a draft of Jews into the army, together with the rest of the population. However, in 1790, it became possible for Jews to be freed from the draft by a payment of 30 Florin by each recruit. This situation lasted until 1804, when it again became obligatory for Jews to enlist together with the Christians. In 1797, the Jews of the district of Myslenice, which included Dembitz at that time, were granted an exemption from all army service, through the intercession of Shlomo Kofler, the lessee of the candle tax at that time. In return for the exemption, the Jews would have to pay 200 kantar of silver [33], or the sum of a million Florin of silver utensils, plus 5,000 Florin in cash.

The offices of the district informed the Rabbi of Dembitz, Rabbi Natan Landau, about this exemption. Rabbi Landau served in Dembitz between 1797 and 1809. However, the government of Vienna refused to negotiate with Kofler about this matter, since the Jews tried to get out of the draft before they paid the required sum.

In 1788, there was a census of the Jews in the areas of Galicia. To our dismay, the census lists of the Rzeszow region make no mention at all of Dembitz – they only show the totals of the entire region.

Already from the time of Polish rule, the Jews had ownership rights to houses and plots within the city, due to the privileges of the private cities. After the Austrian conquest, Jews were forbidden to purchase government and public houses. They were, permitted to purchase houses and plots only within the Jewish quarter. This prohibition was entrenched in the city charter. When the government wished to improve the state of the buildings in Galicia by demanding that the houses of the Jews must be of stone, a decree was issued on March 28 1805 that changed the status quo of the Jews for the worse. Jews were forbidden to purchase any house or plot that had not previously been in the possession of a Jew. Even a home that had previously been owned by a Jew but was later sold to a Christian, could not be purchased by a Jew, even if the Christian would make a profit in the sale. Nevertheless, despite these decrees, the Jews of Dembitz were able to purchase houses and plots from Christians in recognizable numbers. In 1824, the community approached the government with a request to authorize their ownership over their houses and fields as a one time gesture. This petition reached the commissioners in Lwow, the capital of Galicia [34], who in turn sent the request to the Ministry of Lands in Vienna. This petition was answered positively, with the caveat that this was an exceptional situation. Incidentally, at that time, the Chasidic leaders opposed the ownership of homes by Jews. The Chasidic Master, Reb Mendel of Rymanow viewed the permission by the government of Jews to own their own homes as a pretext to insure that the Jews would become comfortable in their exile and promote assimilation (Menachem Zion, p.56-57).

The city grew and flourished economically under Austrian rule, and the Jews benefited as well from this state of affairs. Business contacts were established with many provinces of the Austro-Hungarian Empire. Already from the first half of the 19th century many new enterprises and workshops were established, primarily by Jews. These included flour mills, lumber mills, a match factory, a soap factory, a glass blowing plant, and a liquor distillery. The population made their living from industry, commerce, and labor, primarily from enterprises owned by Jews.

The ownership of Dembitz passed from the Radzibilim family to the hands of the Baron Rozinski, who built his palace in the village of Zawada, four kilometers from Dembitz.

In 1831, a cholera epidemic broke out in Dembitz, which caused great suffering for the population, both Christians and Jews.

In the 1840s, the Poles of Dembitz began to become involved in the Polish movement for the liberation of Galicia. Often, noblemen who were involved in this movement would pass through Dembitz for secret meetings, in particular since the organizer of the 1846 insurrection, Jan Tyosowski lived in Dembitz with his family. He was later declared as the Dictator of the Republic of Krakow.

At the time of the outbreak of the 1846 insurrection in Krakow, an uprising of the farmers took place against the noblemen with the encouragement of the Austrians under the leadership of the farmer Jakob Shela. This was a time of great trepidation and fear for the Jews of Dembitz due to the massacres of noblemen that took place in Jaslo, Sanok and Tarnow, even though nothing happened in Dembitz itself. The Jews of the city were waiting in fear: on the one hand the noblemen who owned the lands would be tempted to take revenge on them on account that a Jew, Lewek Stern was the right hand man of Shela, the leader of the uprising; and on the other hand for the fear that the farmers may have a complaint against them because they supported the noblemen in the oppression of the farmers. The power of the owners of the surrounding property was diminished due to these events. A farmer, Kazimierz Walczak, was chosen to represent Dembitz in the first Austrian parliament, that was set up in Vienna after the 1848 uprisings.

In spite of this, the Polish insurrection left very little effect on the city by 1863, even though the nationalist organizations of western Galicia made great effort to influence the youth of Dembitz to support the revolts.

Slowly but surely the lot of the Jews of Dembitz began to improve, since the Jews of Austria were granted equal rights in the second half of the 19th century. The special laws designed to prevent their increase, and to push them out of economic life were repealed.

{Page 14}

A great factor in the improvement of the economic situation was the construction of the Karel Ludwig railway line, which traversed the entire northern region of the Hapsburg Monarchy from Vienna to Lwow, with Dembitz being one of its stops.

The Jewish population, which numbered 500 souls in 1840 had grown a thousandfold [35] by 1865. In the census of 1880 it numbered about 2,385 people, which was 73.2% of the general population of the city. However, the cultural and societal development was much slower, since the decisive majority of the community in the city were Chasidim, or were wary of starting a conflict with the Chasidim [36].

In the second half of the 19th century, the Chasidic group who were followers of Rab Naftali Tzvi of Ropczyce (1760-1827) [37]. The city eventually became a Chasidic center. After a controversy over the Rabbinate of Dembitz, the grandson of Reb Naftali, Reb Reuven Horowitz, became the Rabbi of Dembitz.

We do not know anything about the Rabbinate in Dembitz until the second half of the eighteenth century. The first Rabbis of Dembitz about whom we have records were Rabbi Shmuel and Rabbi Eliezer of the Horowitz family, who served in the latter part of the 18th century. The were members of the renowned Horowitz Rabbinic family, but they are not to be mixed up with family members of the Chasidic leader Reb Naftali of Ropczyce, who took on the name Horowitz at a later date. When Rabbi Eliezer Horowitz passed away in 1790, Rabbi Natan Landau the Kohen became the Rabbi. He served as Rabbi until 1809. After him, Rabbi Shmuel Henech Gewirtz served as Rabbi until 1820, and he was succeeded by his son the Rabbinic Judge Rabbi Eliahu Gewirtz. After his passing the Rabbinic seat was empty for several years, and only in 1872 did it become possible for Rabbi Reuven Horowitz to settle in Dembitz. He fulfilled the two roles of Rabbi and Admor [38] simultaneously.

The Haskala movement did not have a great influence among the Jews of Dembitz, who generally lived a very traditional lifestyle [39]. The Jews of Dembitz only began to modernize culturally at the beginning of the 20th

century. At that time, some families were brazen enough to send their children
to the Polish public schools, and also the Gymnasia [40]. In 1907 there were
27 Jews among the 406 students of the Gymnasia. Some of them were from
outside the city, however.

A decree was issued by the Ministry of Religion and Education in Vienna
that as of April 2, 1891, the community of Dembitz would be an independent
community within the administrative district of Ropshitz [41]. The community
would have its own communal council. However this communal council only
occupied itself with religious matters, and did not come up with any new ideas
to improve the economic and cultural state of the burgeoning Jewish
population. The economic and cultural situation was degenerating, and many
Jews were forced to leave the city due to the lack of a livelihood.

In 1890, before the establishment of the new communal framework, an
organization for the assistance of the poor was set up. This organization
provided 6 acre plots of land, and loans of 3,000 Guilders [42].

The final communal council before the First World War included: Reb
Mendel Mahler as head, Yisrael Shtarch as deputy, and Yaakov Taub, Yona
Geshvind, Hersch Shuldenfrei, Yaakov Lishe, Chaim Alster, Moshe Sommer,
Avraham Kus as members. The communal secretary was Yehuda Tewel. The
teacher of Jewish religion in the public school, who drew a salary from the
community, was Moshe Wallach. The communal budget for 1914 was 13,000
Crowns.

A Jewish burial society (Chevra Kadisha), and an organization for visiting
the sick (Bikur Cholim) functioned under the auspices of the communal
council. Yaakov Taub served as head. Their was also an endowment fund for
the poor.

The first sparks of Zionism began to appear in Dembitz in the 1890s, when
the movement was beginning to take root in Galicia. However, the movement
only began to conduct its activities on a widespread activities from the year
1907, with the excitement that was generated among the Jews of Galicia on
account of the controversies that surrounded the elections to the Austrian
parliament. At this time the Zionist representatives were elected for the first
time in the general elections.

Dembitz is remembered in the Zionist annals of Galicia as the location of
the founding of the student's organization "Hashachar", which was founded at
a convention that took place on the intermediate days of Passover 5668 (1898)
in the Bornstein Hotel.

{Page 15}

Dr. N. M. Gelber

THE JEWS OF DEMBITZ

   {Yiddish text – pp 15-24. A direct translation of Hebrew text of pp 9-14 of the original Yizkor Book.}

The bathhouse.

The courthouse in the old town

Government High School.

Translator's Footnotes

1. The Hebrew here is "Shiluchei Mitzva" – Emissaries to carry out a mitzva act.

2. A reference to the Jewish laws of family purity, which include separation of spouses during menstrual cycles, and immersion in a ritual bath (Mikva) that follows the period of separation.

3. The Hebrew / Yiddish word Poretz refers to the landowner upon whose land the Jews lived. Here the word Poretz is actually used, but in other places in this document, the word "master of the city" is used to describe such a landowner.

4. Galach is a Christian priest in Hebrew / Yiddish. Literally, it means clean-shaven, in contradistinction to Rabbis, who for the most part would have worn beards. Galachit would mean "The language of the priests".

5. Literally "The Council of Four Lands", which was the central Jewish organization of the Jewish communities of the four lands of Greater Poland, Lesser Poland, the province of Lemberg (Lvov or Lwow), and Volhynia.

6. A Midrashic reference that the events of Joseph's life (including having being hated by his brothers, and being separated from the family, etc.) parallel the events of his father Jacob's life.

7. This phrase is apparently the Latin quote from the book. There are several words and phrases in this article that appear in parentheses, and appear to be Polish and / or Latin words for various concepts. I include these phrase as is in parentheses. Note that all these words or phrases, except for this current one are in parentheses in the main text.

8. There is a city called Sroda in modern Poland south-east of Poznan.

9. A city in the eastern part of Germany between Berlin and the former East German / West German border.

10. Greater Poland was an independent area of Poland that was centered in northwestern Poland around Poznan (Posen). This area was known as Wielkopolska during its independence. Lesser Poland is a term that is often used for outlying areas of Poland, especially Galicia.

11. A Ukrainian monetary unit. The modern day country of Ukraine uses the Grivna as its unit of currency.

12. Kasztlan is a Polish title for head of a city or area.

13. Sejm is the name of the Polish parliament, still in use in modern Poland.

14. Apparently, there were two types of cities at the time: privately owned ones such as Dembitz, and national cities, under the control of the King.

15. Parnas, from a Hebrew word meaning to sustain, is the name of a Jewish community administrator.

16. The monetary term here is 'Tinofot'. I have checked with a Polish native, and it is not a recognizable form of currency in Poland. It also has no Hebrew connotation of any currency unit that I am aware of. I am not sure of the exact meaning.

17. The reference is presumably to alcoholic drinks.

18. Evidently, the role of Parnas was filled by some sort of a rotation system.

19. A Russian / Slavic word for the mayor of a city.

20. It is not clear to what this 33% applies, as 33% of 573 is 191. Perhaps it is a very rough approximation.

21. The English translation of this Yiddish title is "Jews in Old Poland in a Statistical Light". The footnote that appears at the bottom of page 11 indicates that this book was published in Warsaw in 1958, and the page references are 91, 119, 124, tables 11 and 43.

22. Evil Eye is "Ayin Harah" in Hebrew and Yiddish, referring to a various superstitious beliefs that certain deeds or innuendoes would bring evil influences upon people.

23. The Hebrew word used here is 'Sandek', which generally means (rather ironically given the context of the use in this story) the man who holds the baby upon his lap during a circumcision ceremony. Here the word refers to godfather, sponsor or patron.

24. There is a town called Bar in Ukraine. It is not within the borders of pre WWII Poland. Perhaps this is the Bar that is referred to here.

25. The German portion was known as Silesia.

26. A city south of Krakow.

27. Rzeszow is a city to the east of Dembitz, and Tarnow to the west.

28. The Hebrew words used here are in quotes, "Patnatim" and "Dakartim". The meaning is unclear and these may be referring to Polish or German words, however the implication of "machinations" is very evident from the context.

29. A form of church tax.

30. The Hebrew term used here "Baale Hatzaot" indicates some sort of mischievous or non straightforward intention.

31. Apparently, unregistered marriages were common among the Jews of Galicia at the time, as they attempted to avoid the hefty marriage tax. The magnitude of the marriage tax can be seen from the text above, where it is described that the Rabbi's annual stipend was 20 Florin, the same amount as the marriage tax.

32. A kantar is a measure equivalent to 288 kilograms. The required sum of silver was 57,600 kilograms.

33. Lwow (or Lvov), now in Ukraine, was known as Lemberg during the period of Austrian rule.

34. The number 'a thousandfold' may be somewhat of an exaggeration, since the growth from 500 to 2,384 represents just under a 500 fold growth.

35. The Chasidim, in that time as in modern times, would be very wary of embracing modern cultural mores.

36. Reb Naftali Tzvi of Ropshitz was a reasonably well known Chasidic leader at that time. The Polish spelling of the town would be Ropczyce, but the Yiddish transliteration into English would be Ropshitz. In English literature, the Ropshitz version would commonly be used. Throughout this translation, I have generally tended to use the Polish spellings of Polish cities, towns and names (except for Dembitz, where I did not use the modern Polish version of Debica). This should facilitate the identification of these places on modern maps, for those who would be interested. In the vast majority of cases, I was able to find the cities and towns on the maps in the National Geographic Atlas, or by looking them up on the shtetl index available on the Jewishgen website. In a few cases, I was not able to identify the towns. I also generally tried to use the Polish

spelling for names: thus Vladislav is Wladislaw, and Casimir would be Kazimierz, etc.

37. Admor is the Hebrew acronym for Adoneinu, Moreinu, veRabbeinu, which means our master, our teacher and our rabbi. It is the title used for a Chasidic leader.

38. The Haskala movement was the movement of Jewish 'enlightenment' which was prevalent in Europe at that time, when Jews were beginning to loosen themselves from the traditional bounds of shtetl orthodoxy, and to become more acculturated to the world at large. A person affiliated with the Haskala movement was known as a Maskil.

39. Gymnasia is a Polish / Russian term for a high school.

40. I use the Germanic spelling here, since the Hebrew text has this town name spelled differently than it is in all other occurrences in this text, probably to indicate that this is the German name for the administrative district.

41. Clearly, this organization was involved in helping people set up their own means of livelihood, rather than in providing the destitute with their immediate needs.

42. Many communities of Poland were only settled in the 18th or 19th centuries. From the previous essay, it is evident that Dembitz was settled much earlier.

UNTIL THE FIRST WORLD WAR

{Page 27}

The City and its Rabbis

We can gain some insight about the picture of the Jewish community of Dembitz from the fact that in the area surrounding the central structures of the old city – the church and the residence of the Priest – there were no Christian homes at all. There were no barriers at all between the rows of Jewish shops, with the exception of the King's thoroughfare and the courthouse building, which was erected at a later time in the field to the front of the church. The synagogue and ritual bath were located behind the rows of Jewish shops.

The physical and spiritual life of the Jews of Dembitz was not different from the life of the Jews in any other city of Lesser Poland. The Jewish accent has certain clear signs of a unique style, which is a sign that the community is of ancient origin [43]. The vocabulary of this dialect is very reminiscent of the language of the Jews of eastern Galicia, and is perhaps a sign that the first Jewish settlers of Dembitz came from there.

Very little has been preserved in the annals of history about the persecutions of the Jewish community by the governing authorities. We must thank the eminent historian Dr. N. M. Gelber who opened up for us several chapters of history that were previously unknown to us (see the previous essay).

The Jews of Dembitz were not particularly wealthy. Until the beginning of the 20th century there was only one Jewish house which was more than one story high. The residences were generally quite crowded. The Jews generally only managed to make ends meet in business. The Jewish masses used to wait impatiently for the fair of Bartel-Mark, which was a very important source of their livelihood. Many would also travel to fairs that took place in cities that were near and far, in order to bring home their sustenance.

By the beginning of the 18th century, the old city, which bordered on the west side of the Staszowka River, could barely contain the entire settlement. Jews began to settle on the other bank of the river. They began to purchase fields and to build houses in the new city. The square in the center of the new city was known as the Market Square. All of the buildings surrounding the market were built by Jews. Until the beginning of the 20th century, there was only one Christian store in the area. A similar situation existed in the old city. This one Christian store was the general store owned by Sradniczki, which also served as a restaurant for captains of the Austrian army and Polish government officials. The weaving, clothing, and shoe businesses were located on one side of the marketplace. This row of buildings was known as "Di Zeil" or "Di Potshene". The stalls were located beneath a covered area. Underneath the roof were the stalls of the weavers, the clothing merchants, merchants of colored cloth, ribbons, lace, and other material. Hidden behind the colorful display of the marketplace was the poverty and drab day to day concerns of the Jewish people.

The way of life of the Jews of Dembitz, even of the wealthy, was generally modest and restrained. Nevertheless, there were recognizable differences along the spectrum of wealth. There were those that would only taste a morsel of meat once a week. These differences could be discerned from the breakfast meal that the students of the cheder [44] would bring with them to eat during their recess: the children of the wealthy would bring buns or bagels spread with butter, while the children of the more needy, primarily those that lived in the back alleys, would bring two pieces of old bread, singed by an oven, and softened with a bit of garlic on top. Interestingly enough, a daily swap would take place. The eyes of the needy children would pop out with the desire of a half a slice of buttered bagel, and the children of the well-to-do would desire a piece of singed garlicky bread.

That Jewish poverty, which was lamented in "Katzvei Hakrach" [45] was well known in the eyes of the gentiles as well. They would be astonished at the severe poverty of their Jewish neighbors, who would sustain themselves from dry bread and garlic. Some of these gentile neighbors were more attuned to the poverty of their Jewish neighbors than the heads of the Jewish charitable organizations. Jewish people tend to be very discreet, and poverty was considered, even in Dembitz, to be somewhat of a disgrace [46].

The generally held viewpoint among the Jewish population was that poverty and riches are decreed from Heaven, and there is not much that one can do to change one's situation save beseeching G-d for mercy. Jews tend to be merciful people, and supporters of the poor. In Dembitz there was charitable giving, particularly in a discreet fashion. A commonly held view was that poor people were created so that people would have an opportunity to fulfill the commandment of giving of charity. Before the First World War, there was no attempt to form an organized, centralized charitable organization in Dembitz. The charitable giving was conducted on an ad hoc basis.

This pressing poverty was the prime reason for the emigration of Jews from Dembitz to the larger cities and far off lands. At first, the destinations were Germany and London. When the gates of England were shut, the emigration began to the United States of America. This emigration was the cause of the continual dwindling of the Jewish population of Dembitz during the last 70 years of the existence of the community. This dwindling continued despite the large rate of natural increase.

With all this, Dembitz was a city of G-d fearing Jews, who learned Torah without fanfare. No famous Torah scholars arose from Dembitz, with the exception of the Rabbi Reb Chaim Natan Dembitzer of Krakow, who was one of the Torah giants of the 19th century. He wrote many books which bore his name, and testified to his family history from Dembitz.

The sprouting of the Chasidic movement influenced Dembitz. Many of the Jews of Dembitz were disciples of the renowned Chasidic Master Rabbi Naftali of Ropczyce, whose influence was significant in the whole area.

When the Rabbinic chair of Dembitz was vacated by the passing of the previous Rabbi, Rabbi Henech Gewirtz, the Chasidim of Ropczyce wanted to appoint Rabbi Reuven Horowitz as Rabbi. He was the youngest son of Rabbi

{Page   28}

A Corner in the Market Place

Eliezer of Zukow, and the grandson of Rabbi Naftali of Ropczyce. However, there was also a large following of the Chasidim of Rabbi Shlomo Zalman of Wielopole in Dembitz, who objected to having a Rabbi who was not from their own group. Wielopole was also a town near Dembitz [47]. The dispute continued for many years. During this time the Rabbinic activities were administered by the two Rabbinic judges: Rabbi Yitzchak who was called Reb Itche Zilberman, and Rabbi Elizh (Eliahu) Gewirtz, the son of Rabbi Henech Gewirtz, the last Rabbi of Dembitz before the take over of the Rabbinate by the Chasidim of Ropczyce. Rabbi Henech's gravestone, which survived the Holocaust, and is located in the cemetery near the gate, testifies to the fact that he was the last Rabbi of the entire City. His epitaph reads:

    Stones Shall Cry out from the Wall
    Woe to the Loss of this Great Person
    The Rabbi of the Entire City [48]

Rabbi Elizh served as a Judge without any interest in monetary gain. He earned a very good livelihood from his significant business interests, which were looked after by his wife Chanale. Rabbi Elizh's son was Reb Daniel Gewirtz, who was a very influential person in the city. All communal matters were conducted according to his will, and he decided that as long as his father

Rabbi Elizh the Judge was alive, nobody would serve as the chief Rabbi of Dembitz. Only when Rabbi Elizh Gewirtz passed away did Reb Daniel accept Rabbi Reuven, the son of Rabbi Eliezer of Zukow, as head of the Rabbinic court of Dembitz. Several more years of dispute took place until the Chasidim of Ropczyce prevailed over the Chasidim of Wielopole, and the Righteous Rabbi Reuven settled in the city.

The Pious Reb Reuven

In the book "Ohel Naftali" (Lemberg, 5671 – 1911), a Chasidic story is brought down which describes how Rabbi Naftali of Ropczyce promised the Rabbinate of Dembitz to his sons and descendants. The following is the quote from the book: "At one time, the Rabbi Reb Naftali of Ropczyce came to the community of Dembitz, and gathered together the heads of families and their children, and made a great feast for them. He himself gave all the children wine and said: ' The angels were not able to start up with Moshe Rabbeinu of blessed memory at the time of the giving of the Torah, since they had partaken of the feast of Moshe's ancestor Avraham our forefather [49]. You should all know that one of my descendants will be a Rabbi here, and since you all have benefited from my feast, you will not be able to do harm to him.' He then said to one child, whose name was Shneur, and to two others: 'Remember this!'. Later, these three youths became leaders of the community." End of quote.

When Reb Reuven ascended to the Rabbinate of Dembitz, he was still a young man. Nevertheless, he managed to win over the hearts of the residents of the city. When a marriage took place, it became the custom to bring the bride to Reb Reuven in a carriage prior to the wedding ceremony so that he could give her his blessing. Within a short time, Chasidim began to flock to him from all western Galicia in order to break bread with him at his table, and to listen to his words of Torah.

Rabbi Avraham Chaim Simcha Bunem Michaelson describes the character and customs of Reb Reuven in his book "Ohel Naftali". From the time he was twelve years old, he would not sleep on the Sabbath, but would rather spend the day dancing in the presence of the Sabbath Queen [50]. When he settled in Dembitz, the community set up four watches of people to sing and dance with him. He even did so in the week that his mother the Rebbetzin passed away. He explained to his relative Rabbi Michaelson, who was present at that occasion: "Since my standard custom is to do so, if I would not do so on this particular Sabbath, it would be as if I made a public display of mourning". [51] This event took place in the year 5732 (1872).

The first wife of Reb Reuven, the daughter of the righteous Reb Isser of Rozwadow, died in her youth after she had borne him one son. This son was Reb Alter, who inherited the Rabbinical post after him. His second wife, the

Rebbetzin Dvorale, was not of Rabbinical stock. She was the adopted son of one of his Chasidim. After Reb Reuven lost his first wife, one of his Chasidim, who was very wealthy, and owned much property, came to him and said: "Rabbi, G-d gave me much property and money, but He did not grant me children. Therefore, I adopted the daughter of my brother. Please take her as a wife, and I will give you all of my money and riches." The Rabbi took the young woman Dvorale as a wife. Aside from the money and property which she brought into the marriage, she bore him two sons and three daughters.

Reb Reuven, who was constantly occupied with Torah pursuits, did not deal at all with the economic matters of his home, nor with the incidental business of the Rabbinate. The Rebbetzin Dvorale took care of all these matters. She continued to purchase property, in addition to from the property which she had brought into the marriage. Reb Reuven's house was next to the synagogue in the old city. The Rebbetzin purchased property on the other side of the river, in the place where her son Rev Shmuel would later set up his home. She leased this land to the neighboring non-Jews as pastureland. A long time later, after Reb Reuven had passed away, she sold these properties one by one, whenever she had to marry off one of her sons or daughters.

Reb Reuven conducted Rabbinical judicial matters along with the Rabbinical Judge Reb Itche, who was not one of his Chasidim. They generally got along, but there were occasions when there was friction between them.

On one occasion, when two plaintiffs requested a Rabbinical judgement on a certain issue, the Rabbi and the Judge debated the law, and Reb Reuven physically pushed the Judge Reb Itche in the heat of the debate. Reb Itche fainted and had to be brought to his home. Reb Reuven felt very bad about this matter, but he felt that it was not in keeping with his honor to apologize, until the head of the community Reb Daniel Gewirtz ordered him to apologize to the Judge, with the threat that if he would not make amends, "He would send him under guard to Rozwadow", from whence he had come. Even after that occasion, peace did not reign between the head of the Rabbinical court and the Judge.

About this they relate: Once Reb Leibush the shochet [52], the father of Reb Tovia the shochet, came to Reb Reuven with a complaint against the Judge Reb Itche that he had permitted as kosher an animal who had a lesion on the lung in the shape of the letter vav. Reb Reuven called the Judge and requested that he repeal this decision. Reb Itche refused to do so, and Reb Reuven commanded that all the synagogues should issue a declaration that those who had bought this meat should be aware that it is not kosher.

When Reb Itche, who never ate the meat of cattle at all, heard of this declaration, he asked that some meat of that animal be bought for him, and he ate it. A dispute broke out in the city, and the heads of the community sent an emissary to consult with the Rabbi of Lwow, Reb Yitzchak Shmelkes, the author of the book "Beis Yitzchak". He decided in favor of Reb Yitzchak

Zilberman, and decreed a fast upon all those who spread a bad name on the kosher food.

Road to the Railway Station

{Page 30}

The Rabbi Reb Alter

This dispute did not weaken the commitment of the Chasidim of Dembitz to their Rabbi. This commitment continued to grow with the passing of Reb Reuven, when his eldest son Reb Alter inherited his position. Rab Alter had a blend of the qualities of a pious individual with an awareness of the ways of the world.

An interesting description of the wisdom and ways of this righteous person can be found in the book "Zichronot Mechayay" [53] by Mr. Yosef Margusham, who knew the Rabbi Reb Alter during the 1880s.

"In the middle of the winter the Rabbi from Dembitz, Rab Alter Horowitz, came to Radomysl. For an entire week, the Rabbi was the guest of the father of my father-in-law Reb Yudel Steiglitz, who was one of his principal disciples. He was en route to his father Reb Reuven Horowitz, who was the grandson of the elder Rabbi, Reb Naftali of Ropczyce.

Of course, on the day that he arrived, I came to greet him. I stayed in Radomysl for the Sabbath, and I took note of his customs at the table. I was also with him before he returned to his home, and I gave him a kvitel [54]. I also gave him a donation of 50 gold coins of very fine quality.

I was not sure what to write on the kvitel. At that time I was not yet a merchant, and I did not have any children yet. I only wrote on the kvitel my name and the name of my wife, with the words "for success, and physical health".

The Rabbi took the donation immediately and put it in his pocket. However, he read over the kvitel two or three times even though it was very brief. He then asked me: 'Do you really need a kvitel?'

I did not understand the meaning of his comment. I later discussed this with the father of my father-in-law, who smiled with pride and explained to me the meaning of these words thus:

– Since you are still a young man who is supported by his father-in-law, and you are not occupied in business, and you do not have children at this time – with what should I bless you?

However, I understood these words in a completely different manner. Since Reb Alter knew very well that I was a "Maskil" [55] and a man of little faith, so he asked me why I was bothering with a kvitel?

From that moment on I was together with him several times. I looked at him as a very astute Jew, and I consulted with him often about my business affairs. I always gave him a very respectable donation, but I never gave him a kvitel again. He was astute enough never to ask me for one, even though he surely would ask for one from other people.

The Rabbi of Dembitz, Reb Alter Horowitz of blessed memory, was in truth a very precious Jew, who was very wise in the affairs of the world. He was knowledgeable in many different fields, as if he was a very experienced businessman. He would offer proper advice to all of his Chasidim on their business affairs.

Whenever my father-in-law had an important decision to make, he would consult with the Rabbi of Dembitz, who was to him like a close, faithful childhood friend. When my father-in-law left Zagorzyce to look for another property, the Rabbi of Dembitz became involved in the matter in great detail, and advised him on several different properties.

Reb Alter, as I have mentioned previously, was an expert in many different fields. He even was familiar with the horse trading business.

One of his Chasidim was a horse dealer from Radomysl by the name of Hershel. He would constantly fill up many train wagonloads of horses to send to Prussia (14 horses would be placed in one wagon). Since Radomysl did not have a train station, and the village of Czarna did not have suitable facilities, he set up his first warehouse in Dembitz.

He and his helpers would make the rounds to many fairs in many towns, and he would bring the horses he bought to Dembitz, and from there, he would send them by train to Prussia.

Whenever Hershel was about to arrange a shipment of horses to Prussia, he would first come to the Rabbi of Dembitz to ask for his blessing on the business undertaking. He would give the Rabbi a donation of gold coins according to the number of horses that he was shipping in that shipment to Prussia. At times he would ship 40 or more horses in one week.

The Rabbi was not satisfied in simply giving the blessing to his Chasid. Rather he requested that whenever Hershel would arrange a transport of horses to the train station, he should bring them first to his house, so he could take a good look at them.

On several occasions I had the opportunity to be present as Hershel's horses were being displayed before the righteous Rabbi.

Reb Alter would stand outside the gate of his house, near the King's road that led to Pilzno. In the large courtyard in front of his house there would be standing about 40 horses with their drivers. Each horse would be passed in front of the Rabbi, and the Rabbi would ask him how much he paid for it.

The Rabbi would hold a thin stick in his hand, and he would look at each horse with piercing vision and great understanding.

Once in a while he would suddenly say:

Hershel, what is this on its right foot?

Hershel, who previously had not noticed this, would be compelled to admit that the Rabbi was correct: on the horse's right food there was indeed a small wound which required immediate bandaging.

Once in a while, when one of the horses did not please the Rabbi, he would ask one of the drivers to mount the horse and ride it a bit, so that he could "see how it rides".

He would estimate very closely the price that each horse should fetch. At times, someone would say to Hershel:

Hey, they pulled one over you. You will not profit much from this white horse.

Reb Alter did not have any children. He was not a big spender of money. The Rabbinate and the leadership of the Chasidic group would bring in significant sums of money, and he always had more than enough money. Therefore, he would often lend money to his Chasidim at very reasonable rates, and at times it was as if he was a partner in their business affairs.

One of his relatives, Mendel Kelinman, who was a very large forestry merchant, always owed him thousands of gold coins. When he went into bankruptcy – due to a dispute with the residents of Gottwiert – the Rabbi was short thousands of gold coins which he never recovered. Nevertheless, Mendel remained one of his Chasidim, and the Rabbi would continue to assist him in financial matters.

The Rabbi of Dembitz was a very wise and sweet Jew. There are not many Jews like him. May his soul be bound in the bonds of everlasting life!"

{Page   31}

The wisdom of Reb Alter with respect to business affairs was revealed to his followers through signs and actual miraculous events. Once, so they relate in Dembitz, it came to the mind of Reb Alter that one of his Chasidim, Reb Yoel Gritzman, must purchase the house of one of the gentiles in the city. He called to his assistant Reb Yisrael and said: go to Yoel Gritzman and tell him to purchase the house of so-and-so the gentile. When Reb Yoel heard this, he got dressed and came to the Rabbi and complained: "How can I buy that house when I do not have any money?" Reb Alter said to him: "Give him a down payment". Reb Yoel hesitated by the door, then he went, and the next day he found the money to make the down payment.

The Rabbi Reb Alter was weak from his youth, thin, and childless. However he conducted his Rabbinic court with great honor and regal trappings. Since many merchants would bring him a great deal of money, gifts, horses, and all sorts of finery, he was able to move from his original house near the synagogue and build a house on a larger property. This new estate served as the home of the Rabbis of Dembitz until the end of Jewish Dembitz. On this property were stables for horses, wagons for wayfarers and horse drivers. There was a large Sukka [56] for the Festival of Sukkot, which had a retractable roof, and was large enough to accommodate the Rabbi with all of his Chasidim and his entire entourage. There were also sleeping rooms, a kitchen, and a study hall. All of this was surrounded by a large fruit garden in which fruit of the land of Israel grew: grapes, olives, peaches, and cloves which were used for Havdala [57]. The dried clove plants were put on coals every Friday, [58] Reb Yisrael Reiner would bring them on a griddle into all the rooms of the house, so that the rooms would absorb an aromatic odor in honor of the Sabbath.

Reb Alter had four Gabbais: the first, Asher Appel, handled his external affairs and slept with him in the same room, the second would write his notes, and a third would stand near the door. The fourth, Reb Yisrael (Reiner) was in charge of supervising them all. He held this position from the days of Reb Reuven, and he was Reb Alter's private advisor. He was responsible for insuring that all of Reb Alter's many plans came to fruition, in particular with respect to commerce and business.

Reb Yisrael had apprenticed with Reb Reuven. This is how it came to be: Reb Yisrael's mother was a first cousin of Reb Reuven and was married to the Rabbi of Tarnow, who did not live very long after Reb Yisrael was born. What did Reb Reuven do? He married off his widowed cousin to a Chasid of his, Reb Kalman Feffer, who was quite wealthy and owned much property, and the child was educated personally by Reb Reuven. When the child grew up he became his right hand man in all his affairs, and Reb Reuven married him off to the daughter of a Chasid of his, the Shochet of Rieglice.

Reb Yisrael's house was next to the garden and courtyard of the Rabbi. Even though he had his own family, he would spend all his time in the house of the Rabbi, first Reb Reuven, then Reb Alter, and after Reb Alter's passing, Reb Shmuel. The Chasidim of Dembitz used to come to Reb Yisrael for advice in their affairs, whether it be family affairs, business affairs, or communal affairs, in particular after the passing of Reb Alter.

Reb Yisrael Reiner

Reb Alter did not live a long life, due to his weak state of health. His untimely death caused a dispute over the Rabbinate of Dembitz, between Reb Betzalel, the husband of Gittele, the eldest daughter of Reb Reuven, who at first lived with his father-in-law, and later settled in Pilzno, and between Reb Reuven's son Reb Shmuel, who was already a Rabbi in the town of Prystyk.

This dispute shook the whole city, until even the local gentiles became involved. When the Jews would stand in the marketplace and argue among themselves, whether for the side of Reb Shmuel or the side of Reb Betzalel, the gentiles would become involved in the argument, some "Za Shmulem" and some "Za Zalkem" [59]. The dispute continued for about three years until the Rabbi of Sieniawa was brought in as an arbitrator. He decided that the Rabbinate of Dembitz should go to Reb Shmuel, the son of Reb Reuven, and that he was to compensate his brother-in-law Reb Betzalel with 3,000 gold coins, so that he could buy into the Rabbinate of Pilzno. Reb Betzalel did not live long after he took over the Rabbinate of Pilzno. His death caused a renewal of the dispute with Reb Shmuel. After Reb Betzalel died in Pilzno, his relatives and supporters decided to bring him to Dembitz for burial beside his father-in-law Reb Reuven.

Making their way home from the Synagogue

{Page 32}

However, the Rabbi of the city, Reb Shmuel Horowitz, did not agree to this, since he wished to reserve the spot beside Reb Reuven for his own use. Indeed, when Reb Shmuel passed away in 1923, he was buried to the right of the Reb Reuven's grave. Reb Alter was buried to the left.

With the death of Reb Alter, the era of grandeur and honor of that Rabbinic dynasty came to an end, and a new era began.

The Rabbi Reb Shmuel

The Rabbi Reb Shmuel removed all the previous grandeur of the Rabbinic courtyard, with its wagons and horses, and he fired the horse driver. He lived a very modest lifestyle off his share of the Krowka (the communal coffers which came from of the income from ritual slaughter, weddings, burials, etc.) Also living off the Krowka was Rebbetzin Reisa the widow of Reb Alter, the ritual slaughterers, the Rabbinic Judge, the Cantor and the Mohel (ritual circumciser). Chasidim, both rich and poor, would come for Sabbaths, festivals, and vacations, and would eat at Reb Shmuel's table. The table spread was very simple, in accordance with the means of the Rabbinic court, which had diminished in size. On more than one occasion, the Rebbetzin Gitla complained about this state of affairs to Reb Yisrael the Gabbai, who managed the household affairs [60].

Several Jews of Przytiki were among the Chasidim of Reb Shmuel. They became associated with him during the time that he dwelt in that town. However, to his distress, not all the Chasidim of Reb Alter followed after Reb Shmuel his heir. Several of the supporters of Reb Betzalel remained opposed to Reb Shmuel until the end of their days, and they would travel on Sabbaths, festivals, and other days of gathering to Pilzno in two or three wagons. As they passed the courtyard of Reb Shmuel, they would burst out in song in loud voices in order to provoke him. This caused Reb Shmuel great distress.

When Reb Shmuel ascended to the Rabbinical position, the power of the Rabbinic household decreased in another way as well. Slowly but surely the Maskilim, who were few in number at this time, began to strengthen in the city. Winds of change began to take root among the youth. At that time the Rabbinical household began to co-operate with the ruling authorities in the area of elections and other areas. This accusation [61] became much more serious during the time of his successor Rabbi Tzvi Elimelech.

When Reb Shmuel passed away in 1923, a great controversy broke out into the city as to who would be his successor. There were two candidates: The first was Reb Hershele, Tzvi Elimelech Horowitz [62], the son of Reb Shmuel, who had not yet received his full ordination. The second was the Rabbi of nearby Daliowa, a descendent of the Rabbis of Wielopole. This controversy was a renewal of the old controversy that had taken place in the city before the appointment of Reb Reuven.

A committee of Rabbinic sages was appointed to adjudicate this matter. This committee included the Rabbinic Judge Reb Berish Shilai, Reb Ruvele Kluger, Reb Chaim Schlesinger, Reb Chaim Brik, and Reb Alter Pechter. The communal council was in favor of Reb Hershele because of the rights that came to him by virtue of his ancestry, but with the condition that he would first be required to receive his full fledged ordination, according to all its dictates. However the head of the community, Reb Hersh Taub, was not of the same mindset. He wished to appoint the Rabbi of Daliowa as the Rabbi of the city, and he set forth his stand by bringing him to settle in the city. However, the community would not be able to support the livelihoods of two Rabbis. The community was low in means due to the fact that the export of Kosher meat to Krakow had ceased. This endeavor used to bring a respectable sum of money to the communal coffers.

Reb Shlomo Zalman Frankel, the Rabbi of Daliowa.

Reb Hershele was supported primarily by his Chasidim. He would frequently travel to their towns. He also held court in Dembitz, but not with a great multitude of people.

In subsequent elections to the communal council, Reb Hersh Taub was no longer elected. A large number of his supporters went over to the side of the Rabbi. In his stead, Reb Tovia Zucker was elected as head of the community. The Rabbi and his opponents eventually made peace with each other, and they co-operated in their running of communal matters, and in their opposition to the Zionists and their associates.

An additional factor in the diminishment of the influence of the Rabbinical family was a dispute among the descendants of Reb Reuven who still remained in the city.

The family members of Reb Reuven who remained in town included his son-in-law Reb Yisrael Yosile Unger, who gave up the Rabbinate after the First World War to become a loan broker in nearby Tarnow. When his son Eliezer grew up, he became associated with the Mizrachi movement[63] and taught in the Hebrew school of Dembitz. Afterward, he became a communal activist in Tarnow, and he was one of the first people to bring news of the specific details of the Holocaust to the land. This made a great impression, however, we will not elaborate on it here.

Reb Shmuel's younger brother, Reb Naftalchi Horowitz, married the daughter of one of his father's Chasidim, Reb Motele Weinberg, a well-to-do large scale merchant from Dokla. He lived with his father-in-law for quite some time. After his father-in-law passed away, Reb Naftalchi tried to continue his business affairs, but did not succeed, and went bankrupt. He then returned to Dembitz, and acted as a Rabbi "unofficially", i.e. he did not receive a share of the communal coffers.

Another piece of bad luck befell Reb Naftalchi, as related among the Chasidim of Dembitz: From his youth, he had a pleasant voice, and he knew how to sing beautiful melodies, and to lead prayers to the great enjoyment of his listeners. Once, his uncle the Rabbi of Zukow requested Reb Naftalchi to travel to him with his entire family, and he prepared for the journey. His older brother Reb Alter, who was already the Rabbi of Dembitz, told him not to go since there was an ongoing dispute between the communities of Zukow and Dembitz. Reb Naftalchi, however, was adamant. He continued to prepare for the journey, and he certainly would have went. However he was attacked with a sudden hoarseness, and this hoarseness lasted the rest of his life, so that he could no longer be a fitting Cantor. As can well be understood, the Chasidim of Reb Alter saw in this as a sign and punishment from Heaven.

In 1924, after the First World War, Reb Naftalchi left for America to collect money, and he was successful in that endeavor. However, his son Ruvele squandered this money, in his attempts at financial affairs. He went bankrupt several times due to lack of experience, lack of understanding of the workings of business, and an overly generous heart.

From the time that Rev Naftalchi settled in Dembitz until he left there about ten years later, Reb Hersh Taub wished to appoint him as head of the Rabbinical court. However he met with the constant opposition of Rabbi Tzvi Elimelech. In the final communal elections, Reb Naftalchi joined with the Zionists, even though he had been among their chief opponents at the beginning of the century, and he was even among those who arranged festivities at the time of the death of Herzl in 1904 [64].

Rabbi Tzvi Elimelech perished in the Holocaust along with almost all of his family. May G-d avenge their deaths.

Translator's Footnotes

43. A traditional Jewish elementary school.

44. Katzvei Hakrach would mean the "Outskirts of the City". The reference here seems to be to some literary work.

45. Seemingly, many poor Jews would prefer to subsist with little than to embarrass themselves by requesting help.

46. Ropczyce and Wielopole are both towns within a 15 mile radius of Dembitz.

47. This last line is somewhat ambiguous. It could mean "the Leonine Rabbi of the City", where Leonine would be a praiseworthy attribute "like a lion". The context seems to mean that he was "Rabbi of a Gathering of the City", which I have translated as "Rabbi of the Entire City".

48. This refers to a Midrash (Rabbinic legend) that at the time that Moses ascended mount Sinai at the giving of the Torah, the angels were jealous that a mortal human had ascended into their midst.

49. "Shabbat Malketa", a Cabalistic term for the Sabbath. Joyous ecstasy was a characteristic of the Chasidic movement.

50. During the week of mourning (Shiva) following the death of a close relative, several mourning practices are observed, such as sitting on low stools, refraining from greetings, and the wearing of torn clothing. On the Sabbath that falls during Shiva, these public mourning practices are prohibited.

51. Ritual slaughterer.

52. My memoirs.

53. Yiddish word for note – it generally means a written request for Divine intercession for one's needs that is given to an illustrious Rabbi, who would intercede before G-d. This text uses the Hebrew word "Petek" as well as the Yiddish word "Kvitel". The word is used nowadays as well for the notes that people place in the Western Wall in Jerusalem.

54. A person with 'enlightened' thoughts, who was beginning to loosen himself from the strictures of shtetl Orthodoxy (see note above on the Haskala movement). In the present context, it is evident that the person in question remained a religiously committed Jew, albeit with more

liberal ideas than would have been acceptable as a follower of a Chasidic Rebbe. Later on in the text the word Maskil is used to describe those who have broken away from traditional orthodoxy completely.

55. A tabernacle or booth used during the Festival of Sukkot (Tabernacles) in keeping with the Biblical command. The Festival of Sukkot occurs in the autumn five days after Yom Kippur.

56. A ceremony held at the conclusion of the Sabbath, in which a blessing is made over wine, a multi-wicked candle and spices.

57. The Gabbai would be the person who managed the Rabbi's affairs.

58. Za in Polish means behind. "Za Shmulem" means those behind Shmuel, and Za Zalkem, means those behind Zalke (a diminutive of Betzalel).

59. It is not 100% clear from the context what the Rebbetzin was complaining about. It seems to be that she was complaining that the provisions for the guests should have been more abundant. However, it is not impossible that what is meant here is that she is complaining that there were too many guests coming to the household, more than the household could support.

60. Seemingly of becoming too cozy with the government.

61. Hersh is a direct Yiddish translation of the Hebrew Tzvi. Both words mean 'dear'. Thus, the names Tzvi, Hersh, or the diminutive form Hershel, are often interchangeable.

62. The Orthodox Zionist movement.

63. The opposition to Zionism often took on quite radical forms in Chasidic orthodoxy. In fact, this radical opposition to Zionism can still be seen today amongst the Satmar Chasidim.'

64. The Hassidim believe, as do all Orthodox Jews, that the Messianic end of days will bring about a return of the Jewish people to the Land of Israel. The Hassidim here believe that the timing should be left totally in the hands of G-d, and any human effort to shorten the exile and return to the Land of Israel en masse before the Messiah arrives is inappropriate and doomed to failure.

{Page 33}

Enlightenment and Zionism

Translated by Jerrold Landau

We do not have detailed information as to when the secular Haskala (enlightenment) began to take root in Dembitz. The attempt by Hertz Homberg to set up a Government German school for Jewish children at the end of the 18th century failed quickly. The Jews of Dembitz, just like the Jews of other cities and towns in Galicia, would certainly have rejected this new sapling of foreign culture. It is quite conceivable that the number of parents who agreed to send their children to this school was small enough that this institution could not really be called a true school. However, it is important to point out that, due to the unusual persistence of the government, this school was able to function for several years until the central government in Vienna was forced to admit in 1806 that the experiment was unsuccessful, and the government German schools for Jewish children of Galicia were then officially closed down.

The Jewish children of Dembitz were educated in the purity of Torah in cheders and Beis Midrashes (study halls), just as they were in the rest of the cities of Galicia. Their knowledge of the language of the neighboring gentiles was quite sparse, as this knowledge was only necessary in the realm of business and livelihood. Even those Jews who had greater contact with the gentiles and knew how to speak their language – whether because they lived in their neighborhoods near the outer areas of the city, or whether because they intermingled with the gentiles of the neighboring villages due to their business dealings – were nevertheless not able to read the language. Jewish pronunciation was evident in the spoken Polish of the Jews of Dembitz, for the most part.

Until the last quarter of the 19th century, the Jews of Dembitz, just as the Jews of the rest of Galicia, saw no need or value in learning the Polish language, since their dealings with the central and regional governments were conducted solely in German. For that reason, when the Jews decided that they needed to learn a foreign language, they preferred German, due to the need for contact with the governing authorities, the general trend of the Jewish Haskala, and the similarity to their own Yiddish language.

As contact with large cities, both near and far, increased, and as the economic connections with businesses and factories throughout the country increased, the need to communicate in writing arose – the need for a general enlightenment and acclimatization to the ways of the larger world increased in like fashion. Whether they were asked to provide agricultural products to the local area, such as eggs, grain and wood – or whether they wished to buy clothing, cloth, iron products, etc. – at every point the benefit of knowledge of the vernacular, both written and spoken, became more and more obvious. The more well to do, those whose business dealings brought them to the bourse in Vienna, found it necessary to read a newspaper – at first in German, and later, as the administrative independence of Galicia grew, also in Polish. Thus did the gates to secular enlightenment open slowly among the Jews of Dembitz, accompanied by incessant internal debates. The pioneers were, on the one hand the children of the well to do families, whose situation gained them a higher status, and on the other hand the children of the poor families who attempted to improve their lot by means of enlightenment and secular knowledge. At first only private teachers filled this need, such from as the Liprant and Krantz families, and others. Later, as compulsory education in public schools became more prevalent, the Polish schools began to fill this need.

Thus, the Haskala movement came to Dembitz significantly later than it did to larger cities. At that time, the Haskala movement in Galicia began to define the direction of the nation, as it did in the rest of Eastern Europe. The Haskala reached Dembitz in the national sense with the gradual introduction of Zionism. It is impossible to determine exactly at what point, and through whom was the Zionist idea introduced to Dembitz. We can conjecture that Zionism became prevalent in the 1880s, with the national awakening that arose in conjunction with the pogroms in southern Russia, and through the influence of the newspapers "Hamagid" and later "Hashachar" of Smolniskin. These newspapers had a small readership in this city, since most of the Jewish population, although by no means all, were under the influence of the Orthodox. We know from hearsay that the first Hebrew socialist newspaper, "Haemet" published by Lieberman, was also read by the first maskilim of Dembitz.

In any case, it is a fact that already by the beginning of the 1890s there were active Zionists in Dembitz. In 1893, they attempted to organize a Zionist organization, however we do not know whether they were successful, and if so, for how long it lasted. Word of this organization was transmitted by delegates from the Dembitz area to the second Zionist convention of Galicia which took place in Lvov in 1894. At that time there were already Zionist organizations in Tarnow, a city with which the Jews of Dembitz were in close contact, as well as in other smaller towns near to Dembitz, such as Pilzno and Ropczyce. In particular, when the "Ahavat Zion" organization was founded in Tarnow in 1897 with the aim of promoting settlement in the Land of Israel, and became actively involved in founding a moshava in the Land of Israel by the name of "Machanaim", there was great excitement about this also in Dembitz.

{Page 34}

The influence increased further due to the fact that one of the people who intended to settle in Machanaim was Mottel Leibel, the brother of Reb Chaim Leibel, a long-time resident and the son of an honorable family of the city. This matter was a topic of conversation for everyone, especially when he left along with his family to the Land of Israel.

At first many of the locals, including many of the particularly Orthodox people, such as the Dayan Rabbi Yehuda Leib Laufbahn the grandfather of Yitzchak Laufbahn, as well as many Hassidim, joined the ranks of the "Ahavat Zion" movement in Dembitz. However after a short while, the Rabbi and Tzadik of Sziniowa as well as the Rabbi and Tzadik of Belz proclaimed their opposition to the movement, and almost all of the Rabbinical courts in Galicia followed suit. At that time the Hassidim began to wage an open battle against "actively precipitating the end", and a powerful war erupted between the two camps.

The main weapons in this battle was "graffiti literature" [65], a written debate, where both sides did not hesitate to refer to the other with names couched in flowery rhetoric, replete with hints and innuendoes, each side according to its own spirit.

The Zionist movement remained very small, and only a few youths joined it openly. These youths were maskilim, who had rejected the traditional Beis Midrash, including: Eliahu Gewirtz the son of Reb Alter and the great-grandson of Rabbi Elish the Rabbinical judge, and the grandson of Rabbi Daniel the Strong, Nissan Taffet, Shmuel Mahler the son of Reb Chaim, Moshe and David Leibel the sons of Reb Chaim, along with other people who kept their identification hidden. When the most prominent members of this organization left their city, the field of battle was open for several years until a new generation of Zionists came of age. Some of these were people who abandoned the Beis Midrash, and they were headed by Yehuda Bornstein, and later Yitzchak Laufbahn. Others were businessmen and tradesmen who were no longer dependent on the Jewish G-d, and were not particularly concerned with the view of the community.

From this point, the Haskala and Zionism had caught on in Dembitz to such a degree that assimilation was no longer an issue in the communal life, and the opponents of Zionism were found only among the Hassidim. The few assimilationists among the professional intelligentsia no longer had the need or the possibility of organized activity within the community.

The second unsuccessful attempt to establish a Zionist organization in Dembitz took place in 1904, ten years after the first attempt. A hall was rented next to the synagogue, and they even succeeded in arranging a memorial service after the death of Dr. Herzl. However, one morning they found all of the furnishings scattered, and the organization lost its life force. This deed was perpetrated by the Hassidic opponents, who were heartened by the death of the Zionist leader, and even arranged a festive meal on that occasion. This deed was described in the Zionist newspaper "Der Yud" that was published in Krakow. A Zionist meeting hall was not established again in Dembitz until after the First World War, when conditions had changed radically.

A few years later, an article from Dembitz appeared in the above - mentioned newspaper, apparently from the pen of Meir Sapir, with the signature "Yankel le mort" saying: "By us Zionism died in its childhood". A youth could be a Zionist – but when he becomes a groom he loses interest. There was much truth to this adage, and it remained true until the end of the First World War. The means used by the general Zionist organization to raise funds were quite limited: selling of shekalim [66], and Keren Kayemet [67] stamps, a memorial evening for Herzl and an annual Chanuka play (Macabee players). These means were insufficient to sustain the Zionist movement throughout the year. A small local committee was established, consisting of appointed or elected representatives. Every few years there were also elections for the state organizations, such as the parliament and the Sejm of Galicia, as well as for local organizations, such as the city or communal council. With all this, they did not have the means to sustain an organization of young people during the intermediate times, since in addition to all of the difficulties and persecution, there was also the attrition due to emigration.

After some time, an attempt was made to expand the Zionist activities by the founding of a businessman's organization, just as had been done in larger cities. This union would protect the business situation of the merchants of Dembitz, such as the issue as to whether closing of business on Sundays would be obligatory or optional, the issue of taxes, etc., and the setting up of a reading hall, etc. The Zionists were the main force behind this organization, however the businessmen themselves, men of means and influence, did not participate in this organization, and the union only lasted for a short time.

The driving force of Zionism during this period was the enthusiastic youth named Yehuda Bornstein. He did not lose one opportunity to inject the spirit of Zionism into the downtrodden city. What he was not able to accomplish with the elders he was able to accomplish in a great fashion with the youths.

Poale Zion

The first Zionist organization in Dembitz which managed to survive was "The Union of Poale Zion" (The Workers of Zion).

Very few of the Jewish businesses in town hired salaried employees, so most of the members of this organization were employees from outside the city, or local artisans who worked in their parents' workshops. These people would be less influenced by the pressure from the old guard of the city, and they would also be more brazen in going against the wishes of their parents.

The means of sustenance of the workers' organization was wide enough to be able to win over members from the surrounding area, since the mandate of the organization included the protection of rights of the workers, and the raising of the level of culture among the populace, which at first was quite low.

In the newspaper of Poale Zion, "Der Yiddisher Arbeiter" [68], which was published in Vienna (edition 8, from June 1, 1905), the first article was written about the organization in Dembitz: "Even in our small town, Zionism has begun to spread among the workers. Our organization was founded only with great effort, for we were forced to wage war with the local zealous Hassidim, who were not willing to agree in any manner to the establishment of an organization here."

Later, it describes the first meeting which took place on April 23 of that year. The scholar Rabinowitz spoke at that meeting. He was apparently not a Dembitz native. "He explained the principles of Zionism and in particular the principles of Poale Zion, and the purpose of the organization". The speech had a great effect.

{Page 35}

The first committee was established, with L. Wasserman (a tailor) as the chairman, M. Taub as vice chairman, Sh. Lempel as treasurer, Aharon Finn as secretary, as well as other members of the committee.

The articles was signed by the initials Y. B., that is Yehuda Bornstein, who from behind the scenes was the main force behind the founding of the organization.

When the general organization of Poale Zion was established in Austria (The Jewish General Workers Organization), the workers and business helpers of Dembitz joined, and the Dembitz branch became affiliated with the general organization.

In the meantime, there was apparently a significant changeover of the members of the organization due to the massive emigration. In the second general meeting which took place on April 28th 1906, a new board was elected, with M. Schildkraut as chairman, M. Sheinfeld as vice chairman, Sh. R. Wurzel as secretary, M. Israel (a coppersmith) as treasurer, and M. Dar as recorder.

The organization continued to gain in strength. It felt the need to expand the realm of activities to female workers as well. Once again, Yehuda Bornstein was the main force behind this action. On December 29th of that year, an organizational meeting of the female workers took place which was addressed by Yehuda Bornstein. A committee was appointed consisting of Dintfas, B. Kreindel, S. Siedlesker, and M. Siedlesker. This meeting which founded the "Women's Union of Poale Zion", took place on April 5th, and the above mentioned appointees were elected to the committee. It was decide to establish a library (which was never established), and to offer courses in enlightenment to the women members.

After about two years after the founding of the union of Poale Zion, an action took place which had no precedent in Dembitz nor in any other town in western Galicia: a general workers strike. This strike took place after the strike of the needle workers in nearby Tarnow, which was organized by the Z.P.S. (The Jewish socialist workers' organization – later known as the Bund). The many achievements of the strike in Tarnow left a great impression among the workers, and the workers' union of Poale Zion decided to demonstrate that the workers have the ability to improve their living conditions if they put the effort to it. Dembitz was one of the few places where Poale Zion was the only workers' union. At that time, the manufacturing of clothing for the purpose of export was beginning to develop in Dembitz. It was still not possible to rely on the local residents to organize something as major as a strike, so an organizer was sent in from the central organization in Krakow, namely the comrade Piltzer, later Dr. Piltzer, who now lives in Israel.

The needle workers in Dembitz would work in the summer from 5 a. m. until a late hour in the evening, and in the winter from 7 a. m. until 11 p. m., and on occasion until 12 midnight or 1 a. m. The main objective of the strike was therefore to reduce the number of working hours per day to twelve (!).

Twenty-eight workers participated in the strike, of whom only half were participants of the union. One Christian worker joined the strike as well. Financial assistance was sent to Dembitz from the central organization, without which the workers would not have been able to sustain themselves for the duration of a nine day strike.

The employers did not remain silent during this strike. As usual, they turned to a "third party" – the mayor and the governor of the area (Starosta), who ordered the arrest of two of the strike leaders. They were immediately freed due to the intercession of the above mentioned representative. The employers went out to the neighboring cities to seek strike breakers, but they were not successful: no worker from the outside was willing to come to their aid on account of the great publicity that Poale Zion made with regard to the strike. Additional measures taken to frighten the strikers included the searches and other protocols that were ordered to be conducted by the local gendarmes in the union offices. The workers stood firm even after the employers agreed to reduce the workday to thirteen hours, from 6 a.m. until 8 p.m., and the entire city was in ferment.

Finally, the strike ended with victory for the workers – it was agreed that the workday would be from 6 a. m. until 7 p. m. with a one hour break for lunch. The employers were compelled to pay the workers for the days they were on strike, and a condition was made that none of the strikers would be fired.

The victory in the needle workers' strike raised the spirits of Poale Zion in Dembitz and the surrounding areas. However, the governor of the Ropczyce region, under whose jurisdiction such an event never took place again, decided to liquidate the rebellious organization based on the repeated pleas of one of the employers. After about two months the regional government ordered the closing of the Dembitz branch of the Jewish General Workers' Association on the pretext that during the needle workers' strike the song "Red Flag" (Czerwony sztandar) was sung in the offices of the organization, and on one occasion the members of the organization shouted out "long live social democracy!" as they left a meeting. These serious deeds were definitely legal, however who could stand in the way of the will of a governor of a Galician town?

Nevertheless, the opportunity arose to evade the order, and a new branch of the General Workers' Union was founded. At the founding meeting a new committee was elected, with L. Fuchs as chairman, Grinhut as vice chairman, Wurzel as secretary, and Schneider as treasurer.

At first, many members joined the union. However, apparently, the organization weakened significantly due to emigration. In the years 1908-1909, there was no mention at all in the newspaper of the activities of Poale Zion in Dembitz.

In August 1910, a general membership meeting took place and it was decided to establish anew the Poale Zion union after the liquidation of the national workers' union. About fifty members signed up at that time. The temporary committee began the activities of the branch. A meeting took place in order to distribute the Zionist shekels, and a committee was chosen for that purpose, consisting of Naftali Schneur (currently in the United States), Leiner (currently in Israel), and Mendel Wilner. About fifty workers participated in that gathering. Lectures on various topics took place each Sabbath. One of these lectures, entitled "Our Cultural Tasks", was given by Yitzchak Laufbahn, who had returned from a visit to the Land of Israel. Special action was also taken to distribute the newspaper "The Jewish Worker".

After the other Zionist organizations in the city founded a public library, the members of Poale Zion found themselves disenfranchised by the founders, who did not purchase books in Yiddish. Therefore, they were forced to join the library as members, so that they would be able to have an influence on its activities.

The Poale Zion convened a meeting together with the "Zionist Citizens" in the large Beis Midrash in order to deal with the issue of the "Public Library" that was founded by the governing authorities on January 1, 1911. Meshulam Davidson of Rzeszow (currently of Israel) gave a lecture on the necessity of registering Yiddish as the spoken language.

{Page 36}

A new committee was elected at the general meeting, consisting of Schneur as chairman, Leiner as vice chairman, and Wilner as secretary. A nice two room apartment was rented as an office and the cultural activities increased. A. Rivotzki (Shlimovitch), the representative of the central organization, visited the group and lectured. A Chanuka party was arranged with the participation of Meshulam Davidson, who was very active during those years in the activities of the movement in the entire region.

One Sabbath, Tzvi Wolf lectured on "Socialism and the Agricultural Question". The cultural activities did not weaken even though organization lost several of its most active members due to emigration. Lectures were given by local members on the topic of Jewish literature, history, Zionism, socialism, and other such topics. Evening classes were also arranged.

After the local chapter had re-established itself, special attention was paid to youth activities, and a "Jugent" group was established which consisted of twenty boys and girls at its outset. This was the first youth group in Dembitz. After several months this became an organized "Jugent" group with 25 members. Most of its activities focussed on evening classes.

In an article on Dembitz in the newspaper "Yidisher Arbeiter" from that time period, the following fact is noted: "Recently we were informed of an intended lecture by the member Avner (that is Yitzchak Ben Tzvi [69], who is today the president of Israel), however to our distress Avner became ill during his trip and he was not able to come to us. They invited by telegraph the member Davidson from Rzeszow, who spoke on the same topic "Labor and Culture among the Jews of the Land of Israel" ... The lecture was very successful and we thank the member Davidson for his volunteering.

Thanks to the valiant effort of several members, the number of members of the chapter increased. A new committee was elected. At every chance that presented itself, donations were solicited for the Fund for the Workers of the Land of Israel (K. P. E. Y.), which had been founded at that time by the world organization of Poale Zion in order to strengthen the cooperative and labor movements in the Land of Israel.

The efforts of Poale Zion to gain more influence in the public library, which had been founded by the women's Zionist organization "Debora", were not very successful. The Zionist university students, who took it upon themselves to run the library, were not interested in purchasing Yiddish books which were in demand by the common folk. Therefore, it became necessary to found a special library which would serve the needs of masses. The young women of the common folk did not find the atmosphere of the women's' Zionist organization "Debora" to be appropriate for themselves, so a new women's organization "Chavatzelet" was set up with the assistance of Poale Zion and due to the efforts of Ruchama Gruenspan. A significant number of working women were included in its membership.

When the issue of the library came to the fore, the two related groups Poale Zion and Chavatzelet, with the efforts of Yitzchak Laufbahn, established a separate library "Yidishe Folksbiblioteke". The library started with forty books, and became one of the most significant cultural institutions in the city until the time of the Holocaust.

At the general meeting held on October 30, 1911, the following people were elected to the committee: Naftali Schneur as chairman, Moshe Taub as vice chairman, Mendel Wilner as secretary, Pinsk as treasurer, Shtrik as recorder, Parker, Wilner, Hershlag, Bronheim, Sender Bienstock as officers. Ring, Wurzel and Treister were appointed to the inspection committee.

At the conclusion of seven years of the functioning of the committee, a festive celebration took place. The members of Chavatzelet participated, as well as many members of the Zionist youth. For the first time, the Poale Zion choir performed.

The Workers' Organization

Translated by Jerrold Landau

There were very few labor disputes in Dembitz. There were no large factories there who would hire salaried employees. Most of the workers were employed by family members. In the larger plants such as the wood engraving plant of Nathan Grünspan and the foundry of Naftali Eisen, the vast majority of the employees were Christian. From time to time, the Poale Zion union would become involved in a minor dispute between an employer and an employee, however, after the needle workers' strike of 1907 there were few such opportunities for involvement. One opportunity for action came in 1912 with respect to the makers of the upper parts of shoes (oberteilmachers) who were employed in Mendel Leibel's shoe factory, which had only been established a short time before. This factory also employed mainly Christians. Only the makers of the uppers were Jewish, and most of them had been brought in from different cities. After the employer was in significant arrears in the payment of salary, and a written complaint submitted by the union was not answered, a strike was declared. This forced the employer to respond to the complaint after a few days. In the periodical "Der Yiddisher Arbeiter" which described this strike, it is pointed out that "Mr. Leibel is a Zionist, and not a simple one, but rather a flaming radical."

"Debora"

The Poale Zion organization was the first organization, however once the ice was broken in the city, that very same year a second organization was founded due to the efforts of Yehuda Bornstein. This organization, called "Debora", was known as the "Union of Zionist Women". However, the membership consisted only of unmarried women, who were well to do and well educated. This organization's activities were primarily in the educational realm, with a particular emphasis on culture and Zionist publicity. Its endeavors were assisted by several students of the Dembitz Gymnasia and the University of Krakow. However due its use of the Polish language and the social makeup, this organization remained rather small and did not reach out to (and it is not clear if it even intended to reach out to) the masses of Jewish young women whose language of speech was Yiddish and whose way of life was much simpler.

Zionist Women's Circle "Debora"

These differences were instrumental in the founding of the young womens' organization of Poale Zion, called "Chavatzelet", as has previously been mentioned, due to the efforts of Yitzchak Laufbahn. This organization was headed by Ruchama Grünspan who was far more active than the older members of Debora. These differences were also instrumental in the founding of the Public Library of Poale Zion. As has previously been explained, the members of the intelligentsia who headed the Jewish National Library, which had been founded by Yehuda Bornstein, were not interested in purchasing Yiddish books, and also to a large degree they were not interested in purchasing Hebrew books. The situation was such that this library, rather than spreading Jewish national culture, served as a vehicle for assimilation.

"Geula" and "Shachar"

With the development of the two organizations, Poale Zion and Debora, together with the growth of two different approaches within the Jewish youth movement in Galicia, there arose in 1907 two additional Zionist organizations whose influence and impact was well recognized and significant.

These were Geula (Redemption), a group of Dembitz high school (gymnasia) and university students, founded by Yehuda Bornstein; and Hashachar (the Dawn), an organization of Beis Hamedrash (religious school) alumnae, a branch of the national Histadrut of the same name headed by Yitzchak Laufbahn before he emigrated to Palestine. Geula held its meetings privately in its members' homes due to fear of discovery by the faculty of the gymnasia and expulsion from the school for the offence of participating in a secular organization. Hashachar held its gatherings in the facilities of Poale Zion.

Hashachar held its first conference in Dembitz at the Bornstein Hotel during Passover 1908. Yitzchak Laufbahn was one of the featured speakers, and he also headed the second conference. However, he passed away prior to the third conference. During this period many of Hashachar's members and staff emigrated to Palestine, while the remaining members and the Beis Medrash students joined other Zionist organizations. As a result, there was no longer any purpose for Hashachar's special activities. The area organizations, including those of Dembitz, continued their efforts in a smaller scale fashion, until they also ceased to function with the outbreak of World War I.

By 1912, Geula had stopped functioning as the Jewish high school population had declined and there were only five remaining members in the senior gymnasia class.

"Local Committee"

Starting in 1910, a local Zionist committee (known as the "Local Committee") was formed in Dembitz as an umbrella group to coordinate the activities of various organizations including the collecting of the shekel, arranging elections for the Zionist Congress, Jewish National Fund activities, collecting funds from charity boxes (pushkas) in the residents' homes, setting up a Hebrew school and running it, activities regarding the elections, and all other political activities.

{Page 38}

This committee served as an umbrella organization for all of the Zionist organizations with the exception of Poale Zion. For every joint activity, such as producing the population registry or setting up elections, it was necessary to deal with Poale Zion outside of the committee. Mr. Bendet Fett served as the chairman of the Zionist committee at its outset and for many years thereafter. He was one of those who was most committed to the Zionist idea and to the Hebrew school.

The matter of Aliya to the Land of Israel, of all the issues that were of importance to the community and in particular to the youth, was always outside of the realm of activity of the local Zionist committee. Assistance for those that made Aliya was provided by private arrangements, help from friends, and other such venues. It would have been an inadvisable thing to give out an address to the parents of those that made Aliya which could be used for complaints and requests, since most of those that went did so without the permission of their parents. The party line of the Zionist organization was always that the lot of the immigrants to Israel might reflect badly on the movement itself.

Aliya of individuals from Dembitz to the Land of Israel had already begun by 1909. The first of those that made Aliya included: Yitzchak Laufbahn, Tzvi Wolf of blessed memory, and Moshe Taub (who now lives in Kfar Yechezkel), all members of Poale Zion. Afterwards Mendel Wilner, one of the leaders of the movement in the town, made Aliya to the Land of Israel. However he returned after a short time, and after his return he remained as one of the chief activists in Dembitz. He was an individual whose cultural and organizational activities among the youth and the adults remained in the memory of the people of the city for many years, even after his emigration to America in the wake of the First World War.

"Geula" and "Hashachar" organizations

{Page 41}

Memories as Things Were

Jews in the Town Committee

For many years Jews formed a majority of the population in Dembitz. In the last few decades the proportion shifted. In 1921 there were already 1600 Jews in a total population of 4000. The largest part of this increase in the number of Jews was offset by people moving to larger cities, to Germany or America. Besides this, the Galician leadership systematically "increased" the town area by adding nearby villages. Thus they would be able to eliminate the Jewish majority.

World War I and the Russian occupation also helped to decrease the Jewish majority and many residents of Dembitz did not return. Later, during the 1920s, the Polish government established an "Industrial Zone" in Dembitz. The number of Poles grew as they were able to obtain work there. The Jewish workers became the minority.

Gradually, the Jewish majority in management also decreased. Top management in Dembitz was still in Jewish hands and the power was theirs. However, the influx of intelligent people changed the balance.

The Jews did not give up their rights to elect one of them as mayor, but they willingly agreed to forgo the right. It was acceptable for a Pole to hold the position of mayor as long as he was not an enemy of the Jews. This had worked in the past. The non-Jews who held the position were on good terms with the Jews. Later, this situation changed

Prior to WWI the top management consisted of 36 residents from 4 areas with a small Jewish majority. The Jewish representatives were unable to deal with the issues since they did know enough Polish and were unaware of what the town needed. The Jews of Dembitz, whether silent or vocal, did not bring honor on the community.

It was comical to listen to the Jews express themselves in Polish. Their ignorance and struggles caused the younger generation to ridicule them. Nothing really helped.

Mr. Shaul Kerner, a wealthy man, always had the young anti-Semites rolling with laughter with his poor Polish. He had a big disagreement with the mayor. This was in comparison to the merchant Moshe Rosenberg, to Haim Blecher and to Haim Yaakov who were highly respected. There was also Haim Mahler, son of Yehuda Mahler, the former city treasurer. He was an assessor and was regarded with respect due to his demeanor. There were also others.

Reb Yehuda Mahler and Reb Chaim Mahler

Change did not come until after the war when a group of young people became representatives.   They had knowledge and national tendencies-Zionists like Shmaya Viedershpan, Poalei Zion like Dr. Pinhas Loifban and Shimon Grinshpan.   They understood how to protect the needs of the poor and the workers in the Jewish community.   They earned the respect of the Jews and the Poles. By then the Jews in Dembitz became a minority.

{Page 42}

Parliamentary Elections
Translated by Roberta Newman

In 1907, the first elections to the Austrian Parliament took place as per the new electoral law, which had been passed in November 1905 after a general strike called by the social-democratic parties in all lands under the domain of the Austrian crown. The achievement of this victory took place under the influence of the revolutionary events in Russia, which cast a pall of fear over the rulers of Europe and motivated them to consider ways of preventing similar occurrences in Austria.

During the political struggle for electoral reform, the Zionists in Austria, as well as Poale Zion, came out with the demand that a separate election-curia be created for the Jewish minority in order to ensure full representation in the parliament for the Jewish population , and in general, in order to assert the existence of a Jewish nationality claiming the right of national self-rule.

This initiative did not have the slightest chance of succeeding. Against it were arrayed not only the bourgeois segments of all the dominant ethnic groups in the Austrian lands, but also, and not least, the social democrats, who considered it national separatism. Nonetheless, it was a good opportunity for a propaganda campaign about Jewish nationalist ideas.

Even more significantly, the general parliamentary elections were an opportunity to introduce the broad Jewish masses to the idea of Jewish nationalist solutions to issues. Everywhere, there were demonstrations that stirred up the Jewish population and urged it to vote for Jewish nationalist candidates, some of which were organized in electoral districts where a Zionist had not slightest prospects of getting elected. In the Dembitz electoral district, no Jewish candidate ran for office in the first election, and therefore there was no critical mass. Here, the general ruling party, at whose helm stood the conservative aristocrats, fielded the priest Pastor from Biecz as a candidate. In his speeches, Pastor bitterly mocked Jews and in general, represented himself as an open anti-Semite. Opposing him was the secretary of the Dembitz court, Stanisław Dym, whose base of support included Polish liberals and some Jews, among them the lawyer, Fishler. Dym suffered a big defeat and, as a result, so did lawyer Fishler.

Dr. Fishler had never been a Zionist. In local politics, he had originally supported the Mayor, Tsauderer, a Christian convert and the owner of the only pharmacy in the city. Eventually, there was a falling out between them, and in the elections to the "*Gmine*" (community board), the Jewish majority voted for Fishler as mayor. But here, the government stepped in. The Lemberg governorship mounted a protest against the election and mandated that new elections be held.

In the meantime, the Dembitz aristocrats put on a big ball, to which they invited, among others, the two opponents: The pharmacist-convert and the Jewish lawyer.

"When the heart of the king was merry";[1] a few prominent non-Jews attempted to make peace between them. They brought Dr. Fishler over to the convert and waited to see what would happen. Dr. Fishler extended his hand to Tsauderer in peace, but the convert turned away... The laughter could be heard throughout the entire city. That was, it seems, the end of Dr. Fishler's social activism, a hiatus that lasted many years.

During the second elections to the Austrian Parliament in 1911, a Jewish candidate was finally run in the Dembitz electoral district, the Zionist Dr. Sirop from Nowy Sącz. There was no socialist candidate, and the ruling party candidate was a Professor Doktor Jaworski. The Dembitz Zionists, including Poale Zion, mounted a broad propaganda campaign that included the towns in the district. Among the Dembitz Zionists who appeared publicly at demonstrations were Kuba Nichthauser, Dintenfas[2], Efroym Rakover, and Dr. Piltser; and from the Poale Zion were Mendel Wilner, Moyshe Wurtzel, and the young student Pinchas Laufbahn . Rabbi R. Shmuel Horowitz and the Hasidim, along with the Mahazike ha-Dat[3] throughout Galicia, voted body and soul for the government candidate, the conservative Dr. Jaworski.

At the outset, the Zionist candidate had no chance of being elected. Indeed, the electoral district did not have a Jewish majority. Aside from this, the Zionist influence in all of the cities and towns was at the time quite minimal-- by then, Dembitz was considered a Zionist stronghold--and opposing them like a wall was the Hasidic population, who shivered in deadly fear of a "candlestick" (as the militia men were called, because of the metal tips of their head-coverings), and who, in general, had no desire to "mess with erar." ("Erar" signified in Austria the royal treasury and the tax office, but in the small towns it meant the government itself). He who campaigned against the ruling party candidate. or even worse, openly announced that he was voting "against the government," placed himself in danger, placed himself at risk of higher taxes or of provoking a visit to his house by a sanitary commission, who would issue him a penalty or maybe even compel him to put up a wall. (The sanitary commissions had already been immortalized in Galicia in a widespread children's rhyme: "Aaron, pears, carob, up above stands a doctor-- below stands a barrel, ten gulden fine"[4]). As a result, there was a great deal of fear, especially because the *Starosta* (district head) from Ropczyce personally came down and warned the Zionists. The "*Starosta* ," Dr. Heller, a Polonized German, asked the Zionist "election-committee" (as it was then called) to stop campaigning for Dr. Sirop because "we won't permit your candidate to appear on the ballot." He got a sharp enough reply from Dr. Piltser and Mendel Wilner, who, as a result were severely punished: in the next military "review," the regime did Mendel Wilner the service of classifying him as "fit for service," and so he served in the army from 1913 until the end of the war in 1918.

In the meantime, the youth in Dembitz were on a rampage. When an outside Jewish agitator for Professor Jaworski appeared in the town, he had to "withdraw with honor." When one Dr. Margolis from Krakow alit from the train in Dembitz in order to agitate for Professor Jaworski, he found every horse-drawn carriage taken and one young man (Mendel Wilner) delivered to him a "letter of greeting," that for sure brought him no joy... this person, alas, had to go into the city on foot, surrounded by youths who bestowed upon him such epithets as "Moszka,"[5] "Jewish traitor," and others in a similar vein.

In Dembitz, a series of demonstrations took place in the *Prostn besmedresh*[6] and in other locations. Well-known Galician folk orators moved the audiences to tears. And this is how the Zionist candidate in the election district that, aside from Dembitz ,was comprised of Pilzno, Ropczyce, Brzostek, Jasło, Kołaczyce, and Gorlice, got the majority of the Jewish vote, notwithstanding the rabbis and the *Starosta*.

{Page 43}

Once upon a time there was...

by Ruchama

Translated by Roberta Newman

First years

From my earliest years on, I was drawn in to the circle of Zionist activity. Dembitz was one of the first towns between Tarnów and Rzeszów penetrated by Zionism, even before the end of the 19th century. In my era, as far as I remember, the driving force behind the young movement in Dembitz was Yudl Bornstein (may his memory be for a blessing), my future husband and life-companion. Though himself quite young, he demonstrated an ability to inspire large circles of youth in the town with the Zionist ideal, and it is no exaggeration to say that he was the initiator and mentor of almost every important Zionist achievement in Dembitz in this first period. Bravely and without fear of anyone he brought the Zionist idea to the most diverse circles. I myself became acquainted with the fundamentals of Zionism through him.

To this very day, I remember the memorial for Dr. Herzl, on the second anniversary of his death, that was disrupted by a group of Hasidim headed up by Rabbi R. Shmuel Horowitz. I was among the few very young girls who, at the memorial, were distributing black mourning bands[7] to people as they arrived and who were going around with *pushkes* collecting money from those assembled in the synagogue.

These girls were the first members of the Zionist women's association, "Dvorah,"[8] which had been founded that year at the initiative of Yudl Bornstein. Those who belonged to it included: Rivke and Malke Bornstein; Tauba, Tsile, and Salye Eisen; Dobe Gewirtz; Tonka Dintenfas[9]; Mrs. Zilberman; Golde Kriger; Fradl Toy[10]; Ruchama Grünspan ; Anna Bras; Manye Wurtzel; Salye Mahler; Bintshe Leibel; Bronka Nichthauser; Fridshe and Rokhl Sapir, etc.

Almost at the same time, Yehuda Bornstein founded the student association, "Geulah," whose members included: Iser Dintenfas[11]; Marek, Kuba, and Moritz Bras--who were high school students. Later, membership also included students from other places who attended high school in Dembitz: Moyshe Bergner and Gabel from Redim (Radymno); Vistraykh and the Potasher brothers; Taytlboym from Jarosław; and several more who lived with the Dintenfas family and with the Liverant-Blumenkrants family, a family of teachers.

Zionist students from Tarnów came to help the Dembitz students with their work.

The name "Dvorah" was chosen by Yudl Bornstein. Back then there was a rule that a Zionist women's association had to carry the name of a female character from the Bible--Ruth, Miriam, Judith, and so forth.

There were often parties and evenings (*wieczorki*), and in general, it was a merry life.

A constant struggle was waged between young people and their parents, who could not tolerate the idea of girls coming into contact with boys in the associations. In many homes, real tragedies were played out between parents and the young generation.

These problems accompanied the Dvorah Association every step of the way. In the summertime, we used to assemble in the forest on the outskirts of the city; in the wintertime at the Bornsteins', near the train station. Pious Jews spread all kinds of gossip about us and this had an influence on some families who, on their own, would not have minded that their children belonged to a Zionist association.

I remember an incident, when Feygele Kriger, a pious and upright woman, who would string pearls and make "*bindes*" (as the pearl ornamentation on the headscarves worn by pious women instead of wigs were called), came one Sunday into the room at the Bornstein's where a reading about the history of Zionism was taking place. She had come to drag her granddaughter Golde (an orphan raised by her grandmother) home from the association. Upon noticing that there were twenty girls and not a single young man there, Feygele thoroughly checked out every corner of the room, and not wanting to embarrass her granddaughter, said only that as she was nearby, she had only popped in to ask when Goldele was coming home.

Golde and all of us really paid for that visit in blood, but we were lucky that we happened that day to be on our own[12]. At least this calmed down feelings for a while so that we could go on working until we succeeded in getting our own meeting place.

During that same period, a library with Yiddish, Polish, and German books was created at Yudl Bornstein's initiative. The librarian was Kopl (Kuba) Nichthauser, and after a while, Golde Kriger. Almost the entire youth of Dembitz belonged to this library until the Poale Zion founded their own library.

In 1907, once again through the efforts of Yehuda Bornstein, a branch of the "Hashahar" organization, which had spread throughout many cities and towns in Galicia, and whose members were recruited from among former *besmedresh*[13] boys, was created in Dembitz. Members of Hashahar in Dembitz were: Yitskhok Laufbahn; Yehuda Bornstein; Efroym Rakover; Mendl Leibel; Mayer Sapir; Shloyme and Moyshe Wurtzel; Shloyme Dar; Moshe Taub; Moshe Taub (II), today a farmer in Kfar Yehezkl; Vulvik; Gedaliahu Siedlisker, and others, whose names I no longer remember. In the intermediary days of Passover 1908, Bornstein convened the first countrywide conference of Hashahar in the hall of the hotel in Dembitz.

To tell the truth, even though Dvorah was called a "women's association," at first only girls were signed up, or better said, teenage girls. For the most part, once one of them got married, she would leave Dembitz together with her husband. Only later could one find a few who remained in the city and remained active in the movement.

We had to expand our work so that the married members would also have a scope for their activism. Indeed, in Germany, under the leadership of Frau Doktor Ruppin, a "Women's Union for Cultural Work in Palestine" was created. This was, so to say, the mother of today's WIZO[14]. The work principally consisted of collecting money for the social and cultural work in Eretz Yisroel, for the creation of orphanages, medical aid, and so forth. Women's committees were created in various cities in Galicia for this purpose, and Dembitz did not lag behind. In order to make sure that not only a club of unmarried girls would be left, we transferred authority to Frau Doktor Fishler, and this, to be sure, gave us more visibility. I myself remained closely associated with this work even later, when I had left Dembitz and had settled in Wiesbaden (Germany).

The Dvorah Association occupied an important place in Zionist work in Dembitz from the very beginning. In 1910 (by then I had already left Dvorah and had founded the more popular girls association, "Havatselet"), the Zionist local committee (at the time, we would say, under the influence of German, "*lokal-komitee*"[15]) inscribed Dvorah in the "golden book" of the Jewish National Fund in honor of the fifth anniversary of the association. By chance, the "Kaufmanischer" Association (today, one would say "merchants"[16] association) had brought down a well-known Zionist leader from Tarnów, Ḥayyim Neiger, for a lecture, and organized a celebratory gathering, that included welcome speeches. Aside from the main speaker, Ḥayyim Neiger, there were appearances by representatives from all the Zionist associations in the city, including me, in the name of Havatselet, and Naftali Shnier in the name of Poale Zion. I remember how overjoyed Ḥayyim Neiger was with my speech in Yiddish, because all the other women at the gathering spoke in Polish.

Havatselet

The members of Dvorah were, for the most part, from the intellectual and wealthy families of the town. They spoke Polish amongst themselves and associated very little with the other Jewish girls in Dembitz. The social division was too great to allow them to belong to the same association. I myself was an active member of Dvorah but my sense of social justice would not allow me any peace. I couldn't look with indifference at the fact that such a big group of girls who could have been capable of so much social activism remained, in fact, marginal.

I discussed this with a group of friends: Yitskhok Laufbahn , who had just arrived on a visit from Erets Yisroel; Pinchas Laufbahn ; Moyshe Bergner; Gabel; and a couple of members of Poale Zion, like Mendel Wilner, Naftule Shnier; and together we decided to found a Poale Zion girl's association. Yitskhok Laufbahn was the one who came up with the name Havatselet (there was a newspaper called *Havatselet* in Erets Yisroel). I told a couple of good, close friends about it--Fradl Toy,[17] later the wife of Mendel Wilner; Sore Dar; and my younger sister Rekhe, and we took the mission upon ourselves.

In order to recruit members for our new association, we ran around in all the alleys in town. It was hard work. The fathers and mothers would not, under any circumstances, agree to their daughters, God forbid, going to an association. In the study halls, there was a commotion. Girls who had up until then sat at home and had never shown any interest at all in "alien matters" suddenly began to go to lectures ("*fortrege*"), were bringing home books to read, and altogether began opening their mouths and angrily asking why they weren't allowed to leave the house and know about what was going on in the world. It was truly a revolution.

We held "*fortrege*," arranged evening events, and worked hand-in-hand with Poale Zion. We received strong support and assistance for our work from the central headquarters of Poale Zion in Lemberg, who sent us, from time to time, speakers. A few times we even had a visitor, Berl Locker[18], who was then the party secretary and editor of the party newspaper, the "*Yidisher arbeter*" (Jewish Worker).

Havatselet was truly a great success and did a great deal to raise the cultural and social level of the youth in Dembitz.

It was only with the war of 1914 that the work was disrupted, until it was renewed a few years later in different form.

The first *olim*[19]

From Dembitz, as from all other towns in Galicia, there were a few pious Jews who traveled to Erets Yisroel in order to live out their last few years there, but even that was a rare enough phenomenon. It also sometimes happened that a Jew who was unsuccessful in business and went bankrupt, fled,[20] going to Erets Yisroel instead of to England or America. That way he could be sure that he wouldn't stray from the Jewish path. However, what never happened was for a person in the prime of his life, someone who could still wheel and deal and earn a living, to leave for Erets Yisroel. If someone had no way out, because he couldn't make a living in Dembitz (and there were many for whom this was the case), the road to Germany or America beckoned -- and earlier, also the road to London. Erets Yisroel was considered out of this world. In its time, in the years 1897-8, the attempt of the Ahavat Zion[21] society in Tarnów to establish a colony called "Makhanayim" in Erets Yisroel had strong repercussions in Dembitz. Most people, however, waited to see what would come of it. And when the rabbis, with the Belzer rabbi at their head, came out with an statement against Ahavat Zion's experiment, it was a done deal that that not a single Dembitz Jew would move an inch.

Ten years later in Dembitz, it was none other than the great-grandson of R. Itshele Dayn -- Yitskhok Laufbahn -- who would break through this particular ban of the rabbis.

No "Hehalutz" organization existed yet, back then, in 1908, and the Zionist organization, both in those lands and in the world as a whole, was still cold to the idea of pioneering aliyah[22]. Even though the hope that Zionism would realize its aims through diplomatic negotiations with Turkey and other great powers had been all but dashed, the old conception that "infiltration" (slow and all but illegal immigration to Erets Yisroel) would be counterproductive still held sway, especially when it involved young people without means of support. What would they do, poor things, when there was no work over there? The end result would be that they would return and all that Zionism would reap would be embarrassment and disgrace... This is what a few older Zionists thought, those who had the decisive word. A young man who, in spite of everything, wanted to go to Erets Yisroel, had to do it out of his own convictions and not expect a lot of help. He had to take care of his travel expenses on his own and his closest comrades had to help him keep it all secret from his parents: and even when they weren't in favor of it, because they remained behind, they had to bear the full brunt of the bitter hearts of the forsaken parents. Also, not infrequently, the result was that the Zionist organization wouldn't become involved in such matters. And no aspect of raising the money for the journey was easy, even though you could succeed in getting to Erets Yisroel with only a few dozen kroner. Some of the braver young people set off with a lot less. If only you could make it to Vienna! In Vienna, there was the Zionist office at 13 Türkenstrasse and soon or later, after much frugal living on your part, you would obtain there the necessary funds to get to Jaffa. Truth be told, they didn't throw money at you so quickly there. The first thing that happened was an attempt to convince the fervent young man that he should return home. Why should he go off to Erets Yisroel with no means of support? It was unlikely that he would find work there. Or, in any case, he would have to work very hard. But in the end, the person was expedited to Trieste, put on a ship, and he was out of their their hands.

Despite all this, the aliyah of young people from Galicia greatly increased in those years. It had two sources: Poale Zion and Hashahar.

Yitskhok Laufbahn was one of the first in Hashahar to decide to leave home and make aliyah. He might have been able to get his father to agree to it, but he didn't want to take any chances. In one way or another, he managed to raise the necessary sum, and only when he was in Trieste did he let his parents know about the journey. But as soon as the wall was breached in one place, other breaches followed. Laufbahn 's letters from Erets Yisroel to his comrades in Dembitz had an effect. They knew that one didn't lick any honey in Erets Yisroel, they knew about the hardships, but they decided to take the risk anyway.

The next to leave Dembitz for Erets Yisroel after Yitskhok Laufbahn was Hersh Volf (Tsvi Wolf), may he rest in peace, who died in Haifa two years ago at the age of 67. The third was Moshe Taub, who suddenly disappeared, and only later did it become known where he was. Both of them, after arriving in Erets Yisroel, joined Hashomer. After a while, Moshe Taub and a large group of Hashomer settled in Kfar Yehezkel, and were among the first to settle in the [Jezreel] Valley. Tsvi Wolf, who, had been interested in and lectured on agricultural problems even before he left Dembitz, was for many years the *mukhtar* of Kibbutz Bet Alfa and afterwards, an important administrator of the Jewish National Fund in northern Israel, who, through his expertise on the conditions of and relations with Arabs, played a key role in the laying the groundwork for the National Fund in that part of Erets Yisroel.

In Erets Yisroel, Yitskhok Laufbahn , who even in his youth possessed a sharp, biting pen (letters from Dembitz in the Krakow *Yud* and two series of articles in the *Lemberger Togblat,* "Mehaka le-Hatam" and "Mehatam le-hakha"), after a short time as a worker in Rehovot, became a staff member of the Hebrew newspaper, *Hatsvi,* and afterwards, one of the most prominent columnists in Erets Yisroel, editor of the weekly *Hapoel Hatsair,* the organ of the party he joined, and he became one of its most prominent leaders.

These were the first three *olim* from Dembitz to Erets Yisroel.

Afterwards, Moyshe Shtrik left. He, too, suddenly disappeared, the town buzzed. The situation earned me a lot of curses from his fiancee, who was a member of Havatselet. She suspected that I had known about his plan. This was a big blow to Havatselet back then.

Another *oleh* from Dembitz was Moyshe Bergner, who was actually from the town of Radymno, but who had grown to become so much a part of Dembitz that we considered him one of our own.

Bergner, a brother of the well-known writer Melech Ravitch, was a student in the Dembitz gymnasium and was the heart and soul of the student organization, Geulah. He had a lot of influence on the youth of Dembitz, both because of his talent and his fiery temperament. He had an ecstatic personality; once, when the comrades would get together in his room and start to sing, he suddenly grabbed a bottle of alcohol, poured a circle of it on the floor, lit it on fire, jumped into the burning circle, and danced an Erets Yisroel folk dance. He was an inspiration, both for his words and his joy.

Before his graduation, when he had already completed all his written work, he suddenly decided not to take his oral exams, but to leave for Erets Yisroel instead, so as not to get sucked into the pursuit of a diploma. He wanted to be a worker in Erets Yisroel. Nothing his nearest and dearest friends said could talk him out of it. He decided to burn all his bridges to the Diaspora behind him. He didn't even want to take any expenses for the road from his family in Radymno, but first went to Rozwadów, where he earned the money by giving lessons, and only then from went home with his family.

He left for Erets Yisroel in 1911, became a Shomer and a worker and exhausted himself, living in the toughest conditions. The spiritual restlessness in him wouldn't let him adjust to the conditions in any one place, and he began to wander throughout the country, placing himself in the most dangerous situations. And that's how it happened that during those years, he took a walk with another comrade to the top of Mt. Hermon even though it was life-threateningly dangerous. His brilliant descriptions of these wanderings were printed in the Zionist weekly, *Vskhod,* which was published in Lemberg.

Because he was an Austrian citizen, when the war broke out in 1914 he was drafted, and served as an officer in the Turkish [Ottoman] Army. After the war, he came to visit his parents, who at the time lived in Vienna--he was sick, exhausted, and full of doubt, and this is where he tragically died.

During this period, I too went around full of plans to go to Erets Yisroel, and this was also the case for my best girlfriends. But I didn't muster enough strength of will to surmount the tragedy my departure would have meant to my parents in particular and for my family in general. For the time being, I gave it up and tried to think of a way of carrying out my plan without victimizing my nearest and dearest, who I loved as much as life itself.

When I left Dembitz in February 1914 together with my comrade and husband Yehuda Bornstein, we had finally decided to go to Erets Yisroel as quickly as possible. But in the meantime, the outbreak of the war thwarted our plan, and it was not until 1924 that we were able to realize the dream of our lives.

{Page 47}

The Beginning

by Naftali Shnier

Translated by Roberta Newman

I remember Zionism in Dembitz from summer 1904 onwards. At the time, I was hardly even of bar mitzvah age. This was around the time that Dr. Herzl died. Some sort of young man arrived in Dembitz and became acquainted with a few young people, a few students, and they founded a Zionist association. The headquarters was in Alter Gewirtz's house near the synagogue. There, they arranged a memorial ceremony for Dr. Herzl. For a while the association held regular activities, such as presenting speeches and singing *Hatikvah*.

While worship was going on in the synagogue, arguments about Zionism and socialism took place in the vestibule. There were a few young people who worked in Tarnów and who used to come home for the holidays. They brought a smattering of socialism to Dembitz. But Zionism was known about in Dembitz a lot earlier.

One fine morning, when the congregation was entering the synagogue, all the windows in the association were broken and that was it, the association was dissolved; it ceased to exist.

On the second anniversary of Dr. Herzl's death, a couple of high school and college students got together and organized a "committee" of a few of the more progressive householders, like Yehuda Bras, Manek Geshvind, Herman Wurtzel, and I think, also Shemaya Widerspan. And the first item on the agenda was the organization of a commemoration for Dr. Herzl. This time, it was going to take place in the synagogue, and in addition, a speaker from Krakow was engaged, a doctor of some sort. That day, before afternoon prayers, the members of the "committee" and a few young people came into the synagogue all dressed up. Yehuda Bras and Yoynele Geshvind came in top hats. They began the memorial ceremony and the doctor from Krakow got up to say a word. Suddenly, just as he began to speak, in came a gang of Hasidim with a rabbi at their head and they began to loudly recite the afternoon prayers.

This went on for a little while and then Yehuda Bras slapped Yankev Veb, the ringleader of the Hasidim. Nor did the Hasidim remain completely innocent. There was a big brawl. Lecterns were broken, blows flew like boards. As they say, a regular battlefield. Strewn around the synagogue were broken lecterns, yarmulkes, snuff boxes, belts, and so forth. R. Leybish the beadle had a tough time cleaning up the synagogue afterwards.

The members of the "committee" came home as if from a war. Yehuda Bras's top hat was crushed. Manek Geshvind's frockcoat was torn, and the speaker, the doctor from Krakow, barely escaped with his life.

And from that point on, Zionists in Dembitz were hounded. A Zionist in a family was like a black mark. No one wanted to make a match with such a family. Itsikl Laufbahn was thrown out of the Hasidic *besmedresh*[23].

But even though the Zionist idea had barely taken hold in town, it was already too late to uproot it, especially among the students. The leading light, the trailblazer and leader of the Zionist youth in Dembitz from the beginning of the twentieth century until right before World War I was the young Yudl Bornstein (may his memory be for a blessing), about whom one can say that not a single thing of this sort happened in Dembitz without it being his initiative.

It was thanks to him, Yudl Bornstein, that the Poale Zion organization was established in Dembitz. It started with a club of autodidacts founded by Yudl Bornstein, with a membership that included Mendl Dar, and Shloyme Ruvn Wurtzel, and his brother, Moyshele. Later, I, too, was recruited.

The library and the autodidact club was located in a cold, dark *shtibl*[24], lit by a kerosene lamp, and at this point, I don't remember the name of its owner. We sat there every evening and Yudl Bornstein taught us the "theory and practice of Poale Zionism" by Dr. Daniel Pasmanik. Other courses were led by the student, Kuba Nichthauser and so because of the autodidact club I grew into becoming a Poale Zionist.

A little later, we--Shmuel Precker, Mendel Wilner, and I--called together all the tailors, shoemakers' journeymen and apprentices, and founded a Poale Zion organization. A Yugnt organization was set up for boys under 18. Those older than 18 we took into the Poale Zion association, and later, comrades from other occupations (bakers, salesmen) also joined.

The tailors' strike

The membership of the Poale Zion organization in Dembitz consisted, for the most part, of workers in the tailors' trade -- journeymen and apprentices who worked in various workshops, who dealt with both second-hand and custom trade.

The working conditions were dreadful. On Saturday night, right after *havdole*[25], the workers had to go into the workshops, sit down by their machines, and work until late into the night. This is how they worked every day, from 7 in the morning until late at night, until the boss himself told them to go home. As it is said: Need breaks iron.

This went on until the organization got involved. The Poale Zion and Yugnt wanted to wage an educational campaign among the workers and apprentices. Every evening, there were different course and lessons. Every Sabbath, a party, an evening with a glass of tea and snacks. But the garment workers couldn't come because they were working then. What to do? A special assembly of all garment workers was convened on a Saturday and a decision was made not to go work on Saturday night, beginning with that very evening. No one went to work in their workshops.

This was the first shot fired. The bosses did not mount any resistance and that's how it remained. However, eating made the appetite grow. A couple of weeks later, the committee of the Poale Zion organization, together with representatives of the garment workers, came up with a plan to call a strike of all garment workers. The work-hours should be from 8 in the morning to 6 o'clock in the evening, with an hour's break to eat lunch. About wages, it seems, nothing was said. These demands were delivered to the bosses and they, naturally, rejected all of them. What nerve to expect such luxury! And the workers went out on strike-- the first time in Dembitz's entire existence.

There was a bit of a stir in town. All of Dembitz was in an uproar. Naturally, the workers, for the most part, lived room and board with the bosses. So a kitchen was set up in the union headquarters, in Motl Kreyndl's house, and meals were cooked for the strikers. And in the evening, bundles of straw were brought in and spread on the floor and the strikers had somewhere to sleep. The union headquarters became their home.

The strike lasted for nine days. The bosses ran in like lunatics and called in the "*burmistrz*"[26] and the police. Until the mayor came from Ropczyce with a commission to investigate what was going on here. What's going on? A revolution, God forbid? But since the mayor was no help, the bosses blanched and began to cave in. When the central committee of Poale Zion sent a member of the intelligentsia, the lawyer-candidate (junior lawyer) Dr. Piltser, to lead the strike, the bosses really got scared. No small thing, that the strike was now being led by a real lawyer and not just some kids! And so they gave in. Every one of them came to the union headquarters and stood in line to sign the contract that Piltser drew up.

And thus ended Dembitz's first strike.

{Page 49}

Dembitz Jews

by Mendel Wilner

Translated by Roberta Newman

R. Lozer Perlshteyn is the first name that comes to mind when one thinks about the Dembitz that once was. It was too late for me to have known him personally, but what I was told about him is deeply engraved in my memory.

R. Lozer was quite a wealthy man. Suffice it to say, that in those days he was the owner of the Dembitz Uhlan regiment[27] barracks (between the marketplace and R. Yehuda Mahler's house), fields of a few dozen acres, buildings, a steam-powered sawmill, and so forth. There is a story about how a soldier from the garrison wanted to elicit a nice bribe from R. Lozer, but R. Lozer wouldn't have anything to do with it. So the officer up and went to court and gave his "officer's word of honor" that it was the opposite: R. Lozer Perlshteyn tried to bribe him, and he, the officer, would not agree to it. The result: R. Lozer Perlshteyn was sentenced to eighteen months in prison, his property was confiscated, his children driven into poverty, and he himself, the proud Jew, not able to bear the shame of having served a prison sentence, left for London, where he died in dreadful poverty.

His son Itshele was, until his dying day, a passionate *maskil*[28], the first to organize a club in Dembitz for reading German books.

Another instance of the tragic ruin of a family in Dembitz involved the Gewirtz family. R. Alter Gewirtz was the son of the power broker R. Daniel, who, in his time, was the power in Dembitz, and was famous from Krakow to Lemberg. His son, R. Alter, wanted to become a millionaire. He wasn't satisfied with his big machine works and so he invested a lot of money in some sort of fabulous little mill with which he hoped to take the world by storm. This beautiful dream petered out, however, and R. Alter's holdings passed into the hands of strangers. R. Alter died abroad in great poverty, and in addition, to his sorrow, a tragedy befell his son, Eli Gewirtz.

Eli Gewirtz was one of the most capable young men in the town. He was not only a great religious scholar, but was also extremely well-versed in secular literature. About his unbelievable intelligence, wondrous things were recounted. One time, he bet that he would learn Veber's foreign-language dictionary inside and out and he demonstrated his success in the matter of a few days... Eli Gewirtz was the darling of his family, but all their hopes and dreams came to naught because of an unsuitable match. The freethinking *maskil* was matched up with a pious wife, who couldn't tolerate his heretical ways, and the marriage ended in divorce. Eli Gewirtz left Dembitz, and not long afterwards, it was reported in town that he had fallen in with Christian missionaries in London. It was even said that he had become an prominent member of the Christian clergy there.

(Dembitz, apparently, "heard sounds but didn't know from which forest they were coming"... Eli Gewirtz left London and went to the United States of America no later than the beginning of World War I (perhaps because he was a citizen of Austria-Hungary) because already in 1915, a short theosophical book in English by Elias Gewürz was published in Los Angeles. The author was identified in the preface as a "great master" of a theosophical order, with a grandfather who was the "head of a yeshiva in a town near Krakow." This book, which appeared in two editions, is in the possession the Jerusalem professor and scholar of Kabbalah, G. Scholem[29], who maintains that within it, there is no trace of Christianity or Christian influence. So, what then? According to Professor Scholem, Elye Gewirtz was, "like all theosophists," a plagiarizer: he cites old kabbalistic texts, in a way that doesn't make much sense; he uses splendid material from manuscripts that he says he saw in Cambridge and Oxford. But Professor Scholem has read the same manuscripts, and there is nothing of the sort there -- D.L.)

This was the fate of the great-grandson of R. Henikh and the grandson of R. Daniel Gewirtz.

A well-known figure in Dembitz was "Dr. Reis" -- a Jews from western Galicia who settled in Dembitz as a doctor and became just like a native of town. Actually, he didn't have the formal title of "Doctor." He was a "practical medic," a doctor with half an education, which was permitted in the old Austria because of a shortage of matriculated doctors. A happy man, a jokester, he would stop for a chat with anyone, and because of all this, he had a large Jewish and non-Jewish clientele. For a long time, aside from him, there was only one non-Jewish doctor, Benda, in town, and neither of them had trouble making a living. About Judaism, there was a lot that Reis didn't know or didn't care about. He used to say about himself, that he observed only one holiday: "*kishkele* holiday."[30] He was, however, a devoted Austrian patriot, and because he was well-versed when it came to choral music, in order to ascend to "high society," he and R. Simkhe *khazn*[31] (Siedlisker), set their hearts establishing a choir that every August 18th, on the Kaiser's name day, sang in the synagogue and in the street, in the middle of the marketplace. The best singers in the choir were Khananye Vizen, Khayim Zeyden, Berishl Grin, Shloyme Zeyden, little old me, Henek Shnier, the boy from Ropczyce, Shmuel Ulman, and Yisroel Siedlisker . The director was R. Mayerl Gewirtz.

This same choir, but reinforced with soldiers who were former chorists trained by cantors, and who were stationed in Dembitz, sung on holidays in the synagogue. I still remember the great joy of the trustees, who, along with the entire congregation, derived great pleasure from our solos--especially the joy R. Simkhe took in R. Dovid Reder. Because of this, he always invited all of us to his house for *kiddush*[32]. And they're still talking about the concert of prayers that we would give at R. Mendl Mahler's in the old city, with the fine roast geese to munch on...

R. Mendl Mahler was the eternal head of the Kahal[33] in Dembitz. He reigned in the Kahal and ruled over their businesses with a steely stubbornness. When someone brought in a protest against the communal elections, "Uncle Mendl" put it away on the chandelier, that is, he never bothered with such things. And this was an honest man, a respectable man, a regular leader of prayers for the rabbi during the Days of Awe. His brother was R. Yehuda Mahler, the wealthiest man in town, the chairman of the liquor licensing board, with an extensive family with many branches. Another brother of R. Yehuda Mahler was R. Itshe Leyb, and I still remember how he played at Jewish weddings.

Reb Nathan Grünspan

One of R. Mendl Mahler's daughters was the wife of R. Nathan Grünspan , whose home as always open to anyone who sought knowledge. Nathan Grünspan was a quiet man, a miser when it came to speaking. He was endowed with a sense of practicality and effectiveness in his business dealings. Even 60 years ago, Nathan Grünspan was the industrialist of Dembitz. He operated his wheelbarrow factory on a large scale, even for export, and employed dozens of workers, including his own children. His oldest daughter Ruchama later married Yidl Bornstein, one of Dembitz's most important sons.

Melamdim[34]

Without exaggeration one can say that up until World War I, the great majority of children in Dembitz went to school in the *kheyder*[35] of R. Nokhem Neimark, or "The *melamed* from Tarnów," as they used to call him. He was a pious, honest man and an observant Jew through and through.

When I was barely three years old, my father, as was the custom, wrapped me in his prayer shawl and carried me in his arms to R. Nokhem's *kheyder*. This was a narrow room with two windows and a long table, at which dozens of children were compelled to learn about Judaism, from the *alef-beys*[36] to *khumesh-Rashi*[37]. There wasn't enough room for everyone at the table, and so in the summertime, a portion of the students would spend their time outside near the big trash box which served as the boundary of Lorents the pig-farmer's pigpen.

R. Nokhem had two assistants: Yosl, a more refined young man, who did his work meticulously, and an *unter-belfer*[38] Dovid, who was much less well-regarded by us. In the *kheyder*, boys and girls studied together. The *unter-belfer* had the habit of pinching the attractive, well-fed girls, especially those from the wealthier homes, and we boys strongly resented this. We were sure that because of this he would go to hell and never get out. Aside from this, we bore him a grudge because he was the one who made the children "bundles" when they did something wrong.

What did a "bundle" look like? The sinner would have his trousers pulled down, his hat turned backwards on his head, was given a broom to hold in his hand, and forced to stand that way for a while inside the chimney. When the frightened child was taken back out of the chimney, the other children had to sing a ditty and "make a *beh*"[39] at the one being punished. Later, we contented ourselves with putting the boy in a sort of "dress" near the door. And the aggravation of the children poured itself out on the *unter-belfer*, and so we would earnestly sing under our breaths the following ditty:

Belfer gehelfer[40], little clipped tongues,

Be a *kapore*[41] for all boys--

Belfer gehelfer, little clipped dumplings,

Be a *kapore* for all girls.

Sometimes it happened that the rabbi himself, R. Nokhem, would take the errant boy, unbutton his trousers, and whip him. The burning shame was worse than the actual physical pain. Once, R. Nokhem whipped a student, Simkhe Sheynfeld, but he wouldn't submit and kicked out with his feet and cut the rabbi on the tip of his nose with the nail of his big toe. The rabbi went over to the wall, sought out a dusty bit of spider web and put it on his nose for a cure and stuck it there with a bit of brown packing paper. And he went around this way all week long to our great amusement.

Once, when the whipping went on without end, a few boys brought pieces of garlic from home and the rubbed them onto the straps[42] of the whip. This was an amulet, so that the straps of the whip would fall apart. Another time, the whip was stolen and hidden somewhere--but no one had the guts to destroy it entirely.

Aside from R. Nokhem, the *melamed* from Tarnów, we also had a Shiele Gewirtz, a Tuvyele, a Shakhna Pinkes--all of them *melamdim* of very young children.

One of the the *gemore*[43] *melamdim* was R. Yosele Volf, a learned man, a Czortków Hasid--with him it was a pleasure to learn. His Hasidic *nigunim*[44] captured the heart. He was always hungry, but he never succumbed to melancholy. Not to mention, when Rosh Khodesh Elul[45] arrived, we children has wonderful time--the rabbi, R. Yosele took off time to go on foot to see his rabbi in Czortków.

Most of R. Yosele's students were from Hasidic homes. I still remember how we were seated in the classroom. Sender Binshtok, and little old me, who were among those who had good heads for learning, sat right next to the rabbi. When it came to reciting the *gemore* in preparation for the Sabbath examination[46], we were the first. If he was unhappy with the way we answered a question, he would cry out: "Woe to you, *iluim*[47] of Dembitz!"

Our comrades at the time were Shevekh Leibel and Yosele Riter from Kamieniec. More than once, because of the behavior of his students, the rabbi put aside Prophets to wonder aloud, what would become of their Judaism. Some of them, he bitterly preached, were as worthless as mud, and he described hell for them.

Much beloved was studying with Blind Lishele, R. Elishe Lerer. He was blind and you could do whatever you wanted during class--the rabbi could not see where or who to hit.

The *melamed* R. Hersh Dovid Blayvays had a more pedagogical approach to teaching. He was not trusted by the Hasidic fathers, and was even persecuted, but those who studied Bible with him had the Torah of the prophets firmly engraved in their memory.

Some of the other *melamdim* I had later on, such as a Yoysef Preger and R. Itshele Vayndling, should also be mentioned with great respect.

Among the *melamdim* in Dembitz one must make particular mention of R. Binyomin, the beadle of the *Prostn besmedresh*[48], a tall, good-looking man, whom everyone treated with great courtesy. He had the privilege of providing the householders from his study house with wax Yom Kippur candles, and this he did with total finesse: every candle was labeled with the name of the householder in printed letters. And there was a sense of great festivity when R. Binyomin *Shamesh*[49], with a high *kolpak*[50] on his head, walked through the market, from store to store, with one of his sons trailing behind and carrying the wax candles. Even fifty years ago this seemed like a bit of living history itself, a burning wax candle.

A story about a captain

Dovid, the *melamed's unter-belfer,* later on volunteered to join the army and rose to the rank of staff sergeant, until he was finally--according to urban legend--elevated to the rank of captain!

It seems, so the story goes, that a military draft board arrived in Dembitz to sign up new recruits, and they set themselves up in the Rekht Hotel, which was managed by R. Yisroel Mahler. The captain of the board asked R. Yisroel: "Is R. Nokhem, the *melamed* from Tarnow still alive?" But as soon as the captain heard that he was, he told him to summon him and to say: "The captain of the draft board wants to see you!" The first thing that R. Nokhem did when he got the message was to faint. He didn't understand what was wanted from him. First of all, he no longer had a *kheyder* and he didn't want any kind of favor from a captain; secondly, he had no son to send to the army, but what good are wishes? R. Nokhem had to pick himself up and go to the Rekht Hotel to talk with the captain.

When R. Nokhem presented himself before the captain, the first thing he did was to bestow a blessing upon everyone, in particular, the blessing one recites when one see angels.

In short, the captain asked R. Nokhem in German whether he remembered when a Dovid *belfer* worked for him.

"Yes," R. Nokhem replied. "I paid him off and threw him out. He was a real nasty piece of work; he touched little girls." And he would have gone on, but the captain wouldn't let him continue: "It's me, R. Nokhem, your *unter-belfer*."

R. Nokhem was beside himself and in order to mollify the captain, he said to him: "Yes, yes, if you had remained with me, you could have become a *dardeke-melamed*[51] for me."

Teachers

Children in Dembitz, almost all of them, received their first secular learning from R. Lipe Gewirtz, Herr Krantz, and also from R. Yoske Beyer. Of the teachers who we learned from in our riper years, one must with great respect mention Herr Liperant and his sister Libtshe Blumenkrantz.

Mrs. Blumenkrantz had, as boarders, children from the surrounding villages whose parents did not have any way of providing them with a proper education at home. From among them, I remember the two pretty Riter sisters from Kamienec, the future Dr. Israel Sandhaus from near the town of Pilzno (who later married my dear comrade Rechtshe Grünspan) and his brother Dovid (Dovidke).

To Mrs. Blumenkrantz's would often come as a visitor the son of her sister who lived in Tarnów and who was also a private teacher, known as "Pani Zosia." This was the young Karol Sobelsohn, later known as Karl Radek[52], executive member of the Communist International and unfortunately, a popular world personality.

That being said, this did not exhaust all the possibilities for secular education in Dembitz. Together with my comrades Henek Shnier and Moyshe Wurtzel (Koyan), I began to learn bookkeeping from a correspondence course from Royshn's commercial school in Tarnów. Aside from that, there were the Jewish students from the Polish high school in Dembitz--Kuba Nichthauser, Gabel and Moyshe Bergner. From them I learned Polish literature, history, and things like that. German literature we had already started to study with Herr Liperant. He introduced us to Schiller's "Don Carlos," "Intrigue and Love," the "Wallenstein" trilogy, and other German classics. Yiddish literature was not yet widely known in Dembitz, aside from the *Mayse-bikhlekh*[53], which were disseminated by the book peddler. The pioneer in this arena was the Poale Zion library.

The blind baritone

One of the more unusual types in Dembitz was Blind Lishe (Wulvick).

Blind Lishe (Elishe) had lost his sight in both eyes in his youth. Despite this, he became a *gemore-melamed,* and every year a cantor in the *Prostn besmedresh,* where he recited the morning and supplementary services every Sabbath. This, one can believe. But how he managed to recite the morning and supplementary services for all the holidays, including the high holidays, from beginning to end is hard to grasp. He had a phenomenal memory, and what a voice he had! A deep baritone that sounded like an organ.

One evening Jews came to pray the late afternoon service at the synagogue of the new city. Suddenly, just as the service was about to begin, a company of fifteen Austrian officers arrived. They belonged to a military geographical expedition, which was traveling around in the entire surrounding area (Dembitz, Mielec, Radomyśl, Przecław, etc.) in order to draw up new atlases and maps and such. That day they had finished their work in the area and arrived in Dembitz. Not having anything to do and seeing Jews going into the synagogue, out of curiousity, they went, too, in order to see how Jews in Galicia "*machen das gebet*[54]."

The congregation was dumbfounded. They started murmuring about what should be done. To pray in front of the officers in an ordinary weekday way would be unseemly. So they hatched the plan of summoning Blind Lishe, and, indeed, he, with his organ-voice, recited the afternoon and evening services as they should be recited. The officers were pleased and the Jews were pleased: they had done what they had to satisfy the state!

{Yiddish text – Page 53}

Reb Shlomo Mordkowitz

Translated by Ronald M. Miller

by Naftali Shnier

A quite remarkable folk type in Dembitz was Reb Shlomo Mordkowitz, the only fishmonger in the shtetl. They called him Shlomo Monik.

Every summer he would wear a white linen suit. In the winter he would wear a fur coat, also with a white cloth trimming. In all his clothes he had deep wide pockets. From the left shoulder to the left hip he had a rope by which hung a flat tin flask with 93 proof spirit which was closed on top with a tin lid. In his deep pockets he had broken pieces of water bagels. In this outfit he would go out into the villages near the streams where there were fish. This is where he would buy his merchandise. When Shlee–am–ka (that's what the goyim called him) would arrive in a village all the goyim would surround him. He would give everyone a drink and with it a piece of a bagel from his pocket. With this he would buy their loyalty, and they would do anything for him. (Literally: Jump across the water for him).

Every Thursday Shlomo Monik would display his wares in the marketplace. The fine carps for the rich people and the little herrings for the poor souls.

When the holy Sabbath came, Reb Shlomo dressed in a black sheepskin coat in the winter, and a black cotton kaftan in the summer with a shreimel on his head. This is what he wore when he went to shul to pray. But in the shul he only davened shachris; for the torah reading he used to go with a whole group of friends to his shtiebel which they called the tailors' shtiebel because once only tailors davened there. There in the tailors' shtiebel which is called Yad Harutzim, Reb Shlomo and his friends would end their Sabbath prayers – they read from the Torah and recited the mussaf prayer. After davening, Reb Shlomo would invite the entire congregation to his home for Kiddush and a bite to eat. Pieces of buttercake or cheesecake and, of course, it goes without saying, beautiful portions of fish. This was his habit all of his life.

When Simchas Torah came he made a really fine meal in his home. His wife Ita and together with a few other women would roast geese, they would also have fish and shnaps and a barrel of beer wasn't missing either.

Also, when the "chevre yidden" (Jewish group) had their fill of food and drink they would go with candles in their hands, singing, to shul to the hakafos – At the head of the group, the children and the grandchildren would go with simchas torah flags and with a candle in a potato or in an apple.

When the hakafos honors were given out, there would always be a scuffle (or argument) with, who else but the Gabbai, Reb Itche Shlage, for giving one of Reb Shlomo's friend a less than desired hakafos.

This is the way things were all the years until all of the group with Reb Shlomo amongst them, went over the world of truth (all died), before the first world war broke out.

{Page 53}

Jokers

Translated by Roberta Newman

Dembitz never lacked for jokers. Playing a trick on someone was regarded as doing them a big favor, the more so and especially if you could spread the joke around town and expose the victim to polite laughter.

Something like this befell R. Shimele--whose family was known as the "Tsheplyes," for whatever reason I don't know. *Nu,* R. Shimele, may he not be shamed, was known to enjoy a card game--in Dembitz, someone like this was called "A Hasid of Piantek." (Piantek -- a well-known manufacturer of playing cards in the old Austria). Once, on a winter evening, he sat up playing cards until late, but didn't want to stop yet. What could one do to prevent his wife from dispatching him to a bleak end? He went off to the innkeeper, R. Yisroel Mahler, and had him pack up two roast goose gizzards-- a gift for his wife. And so he was feeling confident that he was all set, he was pleased with his ruse, and he put the package under his coat so that it hung out beneath and went off, back to the pack of cards.

But what do his good fellow card-players do? One of them went out into the marketplace, packed together in a very precise way a sort of package of frozen horse manure and swapped it for the gizzards in R. Shimele's coat purse. You can imagine for yourself the welcome that R. Shimele got at home when he opened for his gift for his wife.

Anyhow, the city had a little something to laugh at. But it was worse when a Jew got a hankering to dress like a non-Jew. Then the entire town played with fire.

R. Dovidl Reder, a brother-in-law of R. Itshe Mahler, was a real joker. Once, he wanted to buy a few poles for firewood from a peasant and the non-Jew asked for who knows how much. It wasn't to R. Dovidl's satisfaction, since it wasn't as if the sticks had been raised feeding on the non-Jew's garbage. For sure, it was stolen Jewish labor-- and therefore should he have to pay such a high price for it? So he told the peasant: "Listen up, Kumye, if you sell me the poles for cheap, I'll tell you a secret which can earn you a lot of money." The non-Jew allowed himself to be convinced and R. Dovidl quietly confided the "secret" to him: "You should know, that this year Succoth falls next week already. If you come to the market with *skhakh*[55] then, you will make money without end. But listen, don't tell anyone else about this, so that you will be the only one at market and can set your own price."

The non-Jew was happy but spilled the "secret" to all his good neighbors, and the next Wednesday, the entire village set off for Dembitz with wagons full of *skhakh* even though it was still in the middle of summer.

The deceived non-Jews boiled over with anger: What was the meaning of such a mean trick? One could hardly calm them down. R. Dovidl, naturally, had to avoid the marketplace for a long time so that he wouldn't be recognized by the non-Jew.

There were two Yehude Leybs in Dembitz. One was Yehude Leyb *Dayen*[56] and the other Yehude Leyb, the barber. R. Yehude Leyb *Dayen* was a great scholar and sat studying day and night. Sitting this way and studying in the *Prostn besmedresh*[57] next to the eastern wall near the ark, always preoccupied with philosophical questions, he had quite a stately appearance. When he prayed, he was sedate; he didn't sway back and forth or rave. Apparently, he was a *misnoged*[58].

The other one, Yehude Leyb the barber, was aside from that ,a folk doctor, an expert, and in addition to that, a klezmer musician who played at Jewish weddings. If, God forbid, anyone got sick, the first one they called was Ide Leyb. He would even write prescriptions in Latin and he helped a lot of people. Some held him in higher esteem than a professor. If he told someone to call a doctor, they did. Therefore, the doctors in town were very friendly with him, especially Dr. Reis. He could be found in Ide Leyb's barber shop more than in his own office.

It not infrequently happened that if a Jewish woman fell ill after a heavy Sabbath meal and sent the maid for Ide Leyb, the maid would go and summon R. Yehude Leyb Dayan.

Once, the opposite occurred. In the home of a housewife, milk ran under a meat pot in which a duck was just then being roasted. So the maid, a village girl, went, as per habit, to Ide Leyb Balbirer.

In Ide Leyb's barber shop there was always a group of jokers engaged in jolly conversation. One of the group said to the girl: "Ide Leyb just left. Bring the little duck here and when Ide Leyb gets back, he will determine whether it's kosher or *treyf*[59].

So the girl brought the duck and in the meantime she went to visit a friend while she waited for the *dayen* to come. When she returned, the joker told her that the *dayen* had just then deemed the duck *treyf*, and so the girl left the duck and the group of jokers had a wonderful feast.

Behind the Bridge

{Page 55}

The Jewish Heart

Translated by Roberta Newman

"A funeral"

More than once, Jews of Dembitz (those who were not wealthy) stood up in public for a poor man who was being wronged. Once, a merchant by the name of Tankhem tried to evict, from an apartment, an highly esteemed poor Jew who hadn't paid the rent. A crowd of adults and children gathered around the house making a great deal of noise, and suddenly came up with the idea of "a funeral." Children made a "coffin" out of a few boards and covered it with a black rag, and, banging on a piece of tin and chanting,"*Meys mitzve*[60], Tankhem is dead!" They marched in a long line to Tankhem's business in the opposite corner of the marketplace. Tankhem and his children quickly stopped doing business, closed the window shutters, and only then did a hail of stones rain down upon them.

Tankhem realized that he was no match for Dembitz. The man remained living in the apartment, but it didn't take long for Tankhem and his family to move away to another city. He couldn't live down the terrible shame.

D.L.

Bailing out a Jew

More than once, when a Jew, God forbid, had a business that failed, other Jews came to his aid, above and beyond their own resources.

I remember: Herr Shinagel, the father-in-law of R. Shlomo Bornstein and the grandfather of Yudl Bornstein, a Jew who at the time was considered a rich man, signed a contract with the military board, along with R. Khayim Wilner, to build "the red barracks" on the outskirts of the city not far from the Wisłok River.

These simple, provincial Jews were completely ignorant of the fact that in order to make a profit on a government contract in Galicia, you had to know who to bribe so, indeed, both partners failed miserably. When the commission looked over the work they found so many faults in its construction that instead of making a profit, they lost everything they owned. Herr Shinagel declared bankruptcy. R. Khayim Wilner remained with nothing.Ten Dembitz householders gave written guarantees for 50 guilden apiece -- and with 500 guilden a Jew could get up on his feet again and go back into business.

The ten were: Nathan Grünspan, Mendel Reiner. Wolf Ader, Berish Vizen, Melekh Wurtzel, Moshe Yosef Sommer, Hersh Schuldenfrei, Mendl Volitser, Yisroel Mahler, and Naftali Ulman.

M.V.

Help me, R. Osher

An interesting case of self-sacrifice for a friend happened when R. Osher Taffet, a Jewish householder with a great entrepreneurial spirit, the manufacturer of soda water in Dembitz, died on the operating table in a Krakow hospital. The board of the hospital wanted to autopsy the deceased, something which, in those days, was regarded as desecration of a corpse. Leybush Altman, a wealthy Jew and a good friend of the deceased, placed himself at great risk, and, despite all the prohibitions, carried the corpse out of the hospital on his own shoulders and gave it a proper burial. Before he lifted R. Osher's corpse, he said to him: "R. Osher, I am going to redeem your honor. Help me so that I can carry you."

M.V.

{Page 55}

Theatre

Translated by Roberta Newman

Every few years a circus would appear in town and set up its big tents in the marketplace. Even the more respectable middle class Jews would go to the circus, with its horses and jugglers, since it was an era in which Yiddish theater had the reputation of being a venue where "Jews were made fun of." Therefore it was rare that a Yiddish theater wandered into Dembitz by mistake. It simply wasn't worth it. Nonetheless, I remember that once, Moyshe Rikhter and his famous troupe descended upon Dembitz.

There was no choice. From time to time, you had to perform something with your own resources. I remember one episode in connection with these sorts of theater performances. In an attempt to organize the youth of the poorer classes, Poale Zion hit upon a solution: they would put on their own play. With the participation of some more well-known actors from the Krakow Yiddish theater, they decided to perform "Kol Nidre," "Father and Mother's Troubles," and "Hertsele the Aristocrat."

The time came when three of these actors lusted after an easy serving girl. They committed petty larceny and were caught. When they were brought before the court and one of them was asked where he had gotten the sum of money that had been found on him, he answered that he had received it for playing a part in a play. When they summoned me, the leader of the dramatic club, to the investigation and my testimony didn't square with the claims of the accused, two of the actors were sentenced to short prison terms. And no good came of this for the dramatic club.

M.V.

{Page 56}

The Baking of Matza Shmura [70]

by Yehuda Pechter

Translated by Jerrold Landau

My memories from over forty years ago of the baking of matza shmura in Dembitz will certainly add no novel ideas. Matza shmura was baked in the same fashion in all of the town of eastern Europe. So what can I add? Did the Hassidim of Dembitz follow any law or custom that was different than the rest of the Hassidim of Galicia? Nevertheless, I feel that my description will add one more line to the portrait of the generations that were annihilated, one small iota of the picture of the sublime and holy world which was woven seamlessly together with the secular life in our city, just as it was in all of the towns of Galicia.

My grandfather of blessed memory, Rabbi Chaim Schlesinger, who was the ritual circumciser (mohel) of Dembitz, would go out to a village close to town already during the harvest season in the middle of the summer, in order to visit the one Jewish farmer in that village and harvest with him from a specially designated part of his field the wheat that would be used for the matza shmura. My grandfather and this Jewish farmer were the only ones who would be involved in the harvesting of this wheat.

The wheat was harvested and threshed with holy purity, and was placed in a white cloth. This cloth was not washed with starch, as starch was actual chometz [71]. Grandfather brought the wheat home in that cloth, and later placed it in a special place in the attic of the Hassidic Beis Midrash, next to the house of the Tzadik Rabbi Alter Pechter of blessed memory. There, grandfather spread out the wheat onto well laundered white sheets with his own hands in order to dry it properly. Only between Purim and Passover, once they had dried completely, did he sort out the "heads of garlic" [72], which were also considered to be complete actual chometz, and those who were extremely meticulous in the performance of the commandments would be very careful that not one "finger" should be found among the wheat that is being prepared for the matza shmura.

At this point, the wheat was transferred with great care to Reb Yosef Levi, who was the teacher of the older youths. He owned a hand mill consisting of two round stones one on top of the other, one moveable and the other immovable. There, at the house of Reb Yosef Levi on Lakbencin Street, the grinding would take place. Grandfather and myself, his young grandson, would grind the wheat together.

I became quite adept at pouring the wheat into the hole of the moving stone during the time of the grinding. I was very careful not to G-d forbid spill any of the wheat on the ground, since this treasure was more precious than gold. The milled flour was placed again in the above mentioned kosher cloth, and we brought it back home with good luck. We tied it on a nail near the ceiling so that the active "chometzdik" hands of the children should G-d forbid not touch it.

At the night of the 14th of Nissan between mincha and maariv [73] before the search for the leaven, about twenty members of the Beis Midrash of the Hassidim would go to the nearby brook with new wooden vessels in their right hands and porcelain cups in their left hands in order to draw the "water that rests overnight" [74] for the baking of the matza shmura. This water was brought into the Beis Midrash of the Hassidim and covered over with white clean cloths.

After the congregation finished the maariv service the "water that rests overnight" was brought to the house of Reb Alter Pechter, in order to insure that no drop of chometz would fall into it. Reb Alter and his family were trusted to watch over the "water that rests overnight" as the apple of their eye.

On the next day, on the eve of Passover in the afternoon, the Hassidim would gather into a special bakery which had been made kosher and purged for this purpose several days previously, and everything was ready for the task at hand.

The "water that rests overnight", and the flour had already been brought to this bakery. A large, long table was constructed out of boards supported on a framework. Already from morning, rolling pins made out of strong wood were brought to roll the matzot. Wooden piercers were also available to make the holes in the matzot, as well as baker's shovels to remove the matzot from the oven. Now the "holy work" of baking the matza shmura of the eve of Passover was ready to commence.

Dressed in their silk tunics and armed with their rolling pins under their arms, the Hassidim stood ready and prepared to fulfil the commandment of the baking of the matza shmura of the eve of Passover, their eyes waiting eagerly for the first dough to come out of the bowl, so that they can knead it in haste, in memory of the haste with which the people of Israel left Egypt.

As soon as Reb Chaim Schlesinger lifted up the first dough, it was divided up into pieces and distributed to the rollers, who were ordered to take care that from the beginning of the kneading until the conclusion of the baking of the matza, not more than eighteen minutes would pass, in accordance with the law. During the time that they were occupied with this mitzva, they would sing the chapters of Hallel[75] with great gusto, such gusto that we cannot imagine in our days.

As the pierced matza dough was placed in the oven, each of the rollers would call out loudly "for the sake of the commandment of matza, place the matza in the oven!" in order to goad on the baker.

At the conclusion of the baking of matza, the community would celebrate with toasts of "lechayim" on plum wine (slivovitz) that was kosher for Passover, accompanied by soft boiled eggs. They would bless each other with "Congratulations! May we do this again next year, G-d willing! Next year in Jerusalem!". Each of the workers would be given one or two matzos as a reward for their work.

The matza shmura would be brought home in white sheets, and would be placed in a special place apart from the regular matzos which had been baked about two weeks previously.

Thus did the worshippers of the Beis Midrash of the Hassidim in the holy community of Dembitz bake their matza on the eve of Passover with humility and trepidation.

Reb Efraim Steinhauer, the medic

{Page 57}

Dembitz Cameos

by Daniel Leybl

Translated by Roberta Newman

In Szkola[74]

It cannot be said that there was great joy among the Jews of Dembitz when the authorities in Galicia began implementing the law of universal education. Indeed, it had been about a hundred years since Herz Homberg had tried to bestow upon Dembitz his German school for Jewish children, and (like in all the other cities and towns in Galicia) ran into a wall of Jewish orthodoxy and anti-secularism.

But what is a hundred years finally when faced with a stiff-necked people who keep to their own ways and tremble at any change that might lead their children astray from the path of righteousness?

Truth be told, from the outside, from the big cities--from Lemberg, for example--new winds were blowing. The Haskalah[75] had sown her seeds in Dembitz, too. A group called Shomer Yisroel, which wanted to introduce more modern methods into Jewish education, was suddenly heard of. A few young people, infected with the ideas of the zeitgeist, thought about reforms in the *kheyder*,[76] but they had no real influence. *Kheyder* remained *kheyder*, complete with the same method of instruction and learning introduced into these environs way back in the 17th century. And in Dembitz, of course, there was no civilized Jew who didn't send his children to *kheyder*. Even those who were considered practically converts. Would you pull your children out of *kheyder* and send them to the non-Jewish school, delivering them into the hands of the Gentiles to transform into non-Jews? True, one should know a little German, how to read and write, and a little bit of arithmetic. But for that one didn't need any non-Jewish school. It was enough that they would at age 12 or 13 study for a short while with Krantz or Liverant -- this would be enough to enable them to become a merchant and even a wealthy, successful one. For that matter, which of the big wheels in town had ever attended a non-Jewish school? May it only be said of us, too. This is the way the Jews of Dembitz thought about the matter, and the more prominent among them did everything they could to circumvent the new laws. Only it was bad that youhad to pay a fine if you didn't send your boy or girl to school. It also wasn't easy to defy the authorities. After all, it was only a Gentile school, where the

Jewish child would feel alien and be not so easily led astray as they could be in the heretical schools of Jewish teacher-priests and *treyfnyakes*[77].

From year to year, it became easier and easier to get used to the idea that one had no choice about whether to send one's children to the Polish school. And thus, one all the more kept to the old ways in the *kheyder*, so that there, in the afternoon hours, the child would receive the Judaism that the non-Jewish schools wanted to strip away. All the more since it was the wealthy who were the first to give in -- they, who had the resources both to pay the fine and engage a private teacher in their homes for the Gentile subjects. And so gradually, the number of Jewish children in the Polish school grew.

First, they began to send the girls there and then they broke down and began to send the boys, too. Until it became almost a general school for the Jewish children - a type of morning supplement to the afternoon *kheyder*.

It was indeed difficult for the Jewish children in that school. Okay, you got slaughtered by the non-Jewish boys when leaving the schoolyard--that was nothing. You fought back, war was waged. The Jewish children would make a stand near the courthouse, with stones, on trial.[78] From there it was easier to run home or to go get help. The non-Jewish boys would station themselves across the way. And then the "shooting" would start. Much worse was the "beating of the paw" for the smallest infraction. But the absolute worst was the "*potsher.*"[79] It was not necessary, God forbid, for the Jewish children to say *potsher;* however, you had to press your hands together when the Christians pray to their God. The teacher says the *potsher,* the non-Jewish boys hold up their hands, palm to palm, holding crosses, and say their prayer. And the Jewish children had to stand up alongside them and hold their hands evenly outstretched, palm to palm, and remain silent. This was a bitter silence, as if we ourselves didn't have a God.

And another torture: there were two very assimilated Jewish boys, who held their hands the way the Gentiles did. They looked at their lips to see if they were joining in the prayer. And later, when we had left the school building, we gave them their reckoning. And the non-Jews came to their aid, and the war raged on...

Nonetheless, it cannot be said that the realm did not see to the care of Judaism. For this, a special "religion hour" was set aside, where the "religion teacher," Yidl Tewel, who was also the "registrar,"[80] and sometimes also the Kahal[81] secretary, had to inculcate the Jewish *kheyder* boys with the *"Zakon bozhy,"* the Five Books of Moses, in Polish, in the most abridged way possible.

The Jews of Dembitz would, no doubt, having been willing to give up that Torah--if the religion teacher, that impudent man, wasn't such a fanatic, and made the abridgement even shorter. Of course, he knew it was a pointless exercise.

Despite this, the children held a grudge against him from the first grade on. True, he didn't hit the youngest children "over the paw" with a ruler like the arithmetic teacher, the non-Jew, Berger did. On the contrary, he was nice to the children, just like Pietruszewski, the teacher for Polish. However, he was committing a terrible sin against Judaism and this the children could not forgive.

The school proper was on a small hill in front of the chapel. This was a big, two-story building with a courtyard and garden attached to both the chapel and the school. Here, all the grades learned except for the first grade. The first grade, in two divisions, attended school in the "*shtube*"-- a small hut behind the chapel, on the other side. Nuns were the teachers there, in heavy, brown dresses with white, stiffly starched headdresses, with crosses hanging from their necks. They were very nice to the children, even to the Jewish children, but even though they were also pretty enough, they caused us dread. They kissed the non-Jewish children on their fat hands, while the Jewish children would settle for a "curtsey" and would hold themselves aloof. In general, fear emanated from the entire corner behind the chapel. On one side were the gardens; on the other, the high wall around the chapel, at which you had to gaze up, higher and higher, until the top, over which could be seen the roof of the tower with the cross, which cast a pall over everything. Every day, Jewish children would count the bricks in the wall, to see how every day, the chapel was sinking a little because the earth could not bear the load. The Jewish children took care not to have their hats, God forbid, fall off outside in front of the *shtube* so that they could not be mistakenly believed to be removing their hats before the cross. And it was indeed because of that cross that the animus against the religion teacher Yidl Tewel was so great.

The cross of the chapel peeked into two windows of the first grade. The Jewish children couldn't forget this for a single minute. You want to take a look outside, see how the snow was falling, and you would see the cross; you glanced at a bird flying by, and you would see the cross. All the time. And here comes the religion teacher, who takes off his hat and stands there with bare head. This could be understood, at least. All of us, we ourselves, went bareheaded into the classroom. But then comes the worst, when the religion teacher would sit down and take attendance and would barely have begun to tell us something-- when he would get under the chair behind the table that stood near the window and you would could see only his boots and his short frock coat. Children are curious. We would bend down and peep underneath: what was he doing there? And then one witnessed a terrible sight: Yidl Tewel taking a flask out his breast-pocket, taking off its lead stopper, and putting it to his mouth: glug, glug, glug. He drank, with his bare head, and the cross peered in from outside... terrible... terrible...the hearts of six-year-old Jewish children ached at the sight of such licentiousness.

{Page 57}

Rabbi R. Ruvn's Sabbaths

When Rabbi R. Ruvn was installed on the throne of the rabbinate in Dembitz, he was still quite young. When the holy Sabbath arrived, he didn't know what to do with himself. The spirit of holiness was blocked from him and allowed him no rest.

Well, so, one can pray the Sabbath service with the full melodious sweetness of "Yoytser hameures."[61] What's so bad about that? How much can one make the Sabbath prayer more Sabbath-like than weekday prayers when the weekday prayers themselves are already a Sabbath? Let's say you peruse a holy text. So what more could you want? After all, this is what he did all week long. And would his studying suffice to fulfill the commandment? Only study, study, and what about deeds? Jews, Jews, study is not enough. One needs deeds, deeds... so what should one do?

When a Jew works hard all week long on the road and comes home from the fair to his wife and child for the holy Sabbath, it is indeed nothing but a mitsve[62] if he seeks out a taste of rest and peace. But he whose livelihood comes to him at home and who has rest and peace all week long, how will he observe the Sabbath?

Oy, Jews, Jews, it is bitter to be a rabbi, since he can't sanctify even the Sabbath in a proper way.

Once, he fell into melancholy. But he was, after all, who he was. Would he, God forbid, slip into dreaminess, close his eyes and think about what was up and what was down, when here in his house the Sabbath queen in satin slippers twirled around silently, silently, waiting for his loving glance?

R. Ruvele had been grappling with "weekday Sabbath" and "Sabbath-ness during the week" from childhood on, from when he was still living in the house of his father, the Rabbi R. Eliezer from Dzików. He was a good boy. Sitting over the gemore[63] or a muser[64] book, he swallowed the Torah. You sensed that here was a great man in the making. But on Friday night something of a spirit of rebellion would come over him. At the table, at lunch, he would barely recite a blessing over the piece of challah and fish soup that was put before him. At twilight, when his mother the rebetsin[65] brought him a saucer of broad beans from the Sabbath soup, he barely looked at it. He was on the point of something that, that.... this, this--- He waited until the beadle lit the Sabbath candles in the seven candlesticks and his father began to recite the Song of Songs, the poem of the shekhine[66] who conversed with the Holy One, blessed be He, and who is also, on the other hand, the Sabbath Queen. Now she was once again in the house of the King and not in exile. Now, by the radiance of the Sabbath light, the Land of Israel is in every Jewish home and in every

Jewish home she is there, the queen. Everyone sees her as he deserves. In the home of a householder, there was a Jewish wife with a pair of long earrings and a brooch on high on her bosom: and in the home of a rabbi, a *rebetsin*, a paragon[67] in all her glory; and in the home of a poor man-- a quiet little wife, very charming but with tears in her eyes. One Ruvele, the son of R. Eliezer, saw the Sabbath queen as Shulamith in the Song of Songs: *Mah yofu pemikh b'naalayim,* how lovely are your steps in your slippers of satin... Around him he sensed her whispers: Let him kiss me with the kisses of his mouth--for thy love is better than wine... His left hand is under my head, and his right hand doth embrace me.[68]

When his father finished the Song of Songs and the Sabbath cantors began "O come, let us sing,"[69] Ruvele swayed in his father's *hisbodedus-shtibl*[70] and began to dance. Dance, first in an matter-of-fact sort of way, and then much more passionately, a dance for the *shekhine,* the Sabbath Queen, Shulamith, and all Friday night he danced and danced, first in the *hisbodedus-shtibl* and later in his father's study house when the congregation had already left.

This is how he welcomed the Sabbath. And this dancing opposite the Sabbath Queen remained with him all the days of his life. On the Sabbath, R. Ruvn would dance and sing, come thunder or lightening. Even when his mother, may she rest in peace, passed away, he danced that Sabbath. He had a premonition that if he refrained from dancing on that Sabbath, it would be "*Aveles beparhesia.*"[71] He left praying at the lectern for others, even though he himself had a nice voice for singing. He enjoyed music, he liked to listen. Because when one sings alone, one becomes too preoccupied with one's self, and aside from this become susceptible to arrogance: Ay, ay, ay, how beautifully I sing. But it was different with dancing. When one dances like he did, "All my bones shall say,"[72] one forgets one's self entirely. And even more so, when one was dancing with the Sabbath Queen, opposite the *shekhine.*

This kind of dancing caught on among the Jews of Dembitz. Dancing this way together with the rabbi, it was as if they were dancing into seventh heaven. Just stick by the rabbi's coat tails and you will be freed of all the worries of this bleak universe. Here, on the spot, you will be as one already ascended to heaven. After a week of bustling around at fairs and standing half -days at the opening door of the shop waiting for customers, they sensed the Sabbath, the Sabbath Queen, her fragrant breath.

And so the rabbi wouldn't remain, God forbid, alone, and God forbid fall into melancholy, they mounted watch at R. Ruvn's every Friday night. Some left for the rabbi's right after the Sabbath meal, others took a nap and took the midnight shift, and some slept until 3:00 a.m. and took the last watch. Just so the rabbi could have company when he danced.

From them, from the these long-ago Hasidim, there remains in Dembitz a saying and *nign*: "And a weaver in colors[73]--and lived, only lived with zest."

They weren't lacking a zest for life, that's for sure.

{Page 59}

Skating

There were two study halls in the newer part of Dembitz: the *Prostn besmedresh*[82] and the Hasidic *besmedresh* -- both were on a small hill opposite the synagogue, but the Hasidic *besmedresh* was on the other side, nearer to the gulley and to the *mikve*[83] that was near the gulley.

During their last dozen years or so, there was already no enmity between the two. But during the course of the previous century, there was fiery enmity between them. In the *Prostn besmedresh*, the service was prayed according to the Ashkenazi rite, while in the Hasidic *besmedresh*, they prefered the "Nusekh Sfard."[84] There were also, however, simple Jews, the "*Prostakes*," not to mention the outright *misnagdim*[85], who were not in agreement with this. They fought and fought, and sometimes even came to blows, until they went their separate ways. *Prostake* children at that time would sing anti-Hasidic verses: " Hasid Loshik, take some *proshik*,"[86] or, "Hasid-*shine*, have a *meyse meshine*..."[87] The Hasidim put up a big, wooden study hall and observed the Sabbath on their own. Jews in both study halls would sit all day studying, especially young men *af kest*[88]. When the custom of "*kest*" began to go out of fashion, though, and young men began to gradually start working for a living, the ranks in both study halls, the *Prostn* and the Hasidic, thinned out--and were replaced by *Gemore melamdim*[89] and their *kheyders*. R. Binyomin Shamesh and his students studied in the *Prostn besmedresh*, and Blind Elishe in the Hasidic one.

Nonetheless, both study halls had one thing in common: the gulley. During the wintertime, when the gulley froze over, the town's top skating rink was at the Hasidic *besmedresh*, to which youngsters would come on Fridays after school, about 11 o'clock in the morning, to do a little skating--they had no other free time during the course of the entire week.

There, there was no difference between Hasidim and *Prostakes*, no difference between "fur coater" and "overcoater"; between short *peyes*[90] and long, curled "corkscrews." There, everyone showed what they could do. When a child showed up with "skating-shoes,"[91] it was the cause for great wonder. You skated in your shoes and more than one child ruined his soles.

Indeed, the fathers' shop looked onto the skating-rink. But it did them no good. Boys who studied with the *melamed* from Tarnow near the marketplace took a different route home, so that their fathers couldn't spot them. They snuck down the poorhouse alley and approached the Hasidic *besmedresh* from the back, where the outhouse stood, open with torn-down doors, and snuck in a little skating.

When a father noticed that it was twelve o-clock and his sons were still not home from *kheyder,* he knew just where to find them. He stuck a willow branch[92] into his boots and set off for the gulley.

As soon as one of the gang saw him, he would let out a shout: "Zelig, Zalmen, your father's coming." You would remove yourself to the bank and stand there calmly, trying to look entirely innocent.

Father would arrive and ask , "What are you doing here?" And you would answer: "Nothing, I'm watching." "Did you skate?" "Me? No." But Father wasn't having any of it. He would pick up Zelig's foot: see here, still showing the evidence of skating! And here there appeared from somewhere the willow branch, and he whipped their legs wherever he could reach! Until Father would calm down, take a handkerchief out of his pocket, wipe his junior bridegroom's tears from his eyes and the "candles" from his nose, take both of his sons by the hands, bestow a kreuzer on each of them, and together they would set out for home.

On the way home, Father would ask his sons: "Did you ever see your grandfather, R. Berish, go skating?"

At the time, R. Berish was seventy-five years old.

{Page 60}

Between Two Worlds

About the great "learnedness" of Dembitz's Jewish elite when it came to foreign languages: even though they lived in close contact with non-Jews, just as it was with their proficiency in secular matters, they would, in order not to be put to shame, tell all sorts of tall tales. Perhaps, the same kind that you told about your peers in other cities, but here, it really fit.

Honest Jews, who didn't have anything in the least to do with non-Jews, except for a "*Dzien dobry*" [Good morning] every now and then while passing by--Jews who kept their noses stuck in the Torah and their work all day and night and could read non-Jewish letters only from the title pages of religious books or from the signs on some of the shops--to them, this was irrelevant. They lived in a different world. For them, an encounter with the other world was painful.

About R. Shmuel the Rabbi, they say that once, before elections, the district head decided to pay him a call all the way from Ropszyce, to make it clear that the regime desired that one vote for the ruling party. This was an event of some importance, because the aristocrats were capable of causing much harm, for instance, sending in "a commission" (a *sanitarishe*) and levying fines for anything or everything.

That day, the Rabbi was in a considerable uproar. Boys, messengers, were posted all the way from the bridge over the gulley to the Rabbi's house, so that as soon as aristocrats riding on a *"kolyes"* were spotted, someone would run to the Rabbi to let him know. And that's exactly what happened.

When the Rabbi got the message, he was overcome by terror. As soon as the door opened and the district head appeared with his epaulettes and his entourage of militia men, he grabbed a chair, carried it over to the aristocrat over by the door, and when the latter asked him: *"Jak sie masz, pan Rabin?"* (How do you do, Herr Rabbi?), he quickly burst out in his Polish, barely dragged up from the depths of memory: "Lie down, please." And the rest he indicated with a gesture. Out of great nervousness, he had forgotten how to say "sit" in Polish. And this was a major failing, because the rabbi of a town such as Dembitz was supposed to be able to pass at least a fourth-grade public school exam.

The "heretics" of Dembitz could hardly wait to hear stories like that. They were also fond of repeating the story about the Rabbi's sermon on the "Kaiser's nameday." They would never know the agonies suffered by the Rabbi over this sermon.

On the morning of August 28, there was an assembly in the synagogue with a large audience of the most elite householders in their best Sabbath outfits (a few of them in top hats, and others in their new satin hats); the rabbi; the rabbi's assistants; with the head of the Kahal[93] presiding. Soon thereafter, the non-Jewish mayor, the director of the tax board with a few "financiers," the commander of the garrison in uniform, three militia men with "candles"[94] on their heads, Harnung, the police chief, the *Sędzia* (magistrate), and other dignitaries arrived in the synagogue. The Rabbi ascended the reader's platform. When the beadle, R. Leybish, banged three times on a table, the Rabbi began his sermon: "Gentleman, it has been promulgated and announced that the kingdom is having a birthday. In a chapter of the Mishnah, it is written: 'Pray for the welfare of the government, since but for fear of it men would swallow each other alive.'[95] And afterwards, he gave a translation of the Mishnah chapter, repeating himself several times, and finished up in a few minutes more with the exhortation: "May the Kaiser and all the militia live and be exalted. Now, all Jews say after, after me: exalted, exalted, exalted!"

Right after the sermon, R. Moyshe the cantor sang "Hanosen Teshu'oh,"[96] and the aristocrats approached the Rabbis and thanked him for the fine celebration.

The Rabbi looked them in the eye, not knowing if they were mocking him or if they sincerely meant what they said, the evil-doers, and thought to himself: "*Oy, gotenyu*, may they die as fast as possible. Is it not yet time, Master of the Universe, for the Messiah to come?"

The Barracks

Translated by Jerrold Landau

{This is the only Hebrew section of the article "Portraits from Dembitz" by Daniel Leibel, which runs from page 57 to 61.
The remainder of that article is in Yiddish.}

In the middle of the 19th century, a cavalry unit was stationed in Dembitz, which contributed in no small measure to the livelihood of the Jews of the city. The Malter family operated a special bakery for the baking of the army bread (komis broit). Others supplied meat, and still others provided fodder for the horses. In addition, many of the families of the captains included members of the Austrian nobility who were among the best customers of the Jewish stores.

The main barracks were at first in a building rented from a Jew in the corner of the market plaza. The training grounds for the cavalrymen (reitshul) extended the entire length of the area behind the row of buildings of the market. The Jewish children of the area would spend many hours at the edge of the field watching the training exercises, and on frequent occasions the captains would send the riders after them, so that they could enjoy the spectacle of the hasty flight of the payos clad youths.

Nevertheless, there was one time in the year when the Austrian captains relied on the good will of the young Jews at the edge of the field. At that time, the schoolroom (cheder) of Reb Nachum "the teacher from Tarnow", was located in a poor clay house next to the "reitshul". As the days of Passover approached, the students were learning the Song of Songs [76] with its heartwarming melody. As the sound of the song reached the open windows of the captains in charge of the training field, they would stop their exercises for a while and stand by the windows of the cheder in order to listen to the song. When the cheder assistant (belfer) realized that the gentiles were enjoying the singing, he would encourage the children to sing with greater strength, and the children, who barely needed this encouragement would, with glittering eyes and joyous voices, break out in song: "Shir – a song, Hashirim – of songs; all songs are holy, however this song is the holy of holies; all songs were sung by a king, however this song was sung by a king the son of a king; all songs were sung by a prophet, however this song was sung by a prophet the son of a prophet, a king the son of a king, and a wise man the son of a wise man".

This was just the beginning. The groups of captains would begin to throw coins into the cheder: copper coins and even small silver coins. Thus did the cheder assistant receive a special reward for his efforts. The second verse began. One of the children began to sing "Yashkeini", and the rest of the children continued "he will kiss me, Minishikot Pihu – with the kisses of his mouth", and so on. The captains were enjoying themselves as they saw before their eyes the peyos clad, unruly, Jewish children in a completely different light – in the light of a holy song, warm and living, serious and heartwarming. They tossed in more coins, shouted encouragement, an requested an encore. This was the day of victory of the Moisheles and Shloimeles over the knights and noblemen of the Austrian cavalry.

At the end of the last century, a new, much larger barracks were built at a distance from the city nearer to the Wislok river. The contact with the city dwindled, however the captains would come to town in the afternoons, especially during the summer, to drink and engage in further levity at the establishment of the gentile Srednicki, who made his living primarily from this.

They would sit next to tables that were set up in front of the store. Since the Jewish children enjoyed watching the captains, the captains would enjoy some fun at their expense. Before they would sit down outside, they would all arm themselves inside the store with handfuls of small coins and siphons of soda water. As the children came closer, one of the captains would throw a handful of coins at them. The children would begin to wrestle with each other in the dust of the marketplace. Battles would break out over each coin. This is what the group of captains was waiting for. They would direct their soda siphons all together in one massive stream of soda water in the direction that most of the children were congregated ... to the great enjoyment of the merry donors.

The simple cavalrymen, who were for the most part drafted from amongst the farmers, were not able to permit themselves to engage in this type of fun. They would have been quite content if their honorable captains would play the same stunt with them, provided that they could buy a cheap cigarette "darma" from the nearby store. They had their own fun with the officials in the corridors of the houses between the hours of seven and nine, before the evening song of the guards which was the official song of the entire city. The children would accompany them with the following words: "Reitze, if you strike her she will scream; if you do not strike her, she will not scream".

{Page 62}

Nicknames

by Mendel Wilner, Daniel Leibel

Translated by Roberta Newman

Nicknames held a special place in the life of the town. The wealthy Jews were referred to the way they themselves wanted, but a poor man without a nickname was an exception. Sometimes the nicknames rhymed with one another: such was the case with one--Alter Skarpak, then R. Wolf Petrak, followed by Miriam Khak, Yisroel Hak[97]. One impoverished family, from among the most unfortunate, had a rhyme within the nicknames itself -- Ozhebozhe, with an echo of laughter. All of these nicknames had their reasons, though these were quickly forgotten. But the nicknames remained.

But there were also "political" reasons for a Jew to get given a nickname.

During the census in January 1911, the Zionists and the Poale Zion agitated that Jews should register not Polish, but Yiddish as their "everyday language." This propaganda campaign was a very lively one. Standing in opposition were the Hasidim, headed up by the Rabbi, who maintained that "We don't need Yiddish." If the district head wants us to register *goyish*[98], let it be *goyish*!

A registration-commission from two non-Jewish departments, along with a policeman as a bodyguard arrived in the home of a Jew named Moyshe and they laid out the big questionnaire sheets on the table and began to "research" the Jews. The Jew could barely grasp what they were asking him. He was a habitué of the study hall and knew maybe ten Polish words. But he knew what the Rabbi had instructed: you should write *"goyish."* Outside stood boys yelling through the window, "Yiddish, Yiddish," but Moyshe would not let himself be misled. In answer to the first question, "What is your name?," he answered properly. The second question, "Date of birth?", he also made it through, but when it came to the question, *"Język potoczny?"* (everyday language), he burst out with, "Kakalik." What he meant to say was, that he was a non-Jew, a Catholic, and so long years afterward, that's what he was called: "Moyshe Kakalik."

It was during the elections to the Austrian Parliament that Mendzhe Leibel, a passionate, active Zionist, got his nickname: "Chłopak".... This was on the day of the election. At the polling station police and militia stood guard to make sure that only voters would enter. But who would dream of forbidding entry to such a well-known figure like Mendl Leibel, Mendl who wandered in and out of the polling place escorting Jewish voters and making sure that they voted the way they were supposed to? The district head from Ropszyce arrived and saw this young man with only a trace of a beard lording it over the polling place as if he owned it. He asked: *"Kto jest ten chłopak?"* (Who is this boy?) And so Mendl Leibel remained "Chłopak."

There were also nicknames based on the role someone had played in a Purim play back in his youth. A member of the Fink family, a craftsman and a member of the Jewish community board, had the nickname, "Kaiser," because he had once played a king in a Purim play. And indeed, he always cut a "majestic" figure, with his nice, attractive well-kept beard.

{Page 64}

Images I

Translated by Jerrold Landau

{All articles in this section are in Hebrew. The following is a translation of all articles in this section, with the exception of "In the Line of Hashachar" by Dov Sadan.}

{Page 65}

Yitzchak Laufbahn

Yizchak Laufbahn

Reb Eliakim Getzel Laufbahn and his grandson

Yitzchak Laufbahn, the talented publicist and one of the leaders of "Hapoel Hatzair", was a native of our city, and we are proud of that fact. He was one of the molders of the Jewish youth of Dembitz, as well as of the workers' movement, before he made Aliya to Israel and even afterward. For decades after he made Aliya, the beloved name "Itchele" was mentioned with pride among the many in our midst who were influenced by him, and who took his lessons to heart.

He was born in Dembitz on the 9th of Av 5648 (1888). His father, Reb Eliakim Getzel, was a respected merchant of forest products as well as a learned man, and an expert in Hebrew literature of the middle ages. He was from a long line of Rabbis, whose family tree could be traced to Rabbi Yitzchak Abarbanel [1]. His mother Rachel was the daughter of Reb Avraham Leib Polaner, a zealous Hassid and fighter for justice in his community. His paternal grandfather, Reb Yehuda Aryeh Leib was a Misnaged, and one of the first members of Chibat Zion in Dembitz. He was a great scholar, and served as a Rabbinical judge in Dembitz. He was the son-in-law of Reb Yitzchak Silberman, who was very sharp, and had a vast knowledge, and also served as a Rabbinical judge in the city. Laufbahn studied in the cheder and in the Beis Midrash. He was known as a genius from his early days, and his maternal grandfather did not allow him to occupy himself in secular studies, so that he would be able to devote himself fully to his religious studies. During his youth, he was able to debate Talmud and Rabbinical Responsa in the Beis Midrash as an expert scholar. However, the spirit of the times also affected him in the

Beis Midrash. He began to read the forbidden literature secretly, and studied privately general knowledge. At age sixteen, he participated in a memorial program for Herzl in the synagogue, even though the Rabbi and the heads of the community were opposed. The conflict between the two sides lead to a brief period of imprisonment on the count of disrupting public order. In 1907, he joined the "Hashachar" movement and was one of its noted leaders.

In 1908, after he had saved a small sum of money for his journey to the Land of Israel, and before he boarded the ship in Trieste to travel to Jaffa, he wrote a farewell letter to his father and informed him of his intention to make Aliya.

In Israel, he began to work as an agricultural worker on a moshav, and he joined the "Hapoel Hatzair" (The Young Worker) movement. He spent some time in Jerusalem with the "Hatzvi" organization, as an assistant to Eliezer Ben Yehuda [2]. In 1910, he traveled to Switzerland where he audited philosophy courses at the University of Zurich. He was called to the Land of Israel by telegraph in 1912 in order to write popular science that would be published by "Laam".

In 5674 (1914), he edited "Hapoel Hatzair" along with Yosef Aharonovitch. When Aharonovitch was exiled to Egypt during the First World War due to his Russian nationality, Laufbahn took his place as the editor of the newspaper. He was allowed to remain in the Land of Israel since he was a citizen of Austria, which was an ally of Turkey. When "Hapoel Hatzair" closed down, he edited various different publications. During the time of danger he gave voice to the feelings of the movement and the Jewish community. During the mass expulsion from Jaffa and Tel Aviv, Laufbahn lived in Ein Ganim.

After the British conquest of the southern portion of the land, Laufbahn was active in the reorganization of the Jewish community, and he was an associate member of the temporary council. When life returned to normal in the land, he was a representative to the elected council aleph' gimel', a member of the education committee of the Zionist executive, a member of the central body of the "Hapoel Hatzair" movement. When it merged with "Achdut Haavoda", he became a member of the central workers' organization in the Land of Israel.

In 5681 (1921), after he participated in the Zionist congress, he went out to work on the organization and publicity in Poland. He set up the newspaper "People and Land" in Warsaw. Later, he established the newspaper "Working People" in Berlin. He wrote articles in other newspapers in Yiddish, German, and Polish.

During the course of thirty years, the editions of "Hapoel Hatzair" published Laufbahn's essays and articles. They were very well liked by the readership, and served as signposts for publicists for the duration of an entire generation. Laufbahn's essays also appeared from time to time in "Hashiloach", "Hatkufa", "Meoznaim", and other periodicals.

He translated the two volumes of the book "Napoleon" by Emil Ludwig into Hebrew. He edited the book "The Workers' Movement in the Land of Israel" by Ada Fishman, as well as several booklets of the monthly "The Workers Union", and four books of "Dvarim" (statement) – an anthology of essays of Chaim Weizmann, which was published by "Hamitzpeh" in 1934.

Shortly before his death, he edited and published the anthology "Forty Years", on the occasion of the fortieth anniversary of the weekly "Hapoel Hatzair".

He passed away in Tel Aviv on the 6th of Elul 5708 (September 10, 1948). After his death, a large volume of "An Anthology of the Writings of Y. Laufbahn" was published as well as the book "Anshe Segula" (Extraordinary People).

{Page 66}

The Modest One

by Yosef Shprintzak of blessed memory, President of the first Knesset

I take great pleasure in the opportunity that has come my way to dedicate a few words in memory of Yitzchak Laufbahn in the book that is being compiled by the Dembitz natives, his birthplace.

To be honest, in my mind the names of Dembitz and Galicia never come to mind when thinking about the name Laufbahn. Even his first name Yitzchak is not on the tip of my tongue when I think of him, and it was not often used during my official and personal contact with him. The people of the second Aliya conducted their lives in a new fashion in the Land, and were not connected to their past or to the events in their birthplace. The late Mr. Laufbahn was similar in that matter. The name Laufbahn, as it stands alone, stood for his essence and manner of conduct for all of his days. Laufbahn was close to me for decades as a friend and as a participant in all aspects of our life in the Land – in "Hapoel Hatzair", in Zionism, and in the workers movement – from the time of the second Aliya until the time of the establishment of the state. One can sum up his character very simply: a dear friend, with clean hands and a pure heart [3].

His modesty concealed him so much that even on the precious day of the jubilee festival of the second Aliya, his name did not appear in any way in the list of the builders and activists of the Hebrew workers' movement He was one of our best publicists, the prime spokesman, the accurate spokesman, who publicized and promoted the thoughts and actions – the pains and accomplishments of the era of Zionist renaissance. His publications were fundamental, rich, and full of nuances. In his years of service in the field of writing, he was the voice for the pioneering effort of the nation, who desired the renewal of the Land and to become a working people.

The omission of the name and memory of Laufbahn during the jubilee festival of the second Aliya was completely unintentional, and was not caused by any disrespect for his position and the great esteem in which he was held, but rather because the blessed publicist, who gave so much in such an honorable fashion to the delineating of the path and deepening of the thinking of the people of the "workers' conquest" of Israel – concealed himself and was completely encompassed by his work.

Laufbahn continued the newspaper "Hapoel Hatzair", founded by Yosef Aharonovitch, with talent and honor. This was the first Hebrew mouthpiece of the workers of the Land of Israel. He added content to it, and stamped it with his unique signature.

Yitzchak Laufbahn has left us, however his spiritual legacy has not departed from us. His rich literary creations will continue to serve as a rich source of educational material for years to come.

Yehuda Bornstein

Yehuda Bornstein was only fifteen years old when he first appeared on the Jewish public scene in our city, and he was twenty-four years old when he left. Nevertheless, it is possible to state without exaggeration at all that thanks to his activities and many great struggles, the Jewish community of Dembitz succeeded in awakening from the darkness of the time, and to attach itself in an ever increasing manner to the world movement of renewal, which spread among the Jews of Galicia at the end of the 19th century.

It is possible to state without any exaggeration at all that during these ten years from near the beginning of the 20th century until one year prior to the outbreak of the First World War, no organization in Dembitz was founded, and no worthwhile public endeavor was organized without the efforts, activism and leadership of Yehuda Bornstein.

There were individual Zionists, and even small groups in Dembitz prior to him. But it was he himself, Yehuda Bornstein, who was the first that saw no other issue in front of his eyes, and no other purpose in his life other than the Zionist endeavor. Even his great thirst for knowledge and his love of literature and science did not distract him from his many activities.

Yehuda Bornstein (1904)

Yehuda Bornstein (1930)

The general state of the Jews of Dembitz at the beginning of the 20th century was such that nearly all of the Zionist activists were forced to leave the city, due to the scanty opportunities to support themselves. Some left to larger cities in Galicia, while others emigrated to other countries, particularly Germany. Dembitz was slowly emptied of the good powers of its activists. At that time, as the field remained without anyone to plough, as the saplings of the first activists were about to wither without anyone to cultivate, he arose, a youth of fifteen years, and with great self sacrifice he gave himself over to put an end to the desolation that reigned.

Yehuda Bornstein was born in 1888 to his father Shlomo, who was the son-in-law of the contractor Geshwind, and who owned a hotel next to the train station. He chose for his son the dual education which the maskilim of Galicia gave to their children at that time: traditional and Jewish combined with secular and modern. On the one hand, he studied in the cheder and the Beis Midrash, and on the other hand he prepared for studies in the Gymnasia. He did not go beyond the preparations, for as the son was actually about to be sent to Gymnasia, there was fear of persecution from the religious zealots. In any case, it was possible to consider the students of the Gymnasia to be students from the outside, privatists in the vernacular.

Thus Yehuda was caught between two worlds: half of him was in the Beis Midrash which no longer held his interest, and half of him in the anteroom of the Gymnasia, so to speak. At the end, he left the Beis Midrash but did not make it to the Gymnasia. For even more than his desire to become a lawyer or an engineer, the call of communal duty took hold of him, and that determined his path of his studies. He learned a great deal and read a great deal, however the purpose of his studies was no longer in order to obtain a diploma in the future, but rather to absorb the philosophy of the modern world, in which this nation would be Jewish and Zionist.

During the course of his preparations for the Gymnasia, he established friendships with the Jewish students of the Gymnasia of Dembitz, some of whom were from outside the city, and he was like one of them. He was a reader of "Moria", the newspaper of the Zionist students of the Gymnasia at that time, which was published in Lvov. During the years 1904-1905 he published several essays and bold articles in that paper regarding current events. He also became involved in Zionist activity. A new spirit suddenly broke out in the city. The ice was broken, and fifteen year old Yehuda became more and more involved in his activities. He saw a world of opportunity before him.

There were several Zionist youths in the city who were of the middle of the road, however they were spread out and very few of them were bold enough to proclaim their Zionism openly. All prior attempts at organizing were foiled due to the opposition of the Hassidim. It was necessary to find a means of organization that would not awaken such harsh opposition. Yehuda proposed in his articles the idea of founding a "merchants' union", that would not proclaim itself officially as a Zionist organization, but would open up the opportunity for Zionist activity among its members. This organization was founded and existed for a period of time. The young Bornstein spoke at its opening assembly. However, this organization was not able to take roots, since there was no real need for a "merchants' union" in such a small city as Dembitz. The leaders of this union included Naftali Eisen, the owner of the large locksmith workshop, Nathan Günspan, the owner of the large drawer factory, and Shmuel Mahler, the son of Chaim Mahler and one of the first Zionists of Dembitz.

At that time Yehuda Bornstein was also behind the establishment of the first Poale Zion group in Dembitz. He wrote the first article about that subject in "The Jewish Worker".

This was not sufficient for him. That very same year, Yehuda Bornstein came up with the idea of founding the "Debora" women's Zionist organization, which existed in various forms until the outbreak of the Second World War.

The year 1905 was the most fruitful year for the efforts of Yehuda Bornstein in Dembitz. That year, the organization which served as the foundation for the younger generation in Dembitz was founded due to his blessed efforts. From that time on he had the responsibility of overseeing the existence of all of the new organizations, of directing them in their day to day activities, of maintaining the contacts and preventing disputes among them, as well as fighting the battles against the main opposing force to Zionism from its outset – Hassidic Orthodoxy. He conducted his activities without tiring, with great dedication and self sacrifice. When it came to establishing a Hebrew school and a library, and with every external political activity – Yehuda Bornstein was one of the prime volunteers and workers. He was the recognized head of the movement in Dembitz. He represented it externally, even though it was not in need of such representation. He was a delegate to the twelfth congress in Vienna.

The final effort of Yehuda Bornstein was the founding of the "Hashachar" youth organization, which called itself "The Union of Young Students". It was a branch of the national "Hashachar" organization, which held its convention during Passover of 5678 (1918) in Dembitz, in the Bornstein hotel. Yehuda was one of the participants in that convention.

Yehuda married Ruchama, the daughter of Nathan Günspan in the winter of 1913. She was an activist among the youth of the city. In 1914 the young couple left to Frankfurt, Germany, with the definite goal of making Aliya to the Land of Israel as soon as possible.

Yehuda Bornstein's sojourn in Frankfurt was very short, not more than two months, however he certainly left his mark there: "the Jewish Cultural Union", which flourished greatly for several years.

In April, Yehuda left Frankfurt for the Land of Israel in order to prepare for his settlement along with Ruchama, and he remained there for three months.

He returned to Germany in order to return with Ruchama, however in the interim the skies of Europe darkened. The First World War was looming, and due to lack of any choice, the family moved to Weisbaden, where they resided during the years of the war and the French occupation. Ruchama, who was very astute in organizational and commercial affairs, succeeded in establishing a flourishing business in Weisbaden, and Yehuda gave himself over to his work for Zionism, which won him great recognition among the Zionists of Germany. Among other things, he was very active in the "Organization of Jews from the East" in Germany, which was founded by two Galicia natives, Moshe Waldman from Tarnopol and Ben-Zion Fett from Rzeszow. There was not one Zionist convention in Germany where Yehuda did not represent the Zionists of Weisbaden. At the beginning of the 1920s he was chosen as a member of the executive committee of the "United Zionists of Germany" which was seated in Berlin, Munich, and Strasau.

Nevertheless, the physical success which was due to the changed circumstances, and the Zionist activity did not mitigate the plans for Aliya of Yehuda and Ruchama.

{Page 68}

In 1924, the couple liquidated their business in Weisbaden and moved to Israel, to Haifa, where Yehuda built his home in Hadar Hacarmel. Due to the unstable economic situation, they decided to return to Germany temporarily in order to rescue their wealth there, and apparently for several years he remained there, always hoping to return to the Land of Israel, to his home in Haifa. In the meantime, he continued with his Zionist activity without bounds. Everyone who came to his house did not fail to recognize the great measure of the hospitality of Yehuda and Ruchama, and their willingness to assist whomever required assistance. However, at that time their economic situation deteriorated, and Yehuda, who was straight in his ways and pure in his intentions was not able to continue functioning. On June 30, 1930, the heart of this man, who from the days of his youth only had one direction – Zionism, stopped beating. He did not merit to see the Land of Israel again, Haifa the city in which his home awaited him, and in which he had hoped to educate his two sons. Ruchama, his partner in life did continue on to the Land of Israel, and she keeps his legacy alive until this day.

In the Path of Hashachar

by Dov Sadan

A.

The San River, which traversed the crown lands of Austria known by the pseudonym of Galicia, and served as the boundary between the eastern side whose main population indicated that it had been torn asunder from Ukraine, and the western side whose main population indicated that it had been torn asunder from Poland, also served as the boundary between its Jews. Anyone looking from up close would not miss the covert differences, primarily in mentality. However, even those looking from afar would notice the most obvious differences, particularly in the level of development. Certainly, the network of streams and struggles penetrated the entire space, but not to the same degree and fashion. This difference is noticeable to anyone who studies the founding of the first streams – Hassidism and the Haskalah – and their battles from both sides of the San. The east side appeared as a front of strong bastions of Haskalah opposite strong bastions of Hassidism, with a constant and open battle. The west side appeared as a field of Hassidic conquest with pockets of Haskalah invasion, with the battle being intermittent and partisan in style.

The standard path of the Haskalah from Berlin though Prague and Vienna toward eastern Europe required a passageway, which began through Krakow, Tarnow and Rzeszow, and continued to Lwow, Brody and Tarnopol. However, in truth, the pathway was not like the railway track, but almost the opposite, such that it can be said that the Haskalah in Western Galicia was like an echo of the East.

The difference is also noticeable to someone who studies the foundation of the later streams, assimilation and nationalism, and their battles on both sides of the San. On the eastern side of the river, the Jews were situated between the anvil of a Ukrainian majority and the hammer of the Polish minority who were in power. This tension instigated the consolidation of the national consciousness and political plans. This factor was absent in the realities of the Jews on the west side of the river, where the situation in this case as well was like that of a voice and its echo.

B.

This development, through which the Haskalah and the national movements in Western Galicia were apparently seen as imported from the East, was also a causative factor in the unification of the few, isolated centers of these streams, and the typical failures of their bearers. These trends were particularly prominent in the main center in which these streams converged like a mother and her heirs. This refers to Tarnow, where this characteristic failure was imprinted strongly on the ways of those under its influence. In the large district of Hassidism that was affiliated with the dynasties of Lizhensk and Ropszyce, to which Dynow and Tzanz were later added – a stream of opposition broke through in Tarnow, whose extremist representatives were, on the one side, personalities such as Reb Shevach Almogin, who began as the preacher of the Misnagdim and ended up as the assistant to the circle of Maskilim of Tarnopol (his son was the scholar Reb Simcha Pinsker and his grandson was the author of Auto-Emancipation[4]); and on the other side, the personality of the rabbi of the Misnagdim. Resting atop the stratum of Misnagdim was the stratum of the Haskala and its various representatives, from a serious personage such as Naftali Keller the author of "Habikurim", to a jovial personage such as Mordechai Weisman-Chaies. Between them, there was a person in whom seriousness and joviality were blended with significant talents intermixed with a measure of humor – Mordechai David Brandstetter. Like their friends, the three of them were already standing within the precincts of the beginnings of national awakening, as is clear from their common organization, "Hashachar" and its editor Smolenskin. The stratum of nationalism and its various representatives was layered atop of the stratum of Haskalah. Some of those who had left their Talmuds in the Beis Midrash and acquired their knowledge in secret were already beginning to stand out – including Leibish Rafael's, i.e. Leon Kelner, who was among the first of those who began to follow Herzl. Some of them no longer knew the Beis Midrash, or knew it only as the tip of the fork, as they openly transferred to the precincts of the gymnasium in their city or moved to a city of educational institutions, primarily Vienna. They were taken by the young nationalist movement, especially by the "Kadima" organization, and brought news of such to their friends in their home cities. Of the three primarily representatives of this class, whose images stand out from the photograph of the Basel Conference – Avraham Zaltz, Edward Shwager, and Zygmunt Bromberg-Bitkowsky – the first is known as an active personality in the "Ahavat Zion" movement that attempted settlement in a practical manner with unfortunate Machanaim settlement, and fought for their rights before Herzl. The latter was also one of the Machanaim directors, known as a poet, organizer and pedagogue.

Tarnow and "Ahavat Zion" became synonymous terms in the annals of Galician Zionism. Tarnow in its stratum and "Ahavat Zion" were the pinnacle of influence for the region, particularly in the nearby areas, and a concentration point for all the sparks that were ignited in the towns of Western Galicia. All visions were considered as insignificant if they did not stem from this source of influence and its center.

{Page 69}

Ahavat Zion also became a symbol for the relations between the intelligentsia and the masses. The attorney who led in the denouncing of this was the president of Aguda, whose members were intelligent and pious, and the founders of a Moshava whose builders were Orthodox. With these two foundations came the need for harmony. This path of opposition manifested itself in several incarnations. There was the group of Yaakov Meir (Max) Bienenstock, Zev (Wilhelm) Berkelhamer, and Yitzchak (Ignacy) Schipper. Were you to examine their language of writing and essence, you would see, especially in the former and the latter, a connection to the foreign language as well as a tendency to the language of the masses, particularly in their spoken language.

A convention of "Hashachar" in Rzeszow on the intermediate days of Passover, 5688 (1920). Lower row from the left: Daniel Leibel and Yizchak Laufbahn. Second row, standing at the right: Moshe Worcel and Leibel Szewach

{Page 70}

C.

Before you, in general format, is the way of Tarnow, which had influence on the region, and especially on the city of Dembitz, which was like a suburb of it from this perspective. If you went to speak to natives of Dembitz and those who held it up, chief of whom was Yitzchak Laufbahn, who had their hand in influencing it and its path, it is appropriate to remember the opposition game, and the harmonization between the intelligentsia and the people. If you wished, you could also interpret this as an opposition between the newly minted intelligentsia who were educated in the gymnasiums and the educational institutions, and the homegrown intelligentsia who were educated in the cheders and Beis Midrashes. The opposition against "Ahavat Zion", between the first of those who prepared for the return to Zion in a practical manner, and who supported such, but who were not among those who made aliya, and the others who demanded practical action but failed due to the opposition – was evident after some time even in the small but important "Hashachar" movement which encompassed the organization of Talmudic youths, or those who frequented the Beis Midrash. This was a youth movement that arose from the midst of the original intelligentsia, the youths of the Beis Midrash, who sensed the upheaval in the world and therefore progressed beyond their peers of the same age in the gymnasiums. It is certainly no coincidence that it was not the members of the large organization of Zionist students, but rather the members of this small organization who provided the groups of olim who joined the Second Aliya. In the publication of "Hashachar" containing the minutes of the second convention of that organization that was published by "Neie Folks Zeitung" in Rzeszow, edited by the secretary Naftali Zigel (Drohobycz, 5668 / 1908), we read, "Those who made noise and a tumult became a major factor. Youths gathered together from all corners of Galicia in a small corner (the convention took place in Rzeszow on the second intermediate day of Passover, 5668[5]) in order to deliberate over their situation and their needs and to create an organization. This was a sign that these youths were not seeking renown – as others accused them – but rather practical work, not mottoes but rather activity. Who would have imagined a few years ago that a day would come when the youths of the Beis Midrashes and Kloizes would gather together to speak about general matters? Who would have believed that those who were persecuted, those who were 'in darkness' would suddenly awaken to life and work?" From the words of Moshe Weisenfeld, the founder of the movement, we can discern the rise of self- consciousness: "The value of the youths was also greatly lifted by the 'Hashachar' movement. Previously, every boor considered it praiseworthy to disparage and mock the youths of the Beis Midrash. Today, at least, they look at these youths as productive people, as fine sons of the Israelite nation. Also, from our side, we began to look more upon our situation, our purpose in life and duties to the Jewish nation. The more that we understand the aspirations of the youths, the more that we delve into the questions of our nation, we come to the understanding that these youths are the best of the Jews, the most nationalistic of the Zionists, and that they are the most fitting of the entire Israelite nation to bear the banner of renaissance and the Zionist movement, and that they are the most healthy and fresh element within Jewry." Can we not hear from these words a resonance of the youth movement that arose a few years earlier on the Jewish street in Galicia, and whose self consciousness found its confirmation within the definition of M. Buber, for the youth ensures the fortunes of the perpetuation of humanity? If during the investigations of our times we see presumptuousness in this recognition, the opinion is hidden in a place where this self-consciousness comes more as a sense of fulfillment of duty rather than a demanding of rights. Thus was the way of our youth movement, both in its early, most intuitive manifestation during the Second Aliya, as well as in its later, characteristic manifestation during the Third Aliya and beyond. Just as this small "Hashachar" organization inadvertently formed a connection with the previous generation, the "Ahavat Zion" people of the towns of Western Galicia who made aliya to our Land and took hold of it; they also inadvertently formed a connection with the coming generation, the stream of youths from Eastern and Western Galicia, especially the youths of "Hashomer Hatzair", who were carried upon the waves of the Third Aliya. Indeed, the heralds of the Third Aliya were small groups, such as "Chalutzei Zion" that arose in Brody through the initiative of Yosef Aharonowich, and groups of "Hashachar", as well as individuals who acted as pioneers and came to our Land. A sign of the excellence and seriousness of "Hashachar" was that within a brief period of time after this declaration of self consciousness, its members appeared in our Land. These included the Dembitz native Yitzchak Laufbahn, who became one of the chief publicists of the workers' movement; the editor of "Hapoel Hatzair", Berish Miller, a Jaslo native, who later became known by the name of Dov Kimchi the writer, teacher and editor. (Incidentally, at that convention, he opened with the words, "First, I apologize for speaking jargon"[6]); the Tarnow natives Yehoshua and Yechezkel Brandstetter and Aryeh Lichtiger (Nahir) who became known as farmers and communal activists; and the Dembitz native Tzvi Wolf (of blessed memory) who was faithful to the Land and to Hebrew guarding. Others, later on, were youths of "Hashachar" who, like their predecessors, in the interim spread out to other camps and found their way into the Workers Movement, including the Dembitz native Daniel Leibel, a writer, activist, editor and researcher; the Moszciska native Naftali Zigel, a teacher, publisher, and textbook author; the Belz native Yosef Falk, a writer and essayist; Avraham Kahana (Avrech), a writer and folklorists; and others. However, presently our primary interest is Zion, for the "Hashachar" organization produced pioneers of the Second Aliya.

D.

If we now return a bit to that convention, we will hear several interesting things. Here is a word of sympathy – Avraham Zaltz "works in our camp". Of communal support: "Even the assimilationists agreed to give to us, saying: these are the youths of the future." Here is a word of hatred – "The organization of youths is an abnormal organization. The youths conduct their work clandestinely, so as not to arouse the suspicion of their fathers, the suspicion of the householders, etc." Here is something about the close relations with the students – the Zionist academic youth in Tarnow registered Hashachar as a name in the Golden Book. Here is a something about distant relations from them – "We do not want to give the leadership of labor to the students, we do not want to depend on them." The program was restricted to the unification of the Talmudic youths for the purpose of actualizing the Basel program and its aims, of raising their physical and spiritual status, and educating them in the nationalist and European spirit. Its connection to the Zionist movement was a direct connection to the active committee of the Zionist organization in Cologne, its language was Hebrew, and its secondary language was Yiddish. The battle for self definition and independence was fierce. It is interesting that the refusal to affiliate with the national Zionist organization came through the investigation of the assimilationist character of the local Zionist activist: "We have already seen what type of speeches it (the district) sends to Hassidic areas. Most of them are ridiculous people, for more than they are liable to work on behalf of Zionism, they are liable to denigrate – we cannot give ourselves over to people who write to us in a language that we do not understand." However, the debates already became divisive, especially at the point of contact with Poale Zion (indeed, this was the end of many members who were swallowed up in its midst), and what unfolded from it in the matter of Yiddish (the recommendation to publish "Hashachar" in Yiddish as well was rejected not only out of principle, but also based on the fact that all of the members understood Hebrew; there was also a recommendation to request partnership with "Revivim" of Y. Ch. Brenner, which was rejected. Incidentally Brenner wrote a critical article about the "Hashachar" publication.)

To sum up: Before us is a fundamental Jewish youth movement according to the composition of its members, students of the Beis Midrash, to whom Zionism and the Hebrew Language obviously comes naturally. The members aspire to Hebrew culture that encompasses a general spirit, and protect their uniqueness through investigating the typical archetype of a Zionist, including the young Zionist, who is not concerned with the contradiction between his nationalistic mottoes and his vernacular origins. This was an intermediate movement that prepared its members to self consciousness, pride, and the duty of self fulfillment. If specifically this movement gave rise to pioneers of aliya – this was due to the attitude of seriousness that pervaded the movement.

E.

This arena led to the ascent to greatness of Yitzchak Laufbahn, who was one of the leaders of his movement. From the vantage point of time, we can deduce that it was Berish Miller, known as Dov Kimchi, who delivered the lecture on journalism, whereas Yitzchak Laufbahn delivered the lecture on publicity. However, to us who were accustomed to seeing him, a writer and editor disappeared from our midst, for he had organizational skills[7]. It is appropriate that we should now read his small speech as it was recorded those minutes (pages 14-15), and which demonstrates that he knew how to bring order and clarity to that which was before him.

"Dear friends! The power behind any organization is effective and orderly publicity. Through publicity, the idea will spread and followers will be won. We do not have orderly publicity at all. We do not (did not) have talented speakers and organizers who can travel to all the cities of Galicia and work on behalf of our idea. Therefore, our idea has not spread appropriately. However, this is not the main lacuna. The bad thing is that even there (in the place) where publicity is conducted for "Hashachar", it is carried out without a primary aim, without a methodology and without order. Instead of helping, it has caused a great deal of damage. The members who worked amongst the youths did not know how to walk with them or how to speak to them. Thus, they caused a great loss for our organization, for the youths continued to distance themselves from us and oppose our aspirations.

{Page 71}

In order to conduct appropriate publicity, and so that we will be able to realize the hoped for benefits, it is necessary to found a publicity office whose mandates will be:
   a. To devise a methodology and program for publicity.
   b. To set up branches of that office in all chapters, which will inform the
      central office of the powers who possess the skills to conduct agitation.

Thus, our work will spread out with order and method."

In the minutes, we hear that the president, Moshe Weisenfeld, recommends charging Laufbahn "to execute the publicity program and to disseminate it in letters that will be distributed to all the regional councils." His recommendation was accepted. We hear that Dembitz was among the cities that had a regional council, and the council was headed by Yitzchak Laufbahn. He certainly carried out the task that was given to him, but he did not carry it out for a long period, for we hear from the words of Moshe Weisenfeld, who closed the convention with the following pure words:

"We must remember Jerusalem at the head of our joy. You know, dear brethren, that the settlement of the Land of Israel is developing, and today the possibility exists for every Jew to settle there, not just for the ideological purposes, but also to make money there and to conduct good business. Therefore, we have the duty to travel to Palestine. I am hereby informing you, dear friends, that our friend Mr. Yungerwirt, who worked with us last year on the convention, traveled to the Land of Israel to settle there. In the name of the entire convention, I extend our deepest good wishes to him, and may our wishes accompany him on his journey to our Land (applause). Please, let us also try to follow in his footsteps and travel to Palestine, for that is our ultimate goal. That is the place for our youth. You known several youths who until this time have wandered through Vienna and Berlin, searching for their purpose in life. The time has come for all those youths to travel to our Land. Let our comrades set out for our Land! Summon the strength to form a caravan of pioneers to go there, to work in the Land of our patriarchs, each one in the profession of his expertise.

We young people, with our great love for the Land of our patriarchs, are able to do work a great deal toward the renaissance of our Land. Arise, therefore, to work and action! Before we part, I will conclude with the ancient blessing: Next Year in Jerusalem (stormy applause)."

These concluding words emanated from a proper heart, the heart of the president of that organization – who himself did not merit to go to our Land, but remained faithful to it until his bitter end, especially as the head of the Keren Kayemet in Western Galicia. They penetrated a receptive heart, and Yitzchak Laufbahn was one of the first to respond to it. Indeed, that member Yungerwirt had an important position in his path of life. Not long passed before the voice of Laufbahn was heard among the youth of Galicia in an open letter that left an impression. It took place as follows: After a year, when Laufbahn was already in Jerusalem, issues of the Polish monthly of the Zionist youth in Galicia, "Moria", reached him. In one of the editions, he found an article from his hometown of Dembitz, and he decided to oppose it in an open fashion: To my sisters in the Diaspora (Moria, Lwow, Seventh Year, Issues 5-8, September 1909, Pages 178-189).

F.

The letter itself was certainly written in Hebrew, for the editors of "Hamoria" noted, as they published it, that they have translated it into Polish. We wish now to present that letter, in which his style that he later became known for can already be seen. However, all we can include is a translation of the translation. He opened with the observation that he read that article with great interest:

"For behold I am, Heaven save us, someone who was educated in that gloomy city, and the old shadows of the past envelop me, and trepidation overtakes me... I do not know if you in the Diaspora are at all able to feel what I felt when I read that article, which has more of the character of an obituary. 'It is easy to remember' – a memorial of the dead! – Something that has never existed. I still remember, dear sisters! On occasion, I still recall the Diaspora, the dreams and visions, bursting like soap bubbles! I am not writing a letter of accusation against you, but I want to tell the truth.

You were never serious in your work, never! Therefore, it does not bear fruit. A body without a soul has no life! If at times someone[8] carried out his task seriously, he destroyed his self in body and spirit because he was alone. The others, apparently his supporters and helpers, specifically the 'men of integrity', worked for selfish reasons or pretended to be diligently active. They never possessed any understanding about what it means to be a Jew.

You are distraught for naught, beloved sisters! The People of Israel did not lose anything with them, and the Land of Israel does not need such pioneers, who would only drag the Diaspora here.

Pessimists turned into these visionaries. It is no wonder, and indeed it is now typical, that they call for abandonment, become 'spiritual aristocrats' and promise even more than this... 'A child's game.' 'The party chains me down' – one of them said to me, even before he removed the study cap with the letter G. This was on a winter evening. I rambled with him on and on, looked into his eyes with astonishment, and recognized the odor emanating from this. 'They will bury their dead.'

You with your small group, if you wished to work seriously, you could have done more than provide the masses, millions, of such 'student caps.'"

Invalidating the imaginary activity and thought about true actions; an investigation into evasions, removing the covers and exposing the hidden; setting everything on a reliable basis whose power is great and decisive for the masses – to the point that it was acknowleged that the "Hashachar" movement was a link in this aliya.

Translator's Footnotes

1. A leading Rabbi in 15th century Spain, and an advisor to the king.
2. Eliezer Ben Yehuda was the father of the modern Hebrew language.
3. The phrase "of clean hands and a pure heart" is a quote from Psalms 24.
4. See http://en.wikipedia.org/wiki/Leon_Pinsker.
5. There is a footnote in the text here, as follows: The first convention took place in Dembitz on the intermediate days of Passover, 5667 in the Bornstein Hotel – the editor.
6. A term for Yiddish.
7. I believe that this means that he left the immediate realm of the close knit organization to move on to larger roles – although the wording is convoluted.
8. There is a footnote in the text here: A hint to Yehuda Bornstein of blessed memory – the editor

A group of the "Devora" organization (1908) – The first one in the row of those seated, at the right, is Ruchama Grynspan.

{Page 75}

Between Two World Wars

Translated by Jerrold Landau

War and Exile

A sudden rupture in Jewish life of Dembitz came with the outbreak of the First World War in August 1914. As the Russian army approached Dembitz several weeks later, the vast majority of the Jews left Dembitz. Some left in vehicles and others in wagons, and they only took their most precious belongings with them. The houses with their furnishings, and the stores with their merchandise were abandoned. The Russian army entered the deserted city on a Friday afternoon, a day or two before Rosh Hashana, and immediately began to pillage the stores, starting with the taverns and liquor stores. Since the soldiers of the Austrian army purchased most of the food, sugar, rice, and other such goods before their retreat, there were very few provisions to be had in town. They began to request food from the Jews that remained, and whenever they found some, they ordered the Jews to cook for them, and to taste the food first, lest they had put poison in the pots. There were very few incidents of beatings.

Immediately after the invasion, the raping of young women began. They raped whomever they could find, and the women would attempt to find refuge in the attics. The people were afraid to remain alone in their houses, and each night they would gather in a few houses. The Russian soldiers occupied the abandoned houses, and they lit the ovens with the furniture. One of the schemes of the Russians was to ask a Jew for the time, and as the Jew removed his watch from his pocket, the Russian would steal it from him. The Jews of Dembitz did not imagine that things could get worse than this. Hunger increased at that time, and the Jews would endanger themselves by going out to neighboring villages in order to obtain some food, such as potatoes, etc. They had to grind the wheat into flour by themselves. This situation lasted for eight to ten days. It is told that before the Russians left, a strange Jew entered the synagogue and prophesied that the Russians would leave on such and such a day at such and such a time, and indeed it came to pass exactly in that manner.

The Russians left and the Austrians entered. The Jews danced outside for joy, however this joy was not to last. After several days, the Austrian army was forced to retreat. With them, the entire Jewish population left, and only two or three Jews remained.

The Austrian army provided transport wagons for the escaping Jews, upon which was loaded all of the remaining merchandise and all of the Torah scrolls from the synagogues. The other books were buried in the cemetery[80].

The Austrian government housed the refugees in Bohemia, around Reichenberg, and Teplitz-Schenau[81]. They were brought there in transport trains over a period of several days. At first they were housed in large dance halls, where they slept by the hundreds on straw mattresses.

The Jewish refugees were afraid of the gentiles on account of their unusual dress, their full beards and peyos. Nevertheless, they were politely received by the Germans of Bohemia, without any trace of anti-Semitism. They were offered jobs, since many of the refuges were able to read and speak German. These are the same Germans, that about thirty years later would be among the chief henchmen of Hitler in the extermination of the Jews! Nevertheless, they put themselves out to assist the Jewish refugees in Bohemia with great warmth and boundless mercy.

The refugees slowly began to get organized. Families spread out among the villages of the area. They found themselves modest dwellings, and the government distributed a stipend to them. They slowly began to acclimatize to the living conditions of their new place, and they began to do business in all areas, while at the same time they continued to receive their stipend. The young men of army age were drafted, and their families received a stipend from the army. Their relations with the local population continued to remain polite. They also began to concern themselves with their spiritual life. When they found out that a Tzadik buried in the cemetery of Tachau, they began to visit there in large numbers... Many of them traveled to the Rabbis of Galicia who had also fled, mostly to Vienna. Since the living conditions in the small villages were much better than in the larger towns, the refugees of Dembitz remained peacefully in those places until the government sent transport trains at the beginning of 1916 to return them to their homes. They returned from their places of refuge laden with merchandise, some with less and others with more. Thus, they had sufficient means to re-establish their lives as previously. The city was for the most part destroyed and burned, however they began to set themselves up to the best of their abilities.

{Page 75}

Destruction and Rebuilding

In late August 1914, when the Russian army neared Dembitz, the Jewish population fled to where ever they could. The great majority were evacuated to German-Bohemia.

When the Russians were driven back after the large, second German-Austrian-Hungarian offensive, the Jews of Dembitz began to return home gradually. They found a destroyed and looted town. A large part of the marketplace had burned down. The long arcade and the other arcades were gone with the fire.

The municipal administration quartered the returnees in the government school buildings and erected a big barracks in the marketplace for shops and stores. And thus was Jewish life in Dembitz gradually reestablished. And this became even more the case when more Jews began returning from the evacuation. Some needed their old livelihoods, which other looked for new ones. Of course, not all residents of Dembitz returned home from the evacuation. Some young people who had been drafted into the army during the war fell on the battlefield. Other young people remained abroad, some in Vienna and others in Germany. Some, upon their return, settled in larger cities in Galicia.

The war period and the evacuation had a great impact on the Jews of Dembitz, as well as on the Jews of Galicia as a whole. The war taught everyone that the world in which they lived was not eternal, fixed, or secure. If what had happened to them could happen, if you could suddenly lose everything that you had owned, then it could happen again. During the war, it was revealed that even familiar non-Jews, with whom one had lived together without (may it not happen) pogroms or big conflicts, were not such lambs after all, and that one could expect more and more from them in the future. And the evacuation had also revealed another world: cities and villages with such civilized order and cleanliness, the like of which they had never seen in Dembitz and its environs. Jews, in their own homes, hadn't paid much attention to appearances. For who, alas, did you have to appear refined and civilized? Who, after all, was there to please? But it was different during the evacuation. In alien surroundings, one must perforce be quieter, one must observe the dominant customs, not provoke any snobbish laughter, not call attention to one's difference from the norm. Indeed, there were soon more Jews dressed in German fashions, more trimmed beards, more shaved faces, fewer satin hats--and indeed, more cleanliness, fewer loud voices--more civilization.

Immediately following the war, when the Austro-Hungarian monarchy had fallen and Galicia, along with Crown Poland and Posen were declared an independent Polish state, the Jews of Dembitz, along with all Jews in Galicia, sensed the need, for the first time, for an active Jewish political life to defend their rights and lives. Already in the very first days of Polish independence a wave of attempted pogroms swept western Galicia, and not all of them were successfully repulsed as had been the case with the disturbance in the Jewish town of Brigl[99]. The returning Jewish soldiers organized armed self-defense groups, and at the same time, the Jewish National Board for western Galicia was created in Krakow at the initiative of the Zionists and Poale Zion, with the participation of the Zh.P.S., with branch National Boards in other cities and towns, in order to carry out the defense of Jewish rights and lives, and in general, to see to the establishment of a more organized communal life. The old *kehiles*[100] were not suited to this.

And Dembitz too was menaced with a pogrom. Dark anti-Semitic forces among the Poles were mounting a strong incitement. The fear was so great that even those circles who had never before agreed to cooperate with Zionists, gave in this time and took part in the National Board, which was under Zionist leadership.

R. Naftali Eisen

The chairman of the National Board was Shemaya Widerspan. Meetings were held day and night. A way to prevent a pogrom in Dembitz was sought. At the suggestion of Poale Zion and the General Zionists, a self-defense militia was created. Many returning soldiers had brought revolvers and other weapons back from the war. A member of the National Board, R. Naftali Eisen, took it upon himself to furnish 100 bayonets that were in his lock factory. The self-defense organized itself. The town was divided up into districts. Patrols were sent out day and night to all the roads leading to the town. On the National Board, however, were a couple of Jews who did not agree with the more modern political methods. Without the knowledge of the National Board, this small group, under the leadership of Itshe Kaiser (Fink), began collecting money from among the house-holders, and when they had amassed a considerable sum, they bribed the commander of the militia -- who was, by the way, a Ukrainian who hated Poles. They also offered a considerable amount of money to the chief of police, Hornug-- who also wasn't a Pole, and was, I believe, Hungarian, and also no great friend of Poles--so that neither of them would allow any pogroms against the Jews. It was expected that pogrom was going to erupt at the next monthly fair.

On the day of the fair, the commandant of the militia stationed men on all the roads leading to Dembitz. A few suspects were arrested; a lot just had their weapons confiscated and were sent home. Those who resisted arrest were brought before the magistrate, where Police Chief Hornug was already waiting. He received a few of them in very cordially; that is, he laid them on a bench and gave them 20-30 strokes of the whip. Their screams reached the heavens.

The peasants and the town hooligans were terribly disappointed. That is, what kind of Poland is this that doesn't allow a little robbing and murdering of Jews? In vain, they used to say: *"Poydshe tsos, bedzhe nos?"*[101]

That same day, hooligans who had infiltrated the city tried to break into Leyb Hershlag's bakery. But they met with resistance. Elish Dar and Shaul Morgenendler stood up to the band with sticks and forced them to flee with great regret.

Thus did old-fashioned methods spare Dembitz from a pogrom.

The more Jews returned home to Dembitz, the more pressing were their needs. There was no business and no government. The aid came from the American Jewish Joint Distribution Committee. A representative of the Joint came down from Krakow for a meeting of the National Board and it was decided to establish an aid committee, to which belonged almost the entire National Board. On the committee sat most of the representatives of Poale Zion: Shimon Grünspan, Dr. Pinkhes Loyfman[102], and Naftali Shnier. From America came packages of oil, canned meat, and flour for Passover matzohs. All of them were distributed to the needy Jewish population. Great sums of money also arrived, and were used to purchase sewing machines, which were distributed to tailors who needed them. A school to teach various crafts and professions was opened. This work helped more than anything in the rebuilding of the destroyed town.

{Page 77}

The First Elections After The War

The disintegration of the Hapsburg monarchy and the founding of independent Poland left their marks on the municipal government as well. Already in the first years of the renewed Poland, a significant reformation took place with regard to elections to the town council, to other democratic issues, and to the participation of the workers' party. During the time of Austrian rule, the electoral rights of the Galician towns were very limited. This right was only given to three groups:

    a. those who had higher education and served as overseers,

    b. property owners and those that paid high taxes, and finally

    c. those who paid lower taxes.

Each group would elect an equal number of representatives to the town council. Whomever was not included in one of these groups was not a member of the electorate. Thus, the electorate only consisted of a very small proportion of the populace. This was of some benefit to the Jewish population, where the proportion of taxpayers was larger than that of the Polish population.

With the democratic reforms in the area of elections that took place, a fourth group as added to these three groups, which consisted of the remainder of the adult population. The result was that the proportion of Jews in the electorate decreased further. Nevertheless, the extra privileges which were granted to the first group, in which there were very few Jews, remained as previously.

The first elections in Dembitz according to the new laws took place in 1921. The fourth group chose some candidates from among the workers of Poale Zion, and this was also the first time that the Socialist Workers' Party (P. P. S.), also fielded candidates. These were over and above the candidates of the anti-Semitic Polish "All Polish" party, which had a priest at its helm, and other such parties. The election campaign was very tense and heated. The two groups of workers' parties, the Jewish and Polish, both did very well, since they supported each other. Dr. Pinchas Laufbahn and Naftali Schneur were elected to the town council from Poale Zion. However Schneur did not take his seat, as he decided at that time to emigrate to America. Another member of the Poale Zion list took his seat in his stead.

Before Schneur's emigration to America, a party in his honor was planned by the Poale Zion organization in the city, however, this party did not take place. The events took place as follows: The office of Poale Zion at that time was located in the home of Shemaya Widerspan. An officer of the gendarme also lived there. After the crowd had already gathered around the set tables and listened to the farewell speech of Shimon Grünspan, an officer of the gendarme entered with several policemen, and the entire gathered assembly was arrested on the pretext of "disturbing the public order". The entire group was brought to the town hall, where they were detained for some time and then sent home. Of course, the party did not continue.

This event took place in democratic Poland. The customs of the old Austrian police were not uprooted. Rather, the enthusiasm displayed with regard to this event increased further in the following years, first under the "Andak" government, and later under the government of the men of Pielsodoski – "Ozon", that is B.B.R.

{Page 78}

A Community under Government Scrutiny

The organized life of the community of Dembitz as it was conducted according to its customs did not resume immediately with the return of Jews from their exile in Bohemia. Reb Chaim Mahler, one of the important people of the town, felt that everything should be run as it always had been, and that he was still the head of the community. He remained in this role during the turbulent first years of the Polish state. However, not too long after, the Zionists and those that supported them, headed by Shemaya Widerspan, turned to him and requested that elections be arranged, and that he give over the communal ledgers that were in his possession. He refused and stated: "The communal ledgers are a segula [82] for long life." He continued in his refusal until they frightened him by shattering the windows of his house, and then he gave in. In these elections, the following were elected to the communal council from among the Zionists: Shemaya Widerspan, Dr. Pinchas Laufbahn, Moshe Kerner, Naftali Schneur. Shemaya Widerspan was chosen to head the communal council.

This council continued its activities until the controversy broke out with respect to the issue of the appointment of a new Rabbi for the city after the death of Rabbi Shmuel Horowitz. The Orthodox camp in the city was divided into three groups with respect to their relations to the new Rabbi, Rabbi Tzvi Elimelech the son of Rabbi Shmuel, who fought with a high hand against the influence of the Zionists. Finally, the supporters of the Rabbi succeeded in influencing the regional government to remove Shemaya Widerspan from his chairmanship of the communal council, and to appoint Reb Hirsch Taub in his stead. The secondgroup did not agree to this, as they found reason to invalidate him as well, so Reb Tovia Zucker was appointed in his stead. In 1928, with the end of the term of office of the council, a new election took place and the Zionists again gained the upper hand. Dr. Pinchas Laufbahn was appointed as the head of the council. However, the regional government in Ropczyce did not agree with the election results, and a new election took place. Reb Avraham Goldman, one of the supporters of the Rabbi, was elected as head of the community. He served in this position until the outbreak of the Second World War. He passed away a few years ago in Bnei Brak, Israel.

Reb Tzvi Hirsch Taub

Reb Tovia Zucker

In the census of 1931, as in the census twenty years previous, the Zionists requested that the Jews register their spoken language as Yiddish or Hebrew. In opposition to this, the Hassidim in 1911 urged their supporters to register Polish. This time, as opposed to during the period of Austrian rule, it was permitted to register any language. Nevertheless, most of the Jews of Dembitz registered Polish. The Orthodox did likewise, even though a word of Polish would only very rarely pass their lips. This was done due to fear of oppression by the authorities. This fear was spread by the spread first and foremost by the anti-Zionist Orthodox.

Reb Avraham Goldman

{Page 79}

Assistance and Charity

An assistance organization called "Gemilus Chassadim" existed in Dembitz prior to the Second World War. The organization was founded due to the efforts of Reb Pinchas Kuss, who was one of the chief activists of the organization from the time of its establishment. It operated like a bank, and it was lead in a democratic and popular fashion: There were twelve trustees who directed the organization along with a board of advisors of twenty-four. The organization was headed by Naftali Eisen, with Reb Chaim Schlesinger as the vice chairman. The other directors included Nathan Gruenspan, Baruch Shneps, Liebtshe Liebenheimer, Shmuel Fishler, Aharon David Schuldenfrei, Leib Sluman, Chanina Mahler, Shmuel Taub, Moshe Kerner, and others. The activities of this assistance organization, which had at its disposal several thousand Austrian crowns, stopped with the outbreak of the First World War, and did not resume until 1925.

The organization was able to reopen due to the generosity of one of the residents of Dembitz who turned over 1,000 gold coins to the organization in an anonymous fashion. Now it is permitted to reveal that this person was Meir Schwartz, who was not well to do at all, and who himself was responsible for his own family which consisted of many children. Daniel Kerner the son of Reb Shaul also turned over a sum of 2,000 gold coins to the organization.

The members of the organization were immediately called to a general meeting, and directors where elected. A membership fee was instituted, which resulted in an income of 150-160 gold coins monthly. From that time on, "Gemilus Chasadim" in Dembitz was affiliated with the overseeing organization of the charitable foundation of the American Joint, which provided matching funds to the organization. Loans were distributed in the sum of 300-500 gold coins, interest free and with very small bi-weekly payback rates.

In 1935, the capital of the organization decreased to 20,000 gold coins. In order to increase its income to be able to widen its activities, it established, with the assistance of the Joint, a linen factory which operated thirty sewing machines. The factory employed young women who required work, and was supervised by a special guide. The director of accounts was Yehoshua Shneps, and due to the extra income, the free loan organization succeeded in increasing the number of loans it was able to distribute.

The other credit organization, which was called "The Jewish Bank", was run in a different fashion. Prior to the First World War it was headed by Reb Shaul Kerner, who was quite well to do, along with Yona Geshwind and the lawyer Fishler. Reb Shaul Kerner was a noted merchant with great drive. He built homes for rental, and he owned the building of the post office of Dembitz.

A meeting of the "Gemilus Chasadim Organization".

The office of the director of the "Jewish Bank" received an income of 1,200 guilders (2,400 crowns) a month. It is no wonder that for a duration of twenty years, the directors refused to call elections for a new slate of directors.

{Page 80}

Nevertheless, Reb Shaul Kerner, the great benefactor, returned the ample salary in the form of charitable donations. As long as his wife Ruchtshe was alive, and also for some time after that, he fed at his Sabbath and festival table about twenty or thirty needy Jews. He would also support poor people from outside the city via donations channeled through the nearest large city.

Reb Baruch Shneps

Dembitz also had private Jewish "banks" which were set up as organizations or cooperatives. These were really only a veil for loans with interest. The depressed economic situation worsened as the state encouraged anti-Semitism increased, and there were numerous cases of bankruptcy and economic decline. State sponsored and economic oriented anti-Semitism increased when institutions of "The Manufacturing Triangle" were set up around Dembitz. According to the plans of the government, these organizations would not employ Jews as workers, nor use them as suppliers. Dembitz became stronger, however the Jewish population continued to decline until the outbreak of the Second World War, which brought with it the Holocaust that was worse than any of the bad dreams that were ever dreamt by the dreamers of black dreams.

Assistance for the Poor and Sick

There were very few beggars in Dembitz. Behind the market of Dembitz there was a communal alms-house which served as a shelter for the needy who were from outside the city. This was not a luxurious dormitory. It was very far from that, but nevertheless it served as a shelter for those without anything, beggars from the surrounding areas and from farther away whose numbers continued to increase. Groups of beggars would pass through the city, scatter among the houses, and gather together again. Entire families would arrive in the city on wagons with all of their belongings, sleep in the cemetery, remain in the city for a few days and then continue on their way. Not infrequently, controversies broke out between the beggars and the residents of the city, and not infrequently unpleasant encounters occurred when the beggars would demand their portions in a loud and haughty manner. In order to put an end to this rampant wave of door to door begging that came from outside the city, the idea was hatched to set up an organization that would distribute what would be called "retreat money". Every resident would contribute weekly a fixed sum to this fund, and the needy people who came to the city from outside would be prohibited from going door to door, but would rather be directed to the overseers of this charitable fund and would receive a set sum of money. A person with a family would receive an additional sum on account of the family. The wave of door to door begging stopped, and both sides were satisfied. The charitable overseers included Reb Yerucham Kluger, Nachum Lustgarten, Baruch Shneps, Hersh-Nissan Appel, and Mendel Reich.

This organization existed for many years. "Chevra Mezonot" (The organization to provide food) operated alongside. Its founder and life force was Meir Glickles, and its secretary was Wolf Faust. The money that was collected made it possible to provide a warm meal to whomever was in need. It is important to note that these organizations operated primarily due to the efforts and dedication of a few individuals. As long as there was a person who was "crazy about the idea", there would be no shortage of money for the particular need. In addition, at various times, there were people who entertained guests in their homes in a very generous fashion. We have already mentioned Reb Shaul Kerner and his wife Ruchtcha, in whose home any needy person could always find a warm meal and a place to sleep. Dozens of passers through who were indigent, with torn and worn out clothes, would stay over in their home, and these generous people would make efforts to strengthen them, give them a place to sleep, and even give them a modest sum of money for their journey. In the later years, Reb Itzi Kornreich could be counted among these generous people. He was a simple man who entertained guests in a wondrous fashion. At all hours of the day, pots full of warm food could be found on his stove, and anyone who entered his house would not leave hungry.

Reb Shaul Kerner

Two groups in the city busied themselves with helping the ill, one consisting of men and the other of women. "Chevra Linat Tzedek" was the mens' organization. It would happen that the chronically ill would often require care during the night, on occasion for a duration of several months, and the pressure on their families was too great to stand. In such cases, the people of the city, through the efforts of the "Linat Tzedek" organization would take turns in watching over the sick person and caring for him. When the list of adults who could take a turn ended, and the illness continued, the organization would request the assistance of the youth, who would answer the call.

The "Chevrat Lina" organization was composed of women only, and served women only. This organization never had to turn to the youth for assistance, since the list of volunteers for night duty was long enough. The women would willingly donate their time to look after a sick woman. The care would also be extended during the day, for if a woman took ill, it would be necessary to care for her as well as her children.

{Page 81}

If there were not enough people on the lists to take care of all those in need, a hired person would help out and the organization would pay the fee. Thus, the mitzva was double [83].

Mrs. Bina Salomon

The Orphanage

Recha Sandhaus

Mrs. Susi Siedlisker

"Chevrat Lina" owned all of the sanitary equipment that was needed for the care of the ill, and also ran a small pharmacy from which medication would be paid for by the monthly membership fee. Their institution, which was founded by Lea Yoskim, at first consisted of a small number of women, but as its efforts became more well known, its membership increased to 120 women from all the strata of society. It was run by Perel Faust of blessed memory, and the secretary was Bina Salomon of blessed memory. We should point out also the dedication of Reizele Reich (the wife of Reb Yechezkel the ritual slaughterer), and, may she live and be well, Rachel Reiner, as well as others.

Even when the ghetto was set up in Dembitz, this organization did not stop its work, and the women volunteers offered assistance to anyone who needed even though there were great difficulties in obtaining the necessary provisions.

The Orphanage
and Assistance for Brides

A Jewish orphanage was founded in Dembitz in 1927-1928 due to the efforts of Recha Sandhaus, who was the wife of Yisrael Sandhaus and the daughter of Reb Nathan Gruenspan. The orphanage was supervised by a special supervisory organization. The chairman was Recha Sandhaus, and the general secretary was Baruch Shneps, assisted by Tzvi Hersh Taub. This organization was affiliated with the central organization in Krakow, which provided the bulk of the funds in the form of monthly grants. Since the number of orphans was not that large, this organization also cared for the children of the poor, who received support, textbooks, etc.

At first this institution operated out of rented premises, where the children would busy themselves after the regular school day with amusements and study, and they would also receive dinner. Around 1935 approximately, this organization purchased a field behind the Christian cemetery and build a building consisting of eight to ten rooms, which included rooms for study, a kitchen, etc. The children would only return to their own homes to sleep. During the school vacation the children would stay in the building under the supervision of governesses and counselors, who assisted them with their studies in the Polish public school, as well as in reading and writing Yiddish.

In its final years, the orphanage cared for approximately 50 children. The membership fees resulted in an income of 200 gold coins per month. In addition, there were other sources of income due to galas and performances, etc.

{Page 82}

There was no special organization in the city responsible for looking after the needs of brides. However whenever a bride or groom would be about to be married, if they did not have the means to arrange the wedding, one could find honorable women with their black shawls walking the streets of the city, going from door to door in order to raise the money to provide a silk hat or a streimel for the groom, or a dress for the bride, as well as for bedding. These righteous women included Susi and Chana Siedlisker, Salche Kriger, Sarale Sommer, Chayale Olink from the "old" city, as well as Chaya Shuss, Bina Salamon, Chinka Gruenspan, Perel Faust, and many others, all important women whose names we cannot remember anymore. At all times these women would be willing to give of themselves for anyone in need or anyone ill. There were many charitable organizations, many small in their sphere of activity, and functioning without any fanfare. It was not only the well to do who volunteered for these organizations, but anyone with a warm soul, who loved the Jewish people and loved to do a mitzva. Many tears of those that suffered from ill fate were wiped away in this manner.

Mrs. Chana Siedlisker

Mrs. Perel Faust

Reb Yaakov Taub, the head of the Chevra Kaddisha (burial society)

{Page 82}

The Final Civic Elections

The Orthodox camp, which was always the majority, divided up in the later years into three streams, according to their relationship to Rabbi Tzvi Elimelech, as has been previously mentioned. These streams were:

a. the supporters of the Rabbi,

b. the supporters of the Rabbi of Jadlowa (an echo of the controversy that took place in the days of Rabbi Reuven), and

c. the Hassidim of Rabbi Naftalche, who returned in 1934 after living for sixteen years in the United States. Rabbi Hersh Taub, who appointed Rabbi Tzvi Elimelech to the Rabbinical seat, wanted to make him the head of the Rabbinical court without the approval of Rabbi Naftalche, and thus did the controversy begin again.

The controversy increased greatly until at one point, during a stormy meeting that took place in the office of "Gemilus Chassadim" that was in the Great Synagogue, Hertzke Shuss slapped Rabbi Tzvi Elimelech on his cheek. The matter was brought before the Mizrachi Rabbinical court, whose members came from Tarnow to Dembitz in order to adjudicate the matter. Both sides brought in lawyers from Tarnow. The slapper was given a suspended sentence of six months of imprisonment, on the condition of good behavior for the duration of three years.

With the approach of the civic elections at the beginning of 1939, the factions of the Rabbi of Jadlowa and Rabbi Naftalche united with the Zionist camp, since they did not have suitable candidates of their own. This caused the defeat of the Rabbi, who became actively involved in the elections and set up his own slate. The two sides set up their own slates in the three areas of the Jewish election, however in two of the areas, the candidates of the Rabbi (Reb Naftali Eisen and Moshe Rosenberg) were forced to step down due to communal pressure, so that only Reb Avrahamche Goldman of blessed memory remained (he passed away several years ago in Israel).

Nevertheless, the election campaign was very stormy. On the day prior to the elections, the Rabbi convened a publicity rally in the town hall since he was not sure that he would be able to convene that rally in any other place.

{Page 83}

However the second side, whose headquarters were in the "Merchants' Union", decided not to allow this rally to take place, and prevented the Rabbi from leaving his house after the Sabbath.

Reb Efraim Taffet

Reb Leiser Oling

A street in the old city

The implementation was left to the eighteen year-old youths. After the departure of the Sabbath, a large group of youths entered the house of the Rabbi and informed him that the rally would not take place and that he would not be permitted to leave his house until 11:00 p. m. The spokesman of the group was Reuven Siedlisker of "Hashomer Hadati". The Rabbi told them: "Shkotzim, get out of here"[84]. Reuven answered him spontaneously: "it is better to be a sheketz before the Jews rather than a Rabbi before the gentiles!" A guard of thirty youths was set up around the house and nobody was permitted to leave the house. The rally did not take place.

It was quite conceivable that this action of the youths would generate great opposition in the city, for the house of the Rabbi was always treated with proper respect, even though it did not merit the Hassidic style of reverence. This was not the case. In the elections on the following day, all three of the Zionist representatives were elected – Dr. Pinchas Laufbahn, Shimon Gruenspan (both from Poale Zion), and Shemaya Widerspan. The candidate of the Rabbi, Reb Avrahamche Goldman, only received thirty ballots. This was the response of the Dembitz Jewish community to the cooperation with the anti-Semitic government party (B. B. B., or Ozon).

Two Christians were candidates for the office of mayor – Drolak of the moderates, and the Gymnasia teacher Professor Staron, who was well known for his hatred of Jews. The latter was elected as mayor. He threatened the Jewish electorate that if he was not elected, he would destroy the smokestack of the Gruenspan flour mill, and he would also close down the mill completely. The Jews gave in. After he was elected, Strason behaved exactly the opposite from all the good promises that he made to the Jews electorate.

About one month prior to the outbreak of the war, Strason began to oppress the Jews at every opportunity. When an order was issued to prepare moats to protect from an air raid, the responsibility was primarily placed on the Jews, according to his command. When the Nazis entered the city, one of his first acts was to destroy the smokestack and to liquidate the mill, in opposition to his promise.

{Page 84}

The local Zionist committee during the 1920s

{Page 86}

Images (II)

Bendet Fett

by R.B./D.L[103]

Translated by Roberta Newman

Bendet Fett was, without a doubt, one of the most interesting and popular figures in Dembitz. During the course of more than thirty years, he was active in an indescribably self-sacrificing way in the Zionist movement, serving for years as the chairman of the Zionist local-committee, and never seeking any sort of public recognition for himself. Nonetheless, he never let an opportunity pass by to put his shoulder to the wheel.

Though he was not an orator or himself a highly educated man, he was one of the most devoted cultural activists in town. The Hebrew school had his devotion, above all, to thank for its existence and further development. But this was only one side of his activism in this area.

Perhaps even more important was the role he played in the expansion of the Yiddish and Zionist press in Dembitz; and later, in the dissemination of Yiddish and Hebrew books. On the surface, it was a matter of making a living.

The truth, however, ran a lot deeper: he became a newspaper agent and a book merchant because he had an deep-seated interest in disseminating Zionism and secular culture -- two things that were, in the town, tightly bound together. When he first began to order a few copies of the Lemberger *Togblat*, the *Yud* from Krakow, *Yidishn arbeter,* and *Voskhod,* there was no living to be made from it, so few was the number of purchasers. If he had paid more attention to the small hotel he had, he would have been more successful in business. For him, however, more important than the hotel was the fact that young people came to see him and that something could be done for Zionism, for the progressive youth. Only slowly did the business grow, together with the movement. He became the distributor of newspapers in Dembitz, for Jews and non-Jews alike, and his book dealership was also model business. True, even then, thinking about business was not his main thing--this he left to his wife, Chanale--and he was preoccupied only with Zionist activism. And this was treasured by everyone in Dembitz.

If a man with this sort of exceptional energy had received a systematic education and had not been confined to the milieu of a small town, he could have accomplished a lot more, no doubt. In Dembitz, it took more time to get things done.

Yes, Bendit Fett was a stubborn man. In his youth, when he had opened his hotel, he had come up with an invention: a clock that would wake the guests, everyone at the specified hour, so that the hotel owner didn't have exert himself in the night to wake them up. This was a product of small-town hotel experience. Bendit Fet allowed this invention to be patented in Vienna for the entire Austro-Hungarian Empire, and maybe also in other lands--and for years nearly jumped out of his skin with impatience, waiting for the patent to take off. But no one presented himself, no one in the world needed the patent. His friends and even his nearest and dearest in Dembitz sang a song about him, with a special tune, and that was known by everyone in Dembitz:

Bendit Fett with the clock

Has a face like a carcass.[104]

But this never got in the way of the great respect felt for his great, selfless idealism and communal activism.

He was an eternal fighter for culture, for democratic procedure in Jewish life, and he had much gratitude and love for every person who was educated and knowledgeable and who appeared in the city and did something, And who even spoke of whether it had anything to do with Zionism?

Honor to his memory!

{Page 88}

Dr. Pinchas Laufbahn

by Yitzchak Freiman

{Hebrew text – pp 88-89}

Pinchas Wolf Laufbahn and his brother Yitzchak were my brothers-in-law. I would not have taken it upon myself to describe his illustrious personality if there were in our midst someone who is more expert than myself about this era. A Yizkor book about Dembitz – which was his birthplace and field of activity for the course of thirty years – would be incomplete without mention of him. I will therefore attempt to describe on paper some elements of his personality.

Pinchas Laufbahn was born in 1892. His father was Reb Eliakim Getzel. As his brother Yitzchak, he studied Talmud and Rabbinical law from the mouth of his grandfather, Reb Yehuda Leib the Rabbinical judge, who wished to educate his grandchildren solely in Torah. However, with the three youngest, his will did not stand up to the spirit of the time. Due to the influence of his brother Yitzchak of blessed memory before he made Aliya, Pinchas, who was very diligent and quick to learn, started learning at the Gymnasia as an external student, and graduated after four years of study. Before that time, he joined Poale Zion in the city, and participated in the cultural activities of the local group. It didn't take long for Pinchas Laufbahn, who was still a young law student at the University of Krakow, to begin to rise to the ranks of leadership in the local Poale Zion, along with Naftali Shneur, Mendel Wilner, and Ruchama and Shimon Gruenspan. Already in 1912 he participated in the election campaign for the Austrian parliament as a supporter of the Zionist representative Dr. Sirop. It is important to point out that most of the Zionist lecturers did not yet know how to speak well in the vernacular, and were also very far from words of Torah. He appeared on the scene, as the grandson of G-d fearing and observant Jews, with a sharp and clear manner of speaking, absorbing the spirit of the culture of Israel and fighting for national recognition, for democracy and Haskala.

Dr. Pinchas Laufbahn and his brother Israel

All of these activities, both within the community and outside of it, ceased with the outbreak of the First World War and the exile of the Jews of Dembitz from their city. Only in 1916 did they return and slowly begin to renew their way of life as it was previously. With the end of the war and the disbanding of the Hapsburg monarchy, the opportunity arose again for communal activities, and Pinchas Laufbahn was among the leaders. However, during the war a noticeable change took place in Jewish life in the city. The former leaders, heads of the community and the Hassidim, were at a complete loss as to how to go about the task of reconstructing the destroyed city, and in particular they shied away from the new task of guarding the security of their living conditions, which came to be in actual danger due to the growing Polish nationalism in the renewed nation. From that time, Pinchas Laufbahn, in his capacity as a trained lawyer, became involved in all organizational activities of the Jewish community of Dembitz. He was one of the leaders of Poale Zion, working shoulder to shoulder with Shimon Gruenspan who was his junior, and he was recognized by all of the Zionist streams in the city. He was involved in the establishment of a branch of "The Jewish Nationalist Organization of Western Galicia", as well as the organizing of assistance for the needy of Dembitz. He did not neglect the political and cultural activities either. Later he was involved in every effort to renew life in the city, and to help the Jews gain appropriate status.

Pinchas Laufbahn was one of the chief spokesmen and activists of the new style. He was successful in his leadership and influence upon Poale Zion in Dembitz. He served as its chairman from 1920 until the time of the holocaust. He also played a leading role in municipal politics, as well as in the community.

Along with Shemaya Widerspan, the leader of the Zionists of Dembitz, Pinchas Laufbahn and his comrades worked successfully on behalf of the community. The regional government in Krakow appointed Mr. Shemaya Widerspan as the temporary chairman of the community. When elections took place a few years later, the Zionist party ran and received the majority for the first time. Dr. Pinchas Laufbahn and Shimon Gruenspan were elected to the city council. Pinchas fulfilled his role with responsibility and strong resolve, which was a new phenomenon in the community of Dembitz. When it came time to set the budget for the community, he entered a small allocation, which generated the opposition of the entire anti-Zionist camp – the small allocation was for the Keren Hayesod. When the Hassidim on the town council opposed this powerfully, there were some delegates who wished to forego this for the sake of peace. However Pinchas Laufbahn stood his ground as a matter of faith, and the allocation was accepted.

Pinchas Laufbahn was blessed with an exceptional memory. One occasion where his spectacular memory was displayed was at the occasion when a strike broke out among the ritual slaughterers (shochtim), who demanded from the head of the community that they be allocated two kilograms of meat from every animal that they slaughtered, over and above their monthly salary from the town council. When the butchers complained that this would be impossible, since every animal that is found ritually unfit (treif) is sold at half price to the Christians, one of the members of the council stood up and proposed a compromise: that the butchers give to the shochtim two kilograms of meat from any animal that is found to be kosher, and none if it found to be treif. Pinchas Laufbahn then retorted that, as a lawyer who was not that familiar with this matter, he was surprised that such advice be proposed. This was that since it says in the Shulchan Aruch (Code of Jewish Law) section Yoreh Deah in the chapter dealing with the laws of ritual slaughter, in such and such a clause, that it is explicitly forbidden to differentiate between a kosher and treif animal when it comes to allocating a stipend to the shochet, lest the matter come to permitting a forbidden animal in order to benefit from the allocation. This retort was a topic of discussion for everyone.

Even though he was busy as a lawyer, he did not begrudge his time for communal and Zionist matters. No political or cultural activity took place without his input, or at least without his knowledge. The emissaries of the Zionist organizations knew only two addresses in Dembitz – that of Dr. Pinchas Laufbahn and that of Shemaya Widerspan. They would donate personally, as well as organize events. During all the years, he stood at the helm of the successful Poale Zion library, and concerned himself with its development. He also served as a stage-manager for the dramatic club, which was under the auspices of the cultural committee of the movement.

With all this, his door was always open to anyone in need, whether for charity or for free legal advice. Poor people always found an attentive ear in his office.

As a Torah scholar and an intellectual, he was able to harmoniously blend the spirit of the tents of Shem and the beauty of Yefet[85] in a non-contradictory fashion. Thus he won the trust of all of Dembitz Jewry.

He left Dembitz at the beginning of the Nazi conquest. He moved to the Soviet sector, and traveled with many Jews to a remote area in the depths of Russia. From there, he attempted to get to Israel. Yitzhak his elder brother, did everything in his power to bring him here, however at the time when they he had just about succeeded, when the possibility arose, he was stricken by a serious illness. This tireless activist closed his eyes forever, and did not see the Land.

It is an honor to remember him.

{Page 89}

Tzvi Wolf

by R. B.[105]

Translated by Roberta Newman

{Yiddish text – page 89}

Hersh Wolf

Tzvi Wolf

When Tsvi Wolf died in 1956 in Haifa at the age of 61, it is no exaggeration to say that he was one of the most popular people of the Second Aliyah[106] because of the role he played as one of those who had helped lay the foundations for the present day burgeoning Jewish settlement in the Jezreel Valley.

For 45 years, he lived and worked in the Land of Israel, and for the most part in the most dangerous circumstances. When he made *aliyah* from Dembitz in 1911 as one of the first *olim,* the young man already had behind him several years of intensive party and cultural activism as one of the first members of Poale Zion. And so the organization arranged a fine banquet in his honor, at which Naftali Shnier, Mendel Wilner, and Ruchama Grünspan spoke. Upon his arrival in Israel he joined Hashomer and from then on the matter of Jewish vigilance and defense was always at the center of his interests. From the time of the establishment of the first Jewish settlements in the Jezreel Valley, he served as *mukhtar* of Beit Alfa and Tel Yosef, which means he was the person responsible for the safety of those settlements. At the same time, he served as the emissary of the Jewish National Fund, and especially of Khankin, may his memory be for a blessing, for land affairs, which gradually became exceptionally developed. And he carried on this work for the Jewish National Fund with great care and tact until the last years of his life, earning himself friendship and honor within all the Arab circles which whom he came in close contact.

His funeral was attended by a large crowd, representatives of the city of Haifa, staff of the Jewish National Fund, comrades from Hashomer, and Arabs from the environs.

Honor to his memory!

{Page 90}

Shemaya Widerspan

{Yiddish text – page 90}

In a fine room that testified to the affluence of its owner, a man who was not young paced back and forth, repeating to himself without stopping: "olowek iparon, olowek iparon, olowek", [86] with an expression that indicated that these words did not fix themselves into his memory easily.

He repeated the obstinate word over and over again with the stubbornness of a child until it was fixed in his mind. Then his face beamed. He was happy.

This was Shemaya Widerspan, who was about to visit the land of Israel. He prepared for this journey with energy and enthusiasm. There were few people of Shemaya's age who gave themselves over to the Zionist movement without bounds such as he did. We were never short of people who were dedicated and were willing to accepts tasks for the sake of the movement, however there were very few to whom we could turn at all hours of the day or even the night in order to attract them to a new activity or a new idea.

He was honorable. He did not concern himself with his status in the community, his age, or even accepted principles. On many occasions, it was possible to see him sitting and adjudicating trivial matters with the same seriousness that he would deal with serious matters. He would talk to the youth as he talked to the honorable communal members. To him, there was no difference between a great and small task. He accepted every task with willingness and fulfilled it in its entirety. For several years, he was the chairman of the local Zionist committee. For many years he was the patron of the Zionist youth movement. For many years he participated in every activity and every meeting for the national funds, for the Hebrew University, for summer camps, for Hachshara Kibbutzim [87], and for the Hebrew School. This was all over and above his communal activity for the town and for the general institutions. If a delegate was needed for a convention of the movement, Shemaya would go. If the power of the movement was needed for Sejm elections, Shemaya would provide it. He never was stingy with his time or money. He was not a speaker, he was not an ideologue, but he nevertheless aroused feelings of honor in every place. This was primarily due to his sincerity. In the same manner as he reviewed and studied Hebrew words, he studied problems. He found solutions with utter sincerity. His pleasant sincerity was what endeared him to people. He was far away from zealous extremism. He would play the role of arbiter during any conflict between various factions. He would propose compromises for such disputes, and involve himself whether the matter was large or small.

Until the day of his death, he was the central address for the Zionist movement in the city. When he returned from his visit to the Land, he told us about the beauty and wonders that he beheld. Once again, he exhibited a childlike innocence and boundless enthusiasm. This enthusiasm did not permit him to dwell on the problems in the Land, nor to see the shadows. In his stories, everything was nice. As he described the Galilee and the

Kibbutzim, he saw himself as fortunate that he was able to witness all this with his own eyes.

It was later related to us that Shemaya had planned to make Aliya. Indeed he already had made preparations for such, however death overtook him first. The news of his passing came to us when we – those whom he encouraged – were already in the Land. The news caused us deep mourning. It was written to us that the mourning in the city was great and deep. This can be well understood, since everyone held him in esteem and loved him. It is fitting that his name be remembered by all of us, since he dedicated so much for Dembitz Jewry and for the Zionist movement.

{Page 90}

Ben-Zion Widerspan

by A. Haber

{Hebrew text – pp 90-91}

Ben-Zion Widerspan of blessed memory has been etched in my memory already for dozens of years as one of the most prominent people of Dembitz. His ideas were not hewn out of the Kloiz (Hassidic prayer hall) and the Beis Midrash. He was a man of the people, a worker, and his love for his nation, its language and its future was boundless. He was never stingy with his money, time or efforts as a communal activist. He worked for the benefit of all. He was one of the founders of the local Hebrew School, and one of the main people who was concerned with its upkeep. He expended great effort to acquire a building for this institution, even though the financial footing was not solid. However, due to the efforts of several people who were as persistent as he was, such as Bendet Fett, Meir Steiglitz, Shemaya Widerspan, Yochanan Sommer, Moshe Kerner, Reuven Sommer, as well as, may he live long, Fishel Kessler, Daniel Kerner of blessed memory, and Yudel Gruenspan (Bar-Natan) may he live long, who answered the call of the committee on numerous occasions, a significant sum of money was raised for this endeavor. The building was purchased, and it served not only as the home of the school alone, but also as the center for all local cultural activities, the headquarters for all the different youth groups of every stripe, as well as the pioneering headquarters for all ages.

All the residents of the city and its area, Jews and gentiles, knew the school building. It was even known to the area governor, who was an anti-Semite and attempted on several occasions to close down the school by force of the police.

The institution, which was not yet a full fledged school, stood up to its mission, and many of its alumnae live and are active with us today in Israel. Numbered among the alumnae and teachers are the teacher Weinberg, the author Pinchas Lander, and Chana Gruen.

Ben-Zion Widerspan served as the gabbai (trustee) of the Great Synagogue of Dembitz for many years. Most of its congregants were already Jews who did not wear streimels, who were artisans or members of the free professions.

After the First World War, when the Jews of Dembitz returned to their city, they found the synagogue destroyed, just like the rest of the houses. The Russian invaders used the synagogue as a horse stable. The reader's table, the benches, and the holy ark had been burned. Widerspan did not rest until he had restored the synagogue to its former glory, including various improvements. He paid for a significant portion of this endeavor from his own pocket. He fulfilled the role of synagogue trustee with joy and awe on the festivals and holy days. Whoever witnessed him in his role prior to the recitation of Kol Nidre, along with his counterparts, the Shamash Yisrael Einbinder and the Cantor Reuven the son of Reb Moshe the Cantor, cloaked in their prayer shawls and white robes; or at the time of the distribution of Torah honors (aliyot) on festivals or the hakafa (Torah circuit) honors on Simchat Torah, with their great concern not to Heaven forbid offend the honor or ambitions of the worshippers, both regular and non-regular, could never forget this sight.

However, he also knew how to be sharp in this role. In 1924, a group of zealots of "Keepers of the Faith of Israel" attempted to invalidate the cantor (who is now a cantor in one of the settlements in the south of Israel), since he sang in a choir that included women at a Zionist gathering. They even tried to remove him from the synagogue with physical force. Widerspan, however, did not budge, and the cantor remained in his place. He was brought to a disciplinary hearing before the rabbi of the city, however he stood his ground sharply and came out victorious.

As a member of the city council, he played a significant role in combating overt anti-Semitism, which was at that time spreading out in Galicia in general, and Dembitz in particular. He also knew how to win over Jewish friends for the benefit of the community. Members of the Zionist Widerspan family played a role in the development of Dembitz. In their younger days, they built many of the Jewish and non-Jewish houses with their own hands, and later on they served as contractors and planners.

Ben-Zion Widerspan felt all his days, particularly prior to the holocaust, that the disaster was nearing. He desired to make Aliya to the Land, and he even made preparations for that purpose, however he did not succeed. He was unable to do so himself, however two of his daughters, the oldest and the youngest, made Aliya and fulfilled his dreams.

He educated his children in the spirit of Judaism and Zionism, and some of them went on to higher education. One of his sons-in-law in Israel was Zvi Wolf, a native of Dembitz. He was a member of the Second Aliya, one of the first guards of the land, and a man of the land. Ben-Zion Widerspan did not succeed in escaping the Nazi claws. He was killed along with his childhood friend Yochanan Sommer of blessed memory in the Dembitz ghetto, after their strength had been drained by hard labor.

{Page 91}

Shimon Grünspan

by Y. Bar-Yitzchak

{Hebrew text – pp 91-92}

During the period between the two world wars, three communal activists in Dembitz stood out from all the others. These were Dr. Pinchas Laufbahn, Shemaya Widerspan, and the youngest of the three, Shimon Grünspan.

Shimon was the son of Nathan Grünspan, one of the most honorable and well-to-do Mizrachi householders of the city, and Dvortcha, the daughter of Reb Mendel Mahler. He was born in 1894 and educated in both Torah and Haskalah. He oversaw the intelligentsia group of Cheder and Beis Midrash educated people who became involved with European culture. He had many and variegated talents. From his youth he dreamt about higher education and the halls of science. Like many of his generation, he acquired general knowledge as an "extern", however his formal studies did not go very well. Many stumbling blocks and obstacles interfered with the completion of his studies. In the interim, the place became constricted for him, and he toiled endlessly – as if he was locked in prison – to free himself from his parental home and the town – but he could not do so.

In 1912 he escaped from his home and set out towards the Land of Israel. However he never reached there... A few years later he tried his luck again, he left town, he spent some time in the Diaspora, knocked at the doors of institutions of higher education, and then retraced his steps back again. Thus "one by one, and without being seen, as the stars at dawn, his secret desires were extinguished and ended in silent pain".

Much water flowed at that time in the Wislok River.[88]. He had already reached adulthood, and attained an honorable position in the town, but nevertheless – during intimate conversations with him – it seemed as if he was pining for fundamental changes in his life; he still maintained his pleasant youthful demeanor and attempted to free himself from the town, from the "egg". It was as if "his final desire was concealed within him and he pined for it all his life". An ear can understand words – if one paid attention to the intimate tone of his words, the impression would be that all of his activities in his private life, in industry and business, as well as all of his communal activities – and he had a great many endeavors in these areas – were only a substitute for something that did not materialize, a replacement for dreams that were lost, for desires that were extinguished.

As has been mentioned, he accomplished a great deal in many areas of life. He did not possess a degree for a polytechnic or business school. Nevertheless, on account of his self-study and reading of books he attained a true and deep knowledge of the areas of knowledge that were close to his heart. He was able to translate his knowledge into deeds. (His astuteness was undoubtedly inherited from his father Notele, who was imbued with a sober realism and energy that was very rare among the Jews of the small towns of Galicia. Dozens of years prior to the First World War, Nathan Grünspan founded a large factory in the town, and he was the first in town to install electric lights in his home. Hot water flowed from the taps of his bathtub). Thus Shimon was a "practical engineer" from birth… He extended and improved the activities of his father's factory. He expanded the factory of wheelbarrows, wagons, etc. He built a modern flourmill that served the entire region. He kept the accounts himself, in duplicate and triplicate. If it were not for the holocaust, he would certainly have added further layers onto the business.

Just as he was very active in business life, he was also active in communal affairs. His talents – including great knowledge, industriousness, working according to principals, pleasant demeanor, personal charm and honesty, as well as deep and warm feelings – endeared him to his acquaintances and put him in the front seat of communal activities, along with Pinchas Laufbahn and others.

Even though he was involved in a specific faction – he was one of the leaders of Poale Zion – he knew how to place the needs of the Jewish people at large over the narrow needs of the faction. Love of his fellow Jew was the main trait of his communal activities. This love was displayed in its full glory during the difficult and serious meetings of the town council that took place in the context of the stubborn and ongoing struggle for the rights of the Jews of the town. The Hapsburg era, the era in which the Jewish elders of the city had grown up, had ended and was not to return. New days arrived; new communal leaders arose, strangers came from afar; enemies of the Jews began to come to the fore; serious questions of life darkened the skies of the community and required a strong stand and a struggle. Shimon Grünspan, along with Pinchas

Laufbahn, was ready for this struggle. He did this with an upright posture, social knowledge, and national pride.

Whether as a representative of the public or as a representative of himself; who can tell of all his representations and stands he took for the benefit of individuals before officials and government leaders (whether for the Starosta – the local government, the Wojiwoda – the regional government)? Who can count the number of "requests" that he wrote on behalf of people to civic and national officials? His requests, for the most part, were answered positively, for his pen was sharp, and his style displayed deep understanding combined with feeling. He did not merely utter supplications, but rather words from the heart. His heart went out to those that suffered and were deprived of their rights. He participated in their suffering and took up their case. His words also penetrated the heart. (It is related that only once did he plea and beg for mercy... this was during the holocaust when his family's hiding place was discovered in the house of a Christian worker. He Shimon as well as his wife Rachka and his two sons were being taken out to be murdered, he emboldened himself before his death to request mercy for the life of the gentile who hid them. His heartfelt words influenced even the Gestapo man, and the worker was saved from death.)

If we have been able to present something of the national honor and the pride of the Jewish communal life in our town, it is obvious that Shimon Grünspan played a large role.

Therefore may the natives of our town remember him always for that blessing.

{Page 92}

Rivka Diament (Eisen)

by Henia Grin-Heistein

Rivka Diament, the sister of Tova and Tzila Eisen, was one of the first members of the girl's Debora organization. She was raised on the knees of the Zionist movement of Dembitz. When she was still very young, she would accompany her sisters to various lectures and parties that were presented by the Zionist movement in the city. From her youth, she absorbed Zionist philosophy and became accustomed to organizational activity. Already prior to the First World War, she worked with dedication on behalf of the library and was diligent in her studies of Jewish knowledge and the Hebrew language. However she only really began to participate in communal work in full force after the renewal of Jewish life in the city after the return of the exiles from Bohemia. In 1918-1920, she stood at the helm of the girls' organization which later joined Debora. This was over and above her participation in other Zionist activities, and her directorship of the library. She was also a member of the committee of the Hebrew School, and she participated in the amateur drama club, which did not last for very long. She was able to work on her own, as well as inspire others to become involved. She was able to speak even outside her narrow group.

Rivka Diament's activities in Dembitz ceased after her marriage, when she followed her husband, Mr. Pesach Diament may he live long, to Germany. There she participated in the circle of Chaim Arlozoroff and Georg Landauer. This connection brought her, after many years, to dedicated activity in the realm of the workers' union and the workers' council of Hadera. This was after her family had made Aliya to the Land of Israel, and after many difficult years of working life in Petach Tikva. In Hadera, her husband Pesach served as the director of the cooperative shop of the worker's union.

With her untimely death, she left her good name behind her in Hadera and its surrounding area. Her son Lieutenant Colonel Yosef Yahalom, and her daughter Aliza, who is a member of Kibbutz Gesher, survive her.

Translator's Footnotes

80. This would be referring to other holy books, such as prayer books and bibles. These would be buried in order to prevent their desecration by theRussians.

81. Reichenberg is now Liberec, and Teplitz is Teplice in the Czech Republic. These are in the Sudeten area of Bohemia, which was primarily German at that time.

82. 'Segula' is a good omen, often with a mystical basis.

83. The organization was involved in physically helping the ill, as well as   in distributing money to hire assistants for the ill.

84. Sheketz (plural Shkotzim), is a disgusting creature. Literally, it refers to an insect or a reptile, but it also has the connotation of a 'little devil'. It is sometimes used in a very derogatory fashion to describe a gentile.

99. Brzesko.

100. Jewish community boards.

101. This is not Polish, but "Polish-sounding" gibberish.

102. Pinchas Laufbahn?

{Page 94}

Youth Movements

Translated by Jerrold Landau

{Page 95}

"Debora"

by Rivka Faust

{Hebrew text – pp 95-96}

פון ביבליאטעק קאמיטעט אין דעמביץ תרצ"ז

The Library Committee in Dembitz, 5697 (1937)

After a difficult battle with the orthodox community, and almost simultaneously with the organization of the men into the "Hashachar" organization, the "Debora" Zionist women's organization was founded in Dembitz in 1907. The best of the young Jewesses of the city joined. The orthodox atmosphere of the city in those days was not yet open to the possibility for a joint organization of boys and girls.

Aside from Zionist publicity activities, Debora conducted general cultural programs about Jewish history, Zionism, etc. From its inception, the Debora library had several hundred books. At first, the members of Debora solicited the advice of the Zionist university students regarding the purchase of books. The language of the books was for the most part Polish and German, a language that was still studied extensively by the youth. The best of the books were of academic style. The library was conducted efficiently and it developed well. It also acquired a few books in Yiddish. It attracted two different types of youth – those who wished to read books, and those who simply wanted to enter into a modern social group. The librarians would offer advice as to which books to read. Debora also attracted younger girls. With time it encompassed many girls from all strata of society.

After some time, several girls, headed by Ruchama Grünspan, left Debora and organized a second group called "Chavatzelet". This group did not last for very many years. Debora continued until 1927, that is until it joined the "Hanoar Haivri" movement. Several of its members became involved in Hachshara Kibbutzim and made Aliya to the Land.

For a specific period of time after the First World War, as Zionism was becoming stronger in Galicia, Debora flourished greatly since it had already been around for some time. At that time, it was regarded as "the" Zionist organization of Dembitz. The members of Debora, led at that time by Rivka Diament (Eisen), were active in all areas of Zionist and cultural activities in the city. They were at the helm of the Keren Kayemet committee, which was under the auspices of the local Zionist organization. They worked on behalf of the Hebrew school and kindergarten, the Keren Hayesod organization, the committee for the "shekel" [89]. They worked on behalf of Zionist lectures by ensuring audiences. This effort entailed monetary outlay as well as difficulties in obtaining a lecture hall. The members of Debora founded the club for Hebrew speakers, which flourished with the development of the Hebrew school. They brought Hebrew books into the library, which at that time had a collection of about 2,000 books. As a mark of recognition for all of these activities, the name of the Debora organization as inscribed in the Golden Book of the Keren Kayemet Leyisrael (Jewish National Fund) by the local Zionist committee. This was a significant milestone in the life of the organization.

After the original founders of Debora left the city, due to emigration or moving to different cities on account of marriage, a new generation of girls arose who continued the activities and attempted to broaden the scope of the organization. These included Henia Gruen, Rosa and Simma Schuldenfrei, Eidel Taub, Rosa Sommer, Sara Wurtzel, Breindel Strassberg, Hadassa Taub, and others.

On occasion, parties were organized, particularly on Chanuka, Purim, and the intermediate days of Passover and Sukkot. Naturally, the proceeds went to the Keren Kayemet, however the participatory activity brought with it a spirit of life and friendship. If an appropriate hall could not be obtained, such parties would take place in the private homes of supporters. The decorating of the rooms and the preparation of baked goods was done on a voluntary basis. In a town such as Dembitz, where the young girls were not as accustomed to the pleasantries of life as are today's youth, such events had a great influence.

Debora was connected with the women's Zionist organization, which would send speakers to it once in a while. Among others, Ada Fishman-Maimon of Israel lectured to the members of Debora. She spoke about the active workers movements in the Land. Ada requested that the girls join the active organizations. The political outlook of Debora was free and without party loyalties, and also without a pioneering tendency. However, the girls, after being influenced by the words of Ada, and after a meeting that took place in the home of Breindel Strassberg, asked: "If our objective is to make Aliya to the Land of Israel, why should we not go to the Kibbutzim together with the young men?" At that time, there were already significant changes in Polish Jewry, and even in Dembitz various youth organizations arose such as Akiva and Hanoar Haivri. It became obvious that it was no longer possible to maintain a separate girl's Zionist movement. A group of the younger members of Debora, known as "Hashevia" (called after the number seven – sheva – on account of its seven most prominent members: Bronka Taub, Salka Barr, Rivka Faust, Mania Taub, Rivka Taub, Serel Taub and Chaya Wiezer) decided after great deliberation to leave Debora and join the Hanoar Haivri movement. They dragged along the rest of the girls, and Debora ceased to exist as an independent organization.

The library committee directed the library from that time. It became affiliated with the local Zionist committee, as did all of the Zionist organizations in the city.

During its twenty years of existence, Debora accomplished great deeds, and an honorable page is reserved for it in the history of active Zionism in our city.

{Page 96}

Hanoar Hatzioni (Zionist Youth)

by Aka Zilberstein and Pinchas Sommer

"Agudat Hanoar Haivri" "The Union of Hebrew Youth"

The Hanoar Hatzioni movement was not founded in one day, and it is impossible to specify an exact date of its founding. This was an endeavor filled with difficulties, paved with crises, conflicts, and factionalism.

The first stages were already described in this book. Here, we will describe the awakening that took place in the Zionist youth movements in Dembitz starting from 1925, after a serious crisis that took place in all of the youth movements in the years 1922 and 1923.

With the renewal of Jewish life in Dembitz after the conclusion of the years of exile during the First World War, the youth movement also revived in the city. However this movement, which drew its inspiration from the Balfour Declaration, weakened very quickly and after a few years of cultural activity, reached a crisis situation. The youth movements that had existed weakened and almost disbanded. Cultural activity ceased and the Jewish youth began to become apathetic. In those years, 1922-1923, the same situation prevailed in Congress Poland as well as the two regions of Galicia. Obviously, what was transpiring in the country in general also transpired in Dembitz.

During that low period, only the Hebrew School operated in the city. It succeeded in maintaining itself despite the difficulties, and served as almost the only meeting place for the youth. The youth would gather in the Hebrew School, generally twice a week, in order to hear a lecture in Hebrew or a debate about a literary topic. However it cannot be said that the youth were particularly active and effervescent.

Nevertheless, the youth played certain roles in the Zionist activity of the city, in the leadership of the local Zionist committee and its two arms – the Keren Kayemet committee and the Keren Hayesod committee. The Debora girls' organization also continued its activities to some degree. This crisis did not last for very long. The opening of the Hebrew University in Jerusalem in 1925 gave a strong push to the general awakening. In honor of the event, a festive academic gathering was organized in Dembitz in the movie hall. Greeting telegrams were sent to Jerusalem. Dembitz brimmed with joy and enthusiasm along with the nation in the rest of the Diaspora. The time had arrived for fruitful organizational activity.

The awakening was felt in the entire breadth of Poland. In every city, groups of Hanoar Hatzioni were re-established and renewed. The groups were organized locally without a connection between them. The direction and political leaning of such groups were entirely in the hands of the local organizers and advisors. The new group that arose in Dembitz took on the name "Akiva". Apparently, similar organizations existed in other cities, primarily in Krakow; however at first there was no real connection between them. The effort to set up an umbrella organization for all the groups came out of Krakow . In the newspapers and pamphlets which were sent to the local Zionist committee, we were requested to give our address to the Akiva organization of Krakow. In that manner, the first connection between the Zionist youth groups was set up. Afterward, several meetings and conventions took place that were attended by delegates of the Zionist youth groups of the various cities and towns in western Galicia. Finally, the "Hanoar Hatzioni Organization" was established, and spread out throughout western Galicia. The Dembitz branch immediately began to play a prominent and honorable role, due both to the number of members and their abilities, as well as their successful participation in the organizing committee, where they played an active role in the deliberations that defined the objectives of the "Agudat Hanoar Haivri". Activists of the Dembitz branch would go out to nearby towns in order to organize their youth into a movement. They had successful and unsuccessful experiences in Pilzno, Kolbaszow, and Mielic; but in any case, they displayed the organizational abilities of the Dembitz branch. Vibrant Zionist and cultural activity took place within the branch itself. The main activities included study of Zionist history, writings about the Land (Palestinography!), Bible, general Hebrew literature, cultural history, and similar subjects. The leadership of the branch attempted to broaden the cultural perspectives of the members. Since the activities took place in various groups divided according to age, the head of each group quickly attained his role as a leader and role model.

"Agudat Hanoar Haivri"

"Agudat Hanoar Haivri" Band Alef, 24 Tishrei 5680 (Autumn 1919}

"Hanoar Hatzioni "Zionist Youth" Tammuz 5784 (Summer 1924)

At that time, the Debora Zionist girl's movement still existed in the city. It had joined the "Agudat Hanoar Hatzioni"; however it still continued it independent existence. The oldest chapter of Debora, headed by Chana Gruen, Ita Schuldenfrei, Rosa Sommer, Hadassa Taub, Eidel Taub and others who wanted to maintain a separate girl's organization, opposed the merger with Akiva, which was a mixed group. The younger chapter of Debora, consisting of seven girls in total who did not have a great deal of experience, did not feel it appropriate that there be two separate movements in the city with the same purpose, both being affiliated with "Agudat Hanoar Hatzioni". The younger chapter began an agitation that grew, and eventually led to the breakup of Debora as a separate organization. It merged with Akiva. The final push toward this end was given by the participation of the Debora members in the summer camp of Roska Wizna in 1927. After the Debora members returned from the camp to Dembitz, they dropped their opposition, and the merger took place. Debora ceased to exist as an independent organization after many years of dedicated and vibrant activity. With the merger, the organization grew greatly, and numbered 150 members, both male and female.

In those days, the headquarters of "Agudat Hanoar Haivri" in Krakow merged with the similar headquarters in Lvov, and the new group that arose from this merger took on the name "Hanoar Haivri". The Dembitz chapter was one of its first branches, and became the regional headquarters. The activists of that time included M. Hakeh, Bronka Taub, Rivka Faust, Shmuel Sommer, Miriam, Rivka and Serel Taub, Shaul Taffet, Aharon Sapir, Moshe Grünspan, and others. The regional activists would often visit neighboring towns for lectures, organizational activities, etc.

"Hanoar Hatzioni" in Dembitz, Band Alef, 16 Tevet 5683 (January 4, 1923)

"Hanoar Hatzioni"

"Bene Zion" Association "Sons of Zion" Tammuz 5684 (Summer 1924)

A Chalutz organization of Dembitz

A new reformation took place in the movement when the Galicia headquarters merged with that of Congress Poland. The movements combined and took on a new name – "Hanoar Hatzioni". The movement continued with that name until the outbreak of the Second World War. Hachshara Kibbutzim were established in the Diaspora and in the Land of Israel with that name. Under that name, members of the movement fought in the underground against the Nazi enemy.

The movement had a scouting orientation, and according to all opinions, that was a very pleasant orientation. It set the tone of the educational Zionist activity of the organization, and also was very attractive to the group. The movement was divided into branches, and each branch into individual groups. A leader and a council headed the movement. All of the people responsible for the various tasks of the branches were members of the council. The members wore robes, at first gray and later khaki. They also wore shawls and ties, with each branch having a different color. Roll calls were conducted weekly. Hikes and summer camping expeditions, both central and local, were important activities. It is particularly important to mention the local camps that took place for two or three days at a time in one of the neighboring towns (Stobierna and Gumniska). This was a great insult to the feelings of the majority of the people of Dembitz, who had not yet become accustomed to the new winds, and did not always look positively upon girls and boys going out together outside the city for entire days.

On Sabbaths and festivals, the fields and forests surrounding the city called out, so to speak, to the members of the groups. In the forests of Kawenczyn, Lisa Gora and Wolica, and in the fields near the small brook of Krynica, it was possible to see many groups of youth surrounding their leader, who would be reading to them from the works of Ahad Haam, the poems of Bialik, a story of Fierburg or a section of the book of Adolph about the history of Zionism. People would sing, and every expedition ended with a rousing dance of the Hora.

The movement had its meeting place in the building of the Hebrew school. This quickly became the second home, and some would even say the primary home, of dozens of young people. "Lukal" [90] had an uncanny attraction. There were occasions where the groups used the rooms in the attic, and other times where they used rooms on the lower floor. An elderly Christian woman, who became an inseparable part of the landscape of the group, occupied one of these rooms for many years. She was the elderly Kanina who waited on the youth with faithfulness and dedication. Every one of us most definitely participated in the tricks that we played on her.

Consecration of a Flag

Shemaya Widerspan at Consecration of a Flag

In those rooms, dozens of young people milled about. Each group occupied its own corner, engaged in lively discussion, listened to the works of the counselor, and attempted not to disturb the other groups.

Sabbaths were very interesting, particular the silent time, the time of the departure of the Sabbath Queen, prior to the putting on of the lights in the rooms. In the darkness of evening we would sit, crowded together on the floor, and we would sing songs filled with longing for the homeland. I still remember the following songs: "The Evenings are Lovely in Canaan", "The Jordan", "Bring me in", and others. Everything was very fine and pure. Many years have passed since then. Our hair has become white; however to this day, we still remember the dreamy faces of the young boys and girls, and until this day we can still feel the special and pleasant atmosphere of sitting together in friendship.

The relationship of the parents of the members to the movement was not that negative. It is even possible to say that they admired it. At that time, there were no incidents of zealous opposition to the movement among the adults of Dembitz. There was also no vehement opposition by the confidantes of the rabbi, and by other rabbis. The main complaint was that we came home too late.

The Zionist youth was a part of the landscape of the city, and nobody fought against us in an organized fashion. However we should point out that, due to our concern for maintaining proper relations with our parents, we avoided any activities that would violate the Sabbath or offend the feelings of our parents. There were also occasions where we arranged special tea parties for the parents of our members.

In terms of numbers, and in terms of organizational prowess, we took first place from among all the youth groups in the city. There was no communal, Zionist, or cultural activity in which the members of our group were not prominent. We should particularly point our participation in the founding of the Hebrew school. We stressed its importance at every opportunity.

The activists of the movement participated in the governing of the general Zionist library (there were two libraries in Dembitz: that of Poale Zion, and ours). In the library committee, which was composed of delegates of the various movements, our members were prominent. They accepted responsible positions, which demanded dedication and time commitment. Most of the books in the library were in the Polish language; however there were also a significant number in Hebrew. The movement encouraged its members to read those books.

The organizational abilities of the Hanoar Hatzioni group found expression in a festivity that took place to the great enjoyment of all the people of the city, both young and old. This was the festivity surrounding the consecration of the flag of the movement. The day of the consecration of the flag turned into a day of general festivity. The leaders of the group made sure that the appearance of the members would be particularly festive. Cloth was purchased, and special robes were made for all the members of the group. The Zamir band was invited from Kolbaszow.

The important people of the city as well as activists of the Zionist movement, organizations, institutions, and even representatives of the local and regional government were invited to the festivities. Every invitation was accompanied by a silver nail. The invitees were to be honored by nailing these nails into the flag at the dedication ceremony.

On the day of the festivities, a youth parade took place through the streets of the city. The band was at the head, and following after were long rows of youth dressed in their robes, shawls and ties colored according to their specific group.

The ceremony itself took place in the tennis courts of the Bar Kochba sport organization. Tzipora Taub, the head of the organization at that time, led the parade. The head of each group stood before each group. Bronka Taub and Rivka Faust were among these group heads.

A group of "Hanoar Hatzioni

"Kadima" 5682 (1921/1922)

The splendid blue and white silken flag was placed on top of a beautiful pole that was capped with a gilded fluttering Magen David. After that, the speeches took place. Then the flag was given by the head of the local Zionist committee Shemaya Widerspan, and the representative of the central organization Yaakov Bienenstock to the head of the movement. The invitees were then called upon to hammer their silver nails into the pole. The participation of notables of the local and regional government made an impression, for such participation was considered significant in those days.

This was a great day for the movement and a great day for the Jews of the city; for on that day, something of the spirit of freedom was felt, and signs of independence were displayed among the youth movements. It is possible to say that on that day, the bent backs of the people were straightened to some extent.

The Noar Hatzioni movement in Dembitz sent its members to Hachshara Kibbutzim. Some of its members succeeded in making Aliya. The first group of Noar Hatzioni from Dembitz made Aliya in 1929. After that, various individuals made Aliya every year. The numbers of those who actually made Aliya where nowhere close to the numbers of those who wished to make Aliya. The number of Aliya permits issued by the British Mandatory government in the Land of Israel was few, and in Poland, many thousands waited their turn. In Dembitz as well, the numbers of those who returned from Hachshara Kibbutzim each year grew. As the months and years passed, and the chance to make Aliya did not yet come, despair began to enter the people's hearts, and people began to search for a "purpose" in life. Such people no longer found their place in the movement, and the situation had a negative influence upon its activists. Many left the movement, and several finally made Aliya on the Illegal Immigration (Haapalah) ships.

In order to find a place for those who left the movement, the Bnei Zion movement was established. It opened up reading rooms and organized lectures on occasion. However its organizational scope was not nearly as broad as that of Hanoar Hatzioni. In the movement itself, there were ups and downs corresponding with the situation in the Land. If there were possibilities of Aliya, the situation of the movement improved. If possibilities for Aliya closed down, there was a decline in the movement.

With the passage of time, the leaders of the movement, Bronka and M. Hakeh, and Rivka Faust, made Aliya. Their roles fell to the younger people, including Tzipora Taub, M. Grünspan, N. Lustgarten, P. Sommer, P. Salomon, and others. The movement continued its activities, free of difficulties in searching for its path and purpose, and free of stormy ideological debates. The countrywide movement was set up with regional headquarters, Hachshara Kibbutzim, as well as Kibbutzim in the Land of Israel. Some of our own members joined those Kibbutzim. The Dembitz branch was not affected by the disputes that were common in those days. There was a serious dispute in western Galicia when Yehuda Orenstein and Yaakov Frand left the movement and renewed the Akiva movement. There was also a dispute in Congress Poland when Moshe Kolodny set up an independent youth movement. The Dembitz branch maintained its affiliation with the headquarters in Lvov, which was headed by Yitzchak Steiger.

A Hachshara gathering at "Hanoar Hatzioni"

Bronka Taub-Chaka of blessed memory

The high level of activity and capabilities of the organization were expressed in the founding of a Hachshara Kibbutz in the area. This was not the only Hachshara Kibbutz in the area. Other movements, due to the spirit of competition (at times healthy, and at other times, not healthy), brought Hachshara groups to the city. Hachshara groups were founded for Hashomer Hadati and Gordonia. Our group was at first located in the village of Zminne between Dembitz and Mielec, and occupied itself with the production of peat. The work conditions were quite difficult at that time, for the members of the movement were not provided with appropriate clothing for work in the bogs. The bunks were terrible, and the salary for the work was poor. The members were not able to continue under such conditions, and they returned to Dembitz, where there was no possibility of actual work. The members of the movement occupied themselves for the most part with the cutting of trees. A few worked in the flourmills. Others found some employment in agriculture. Despite all this, even with the poor work prospects, three Hachshara groups were set up in this manner in the city. Finally, when the gates of Aliya were shut, there was no further purpose to their existence, and their members went their own ways after they had worked for a few years under particularly difficult conditions. Only a few merited to make Aliya to the Land and to witness its comfort.

Thus did hundreds of youths work in our city, thus did they dedicate their time and energies in order to merit a better life in our land. A few merited, and most did not merit. Fate caught up to them during the holocaust. Let us remember forever the young men and women, pure and unblemished, who dreamed of Zion and now are no longer. They do not have a grave or a grave marker. They only have the memory of a sublime desire and a collective dream.

A group of "Hanoar Hazioni" members from Dembitz on their way to make
Aliya to Israel, in Trieste

{Page 105}

Mizrachi Youth

by Asher Salomon

{Hebrew text – pp 105-107}

"Young Mizrachi" Torah Vaavoda

The dream of the return to Zion, which attracted the Jewish youth of Dembitz, to a large degree also spread among the youth of the Beis Midrash, and created an excitement within their ranks. Most of them joined up with the non-religious youth movements since they did not see the atmosphere of the vision of Torah and Work [91] in the Land of Israel. As they entered Zionist activity, they became cut off from the Beis Midrash and religious tradition. Only later, a group of young people from the Hassidic Beis Midrash founded a youth group that combined the Zionist idea with life in the Beis Midrash. This innovation was viewed by the young men of the Beis Midrash with a bitter spirit and fierce opposition.

The members of this group were: Meir David Weizer, Yeshaya Taffet, Yitzchak Metzger, Yechiel Faust may his blood be avenged, Yitzchak Frieman, Yehoshua Zilberman, Avraham Freidman, Tzvi Diller and others. This was the first organized cell of the Young Mizrachi movement of Dembitz. In the year 5683 (1923), they established a reading hall in the house of Mendel Poloncki. At the opening of the hall, a young man from Tarnow, by the name of Salomon, gave a lecture about the basis of the ideas of the Young Mizrachi movement. At that meeting, organized activity began.

With the passage of time, many younger boys joined the group, including: Asher Salomon, Tzvi Siedlisker, Avraham Siedlisker, Yisrael Bek, Chaim Shneps, Chanoch Kukuk, Tzvi Faust, Avraham Schwartz, Moshe Taub, Moshe Siedlisker, Yeshayahu Geminder, Shalom Wiener, Moshe Shneps, David Koss, Shmuel Ferber, Tzvi Frieman, the brothers Avraham and Yaakov Kriger, the brothers Chaim and Shraga Tenenbaum, Moshe Zilberman, and others. Shlomo Strassberg was elected as the head of the group.

The activities of the group were centered around organized study, the spreading of the religious Zionist idea to the youth, and the consolidation of the Zionist and religious personalities of the members. They established classes for sacred studies, Zionist history, and knowledge of the Land. They also conducted free discussions about various news items. The classes of sacred study were conducted at an early hour in the morning. The evenings were dedicated to general study and conversation between friends. The activities on Sabbaths and festivals were particularly interesting, in that all of the members of the movement participated, and on occasion speakers from other cities, and representatives of the headquarters in Krakow would visit to give lectures. Later on, emissaries of the Hapoel Hamizrachi from the Land of Israel would also come.

The renown of the movement's activities spread quickly, and even people who had no direct connection to the movement would come to attend the classes and listen to the lectures. The class on the weekly Torah portion, given on Sabbath eves by Mr. Yitzchak Messer, was particularly well attended.

Aside from the study groups enumerated above, there were also special groups such as the group for the study of the Eight Chapters of Maimonides [92], the book "Duties of the Heart"[93], Bible and Hebrew literature. Many of the participants gathered together for Oneg Shabbat festivities with song and Torah discussions. The nearby mountain area of Lisa Gora had an honorable place in the activities of the group. People would go out there for a hike during holidays, and there they would hold discussions on various topics. There, the youth were taught the songs of Zion. The parties in the natural setting lifted the spirit and created a festive experience.

Almost all of the members of the movement participated in the cultural activities. The members attained lofty heights in the knowledge of the Hebrew language, in their depth of general knowledge, and in particular in the broadening of their cultural and Zionistic perspectives.

Members of the Dembitz branch of the movement were active in the activities of the headquarters in Krakow. Yitzchak Frieman and Meir Wiezer were elected as members of the national council.

Young Mizrachi participated in all of the Zionist activities of the city, in particular in activities for the national funds, the shekel, etc. On occasion, they served leading roles in those organizations, such as conducting the collection of the shekel; special roles for the various funds; and for a specific time, the leadership of the library, which was located in the building of the Hebrew School.

Their activity was not limited to the sphere of Mizrachi alone. Members of the group were active in other organizations, such as Debora, the women's Zionist organization, and others.

In all realms of activity of the Zionist movement in Dembitz, the members of this group were prominent. Members of Mizrachi displayed a special interest in various municipal institutions, such as: the local Hebrew congregation, and the city council. At time of elections for these institutions, and in particular for the Polish Sejm, all of the members of the organization were enlisted and worked hard to ensure votes for the Zionist lists.

The Zionist activities of the Mizrachi youth movement generated fierce opposition from the orthodox and zealot groups who were centered in the Hassidic Beis Midrash. Due to a desire not to cut themselves off from the Beis Midrash where they had spent their best days, and despite the unceasing persecution in various forms, the members stubbornly, and even with suffering, continued to visit the Beis Midrash and set aside times to study Torah. However, when the persecution increased and reached the point of the dirtying of the benches upon which the members sat and the disappearance of the Gemara books from which they studied, they had no choice but to exchange the Beis Midrash for another meeting place where they would be able to continue their studies and communal work. The Moadon (meeting place) filled this role. All of the Torah and organizational activities began to center there, and with time, it became the replacement for the Beis Midrash.

The activities of the movement moved at first to the halls of the Hebrew School, where all of the Zionist youth groups were housed with the exception of Poale Zion. However after a certain time, they had to leave there for a separate place, since it was difficult for the young people who were educated in the Beis Midrash to accustom themselves to the spirit that pervaded the school.

When they moved to their own meeting place, the organizational activities of the movement expanded greatly. They gained new members, and their influence was felt in all spheres of Zionist activity in the city.

Later, the movement organized a group of supporters from among the adults of the city. Members of this group included: Reb Avraham Goldman, Reb Mendel Taub, Reb Efraim Taffet, and others. This group often supported the movement with financial and other assistance.

A group of members of "Mizrachi Youth"

Meir Weizer

Visit of Mr. S. Z. Shragai from the land of Israel

A group of "Daughters of Bruria" with "Mizrachi Youth"

A group of "Mizrachi Youth" with the teacher Pinchas Lander

In the elections for the Zionist Congress, Mizrachi in Dembitz obtained the second largest number of votes.

In 1929, there was a pioneering awakening in Dembitz. Even though there was Aliya of individuals from Dembitz in all of the previous waves of Aliya, there was not yet an organized pioneering movement. The Zionist education that took place in the prior years gave a push to this movement. The first attempt at pioneering Hachshara took place a few years previously. A few young people went out to study the building trade with the Widerspan brothers building contractors. The first of these pioneers were from Young Mizrachi. They included Yitzchak Frieman, Tzvi Diller, and Yehoshua Zilberman of blessed memory. Due to a lack of organizational prowess, this first attempt failed. Members of Young Mizrachi were among the first who went out to the Hachshara Kibbutz in eastern Galicia. These included Tzvi Siedlisker, Asher Salomon, and Avraham Schwartz of blessed memory.

Thanks to the activity of the Dembitz group, a Young Mizrachi Hachshara Kibbutz was also established in Bielsko (western Galicia). This Hachshara Kibbutz was organized and led by members from Dembitz. The going out to Hachshara engendered fierce opposition from the parents of the members, who attempted via all manners to prevent their children from going.

The Aliya of the first members of the Hachshara Kibbutz of Bielsko made a deep impression on all of the members of the branch. The awakening that came in its wake caused an expansion of the pioneering activity and the setting up of a Hachshara Kibbutz for the movement in Dembitz. This Kibbutz was located in the home of Reb Moshe Kanner, and numbered fifteen members.

With the widening of the activity and the growth of the membership, the branch moved to a more spacious headquarters. A group for orthodox girls was also founded. It was called Bruria, and had fifteen members at the outset. At that time, a branch of Hashomer Hadati was established for younger boys. This became one of the largest and most prominent branches of all of western Galicia. It was not for naught that the branch of Young Mizrachi of Dembitz was numbered among the largest and best organized of the entire region. Our friend Yitzchak Frieman represented it at the Mizrachi headquarters in Krakow.

The members of the group developed branch activities in the neighboring towns, and organized branches in Ropszyce, Sedszizow, Wielople, and Pilzno.

{Page 108}
The Hashomer Hadati movement of Dembitz

by Moshe Sarid-Siedlisker

"Young Mizrachi" and "Hashomer Hadati" taking leave of those that are making Aliya)

{Hebrew text – page 108}

With the expansion of the pioneering movement in the ranks of Young Mizrachi of Poland, and the growth of the areas of pioneering Hachshara, the need arose to organize the youth of age twelve and thirteen, and to educate them in the spirit of Torah Vaavoda so that they could serve as the future for the older movement.

In 1928, the Hashomer Hadati movement arose in Poland, and branches were set up in all the cities of the country.

The headquarters in Krakow made a request to the branch of Young Mizrachi in Dembitz to organize a Hashomer Hadati branch in the city. This task fell to Moshe Tovia Taub may G-d avenge his blood and to Moshe Siedlisker Sarid. Their organizational activity bore fruit very quickly. Dozens of youth joined the ranks of Hashomer Hadati, and began their educational and organizational activities. They excelled in creating this organization.

The Dembitz branch became the regional center, which worked to spread the movement in the region. Branches were set up in Ropszyce, Mielec, Sedziszow, Wielpole, and other towns. Regional conventions of Hashomer Hadati took place in Dembitz. The representatives of the Dembitz branch were also members of the national committee, and often visited branches in the neighboring region in order to assist with organizational work and conducting of activities.

The influence of the movement upon the youth of the city was quite recognizable. The following people led the branch with great energy: the brothers Yaakov and Avraham Kriger, Moshe Tovia Taub, may G-d avenge his blood, Yehoshua Shneps, Moshe Zilberman may G-d avenge his blood, Chaim Tenenbaum may G-d avenge his blood, Miriam Kriger, Chana Geminder, Moshe Siedlisker-Sarid, Shmuel Ferber, and other from among us.

The branch was bubbling with life. Daily, various groups participated in activities such as the study of Hebrew, the study of holy subjects, and discussions about educational and pioneering issues. An independent library was established, and a newsletter was published weekly. There was also significant activity in scouting: hikes and sporting events played a significant role in the activities of the group.

Yearly, dozens of youth of Hashomer Hadati went during their summer vacation to camps in the Carpathian, Tatra, and Beskid Mountains. They returned full of enthusiasm and energy for the activities of the movement. Thus did the movement grow and develop from year to year.

It also excelled in the realm of general activity, such as work for the Keren Kayemet and Keren Hayesod, joint activities with the other Zionist youth in the city, and celebrations and parties. They would organize and arrange such activities.

The pioneering awakening left its practical mark. Many of the graduates of the movements went to the Hachshara Kibbutzim of the movement; however only a portion of them merited to arrive in the Land of Israel to realize the vision. A significant number of those who went to the Hachshara Kibbutzim were prevented from making Aliya to the Land due to the shutting of the gates of Aliya by the police of the British Mandate. Thus did the end come to most of the members of the wonderful movement – which left a brilliant page in the religious Zionist life of Dembitz. Only a few survivors of the terrible holocaust succeeded in evading the apparatus of death and joining the builders of our land.

Taking leave of friends who are making aliya

Asher Salomon and Tzvi Siedlisker on hachshara on the collective far of
"Hechalutz Hamizrachi" in Ndworna

{Page 110}

"Gordonia"

by Yehuda Grünspan

{Hebrew text – 110-112}

The Gordonia movement in Dembitz was preceded in the city by movements from almost the entire spectrum of Zionism, from Mizrachi to the General Zionists, concluding with Poale Zion. Furthermore, the founders of Gordonia were themselves alumnae of these movements. The unique situation that prevailed in the state of the Jewish youth of Poland during the mid 1920s led them to abandon their former movements and to build a new movement. Masses of Jewish youth in Poland and Galicia at that time were prepared to tie their futures to the future of Zionism and the establishment of the homeland. Many of the young people of Dembitz felt that there was no other way. The founders of Gordonia felt that with the new conditions, it was not sufficient merely to spread the Zionist idea and create the "romantic" atmosphere of various Zionist "clubs", but rather that it was necessary to educate all of the youth to fulfil the Zionist idea in its practical expression – that is to make Aliya and realize the vision. G-d forbid do we mean to imply in this that the other Zionist movements in the city did not educate toward Aliya and practical Zionism. The opposite is true. It is a fact that the first person who made Aliya from Dembitz at that time was a member of Poale Zion – Emanuel Grünspan Yarkoni, a member of Givat Hashlosha-Einat for the past 33 years. As well the first pioneers who displayed their strength of spirit and went out to Hachshara to work in backbreaking labor in the city itself were members of Young Mizrachi – Yehoshua Zilberman of blessed memory, Yitzchak Frieman and Hershel Diller. Similarly, the following members of Hanoar Hatzioni preceded the Gordonists in Aliya: Bronka Taub Hakeh of blessed memory, Mordechai Hakeh, Shmuel and Rivka Taffet, Henia Gruen, Rivka Faust, and others. Nevertheless, despite the reality of those people who made Aliya and actualized the goals of the Zionist movement in the city, there was still abstract, verbal Zionism which enabled people – without expending any effort – to remain in the Diaspora and still call themselves Zionists.

"Gordonia"

""Gordonia" 1933 in Dembitz

The founders of Gordonia were against this type of Zionism, this light Zionism that permitted its members to remain in the Diaspora. The most sublime idea, they claimed, was that the movement itself had no intrinsic value, but rather its entire value rested in its power to create a new reality. The Zionist idea only had value if it would lead to a renewal of the nation by renewing the lives of its members; if it would lead to a personal revolution in the lives of all its adherents. This "personal revolution" was described first and foremost as: uprooting oneself from the exile and from the Diaspora lifestyle – where one would be supported by parents and in-laws and help them in their business – and renewing the connection between the people of Israel and its homeland by returning to a life of work and creativity in the Land of the Patriarchs, and returning to the original environment of the nation. In short, it must lead to a definitive change of conditions. This general "change of conditions" was not foremost in the minds of the members of the other youth movements during the middle of the 1920s, and therefore Gordonia was founded.

The youth from all streams, in particular from the middle of the road streams, who found the Zionist organizations that existed in the city to be not appropriate for them – whether because they were too "aristocratic", too religious, or too "left wing" – joined Gordonia. It presented itself as a popular pioneering movement, tolerant of religion, and fighting for an authority free of slavery and oppression, yet without the internationalist idea.

To a large degree, the founding of Gordonia was due to the ideological and primarily organizational preparatory work that was performed by the founders of Hitachdut in Dembitz, Akiva Elster, Koppel Kreiswirth and others (for a period of time, the veteran Zionist Bendet Fett participated with them). These faithful and dedicated members spared no effort to bring people toward the new movement, to spread its newspaper ("People and Land"), and to represent it to the institutional committees, the library and other nationalistic and cultural organizations in town. They also displayed vigilance and great effort in the election campaigns for the Zionist congresses and the Polish Sejm, in that they worked hard for the nationalistic Hitachdut party. In civic elections, members of Hitachdut generally elected members of Poale Zion, who joined forces with them in "Faction of Working Israel", and the "Palestine Worker's Fund". Nevertheless, the crowning glory of their communal-nationalistic activity was without doubt their practical and dedicated assistance in the founding of Gordonia, which, with the passage of time, inherited the place of Hitachdut. Its members, along with the members of Boslia, which was founded in the interim, fulfilled all the roles of the Hitachdut party locally. Its members included: Avraham Elster, Tzila Brenner, Seril, Rachel and Shalom Lishe, Rivka, Yocheved and David Diller, Tonka and Beilka Bodner, Fetzi Weizer, Bielke Freidman, Henka Blaustein, T. Bornstein, Yaakov Forstiher, Shmuel Jakub, Shmuel Mahler, Hadassa Jabner, and others.

The beginnings of Gordonia were very restricted. In the year of its founding (1926-1927) it did not even have twenty members. Its first members included: this writer, Yechiel Faust, Chana Grinberg, Moshe Perel, and others. Its new ideas that it attempted to instill in its members – working and pioneering Zionism, constructive Socialism, and faith in the correctness of the new movement – were somewhat strange to the ears of the conservative youth of the city. Many of them were actually looking for the youth movement to provide palliative help for their physical needs. At an older age they primarily looked for an opportunity for amusement and friendship. The heads of Gordonia saw these needs as secondary to the main task of instilling the new life as Jews and human beings into their members. This work was not easy at all in the old atmosphere of provincialism.

The housing conditions of the group also became very difficult. The group moved from place to place. At first all the groups were squeezed in together – Hanoar Hatzioni, Young Mizrachi, and Gordonia – in the building of the Hebrew School. Gordonia was allotted two tiny rooms, cubicles literally, in the attic above the living quarters of the Tevel family. These rooms had to serve as rooms for the youth movement... There were even days where even these rooms were not allotted to the group, and the group only had permission to use the large hall of the school for certain times during the week... From there, Gordonia moved to a rented room in Feigele Hakeh's house, and from there to a small wooden room in the Reb Wolfe Ader's lumberyard. At that point, the movement had already reached significance in numbers, but had no comfort in terms of location... In the interim, the ranks increased. The number of members increased by multiples, and, of course, the noise and tumult also increased proportionally. The Horah, "Mi Yivneh Hagalil", "Mi Anachnu? Yisrael", and other similar songs of that era bellowed forth from that room until late hours of the evening. Echoes could be heard throughout the Wanka area. Sleep was deprived from the eyes of the neighbors, and the owner of the property threatened us regularly with forceful expulsion... Nevertheless, Reb Wolf Ader is remembered for the good, as he sufficed himself with mere threats for all those years.

The Hora was danced outside, and in the room itself we conducted numerous education and cultural activities every evening under the direction of the leaders of the groups. (Aside from the original people, with the passage of time new people, even younger people, began to take part in the educational and organizational work. These included Shlomo Yoska Taub, Mendel and Henia Wilner, Blima Lishe, Beltze Kriger, David Faust, Tzvi Grinberg, Yechiel Goldberg, Naftali Tenenbaum, Chaim Lederberger, Naftali Mantel, Moshele Sommer, Itzo Bodner, Anku Wind, Yechiel Derfler, Sara and Avtza Kanner, Avraham, Akiva and Hinda Feder, Henech and Rivtza Wilner, Henech Kukuk, Meir Licht, Yocheved Mantel, and others.) Most of the activities of the group leaders centered on the education of the members. However the types of people that joined Gordonia frequently forced the leaders to concern themselves also with the civilizing of the members. Yechiel Faust, Moshe Perel and others made a very productive effort in this area. They also tried to teach all the members a minimal knowledge of spoken Hebrew. Those students who did not visit the Hebrew school were placed into a "Hebrew Circle" club. Members of Poale Zion also benefited from that club. The participants also studied Bible, Hebrew literature, and knowledge about the Land of Israel. The group discussions focused on topics about the Jewish people, Zionism, Socialism, economics, the literature of the workers' movement, and other similar topics. During the numerous hikes, the leaders tried to bring the members closer to nature, to teach them to appreciate it, love it, and become connected to it. During the summer camps and leadership seminars, members came into contact with representatives of Hapoel Hatzair and Chaver Hakvutzot from the Land of Israel, who taught them about practical Zionism, and instilled in them a feeling of responsibility for the future of the nation and the lot of the homeland. Finally, there were Hachshara Kibbutzim in Chodorow, Rohatyn, where the members became accustomed to leaving their birthplace and their parents house, and got used to communal working life in preparation for making Aliya to the Land. There, the members Blima Lishe, David Faust, Sarah Kanner, Avraham Feder, and others, prepared to make Aliya.

Thanks to all of this activity, a group of dedicated young men and women arose in the city who were given over with their hearts and souls to the movement and its ideas. They later established a Hachshara group in Dembitz, which served the needs of the national movement, and concerned itself with finding work for the dozens of pioneers. This also brought the message of the movement to neighboring towns. With the help of the members from Dembitz, branches of Gordonia were established in Pilzno, Mielec, and other towns in the area.

However, the faithful members regarded all of this blessed activity as merely "study". The most important matter was the "actualization"... and they were prepared for this actualization and thirsted for Aliya. If it were not for the locked doors of Aliya at the beginning, and the destruction which took place at the end, most if not all of them would be alive with us here today, with each one finding his or her place – each according to his or her ability – in the rebuilding of our nation, and in carrying out the dream of our people ... To their sorrow, and to our sorrow, they did not merit, and we did not merit. May their souls be bound in the bonds of the life of our nation and our homeland forever.

The "Atid" group of "Gordonia" 5680 (1919/1920)

{Page 112}

"Young Borochov"

by Manya Grünspan

In the years 1917-1918, while the First World War was still in progress, my brother Yehuda (Idek) dedicated himself to the founding of a youth group called "Borochov Youth" (Borochov Yugent). Some of my oldest friends, including Perelmutter, Sheinfeld, Lempel, Ita Twi and others whom I met during a Hebrew course joined this group. Since I knew a little Hebrew, and I was a girl of 9 or 10, I did not study with children of my own age, but rather in a higher class, with girls of age 13 or 14.

From among the prisoners of war who were employed by the state in setting up our factory, Yehuda found a stubborn prisoner who was an excellent artist. After the death of Borochov, a photo of the late leader was given to him, and he was requested to enlarge it to life size. The picture was drawn in our workshop, which was located beneath our living quarters. My father of blessed memory, who had a fine sense of art and was drawn to unusual matters, permitted this stubborn captive to draw the picture with expenses being paid from the accounts of the "black market" work. The picture was later given as a gift to the "Yugent" group, and hung in its headquarters for many years. I was a witness to the entire goings on regarding this picture, and I was jealous of my brother's activities. On occasion, I accompanied him when he went to the group's headquarters, and I took note of its activities. I had the idea of organizing my friends, girls of my age, into a similar group. We gathered together, Rivcha Perel, Esther Kanner, Sara Grünspan of blessed memory, Rivcha Zeiger, Gita Widerspan, Polonitzka may she live long, and others, and we decided to found "Young Borochov". Our plan was to meet together once a week to sing, to hear a lecture, and also to present lectures and to gather money for a library that would be fitting for children of our age. The support of my brother Idek was guaranteed. Our teacher Weinberg, whom we cheated slightly by telling him that we were founding a center to speak Hebrew, permitted us to use a classroom in the Hebrew School, which at that time was located in our house. We elected a committee. Rivcha Perel of blessed memory was elected president. We gathered on Sabbaths at 1:00 PM in the Hebrew classroom, and there we held our lectures. The first lecture was about the book "Ben Hur" which I read at that time. Eventually we decided to arrange an evening activity in order to collect funds for our library. The program of the activity was as follows: an opening speech by my brother Idek discussing the aims of our group, which was the youngest in the movement, a general lecture by the president Rivcha Perel, poetry readings, a choral presentation, and most importantly, refreshments. Two boys who were members of our Hebrew class, Zeinvel Shlep who was called that because of his injured eye [94], and the brother of Cantor Wechsler, who both sang well, trained us in song. Each night for the duration of several weeks, we would gather in the workshop for our rehearsal and singing practice. It seems to me that our small choir, numbering about twelve girls, was quite good. Esther Perel and Esther Grünspan baked the cookies and other pastries. The members donated the ingredients. Finally, after much effort, the council of Poale Zion, whose members included at that time Pinchas Laufbahn, Shneur, and others, agreed to let us use the Poale Zion hall, which at that time was located in the house of Ascheim, in order to arrange our evening. We were very successful, and the funds raised by the event were substantial. The income was several hundred crowns. Instead of founding our own library, we decided to donate the money to enlarge the Poale Zion library. A delegation of members, headed by Rivcha Perel, gave the money over to Pinchas Laufbahn. Our organization continued to exist for a while longer; however in the interim, other movements arose, such as Hashomer. These were headed by older counselors, and attracted our members. The group disbanded. This was an episode in the life of children of a small town.

A group of "Dror-Borochov"

{Page 114}

"Young Poale Zion"

{Hebrew text – pp 114-115}

The "Bar Kochba" Sport Organization

This writer does not have clear knowledge as to when the Jewish Bar Kochba sport organization started in Dembitz. Nevertheless, it is possible to surmise that it did not begin earlier than the first years after the First World War. In those days, the only field in Dembitz that was open for Jewish sporting activities was the large, ownerless field that was surrounded by a fence and located three kilometers away from town. It was called "Blonia", which means meadow in Polish. It is obvious that there was no bus or taxi service available for the use of the Jewish soccer players in Dembitz. Even so, the members of Bar Kochba always arrived there at the time that was set for practice and activities. The spectators also arrived at the right time. Given the Polish climate, which had no set seasons due to the constant possibility of rain, some sort of shelter was necessary, since the nearest shelter from rain was three kilometers away. This was no laughing matter. After a while, even this possibility for activity was taken away from Bar Kochba, when the government confiscated the entire field for use as an army airfield. Another sport field was opened up in the camp of an infantry division that camped in Dembitz, however its use was only permitted for groups that were members of the P.Z.P.N., which entailed the payment of taxes for the benefit of the Polish organization. At first, Bar Kochba accepted this burden upon itself, however when debts accumulated it was forced to change its name to Hakoach in order to free itself from the debts. Debts accumulated again, and after a few years it returned to its name Bar Kochba, which stuck with it until it disbanded in 1939.

With the passage of time, a civic soccer field opened, for the use of all of the sporting organizations of Dembitz. However, the situation did not improve even with this. Even though most of the taxpayers of Dembitz were Jews, the Jewish youth were not permitted to conduct practices there, but only to appear for their competitions.

Of course, without being able to practice, it was difficult to maintain the physical abilities of the members. Those who were responsible for the field did everything in their power to make things difficult for the Jews.

The most fruitful activity in the realm of physical education for the Jewish youth of Dembitz was between the years 1930-1939. During that time, the leadership of this activity was in the hands of people who possessed exceptional dedication. They rented a field from the Kanner family, and thus opened up the possibility of setting up basketball, volleyball, and tennis courts. The table tennis games that took place in the Poale Zion hall were very popular. A group for light athletics was organized under the direction of Shaul Morgenlander. Today, he goes by the name Shaul Artzi and lives in Haifa. He used to appear on occasion in exhibition parades. Under his leadership, the organization struggled with financial difficulties, which on occasion threatened any possibility of broadening its activities.

The soccer team once was going to compete against the Hakoach team in Krakow, however the leadership refused to permit the travel due to a shortage of money. The disappointment was very great. We decided to organize the travel to Krakow ourselves, a distance of 120 Kilometers, through the use of Polish railway tickets, which would enable us to transport the team there and back at minimal cost. This adventure was quite dangerous; however we succeeded, and the competition took place at the Macabee field in Krakow.

On another occasion, the team traveled to compete against the Macabee team of Mielec, 32 kilometers away. The team traveled in a regular wagon due to the lack of money for travel by train. In most cases, the members themselves paid for their own travel and provisions.

As it was in Dembitz, the sport of soccer was the most popular. Throughout the course of the year, there would be major competitions between the Bar Kochba team and other sporting teams, such as Macabee and Hashchorim in Jaslow, Macabee and Haorvin in Mielec, and Shimshon, Hashachar, and Mattel in Tarnow, aside from games against the Polish Wisloka team of Dembitz.

Until the liquidation, the following people were very active in the maintenance and development of our organization: the dentist Yaakov Krantz, Reuven Dar, Aharon Ganz, Elimelech Shuss, Yitzchak Taub, all of blessed memory, as well as the following people, may they live long: Moshe Siedlisker (today Sarid, of Petach Tikva), and Reuven Pritzker (today in Tel Aviv), as well as many others who did not merit to witness the founding of the State of Israel, may their memories be blessed.

"Bar Kochba" Tennis Court

On a Shabbath Stroll

{Page 116}

The Keren Kayemet (J.N.F.) Commission in Dembitz, 5684 (1924)

Translator's Footnotes

89.   The "shekel" (incidentally the modern unit of currency in Israel), in this context refers to the basic dues of membership in the Zionist organization.

90.   "Lukal" is seemingly a nickname for the group's meeting place.

91.   Torah Vaavoda, literally Torah and Work, is the vision and motto of the religious Zionist movement that encompasses both Torah and work for the Land of Israel.

92.   The Eight Chapters (Shmona Prakim) is Maimonides' introduction to his commentary on one of the chapters of the Mishnaic tractate of Sanhedrin (chapter Chelek). Due to the esoteric material of that Chapter and deep philosophical nature of the introduction, Maimonides' introduction is a topic of study

93.   Chovot Halevavot, Duties of the Heart, by Bachya ibn Paquda, is a medieval philosophical and ethical work.

94.   Shlep in Yiddish means 'to drag'.

{Page 119}

{Hebrew text – page 119 top}

The Field of Education

After the First World War, when the refugees from Dembitz returned home, most of the Jewish children, with few exceptions, such as the children of the clergy and other such people, attended the government public schools. In the morning, they would attend school, and in the afternoon they would attend Cheder, the Talmud Torah, or the Hebrew School, which was not really a school but rather a place with classrooms for the study of Hebrew.

In the Polish schools, there was no particular anti-Semitic feeling that was felt from the teachers, but the "battles" between the students, Christians on one side and Jews on the other side, continued as previously. The schoolteachers imparted to the Jewish girls the ability to take part in Polish culture, and promised them that they would help them even after they graduated school, and enable them to become teachers in the Polish schools. Even though the Zionist youth movements did a great deal to counter this danger, there were nevertheless those who were enticed, and reached the brink of assimilation.

In those years, a fundamental change took place in the education of the Jewish youth. Due to compulsory education in the Polish schools, the traditional Jewish education was pushed off to the afternoon hours. On the other hand, as Polish education was imparted to the children, the parents and students alike felt an inclination toward Jewish education. This caused an increase in the number of students who attended the Beis Midrashes and Yeshivos, as well as the numbers of students who studied Hebrew. In addition, whereas previously German writing was taught with Hebrew characters, now the education took place in spoken Yiddish. There were very many teachers of children in the city, but it cannot be said that this satisfied the wishes of the parents, even those who wished to give their children a serious religious education. Therefore, in the early 1920s, a group of orthodox activists banded together to found the Talmud Torah, which was subject to communal supervision. These activists were: Reb Hirsch Taub, Yisrael Siedlisker, Reuven Horowitz the son of Reb Naftalchi, Moshe Salomon, and Reb Yosef Levis (Brenner). The students were aged four and above. Each Sabbath, the students were sent for an exam in Gemara with one of the accepted "examiners of the town – Reb Leizer Oling, Reb Hirsch Nissan, Reb Yosef Levis, who later became the teacher of Przeworsk.

Reuven, the son of Reb Naftalchi, was very dedicated to the Talmud Torah. He would go there first thing in the morning, during the time of classes.

During the time when he was successful in business, he established a prize for every student who knew a page of Gemara by heart – a bundle of chocolate.

During the middle of the 1930s, there were already parents who sent their children to study Hebrew (with the Sephardic pronunciation) [95] in the Hebrew School, in addition to the Gemara studies in the Beis Midrash.

The number of Jewish students in the gymnasia remained at almost the same level as it was previously. There were about 10 students in all of the classes. The main impediment was the studies on the Sabbath. Even though there was already permission granted for Jewish students to not write on the Sabbath, attending gymnasia during the times of synagogue services on the Sabbath was regarded as too great a breach in traditional family life. For this reason, a few people began to teach their children gymnasia studies outside the gymnasia, and arrange for annual exams. The two Jewish teachers who taught in the gymnasia had no connection at all with the Jewish community.

The majority of the youth broadened their secular knowledge after public school through reading as well as the cultural activities of the youth movements.

{Page 119}

The Hebrew School

by Avraham Weinberg, Haifa

{Hebrew text – pp 119-121}

The first Hebrew School of Dembitz was founded in 1910 through the efforts of Yehuda Bornstein and the great dedication of Bendet Fett the chairman of the local Zionist committee, as well as others. The first teacher was Mrs. Mendel Hochman. However it was only in 1912, with the arrival of the teacher Mr. Moharber, that the school began to consolidate under his direction. Then the First World War broke out. The Jews of Dembitz were exiled from their homes, and the school ceased operation until 1917. When the exiles refugees returned from their exile, the Zionists of Dembitz, headed by Mr. Bendet Fett and Chaim Freidman, made efforts to re-establish and strengthen the school. They preceded even such an important city as Tarnow, whose Hebrew school was only renewed after the end of the war.

The members of the committee that year were: Bendet Fett, Moshe Kerner, Chaim Freidman, Ben-Zion Widerspan, Mrs. Perel, Pesach Diament (today an important activist in the cooperative workers' movement in the Land), Rivka Eisen-Diament of blessed memory, Yochanan Sommer, and Reuven Sommer.

In the middle of the First World War, in the year 1917, when the Russian front eased up and the peace negotiations began, I was imprisoned as a Russian subject in one of the camps in Silesia. An invitation to Dembitz arrived signed by Bendet Fett and Chaim Freidman, requesting me to come and accept the position as a Hebrew teacher in that city. Due to that invitation, I was freed from prison, and I immediately sent a telegram to those that invited me informing them of my arrival. The two of them met me at the train station, and from our first contact, a full beneficial understanding was established between us. The news of the arrival of the Hebrew teacher spread as fast as lightning. The committee prepared everything that was needed with alacrity and great success, and within a few days, the school was opened in a rented hall in the home of Mr. Nathan Grünspan. Classes and courses in Hebrew were opened during three times – morning, afternoon, and evening. The number of students increased weekly.

Hebrew School with the Committee

For educational reasons, I decided to speak Hebrew not only at home, but also in my private life. My "strange" behavior did not cause me any difficulties in my interpersonal relationships. Whenever I started speaking to someone in Hebrew, I would be answered politely, whether in Yiddish or in broken Hebrew. Only the members of Poale Zion did not look favorably on my behavior, and my relationship with them became difficult. At one of their meetings, they accused me behind my back of contradicting the language of the people and dishonoring the Jewish workers who only read and speak Yiddish. Shimon, the elder brother of Yehuda Grünspan, rose to my defense. He was one of the top students at the school. He defended me, saying that the Hebrew teacher has no intention to disparage Yiddish or to negate it. The proof for this was that I does not converse in Polish either. Thus was I exonerated in their eyes, and the relations between us returned to normal.

The number of students in the Hebrew School grew, and the hall was too small to hold them all. During their meeting, the members of the committee decided to establish a fund to purchase a house. The next day, it became known that a fine large house went up for sale on Garzilow Street. Chaim Freidman, as a member of the committee, hurried to make contact with the seller. The seller agreed with the conditions that were presented to him. However, from where would be found the 2,000 gold coins that were required as the down payment prior to signing the contract, when the committee's fund did not even have one cent? Salvation came from a member of the committee, Mr. Fishel Wechsler, who donated 2,000 gold coins from his own money. The contract was signed that day, and the committee bought the house. The school left its small rented premises and moved to a place that was large enough for its needs. The school grew again. Additional classes were opened, and additional teaching staff was required. The committee looked toward the young Dembitz native Moshe Rosen, and he was hired as the second teacher for the school.

Moshe Rosen was from poor stock. His parents made their livelihood with difficulty by selling vegetables. The lived in a small hut on Garzilow Street, which stood up by a miracle, and served as a store as well. The son, who excelled at first in sacred studies only, became enthralled with the Haskalah, and after a few years, due to his great diligence, succeeded in gaining knowledge in many subject areas: history, mathematics, grammar, literature, Biblical criticism, and philosophy. His sight became impaired due to the great deal of time he spent pouring over books to the light of a dim lantern. Even though the doctors ordered him to refrain from reading at night, they could not quench his great thirst for knowledge.

He was a top-notch speaker. His lectures in the Debora and Noar Hatzioni halls were clear and straightforward, and they covered the topics completely. Later in life, he became blind due to his great diligence in his studies.

The school developed well, and it became known in the region. One year, the principal of the local Polish gymnasia participated in the annual final exams as a guest. He was a Christian. Chaim Freidman, who was one of his students, served as the translator between him and the students. The honorable guest expressed his satisfaction with the knowledge and expertise that the students demonstrated in literature, Jewish history, and Bible.

The school, including all of its halls and rooms, served as the center for all cultural and communal activities of the local Zionist organizations. The well-stocked library was in one of its rooms. At night, lectures, gatherings, and meetings took place. It served primarily as the organizational center for the youth. The students of the school set up a drama club and presented plays about Biblical topics. A few of the many students of the school became teachers, and now serve as teachers in Israel. These include Yehuda Grünspan in Jerusalem, Chana Gruen, Tova Kanner, and others. For a certain period, one of the alumnae of the school served as a teacher there. This was Tova Kanner. She filled my place for a certain period when I served as a teacher at the school in Tarnow. After I left the school in Dembitz, several well-known people served as teachers there, including the poet Pinchas Lander, and Eliezer Ungar, as well as others.

I carry in my heart pleasant memories of those days. I remember fondly the students whom I merited to teach Hebrew, including those who are alive with us in Israel today, as well as those who perished in the flood of blood perpetrated by Hitler, may his bones be ground up. These memories will never depart from my heart forever.

Yochanan Sommer, an activist for the Hebrew School, and a member of the Community Committee

Weinberg the Teacher giving a lesson

The Hebrew School of Dembitz

Scher the Teacher with his pupils

{Page 123}

My Hebrew Schools

by Manya Grünspan

{Hebrew text – page 123}

The Hebrew School of Dembitz

It was before the First World War. I was still very young. Ruchama, my older sister, brought me to the Hebrew School, which at that time was located in a rented room in the house where later the family of Nathan Taub lived. We would go up to the schoolroom on a wooden staircase that was on the side facing the road near the entrance to our factory. I don't recall the name of the teacher. They tell me that it was Mr. Hochman. However, I do remember this: he taught us Hebrew in Hebrew. I remember one explanatory illustration as if it was before my eyes. He was attempting, apparently, to explain to us the meaning of 'masa' (burden) or 'laseit masa' (to bear a burden). What did he do? He lifted up a chair, placed it upon my shoulders, walked me around the desk, and explained during the course of the walking what I was doing.

After a certain time, before I started going to the Polish school, I attended the Hebrew School that was in the home of Reuven Sommer. I was in the same class as my sister Bronia, Altek Bornstein, Ita Twi, Chaya Twi, Minda Freidman, Mania Chaim, and others. The large map of the Land of Israel that was hanging on the wall made a deep impression upon me. Our teacher Moharber, who was very handsome, influenced me greatly. It is certainly because of him that I one of the best students in the class. After some time, the school moved to our home. I would sit in on various courses, listening and understanding. I remember one course in which my sister Recha, Fela Bornstein, Rivka Eisen of blessed memory, and others participated. With the outbreak of the First World War, the school disbanded.

After the First World War, we returned home from our exile. The Zionist movements in the city once again began to concern themselves with Hebrew education, and they found a Hebrew teacher who raised our spirits. This was Mr. Avraham Weinberg. I will never forget how he labored to spread Hebrew language and culture in our midst. Perhaps it is only now that I can adequately explain the great and dedicated work that he put into our school. Weinberg was a fine teacher. His classes were full of content. He knew how to attract the hearts of the students to love of the language and the book.

I especially remember his Sabbaths, which I loved greatly. Every Sabbath afternoon he would gather us together, talk to us, and we would sing, play and dance (today they call this an "Oneg Shabbat"). In such a manner did he impart to us the literary and day-to-day language simultaneously. I still remember the songs that we sang with him. When we got a bit older, he would arrange choirs, plays, and celebrations, the proceeds of which went to support the Hebrew School. There were people who understood his ways and valued him. In his merit, it is possible to say, the mission of the school expanded. There was a need for additional classrooms. A house was bought, a respectable library was established, and additional teachers were hired. The youth movements also gathered in this school.

In addition, I should mention that Mr. Weinberg used to conduct lessons in his home in the old city, as if it was an additional school.

{Page 124}

Meir Stieglitz of blessed memory

The Hebrew School in our town was established thanks to the boundless dedication of several activists, who were generous with their time and effort in order to establish that cultural institution.

The most prominent of them was Meir Stieglitz of blessed memory. He was an upright, warm-hearted man, who saw no other aim in his life aside from this school.

He had no children, and when he went to the school, he claimed that he was going to his children.

He loved us, he loved to sit and listen to the Hebrew words – whenever he was free from his activities he spent time in the school. He concerned himself with the budget, he worried about the teachers, and every setback affected his soul.

His activities were not limited to the school alone. He also participated in the local Zionist committee, as well as the Jewish National Fund (Keren Kayemet), and Keren Hayesod. If there were any need for a volunteer for a small or large matter, it would always be Meir Stieglitz.

Along with Bras, Yochanan Sommer, Ben-Zion Widerspan, and many others, he established a glorious institution.

He dreamed about making Aliya to the land, however this never materialized.

He often spoke about his plans with tears in his eyes – for he had a pure and warm heart. Steiglitz takes a prominent position among the activists in the city who concerned themselves with the renewal of the language.

We who merited to hear and speak Hebrew in the school that he founded remember him with love.

Meir Stieglitz, one of the chief activists of the Hebrew School and one of the most dedicated workers for Zionism in the city

(Hebrew text – page 124 right column)

(Photo page 124 top left – A group of youths with the teacher Schechter)

{Page 124}

Beis Yaakov

by P. Salomon-Grosman

{Hebrew text – page 124 left column}

In 1932-1933, a Beis Yaakov [96] girls' school, affiliated with the network founded by Sara Schenirer, was founded.

This was the first school of its type in Dembitz. Its purpose was to teach girls the depths of Judaism. It is strange how backward was the national, and even the religious education of the girls. This was the fault even of the parents. There was no other aim in Judaism other than to be raised in a religious, traditional home.

This was the case until a small group of people banded together and made efforts to give to the Jewish girls what was missing from the Polish public schools and from the homes. Among those who set up the foundations for this school in Dembitz were Bina and Moshe Salomon, Moshe Weiss and his wife, Perel Faust, Buxbaum, Reuven Schlessinger, Hersch Taub, and Miriam Balsam. These people worked with unusual dedication to develop the Beis Yaakov School, even though they were burdened with the heavy yoke of earning a livelihood. Even so, they would meet in the evenings and dedicate their precious time and activity towards this idea.

At Beis Yaakov, education, history, Jewish customs, etc. were taught. In addition to the regular course of studies, which was full enough, we began, in the manner of the Zionist youth movements, to arrange festivities at the times of each holiday. This had great value, since this breathed a spirit of life into the circle of orthodox girls, who had no other opportunity for organizational and social activity.

As was the case with most of the other Jewish institutions of the Diaspora, Beis Yaakov suffered from significant budgetary challenges. In order to make up the deficit, many lovely festivities were arranged for the community, and people would also go out to collect money. This was the situation until I made Aliya to the Land.

Translator's Footnotes

95. Hebrew can be pronounced in both the Ashkenazic and Sephardic style. The Sephardic style, which was prevalent in North Africa, is the style of modern spoken Hebrew in Israel. The Ashkenazic style would have been more in vogue in the traditional Cheders and Yeshivos. By teaching the Sephardic dialect, the Hebrew School was attempting to educate the children in modern spoken Hebrew.

96. Beis Yaakov is the name of the Orthodox girl's school network, which still exists today.

{Page 126}

Recognition of Awakenings

Translated by Jerrold Landau

{Page 127}

Awakenings in an Alien Land

by Yehuda Grünspan

A. From the Early Days

Only very few memories remain from those peaceful days that preceded the First World War, when the town was still built up. My memories are centered on the precincts of the large Market Square, which was surrounded and closed in by rows of stores from all sides. I particularly remember the large and beautiful store of the "Erer Brothers"... When we returned from cheder, we would often gather around the entrance and glance inside. We would look inside with awe as our eyes beheld its beauty. However, even the brave ones from among us did not dare walk through the entrance. This was due to a few reasons:

a. the owner of the store went around "bareheaded" [1];

In the store, they spoke German even to the Jewish and Polish customers;

b. the main reason: Red carpets were spread out on the floor, and these inspired fear in us, as if they declared: "go around, go around, do not draw near".

My first memory from those days is connected with the cheder of Reb Shlomo the teacher and Yosele, his teacher's assistant. The portrait is alive and well before us: a group of young children of age four or five making their way slowly along the "Potszina" to the other side of the "Tepper Lane". For the most part, their noses were not clean. The bottoms of their shirts stick out from their pants in the back, and they have salted bagels spread with butter in their hands. Yosele the teacher's assistant will guide us. Our dear mothers gave us over to the faithful hands of this good-natured man, who was of somewhat dull intellect. We came and went by his command. He recited the "Modeh Ani" prayer with us in the morning, he read with us the "Shema" prayer in the evening, and he reviewed with us the aleph beit during the day – kametz aleph – o, kametz beis – bo, patach shin – sha [2]. He also taught us the vowels and the trop [3] – in short, the entire difficult Torah was taught to us by Shlomo the children's teacher with the help of his pointer and his belt. I do not remember if we were happy in cheder (the nickname of our teacher, "Shlomo Shlep", which was always on our tongues, perhaps indicated that we might not have been [4]). However, we were certainly not bored there. This was thanks to the blacksmith shop of the neighboring gentile, for we shared a common courtyard, us brats and the blacksmith's shears (a match from heaven! Is it not? This device was a constant source of pleasure. Not only did it serve for us as a device for practicing our cutting skills – in particular on their holidays when the entire family of the blacksmith went to the "impure place" [5], but it was also a treasure house of all sorts of blacksmith remnants. We filled our pockets with them and tore them to smithereens. It is obvious that this cutting device did not only bring us great joy but also much suffering and pain. The blacksmith would cut very hot iron. He would take what he needed and leave behind the rest. One of us would run to grab the "find", and the screams reached to the heavens... The Rebbetzin Sarah Gales would hurry to the victim as a redeeming angel and immerse the burnt hand in a pot full of milk to heal it. On such occasions we learned that one places on a wound flowing with blood (i.e. "a cut in the head") bread and butter and a spider's web; a sure remedy for perplexity and fear was to lick the forehead seven times and after each lick, to spit on the ground; if one is injured in the eye, one removes the upper eyebrow with honey and spits three times upwards, and it is cured... It is obvious that these "first aid" lessons from the Rebbetzin were not part of the official curriculum. Also included among our activities were visits to the homes of newborns. The babies were washed thoroughly (incidentally, we were surprised that Tauba "the chubby", the daughter of the rabbi, was able to "wash" all of us with one splash of water. We would often be taken by our teacher in the evenings, as we made an orderly procession to the house of a newborn to read the Shema together and with a melody. We were rewarded with sweets and "stars" (a type of pastry). Our joy was great. These evening hours were the most enjoyable times at the cheder of Reb Shlomo the teacher.

During the evening hours. To the west of the courtyard of the cheder, there was a wide pasture ("di lonke") which was surrounded by rows of tall trees. During the evening hours, it seemed to us young children that the tops of the trees reached to the heavens, that the borders of that field were the "ends of our earth", and that the redness of the sky was the fire of hell.

With regards to the "hell", we were correct, for soon enough, hell would open up before us. The fire of the First World War was ignited. The also signified the beginning of the end of our "ends of our earth". The boundaries of our pasture expanded all the way to Western Europe.

Things transpired with suddenness. On one summery Sabbath afternoon, news spread about the "final train going to the west". A great panic ensued in the city. Father of blessed memory hastily came home from the Chevra Mishnayot Synagogue. His face exuded deep agony that he had to leave the customary lecture of Reb Leizer Zeldales, and that he had to occupy himself on the Sabbath with things that were forbidden as not being in the spirit of the Sabbath. However when he saw the perplexed face of my mother of blessed memory, he surely remembered the adage of the holy Talmudic sage: "Negate your Torah since it is a time of action" [6].

A few moveable belongings were packed onto a wheelbarrow, and I followed along behind it. The Street of the Train was full of men, women and children covered in sweat and full of panic. The burning sun spread its full light upon the square, shiny tiles. Suddenly, as if to "anger" us, the weather changed and rain began to fall. It was a poor opportunity for the song "a son with a rain, the bride has been born". The time was not fitting for this, for how can we sing our songs as we were going out to a strange land.

When we arrived at the train station, we found the train cars filled to the brim with no space. Cramped and pressed, we remained outside on the platform between the coaches. There was fear and also excitement – it was our first ride in a train: There were deafening whistles, pillars of smoke and steam, sparks coming out from under the clanging wheels: fields, trees and houses raced backward and speedily disappeared, the world and its contents were in dizzying movement. At the stops, our older brothers would hurry to bring some water or to pick some ripe fruit from the sides of the track. Suddenly the train would start to move and those that were late would succeed, of course, in jumping upon the rear cars. In the meantime, the mothers would sigh over the "loss" of their children. Refugee organizations would greet us with hot cocoa and baskets full of fresh and tasty rolls. We were quite happy with this. Suddenly, a shriek would come out from the midst of the coach: "Oy vey, I am broken, it is with lard!" [7] Suddenly, people would start to spit out and cough... "Foo!" "Oy Vey". The agony of even the young children who did not yet understand the difference between permitted and forbidden food was great. All at once, the joy ceased. The tender heart brought bad news: "From a gentile... bread of gentiles... not kosher."

Things changed as time went on. Our return to the town was not like our exit. It was no longer the same town, and there were no longer the same townsfolk. The splendor and glory had departed. The face had changed and the clothing had changed. Some people had cut of their peyos and others shaved off their beards. Some only put away their shtreimel and others cut their cloak in half. In brief: the small town of Dembitz looked at the wide world and was damaged.

{Hebrew text – pp 128-133}

B. In the Cheder

We studied Hebrew with Reb Shlomo the teacher, and Chumash and Rashi with Reb Chaim Yoskis. This cheder left strong impressions on many of us, for it was one of a kind. This cheder had everything. It was on the ground floor (if not below). From the main street, the Kaiser Weg, we went down to it on twelve extremely shaky steps. In the winter, when the high snow covered the steps, the pranksters from among us would sit on metal plates and slide all the way down from the street. They would go directly into the cheder, breaking through the door with the force of their bodies. I should add that this 'beating' of the door caused other beatings, this time from the Rebbi [8]. The cheder room was long and narrow, and it was always gray. However we did not feel this, for we had a great light in our hearts, and we even merited having many hours of happiness. Our prime time of happiness was the time between the Mincha (afternoon) and Maariv (evening) services on the long winter nights. The Rebbi would go out to attend the service and we would make haste to return to the cheder armed with flashlights and food. Incidentally, just as the flashlights differed from each other, the food also differed. Those who had flashlights "purchased in Tarnow" with thick, polished glass and a receptacle for fuel and a wick would bring a nice piece of bread (made from sifted flour) spread with butter or duck fat, a good piece of salted fish, and dried fruit for dessert. Those who had the flashlights designed for candles made by the local glassmaker with simple pieces of glass, brought with them to eat half-dark bread spread with "kornol" (a type of margarine and the head or tail of a salted fish. There were also those who did not have any flashlights at all. They brought with them only a piece of bread made of course flour, and no more. Even with the "class differences", friendship and brotherhood pervaded; and probably for this reason, the swapping and "barter" took place – three "scratches" of the turnip were exchanged for a bite of the white bread or a dried pear. There were many other similar transactions. Of course, there were also instances of heard-heartedness and selfishness. Someone may have been stubborn and refused to share even a small taste with his friend who was like a brother to him. What would he do? He would quickly lick it on all sides with his tongue, thus preventing others from benefiting from it. However, such not-nice instances were rare, and for the most part, a good spirit pervaded among us. This was particularly true during these desirable times between Mincha and Maariv when the Rebbi was away from the cheder, and the center of activity moved from the study table to the two beds that spanned the length of the wall. These beds spanned all the way from the table to the baker's oven, which was also an integral part of our cheder. It is appropriate to dedicate a few words to these two beds. Ezra, the son of our Rebbi, slept on one of them. On the second one slept the two sons of Chamia "from across the water", our classmates. During the six weekdays, the cheder room also served as a dormitory for them. During the day, there was nothing on these beds aside from the mattresses, so we saw them as "open" for pranks. We turned them into a "battlefield". This was particularly the case with the bed of the sons of Chamia, which were set apart because during the nights, fish were drawn from them. You might ask about what fishing had to do with the "battlefield"? This was the way it took place for the most part. After we ate appropriately and satiated ourselves with tasty morsels, we began to deal with the "matter". Someone from the group was intentionally pushed upon the bed of the "pensioners", and immediately the sequence of events [9] began. Right away, the pusher also lay down on the bed, and then the next person, the third, the fourth, etc. until there was a large pile of bodies and winter coats on the bed. We all rolled around, there was laughter and muffled grunts as those underneath made their way to the top of the heap, and those on top made their way to the bottom of the heap. Thus began a long session of "oy"! One could cut the atmosphere with a knife. The "trouble" was reserved for the one with bad luck who would be at the top of the pile at the moment that the Rebbi entered the room and the whippings began. Reb Chaim Yoskis was quite expert at administering whippings. He would whip our fathers on the eve of Yom Kippur at the Beis Midrash of the Hassidim [10]. During my childhood, for some reason, I would enjoy seeing how Reb Alter, for example, or Reb Chaim Alter would bend down and fall on their faces as our Rebbi would whip them with his strap as his mouth enunciates. "And He, being all merciful, forgives transgression." The whipping in the Beis Midrash was similar to the whipping in the cheder; however here he would do it both above and below, and was not accompanied with the recitation of "And He, being all merciful".

All of this took place in the first bed of Shlomoke and Leibke. The second bed served as our "club house for storytelling". We sat on it and eagerly listened to the stories of Ezra the son. What did he tell us, and what did he not tell us? He would tell us about the spirits and shades; a story about the mischievous girl with an umbrella in her hand who would walk back and forth to the walls of the nunnery; the story of the lazy person who stood with one foot on the roof of the house of Hinda Hauser and with the other foot on the house of Efraim Hakeh, with a pipe in his mouth that reaches to the ground; a story about the shoe merchants who traveled to the fair in Pilzno and brought with them sacks filled with boots. When they arrived at the Pilzno Bridge, one sack fell off the wagon and disappeared under the bridge. We liked in particular to hear the stories of the wonders performed by the Tzadikim of our town, in particular of Rabbi Reuven of blessed memory, who once went out on his shaky wagon with two pairs of horses, and chased away a band of spirits that had taken root in the town with his whip. Another chapter in Ezra's collection revolved around the dead. There were many stories of dead people who knocked on the doors of the members of the Chevra Kadisha (burial society) complaining that their burial shrouds had been exchanged, damaged during deeds of the "do-gooders", or other such complaints. There was the story of the dead people who worshiped at midnight in the Great Synagogue, which inspired us that night to grab our Tzitzit [11] and recite the Shema prayer with extra intensity. We were not so brazen as to glance with our eyes toward the tall windows of the synagogue, lest we see the worshipping corpses dressed in their white shrouds enwrapped in their tallises. Ezra the son did not only expound about the dead, but also about the living. Living people love treasures, and Ezra loved to tell stories about hidden treasures. In truth, with regard to hidden treasures, I must state that our friend Shaya David (Lisha) was even more expert than even Ezra. There was no item in the world, literally from the horns of buffaloes to the eggs of lice, including of course buttons and letter molds, for which Shaya David did not know the location of their hidden treasure. There are also interesting stories about Beinish and his group. We had a strange pleasure in hearing, for example, how Ezra once found himself at one of the abandoned houses in the town and found Beinish in great trouble. Only after he, Ezra, ran to the store and brought him "ten measures of butter" was Beinish relieved from his trouble. Our small eyes stood out and our mouths were open to drink with thirst more and more from this overflowing fountain. And then suddenly the opportunity passed, for the Rebbi returned.

For one more moment the observer looked around in astonishment until he caught sight of the flame of the oil lantern that was standing on an overturned pot in the middle of the table. However, everything was forgotten very quickly. The mouths of the "holy flock" broke out in the holy chant: "And I, Jacob, even though I am burdening you with my burial", and continuing on with the voice of victory: "Shimon and Levi are brothers" [12]. With regard to the education of children, what can be compared to these holy feelings which we felt as we studied the Torah portion of Vayechi on a winter night in the cheder of Reb Chaim Yoskis? The study material was comforting to the soul, and therefore even the "day of judgement", that is to say the exam which took place on Fridays, was not difficult for us. There was also another satisfying time just prior, for in the "Chevra Kadisha Shtibel" the congregation would finish the Psalms of David the son of Jesse every Friday morning. We the cheder children would try to get up early in order to participate at least in the final daily portion and the recital of the "Yehi Ratzon" prayers that are recited after the conclusion of the book of Psalms. I did not know and I still do not know what intention our fathers had when they stayed up all night and cried out with heartrending cries: "and may Your nation of Israel not need help from each other, nor from another nation". What I did know was that our intention was that the exam should go well and we should not need the support of one another for the "reprimand" or other difficulties. In addition to the Psalms, we made sure to kiss the mezuzah three times upon leaving the Shtibel and to say with great devotion: "Our Father, our King, may this hour be a time of mercy and a fortuitous time before You" [13]. If that was not sufficient, we employed the smoke of the tall chimney of the factory of Uncle Notele in order to make predictions. If the smoke goes straight up, it was a sign that the "doctor is good" (Shaya David nicknamed the exam on Chumash and Rashi – "asentirung" [14]). If the smoke bent to the sides, Heaven forbid, then "it is bitter".

As a small consolation for the times of "fear" on Fridays, the large baker's stove played a significant role in the cheder in which we studied. How good was it, after we succeeded in the exam, to stand in front of the lit stove and look inside as the flames lapped up the frozen, wet sticks of wood, as the water boils and becomes red, and suddenly the sound of breaking as the as a shower of sparks spread out in all directions. How fortunate were we when the Rebbetzin Lea Yoskis would come to our assistance to serve us a piece of honey pastry or some other delicacy. However, our greatest pleasure from this oven came during the days between Purim and Passover. Our joy was double at that time. This was "for G-d and for the people". We studied the Song of Songs with great enthusiasm [15]. "Song" – the song which King Solomon sung. We also studied the Passover Haggadah. "Kadesh" – when the father comes home from the synagogue on Passover night, he puts on his kittel and rinses out the cups. Then he sits down in a reclining position and recites the Kiddush. "Urchatz" – we wash the hands and do not make the usual benediction upon washing, since this washing is not followed by the meal [16]. This was the portion for G-d. The portion for us was even more enjoyable. For two or three weeks before Pesach, our Rebbi used to rent out his stove to various homeowners, and every family baked their matzos with the help of their friends and acquaintances. The matzo shmurah was baked first thing in the morning, and then the regular matzo was baked throughout the day or in the evening. One could discern the status of the family baking by the hours of baking. Of course, the more prominent people baked their matzos earlier and the poorer people later, as was customary. In any case, the cheder was very busy at that time, and our assistance was greatly needed. The jealousy of the children of the nearby cheders was very deep, for only we had the merit of turning ourselves during those two weeks into "hewers of wood and drawers of water" literally. It was our duty to bring in firewood from the woodshed in the yard in order to fuel the oven, as well as to draw the "mayim shelanu" [17] and bring it in. We were also responsible for scrubbing the rolling pins and baking pans, and pouring the water for those who were kneading the dough. On occasion, we had even more success, as the person who was responsible for making the perforations in the matzos (der shtupler) would permit us to make the perforations and put it in the oven, as we shouted out loud: "hurry, put a matzo in the oven!". Is it any wonder that the children of the other cheders were jealous of us?

Our cheder was able to arouse jealousy not only during the time of the baking of matzos. At other times of year as well our cheder had it attractions. This was thanks to the manifold occupations of the Rebbetzin Lea Yoskis. For example, a few weeks before Chanukah, our cheder room was filled with the noisy quacking of ducks. This let us know that the time for the preparation of duck fat for Passover was at hand. The Rebbetzin did a great favor for us in that the skinning and cutting up of the slaughtered ducks took place at the edge of our table. This was an excellent practical lesson in anatomy for those of us who would eventually study "Yoreh Deah" [18]. At this time, we all tried to have some benefit from the organs and limbs that were placed beside us. If the Rebbetzin removed her attention for a moment from the "operating table" one of us brats would snatch a crop or a throat and put it into his neighbor's pocket. However when he noticed that the Rebbetzin was looking for it, he would quickly return the lost object. I already mentioned the status differences that existed in our cheder. Indeed, with the extra insights that we gleaned from this work of the Rebbetzin, we were able to distinguish between for types of purchasers. First there were the well to do people who would purchase whole, fat ducks. Then there were the simpler folk who would purchase skinned ducks that were missing certain limbs. Next were the "women" who satisfied themselves with the limbs and giblets – this was also "in honor of the Sabbath". Finally there were the poorer people who ended up with the leftovers, primarily the heads, intestines, etc. Furthermore, we learned how to classify the purchasers of fish in honor of the Sabbath. We could differentiate between those who ate carp and pike; those who purchased whitefish, sole, and tench; and those who satisfied themselves with sprats and even simpler fish.

During the summer, we enjoyed another of the occupations of Lea Yoskis. She would make raspberry syrup. The Rebbetzin needed our help for this. This is how the syrup was made: after we removed the stems from the raspberries, we put them into cloth bags, and squeezed the juice with our hands. We did this work very eagerly, for there was a double or triple reward for our labors. First of all, we were free from our studies. Secondly, there was the leftover fruit, which we sucked dry and then made into "balls" that we left out to dry in the sun. This was in lieu of gumballs that we did not have during our youth. However, from this "sweet" there was also "bitterness" when our fathers recognized from the redness of our hands "the hands of Esau" that the "voice of Jacob" was stilled in the tents of Torah [19]. They placed their hands "the hands of Jacob" upon us. It should be known that during that era, our fathers took many opportunities to fulfill the verse "he who spares the rod spoils the child" [20]. The fault did not lie with us, however, but with the river. That is to say, the river that separated our cheder from the cheder of Rabbi Lisha, and which was a source of enjoyment to us all. It was, however, also a place of serious problems on occasion. Its two banks were created, literally from the six days of creation, to serve as excellent toboggan hills in the winter. It was divided up so that we brats "the children who study Chumash and Rashi" would get the lower left bank, and the students of Rabbi Lisha, the "students of Talmud" would get the high right bank. We would sit on metal sheets, and when they were not available we would use only our pants, and slide down. The others, the older children, would slide on ordinary boards, but in order to irritate us, they would refer to them with honor as sleds. There was also a division on the ice. There were two areas, one narrow one for us beginners; and a longer one smoothed out, for the "experts". There were often collisions and bruised faces. Worst of all, if the ice broke, we would get our shoes and pants wet. Then there was grief and woe, trembling in the bones as the knees banged together. The only choice was to go home or back to the cheder. That is to say: woe from my father or woe from the Rebbi. If such an "immersion" took place during the summer, whether due to slipping while crossing via the rocks in the river or whether due to being pushed on purpose, the solution was simpler: it was possible to stand in the clothing of Adam and Eve under the tall bridge as the clothes dried in the sun. This bridge would hide our "shame" to a large degree. However, once in a while, it itself would be the cause of embarrassment. This would be the case if one of the reckless people would stand on top of the bridge, and prove, by means of "making a bow" to the innocent people standing below that what was written in "pitum haktoret" was applicable for them [21]. Of course the matter became known to the Rebbi, and the misdeeds of this mischievous person was turned on his face; however this was a small comfort for the victim of the embarrassment. "Accidents" of this sort were obviously quite rare, and for the most part, the river was for us a source of enjoyment and fun. How good was it to jump from the banks into the river! Near the bathhouse, the water was deep and it was possible to swim, do somersaults, splash around in the turbulent water and hunt for fish (for the most part, these were tadpole and leeches; and occasion we would catch actual small fish, however these caused us only distress, for they were without scales – that is to say it was impossible to take them for they were not kosher, and it was it distressed us to put them back).

There were only two people who were not happy with our frolicking in the water: one was Junio, the stoker of the bathhouse. He was a tall, lean gentile who was as thin as a lulav, quiet and goodhearted. He suffered greatly when he saw the water, which he came to draw for the bathhouse, dirty and filthy. Nevertheless, he never told us off nor laid a hand on us. The second one was "the fat kashke", Mrs. Lorenc, for we disturbed her ducks and swans in the waters of the river, or we used them as targets for our slingshots. Mrs. Lorenc obtained the nickname "fat kashke" from our friend Pinchas Wolf ("Tshop") when she caught him once and began to go through his pockets to search for the ammunition, and he began to shout in a crying voice: "Shokai, Shokai, ti grobe (fat) kashke, ya nia mam protza."

In general, these two or three Christian families who were neighbors of the cheders and Beis Midrashes were "in exile" among us. To their credit, they bore their suffering, which must have been quite great, for they were obliged to hear day and night the sounds of singing and prayers. However, on occasion a duck wearily came back to Mrs. Lorenc' yard with a broken wing or leg. The patience of this gentile ran out, and she went to the cheder to complain. Then, we were in exile. However, G-d prepared the medicine before the plague, and the distraught Polish women said to our Rebbi something like this: "Juzs dobze, prashe pani, ja mu dalem glowe wu bzszoch – a head in the book." With her smile, it was obvious that she was somewhat assuaged by the beatings which were administered to us. There is only one thing, which is a mystery to this day: how did our Rebbi, with his minimal fluency in the vernacular, know how many whippings to administer in accordance with the severity of the crime? (We knew the level of his knowledge of the vernacular from his statement to the woodcutter: "vi kodem kol rombtshe, maia Lea poshla lashuk, achar kach maia Lea zaplatshe" [22]). In truth, it seemed that he did not know how to set the right number, but rather used the adage: "whomever does more is praiseworthy" [23].

When we graduated from the cheder of Reb Chaim Yoskis, we transferred to the cheder of Rabbi Lisha to study Talmud. Even though he was blind, he succeeded in teaching us one page of Talmud each week and in instilling his fear into us. He had an exceptional sense of hearing. Not one secret was hidden from him. If one of use tried to disappear from the study table for even a few moments, he would immediately sense that the person's voice was missing from the chorus of study, and an interrogation would begin: "Yidel, where are you?" Or, he would go outside, wave his hand and threaten, shouting loudly into space: "Moshe, do you think that I told you that you should leave!", "Mottel, tonight, your father will know!", "Remember Mottele!". Of course, these threats worked immediately. We quickly surrounded him, and even before he could return to the cheder, we already were sitting around the table like innocent lambs, not knowing what the Rebbi wanted from us. At that time, the Rebbi would stand aback from us, massage his hunched back with his fist, and say: "Nu, say already!" For the Rebbi certainly knew what he wanted from us. He wanted to instill sadism in us. Perhaps it was natural that we, eight or nine year old brats, would arouse the ire of our Rebbi on occasion. One afternoon during on a hot summer day in Tammuz, Chaitza, the only daughter of the Rebbi, a girl of marriageable age, very refined and intelligent, was sitting on her bed for many hours without moving, with her back toward us and her face to the wall. Her strange position instigated the mischievous boys among us, who began to throw cherry pits at her. The first few hit her and she did not move. However when it began to bother her, she moved her head a bit toward us and said: "Daddy, the youngsters are throwing". As soon as the complaint left her lips, her mother Perla began to curse: "we should throw them high and low, such apostates!" This was the manner of Perla (it was strictly forbidden to call her Rebbetzin). She bore her suffering quietly. If a hat flew onto the boiling pot over which she was stooped and filled the room with smoke; if a piece of gum or kutzuk [24] which was placed on the pots gave off an odor; if a pot of waste was turned over "by accident" – she quietly overlooked all of these. However when Chaitza who "would not hurt a fly on the wall" complained at all about the youth (we were eight or nine year olds!), Perla immediately began cursing. Once her mouth was opened, the stream continued like a waterfall. All in all, Perla was a good woman. She witnessed many of our pranks, and she knew our secrets and did not tell. When one of us brats tied a kite tail on the back of the Rebbi's long cloak and ignited it, we began to shout: "Rebbi, the Rebbi is burning!" We hurried to extinguish the burning papers. Or in the evening, we would study a verse from the Early Prophets (in general, we did not learn much Nach [25]) without much enthusiasm, for we had spent an entire day in the cheder, and we were anxious for freedom, for fresh air, for a dip in the Wislok River, or at least to be able to play a bit of "kampes" or "Reitshul" before Mincha and Maariv. However Rabbi Lisha did not skimp on his labor and would not free us as long as there was any sunlight coming in from the windows. We found pretexts. Someone would slowly steal out and cover the window slowly with his coat, as we inside would begin to say that it is getting dark, and shortly the time of Maariv would arrive. The trick worked and we were freed about a quarter of an hour before dismissal time. Later that night our fathers would punish us, for Rabbi Lisha made certain to find them all in the Beis Midrashes or Shtibels and to complain to them about the neglect of Torah that we had caused. It is evident that Rabbi Lisha did not cheat on his work. He was one of the better teachers who knew how to explain a page of Talmud appropriately. As opposed to the other teachers, he rarely had to resort to other methods, such as stories about the wonders and signs of the angels and Tzadikim, etc. One should not deduce from here that we knew no time of relaxation in this cheder. On the contrary, we had times of relaxation in the spirit of mitzvah. Rabbi Lisha's side trade was as a cantor – in our Beis Midrash, the "Frosten Beis Midrash", during the year and on the High Holy Days in the neighboring villages. He was part of the clergy of our city, and he would participate in most of the weddings, circumcisions, and other joyous occasions. He would recite some of the blessings, and receive an honorable stipend for his services. These "joyous occasions of mitzvahs" were indeed fitting of their name, for they would make use students happy, in that they were the only time off that we would have. These occasions improved the lot of those among us (such as Archi Brik, Moshe Shochet, Shlomo Kalb and others) who already wore a long black cloak and hat. For the Rebbi would always choose those boys to accompany him to the joyous occasion. He did not neglect the rest of us completely. The Rebbi would take council with Benno, the son of a well-to-do merchant, in financial matters. He would return from the festivities hastily, and without changing from his festive clothes, he would immediately pick up the lesson and make up what we missed during his absence. Since his sense of hearing was exceptional, and he would hear every word that we uttered, he would simultaneously feel his pockets and count his "honorarium" item by item. He was not able to always make out the value of the paper money, so he had to quietly take council with his "faithful" one and ask. If the amount of the bill was large, our Rebbi would quickly hide the bill, apparently out of fear of the evil eye, and also to protect it from the eyes of his wife Perla, for she was always led to believe that her husband earned his livelihood with difficulty. She would work hard always until a late hour of the night, sewing and plucking feathers in order to earn some money to make up the shortfall. Perla certainly was not lazy in her husband's home. She should be remembered for good, for she looked after her house well and it was always tidy, even though the entire house was one room. This room included our cheder. When we got older we read "The Miser" by Moliere, and we saw in it a picture of our Rebbi, stooped over the chest that nobody else would touch. In our childhood imagination, it was filled with treasures. We felt sorry for Perla and her difficult lot. In any case, these memories certainly do not affect the feelings of respect and reverence that we had for our blind Rebbi, Rabbi Lisha of blessed memory.

After we finished the cheder of Rabbi Lisha, we moved on to study Talmud and commentaries with Reb Yosef Parker and with the "teacher of Przeworsk". With this transition, most of our antics ceased. for we were now "Gemara youths" (ten years old!), and these types of antics were no longer appropriate for us. Furthermore, these new cheders were not the same as the previous ones. Our first Rebbis were natural teachers; however Reb Yosef Parker was actually a merchant of fowl and eggs. Since he was a small-scale merchant and a great scholar, he opened up a cheder, and the teaching fees were a supplement to his income. Therefore, he chose a small number of students from well to do homes (the Siedliskers, Shaul Taffet, Avraham Kanner, Shlomo Fischler, Chaim Schneps and others). Some were intelligent and diligent, and others were such that their fathers "were able to permit themselves" that their sons be considered among the intelligent and diligent ones. Along with myself, Itzu and Ansheli Taub of the new city studied with me. I would go to their house every morning, so that we could walk together to the old city, to the cheder, which was some distance from our homes. It was not easy at all to awaken Itzu from beneath his warm blankets at 5:00 a.m. (Incidentally, even at such an early hour in the morning, I was overtaken by jealousy: their blankets were of excellent quality - in our home we had no similar blankets – they were colored and inscribed with the inscription: "Good Morning". There were also many coins in the blankets, as a good omen for riches.) Then, at that time when even the early morning risers were not up yet, we set out toward the old city. Even though we walked together as a threesome and attempted to portray ourselves as brave and strong, we were greatly afraid along the route. This was particularly due to a tall priest, dressed in black, who would be walking from the rectory to the monastery for the morning prayers, and he was reciting his prayers along the way. At such an early hour, with deep darkness still pervading, he would seem to us as someone of unsound mind muttering to himself. We used all of the good omens, we circled out buttons, we exposed our fringes, we recited three times the verse "you shall surely consider it an abomination" [26], and we spat perhaps nine times. Mainly, we began to run as we made an arc around "the statue of the saints" in front of the courthouse, for even it appeared to us at that hour to be waving toward us and threatening us with its raised hand. We were very happy when we arrived at the cheder. These encounters with the powers of "impurity" during the early morning were very unpleasant to us, and we attempted to forget these events by immersing ourselves in a page of holy Talmud. Our Rebbi helped us greatly in this, for he would leave the study of Tosafot [27] for the early hours of the morning "when the mind is still clear". With his explanations, he often succeeded in arousing joy in us when we would be able to master a certain difficult Tosafot, and this would help us forget about the world at large. The lessons with Reb Yosef Parker were very focused, and they were lacking entirely in stories and other time wasters. The few antics which we permitted ourselves at that time did not take place within the walls of the cheder. They took place outside of the field of vision of our Rebbi. I only remember two of these types of antics: the "battles" between the "czarkses" and the "boszniaks", that is to say between those from the new city and those from the old city. How did these "battles" take place? In general, we got along in a brotherly and friendly manner, and right now, I cannot think of any reason that caused the contention. Nevertheless, this type of battle broke out on occasion, and we "the czarkses" who were the smaller group were always on the losing side. I only remember celebrating "victory" once. This was as we were being hotly pursued through light mud in one of the well-known marshy areas of our town which was called "a roshtshine", and Shlomo Fishchler fell down flat on his whole body. This fall ended the battle. The boszniaks not only stopped chasing us, but they also called us back to help their "commander" clean himself up. Our friend Shlomo at that time needed a great deal of help and words of comfort. We cleaned him up and comforted him. Only one of us did not lift a finger to help and did not offer any words of comfort – this was Itzu, of course, who spent the entire time stifling his laughter at seeing our friends "dressed up". Seeing the "commander" in this type of situation could only cause one to laugh or cry. Itzu laughed.

We put on performances in the attic of the home of Shaul Taffet. The admission fee to the first row was two buttons, and to the second row, one button. Whoever purchased one ticket was allowed to bring his younger brother. We prepared the performance a short time before the first members of the audience arrived. The costumes were prepared very hastily, and they were very simple: we turned our coats, hats, or lining inside out, and wore the visors of our caps facing the back of our necks. We were "robbers" from our earliest youth. The show ended in discord, and the victor would lie prone on top of the victim. The screen would then drop, and everything would be okay. Entry to and exit from the "theater" were a big problem – at least for the writer of these lines. This was the way we entered: from the back of the Taffet house, we would climb up and reach a small shaky roof. On it there would be standing, miraculously actually, a ladder from which we would go up to the attic. Why should I lie? I trembled as a lulav as I entered and left. If everything went peacefully, it was only because "G-d protects the foolhardy" [28]. When the era of our studies with Reb Yosef Parker ended, the era of the "theater" in the attic of Reb Efraim Taffet also ended.

With our Rabbi Yosef Parker, the roles of householder, merchant and teacher were all rolled together in one personality. On the other hand, with Rabbi Blaustein, who was known as the Przeworsker teacher, the role of "children's teacher" was not prominent in his personality. His externals exuded honor and the etiquette of an important householder. The learning with him, which consisted of Talmud, Tosafot, and the commentaries of the Maharsha, was completely learning for its own sake, and the only breaks were the moments when the Rabbi prepared for himself a half a cigarette. He did this with a sense of importance, as if he was offering incense. In his presence, we did not even wink with our eyelashes. We did not misbehave, for the entire surroundings exuded seriousness and refinement. The natural and necessary diversions for children of that age were satisfied by the rabbi himself, as he interspersed the learning with stories from the lives of our sages, rabbinical legends relevant to the time of the year or even – especially during the months of Elul – the study of the melodies of prayer. This was in a tune slightly different than we were used to, but it was very pleasant, as our rabbi used to serve as a prayer leader on the High Holy Days in one of the small neighboring communities. Once, after returned home after the festival, he caught a cold on the journey that developed into a serious case of pneumonia. He died suddenly. His death deeply saddened us, for we honored and loved our "Przeworsker teacher". Until this day I see it as a great thing that I merited to be among those who participated in his burial.

If the two latter cheders were different in style from the first ones, the cheder of Reb Hirsch David was completely different than all the rest. The mouths of the various detractors and maligners of the "cheder" in the Diaspora in general would be immediately shut if they had only seen this cheder. It was literally the Garden of Eden: it had many fruit tries, a large vegetable field and at the edge a flowing stream. There were goats that we could care for during our free time, and the warm goat milk improved our health. The study itself took place in the summer under the open sky in the shade of thick trees. The content included a great deal of bible with the commentary of the Malbim, Ein Yaakov [29], grammar and a bit of Hebrew. When we came into the cheder of Reb Hirsch David he was already elderly.

The hair of his face and his peyos were already white as snow, and his eyesight was quite weak. He would bring the book he was reading from close to his left eye and read diagonally. It was always a wonder to us how even with his myopia he was able to discern all of our mischief, and with a heavy punch from three fingers (his thumb and pointer finger were always holding a pinch of snuff) he was able to immediately return us to the good path. Despite his advanced age, he was healthy, he had an erect posture, and he was wide boned. His appearance was more like a large-scale farm owner than a teacher of children. In terms of his character traits, he was pleasant, perhaps slightly proud, and extremely knowledgeable. For who in our town could compare to him with regard to the knowledge of the Hebrew language and grammar? He particularly had a great understanding of the liturgical poetry, those prayers that we knew how to chant but were difficult to understand. Without any doubt, Reb Hirsch was the first to awaken within us an interest in the Hebrew language, which we later supplemented with "courses in culture", which we were only able to take with much tribulation.

Why were there tribulations? In the meantime, new things were happening in the city. Several important householders (Reb Hirsch Taub, Reb Yisrael Chaim Schiff, Reuveli Naftalczes and others) founded the "Talmud Torah Organization" headed by a principal, who was from outside the city. (He looked a bit like Chanan from "The Dybbuk".) He was a great scholar and also a zealot. He knew how to gather around him other zealots, such as Mendele Reich, and was able to act as a buffer against the group of "apostates", which was also founded at that time. This group sponsored "Tarbut" courses in the Hebrew language under the direction of our honorable teacher Mr. Avraham Weinberg, who lives today with us in Israel. The means of battle were variegated. There would be public gatherings in the Great Synagogue where Rabbi Shmuel of holy blessed memory would deliver a lecture warning about the dangers lurking in the educating of the young generation. In his lecture, he would compare us, the orthodox children for whom the dangers of the "Hebrew School" were lurking, to a young sapling that was liable to become bent over as long as it was still small. His voice, saturated in anguish, apparently moved the hearts of his listeners, for his words were accompanied by sighs, which came primarily from the women's section. In the Beis Midrashes they attempted to prevent those fathers whose children went to the Tarbut courses from serving as prayer leaders on the days that they observed yahrzeit [30], or from being called to the Torah. These types of activities were accompanied by disputes and mutual accusations in matters of spirituality and business. The main sanction, which was also suffered by this writer, was being banned from the Talmud Torah. On one occasion, the powerful trustees of the Talmud Torah were forced to give in. One of them threatened Shulek Morgenlender (my brother Shimon, who headed at that time the "Jugend" organization, drafted him into the "battleground") by threatening him that he would publicly expose the deeds that he did when he served in the Austrian army. Reb Yisrael Chaim Schiff was overwhelmed by the warnings and threats from his wife that she would not permit him to enter the threshold of his house unless he would not stop acting as "G-d's policeman". (My mother of blessed memory drafted Malka Schiff, even though she was not at all happy with the "Hebrew School". However, she was quite perplexed: How could it be that they would expel her son from the Talmud Torah? Such a thing cannot take place!) Therefore, I was allowed back in to the Talmud Torah. However at the end of the semester, I and some of my friends wanted to study in the spacious and illuminated cheder, upon whose walls there were pictures of animals, plants, fruit, workers, and various work tools. We wished to study from an illustrated book ("Sfateinu", volume I). Jampi was the new teacher. He had an enthusiastic smile and a unique expression which rung in my ears like a constant refrain. He was a teacher who, immediately upon arriving to our city, attracted a group around him who never heard a word in any language from him other than Hebrew. (When I heard for the first time, after many years, his vivacious Yiddish, his honor increased even more in my eyes. Only then did I understand the unusual success of Mr. Weinberg in instilling the Hebrew language to members of our city.) Thus, we were distanced from the Talmud Torah and our studies in cheder terminated. However the blessed memories of our rabbis is still with us. May their souls be bound in the bonds of everlasting life.

{Hebrew text – pp 133-137}

C. In School and Gymnasia

Our parents were all true to their Jewish faith; however the vast majority of them educated their children with a mixed education. That is to say, Torah along with the ways of the world (or as they would say in their language "for G-d and for the people"). With the exception of the children of the rabbi, the rabbinical judge, and a small number of "children of holy people", we split our days between the cheder and the schools. (It was not an equal division, for the early morning hours, the entire afternoon, winter evenings, and of course the entire day on Sundays and gentile festivals were dedicated to the cheder.

I remember very well the first days of September 1916 when I was in grade 1 in the public school under the direction of Pietraszewski. The teacher was a young woman by the name of Brobolkowa, who had a wonderful ruler. Her "laps", that is to say her whippings on the palm of the hand with the ruler, in particular on frozen hands in the winter, had their intended effect. Since there were no desks – the war was still at its height, and the town had been pillaged and partly destroyed – we sat on the floor in an unheated room. In sub-freezing temperatures we studied reading, writing, the Polish language, arithmetic, etc. We did not suffer too much from the cold, since we sat crowded together. The hunger did affect us greatly. We finished the paltry ration of bread during the first recess. From then, we waited for the conclusion of our studies and for lunch. As time went on, the conditions of the school improved, and even the food situation at home improved significantly. However, we Jewish children did not know anything about comfort, and certainly nothing of the joy of childhood during all of our time at the public school. The reasons for this were many and variegated. One of them was the Polish language. To be more precise: the proper and appropriate pronunciation of this language. Most of us had difficulty with this, and this caused us punishments and embarrassment over the course of the years. Our gentile classmates accompanied our reading and stories with much laughter and thereby humiliated us. Every time we would mix up the 'sh' with 'z', the 'rz' with the 'zs', when we would read 'zymno' instead of 'zimno', 'ziemia' as 'zemia', or 'snieg' as 'szneg', there would be rejoicing among the gentiles and sorrow weeping among us. Our faces were yellowed like the bottom of a pot, and if only the ground would have opened below us we would have jumped in.

This was the first tribulation [31] that the exile injected into our warm souls. After some time, at the time of the establishment of independent Poland (or as our unforgettable friend Aharon Sapir would say: "okad Polska wybuchla" – "from the time that Poland broke forth") and the beginning of the hooliganism of the Hallercziks who cut off the peyos and beards of Jews and threw Jews off of moving trains, we children realized that what was happening to our parents should be a sign for us. Our school friends added physical violence to their antics of humiliation. This began with "light" mischief, such as pulling the peyos, cutting our tzitzit (ritual fringes) and inserting pork into our mouths, and moved on to more severe mischief that included beatings. The situation reached the point where no Jewish student would remain in the schoolyard during recess. With the sound of the bell, we would be the first to leave the classroom. (Our "educators", who were themselves not known for their love of the Jewish people, would seat the Jews in the rearmost desks, close to the door.) We fled for our lives to an area outside of the schoolyard. There, for the most part, rather than playing games, we discussed our tribulations and attempted to figure out means to foil our oppressors. For some reason, one "decision" is etched in my memory: To choose a delegation who would present themselves before the "Pan Direktor" (Mr. Principal) and request that we Jews be exempted from the study of Polish history. For what do we have to do – we claimed – with Mieszko or Boleslaw Chrobry? We have to know who King David and King Solomon are, and not Stefan Batory! If he were to ask us: "Fine, but what does 'the study of history' have to do with 'troublemakers'?", we would answer with a question: "And what do 'beatings' have to do with 'Polish independence'?". It appeared that in our subconscious, we objected to anything Polish. We never appointed this delegation. Salvation came to us from another source – to our good fortune, that year, among the older students, there were a few brave boys who knew how to pay back a double portion. These included Moshe Goldblatt, Melech Schuss, "the black Josef" and others. These friends of ours went with our older brothers and organized an "independent defense league" within the school. From that time, anyone who passed by the "impure place" in the afternoons after the conclusion of classes would witness a battle between the "shkotzim" and us. [32] Only our "beloved" teachers, Berger, Klamot, Skywa, Leszniakowa, Woroba and others did not notice and "did not see" what was taking place under their noses. At first, we used fists and belts with buckles, and mainly stones. However when the "shkotzim" threatened us with "mass death" on the day of the distribution of report cards, our strong friends armed themselves with boxing gloves and passed judgement upon those who started up. From that day and onwards, it was sufficient to threaten a "sheketz" with the warning that we would call "Mielacha" or "Goldblata", and he would back off immediately.

Thus passed our first years in the gentile school. We suffered greatly there, especially during times of increased Jew-hatred in the country, such as during the war between Poland and the Bolsheviks in 1920. We felt the effects physically, but when the ill winds abated, we also had a reprieve, and we forgot about the tribulations. We played our games (buttons, "Eretz", etc.). We enjoyed ourselves, wasted time, and were not always careful with the honor of our friends. One serious incident of a prank, which even had a trace of desecration of the name of G-d [33], is etched in my memory to this day. This took place with Moshe Shtimler, the son of Reb Tovia Shochet (the ritual slaughterer). This "Moshe Shochet" was a pious boy, quiet and good hearted, who would not even hurt a fly on the wall. It was obvious that only the decree of the government brought him into a gentile school where there were crosses and idols of "their messiah" decorating the rooms. Obviously, he was numbered among the few of us who wore a skullcap (yarmulke) while sitting in the classroom. The "shkotzim" tugged at his long curly peyos dozens of times during the day. They would knock down his yarmulke, and he would not react at all. (Shlomo Fischler also wore a kippa in class, however, he answered every incident with a stream of invective: "Ty psiakrew azeby cie jasna cholera wziela". [34]) The class opened with song, and Kalmut called upon Moszez Shtimler in a festive voice to ask whether he had cleaned off the feathers from his yarmulke, as had been ordered in the previous lesson. Moshe "Shochet" arose perplexed, for he did not immediately understand the Polish request. However at that moment, one of the brats from among us came to his assistance and whispered to him that the teacher wishes that he sing "Deror Yikra" [35]. He of course wanted to fulfil the "command of the teacher", and Moshe broke out in song, as we Jews burst out in laughter. A few years later, poor Moshe perished in a typhus epidemic. Our laughter was replaced with bitter weeping due to our great distress and embarrassment. Since the death of the righteous atones, we hoped that Moshe would have forgiven us for our disgusting prank, for we did not know what we were doing.

Among the "diversions" that we enjoyed in the oppressive atmosphere that pervaded in the gentile school, we must include the reactions of Shlomo Fischler, Avraham Siedlisker (the son of Reb Leib) and others during the time of the recital of the "pacierz" (prayers). These cordial people accompanied the prayers of the gentiles with their own ditties, such as "Yossel Pandri and the Aunt Miriam" [36]. For them, this was a chance to take private revenge against the defilement of their souls, and we who listened had to make great efforts to keep from bursting out in laughter, for this moment of "desecration of holiness" was fraught with danger. However, the verse "G-d protects the foolhardy" was fulfilled for us.

Such were our diversions in the public school. What about in the gymnasia? A few of us transferred to the gymnasia after grade four in the public school. When my sister Estshe of blessed memory brought up the idea in our home to transfer me to the gymnasia; the reaction was as if this was a suggestion to remove me from my religion. There is no wonder in this matter: my mother of blessed memory, who was the daughter of pious Hassidim, was always very proud of her name that was given to her by the Tzadik of Tzanz himself, and of the fact that her father (grandfather Reb Moshe Asher Padwar of blessed memory) used to lead the morning services on the High Holy Days in the courtyard of the children of the Divrei Chayim, could not imagine that her dear son would have to attend gymnasia on Sabbaths. However with the passage of time, by seeing others follow in that path, and the intercession of various people (especially my brother Shimon in America, who supported my parents financially, and as the person who had the money, he also had the say), and finally a solemn promise that I made to my grandfather as he was lying on his sickbed that I would not, Heaven forbid, violate the Sabbaths – all of these together had their influence, and after two years, succeeded in silencing the opposition of my mother. Her silence was a form of approval. Thus, I entered "at a good and propitious time" the third grade of the gymnasia. I should mention here for the good Manka Tewel of the seventh grade. She was a competent young woman, and all of her "private" students succeeded in their entry exams, with the condition that they would agree to receive private lessons in the natural sciences from Zaworski. This teacher knew how to make his profession into a moneymaking activity. Nevertheless, to his credit, it should be said that he knew how to teach quite well. His lessons were very interesting and engaging. This dedication trapped me up on one occasion, even before I was officially a student. I will not forget this until they shovel earth over my grave. The situation was as follows: Zaworski decided to include me in an educational excursion for grade two on one Sabbath afternoon. His intention was certainly positive. Could that gentile have imagined what problems such an invitation would have for me? I decided to hesitate and attempt to get out of it by claiming that it was the Sabbath today, and I could not carry either a pen or a spade [37], I could not write or cut. However it was all for naught. He did not request that I cut or write, just that I listen and learn. Having no other choice, I appeared at the appointed time in the yard in front of the gymnasia, dressed in my Sabbath clothes but with a subdued spirit (father and mother of course did not know anything about this). I recognized a few of the gathered students from the public school, however they all acted strange toward me and were wondering: Why is this mourner among the bridegrooms? Only when one of our Jewish brethren made it known that I was a student of Zaworski did my honor suddenly rise in their eyes. They began to converse with me, for they were all deathly afraid of him. It was only my Jewishness that prevented me from being put, G-d forbid, in the first row. However, as the Poles say "co ma wisiec nie utonie" ("who is to be hung will not sink"). Even though I attempted to remain inconspicuous and lower than the grass as we marched along the main street singing songs, Pinchas Wolf ("Tshop") noticed me as he was walking at that time to recite "Perek" [38]. He began to shout: "Oh, oh, there we have Yidel Chinkeles, going out on the Sabbath to the field with shkotzim!" He concluded with a curse: "Behold, look what you have become, a sheketz!" What shall I say. My eyes darkened. From that moment, I no longer recognized my soul. Of course, the matter was spread very quickly in the Beis Midrash of the Hassidim and in the Shtibel. When I arrived home, I was welcomed with "a warm welcome". My mother shouted at me: "I have no need for a student!", "the entire town will be talking about me!", and other strong words. It was no wonder that on the first Sabbath that I went to the gymnasia, my good mother did not leave me any lunch. And what a "Sabbath" that was! It was "Shabbat Chazon", that was actually Tisha Beov, an appropriate festival for that Sabbath [39]. This was the first time that I recited the Sabbath prayers early in the morning, and by myself. I hid my books under my coat, crept out of the house as if I was a thief, and went on a roundabout route, through the "Reitszal", to the gymnasia so that nobody would see me. However, as if to incite me, wherever I went there were people that I recognized. It seemed as if that all of the people of the town had gathered together, so to speak: the men: some going to the mikva (ritual bath) and others returning; the women: some going to get the coffee from the oven and others returning with full bottles of coffee in their arms. "The hat was burning on top of the thief". It seemed to me as if they all knew where I was headed and that there were gymnasia books hidden under my clothes. In short, I tasted "the taste of gehinnom (hell)" on those first Sabbaths due to my desire to study in our gentile gymnasia. I "did not lick honey" during my years of study there. The difference was that in the first weeks of my study, the reason for my suffering was "the voice of Jacob", the words of reproof from the faithful Jews; and during my six years of study the problem was with Esau, who embittered my life and the lives of many of my fellow Jews who studied in that institution.

When I began my studies in the gymnasia in September 1922, there were about 80 Jews there. The number of boys and girls was approximately equal. They constituted 12% of the student body. Each year, the number of Jewish students dwindled. In my final year of study in 1929, there remained only about 30 students, including seven girls, which consisted of 7% of the student body. That is to say that during those six years alone, the number of Jews studying dropped by 50%. It is clear that we should not look for the reason for this drop in the unwillingness of our townsfolk to acquire a secondary education, but rather in the open hatred of Jews that was exhibited by several of the teachers of that institution. For many of us, the study in the gymnasia turned into a veritable nightmare. As an illustration, I will mention only two or three points: every year a few of us, especially from among the assimilationist families, excelled in the class (Oestern, Schneider, Nichtheizer, and also Dora Mahler, Srulek Tewel, Mania and Munek Gruenspan, Naftali Tennenbaum, and others). They accounted for approximately 12 % (!) of those that excelled in the school. However in the year 1924-1925, there was only one Jew (Oestern) among those that excelled, that is to say .5 % (!); indeed several of us remained in the class, and no fewer than eighteen of us took our matriculation exams. You might say: "perhaps this is a coincidence. This was no coincidence at all. The national day of Grawowski and the civic day of spoldzielczosc (the cooperative movement), days that hatred was expressed against our parents and us, were still echoing in the venomous words of our teachers Kita and Staron. They lectured at the end of the study year about the topic of spoldzielczosc and instilled in the minds of their pupils that the spoldzielczosc would redeem the nation from poverty, free it from parasitical middlemen and help the national economy. Our motto had to be: swoj do swego po swoje (one goes to one of his kind for things of his kind.). In the mornings, our teachers would lecture well, and in the afternoons, during the grading sessions, they would fulfill their words. Therefore, suddenly our light dwindled and even the best of us were considered to be poor students. That year, the drop in grades became so drastic that even the excellent students (such as Mania G., Rivcha Perel and others) were forced to leave the institution at the threshold of the eighth grade, and go to Tarnow or Krakow in order to finish their course of studies.

That year, there was an open outbreak of anti-Semitism. Indeed, our teachers never pampered us during all of our years there. In the first year, Rusinek made our lives difficult by mocking our Polish. In the second year, Piotrowski took his place. Only the One in Heaven and another few of us on earth knew how we were saved from his claws. In the next day, we were afflicted by Kita. He tormented us, may G-d have mercy. Each Sabbath we were called up first to the blackboard, deliberately and not according to the customary order (there were two of us in the class, Shaul Taffet and myself, who did not write on the Sabbath). After we told him each time briefly that we do not write on the Sabbath, he launched into a long and bitter lecture. He paced strongly with his shiny boots all around the classroom, staring upward as if he was standing in prayer, as his continued his lecture. What fault did he not find in us? As my mother would say: "every possibly evil is occurring". Every possible bad trait... "We live on Polish land, we eat Polish bread, but we do not follow Polish customs Is it possible to ask for special privileges for ourselves?! Here you are, you have new privileged citizens, oh Poland! The young descendents of Moses!", and more and more. Words like an overflowing spring, without stop. And as one stands and listens to all this, one feels as if his flesh is being cut by a knife. The shkotzim were deriving great enjoyment.

This took place Sabbath after Sabbath, innumerable times. If there was not enough pain and agony, we were immediately embarrassed further with the desecration of G-d's name, for the third Jew in the class was called up to the board, and he went up, wrote, and was successful.

There was a great deal of pain, bitterness, embarrassment and setbacks, which dampened our spirits significantly and drained the joy out of our youthful days. However the feeling of a nightmare was mainly caused by the stifling social environment that we found ourselves in for all the time we were in the gymnasia. I am referring to those among us who were active in the Zionist groups. We who were full of youthful enthusiasm for free nationalistic activity and all that that entails had to live during the 1920s in a social "bunker". In the eyes of the authorities in general and the leaders and teachers of the gymnasia in particular, Zionist activity was identified with Bolshevism. We were strictly forbidden to join any Zionist group in town. Anyone who would transgress this would be expelled from the school, which was the only one of its kind in town. We, who understood the lie of identifying Zionism with communism, did not accept this. We secretly belonged to various Zionist movements, and put as much effort as we could into them. This was not a simple matter. The town was small, and with every footstep one would run into some professor or colleague from the class. Our "house of life", the Hebrew school itself where all the various Zionist groups, Hanoar Hatzioni, Hashomer Hadati, Gordonia and others were crowded together, was right next to the Bursa, the area where Kotpys, the director of the gymnasia, lived, as well as dozens of other students who knew each of us personally. Perhaps one would be leaving the building together with a group of boys and girls who were not students, immersed in a lively conversation about Zionism and socialism, Herzl and Gordon, Borochov and Karl Marx, the Keren Kayemet or Fund for the Land of Israel, all, of course in a loud voice as befits Jewish people; and suddenly the warning would be shouted out "Staron!" or "Rusinek!". You would quickly attempt to separate from the group and to flee with your neck facing downward, as a chicken whose cock-a-doodle-do has been stifled, as you fled from the "evil visitation". In truth, it is not clear to me to this day if these "angels of destruction" who met us under suspicious circumstances dozens of times, really did not know of our activities, or on the other hand, knew of our activities but were loathe to take action against these young Jews alone. I suspect the second possibility. Indeed, they did not lay hand upon us, however there were many times were we were almost hurt by them. I will tell of two incidents that took place to me and two of my friends. This first incident took place with me along with my friend Aharon Sapir of blessed memory (a wonderful boy whom I pine for as I often remember him. I loved him dearly on account of his good heart, his pleasant ways, and sense of humor.0). Once we made the rounds in town to empty the Keren Kayemet (Jewish National Fund) boxes. We were both dressed as usual in our student uniforms, with our four cornered hats on our heads. That is to say, there was no room here for error. We arrived at the Street of the Train, to the home of Mrs. Reich. We knocked at the door two or three times. There was no answer. We attempted to open the door. It opened and we found ourselves in the spacious kitchen in which there were no people. We heard some whispers from the parlor. Aharon began his usual routine, speaking with various voices in Yiddish and calling into the room "come already". In order to put an end to his pranks, for it was difficult for me to refrain from laughter, I knocked loudly on the kitchen door. The voice of Mrs. Reich was heard from the salon asking, in Polish of course, "who is here"? Aharon answered in his clear voice "we are from the Zydowski Fundusz Nardowy (Jewish National Fund)!" At that moment, the mistress of the house opened up the door of the parlor widely in order to give her donation, and who did we see sitting on the sofa? Our dear Piotrowski. What can I add? We literally froze like stones. To our good fortune, the door closed slowly, and after we regained our composure a bit we began to make motions and hints as if Heaven forbid our clothes had caught on fire. Mrs. Reich was quite astute, and she immediately realized what was going on. She raised her voice intentionally and turned to some sort of imaginary third person who was, so to speak in the kitchen, saying to him: "Please sir (in the singular!) register me for two gold coins!". After a brief pause, as if she only had only just then noticed us, she turned to us with a heartwarming voice, as if she was greeting dear guests who frequent her house: "And as for you, young men, you are surely here to see my son? He is not home now. Perhaps you wish to wait for him?". With great difficulty, Aharon mumbled: "No thank you, we will return later this evening.". We both left quickly as if fleeing from a snake. Not only was her box not emptied that month, but no other boxes on the Street of the Train were emptied that time, for we left there as quickly as if fleeing from an earthquake. At that time, we deliberated over one question only: did he see us or not? Thank G-d, there were no consequences to this "pleasant" encounter, and perhaps the merit of Mrs. Reich was the cause of this.

Shmuel Sommer, one of the founders of Hanoar Hatzioni

The second incident took place literally at the threshold of liberty. During one of the written matriculation exams, Buszko, the secretary of the gymnasia approached and whispered in my ear that I must present myself at three in the afternoon before the directors of the gymnasia. My good friend Shmuel Sommer of blessed memory received the same notice. (Incidentally, my connections with Shmuel went beyond the normal relations that we would have had as being fellow natives of the town; our connection became stronger when we left the city, when we studied together with Reb Yerucham Kriger of blessed memory, and later at the Hildesheimer Boy's School in Berlin. Shmuel eventually studied dentistry, and was a very successful dentist in our city. This success expressed a fundamental element of his personality – every endeavor that he undertook he did with whole heartedness and dedication. His enthusiasm in his work for the Zionist idea is remembered by all of us. It is too bad, too bad, that he did not merit seeing the realization). Of course, we attempted to figure out the reason for this strange invitation, but to no avail. When 3:00 p.m. arrived, Shmuel was ushered alone in to the principal's office, and some suspicions arose in my heart. Shmuel spent some time in there, and when the door opened again, the secretary stood there and gave me the sign to enter, in such a way that I did not even have a chance to exchange a glance with my friend who was exiting. As I entered, to my great surprise in addition to the principal I saw there our teacher Piotrowski, who fulfilled the role as registrar, and Staron, who conducted the interrogation. After I gave the customary bow and stood at attention, pale as whitewash, I was requested by Staron to tell about my activities in the "Communist organization". I should point out that I was very slightly relieved. An accusation of Communism was easier to deal with than an accusation of Zionism. I thought that an accusation of Communism was only some sort of "libel" and it would be easy to push it off. I opened my eyes wide in astonishment, and strongly denied any connection to the matter. In order to strengthen my claims, I tried to gain assistance from the testimony from the "Priest Principal" himself who would often see me in the mornings returning from the synagogue with my tefillin bag under my arm. I asked: "What would a Communist be doing in the synagogue?". Father Kotpys then started to talk and said to me: "An ox like you Psziakraw" – this was an adage he often used – I myself saw you innumerable times standing on the steps of the Hebrew School with Sommer and other young Jews!" I had a prepared answer to this claim: "We came there to see our mutual friend Yisrael Tewel". I felt that my explanation did not convince him very much. During the entire time of the interrogation, Staron tried to trick me by claiming that Shmuel had admitted to everything. I knew, obviously, that this was a lie, and I stood by my original claim that I did not know "either from an interpretation or from a dream" anything about the matter. Then the cat was let out of the bag: Piotrowski presented me with a folio, written on two sides. On the first side, there was the large seal of the Regional Education Office of Krakow. He told me to read what was written.

The first thought that I had was that the handwriting was very familiar to me. It was a letter of slander to the regional education offices stating that despite the numerous rebukes from the directors of the local gymnasia, the two above mentioned students continue with their Communist and anti-government activities. This document eased significantly my job of defending myself. I explained that, according to my estimation (I knew this as a definite fact), this was a slandered document produced by a boy who was jealous of us, and therefore accused us of this deed in order to make us fail the matriculation exams. I added: "indeed, here there is also slander about the leaders of the gymnasia to the regional offices, in that they were derelict in their duties. In order for the directors of the gymnasia to clear their own names, and to prove to the regional offices that there was no basis to these accusations, they should turn the entire matter over to a police investigation." My intention was, first of all, to bide for time so that we could complete our exams and be freed from the authority of the gymnasia. I was sure that we would easily be able to prove to the police that we were simply two boys in a Zionist youth movement; a fact that we were not able to even mention to our teachers who were interrogating us. To them, as I have already noted, the Communist organization and Zionist youth groups were one and the same. I don't know if we convinced our teachers with our explanations. As Shmuel explained to me later, he also denied everything. I do know that on the very same evening, the intercession of Dr. Sandhaus and Reb Yochanan Sommer of blessed memory succeeded in clearing us in the eyes of our investigators. The investigation was indeed turned over to the police, and eventually took place. In the meantime, we both finished our matriculation exams along with thirteen other graduates. We breathed a sigh of relief and made a celebration when we left in peace and were finally freed from our "beloved" gymnasia, which was housed in a large and imposing building, open and full of air. Only we, the Jewish-Zionist students, felt stifled there.

{Page 137}

From My Memories

Edna Perelberg

As a native of Dembitz, and having lived there for half of my life, I wish to describe here a bit about the life of the youth in our town.

I was born at the end of the First World War, and there are only a few events that I remember from my earliest childhood. I can still see before my eyes my family's home in the old city behind the bridge. The houses were one story high, and the alleys were narrow and not particularly clean. Transport wagons passed through the main street daily, bringing provisions from the nearby villages to the residents of the city. Children of all ages, with schoolbags on their shoulders, would pass by our store on the main street every morning and afternoon. Our store was not far from the public school, where at that time boys and girls learned in separate buildings. The new church with its tall spire was across from our house, and I can still hear in my ears the clear and strong ringing of the bells during the mornings of the month of May, when the religious Christians would pray early in the mornings and in the evenings. These prayers, which were accompanied by singing and the playing of the organ, mingled with the chirping of the birds and the ringing of the bells in a wondrous harmony instilled in me, even as a young girl, a longing for our homeland, the Land of Israel, which was so far away yet near to the heart. This was the unknown but longed for homeland from my earliest youth.

Near our house, there was a large field colored with wild flowers of various types. This was my favorite place to play. There, among the wild flowers and golden stalks of wheat, I silently expressed my pain, the pain of a Jewish girl in an alien place, downtrodden and persecuted, only because she was a Jewish girl.

These experiences, which were common among the Jewish girls in the town, were what later fed the youth movements, which set us along the path to adulthood.

The Jewish youth in Dembitz was for the most part organized into Zionist organizations, even though there were some who belong to the other streams which were common in Polish Jewry. Along with the general Zionist youth organizations, Gordonia, the right leaning and left leaning Poale Zion, there was also Agudas Yisrael, the Bund, and the underground Communist youth. The strongest movement was "Hanoar Hatzioni". Many of its members knew not only how to lecture well, but also how to make things happen. They left the comfortable homes of their parents and made aliya to the Land to live a life of toil and freedom. I received the direction of my soul from these people in my youth. They taught me to respect a life of toil and freedom, to walk among the gentiles with a high head and not to submit to oppression.

I remember the parade of the 3rd of May, the national holiday of the Poles, which was organized with great festivity during the time of the rule of Pilsodski. We, the Jewish youth who still studied in the Polish public school, already belong to the Jewish Scouts organization. We wore our scouting costumes with great pride, held the blue and white national flag in our hands, and marched together with the Polish youth on the parade of the 3rd of May. I will never forget the joy of my friends who are no longer alive: Mina Schuldenfrei of blessed memory the daughter of Yoel, Reizel Polaner of blessed memory, Dincha Mahler of blessed memory from the watchmaker's store of the old city, Belka Siedlisker of blessed memory the daughter of Gedalia, Mina Lisha of blessed memory the daughter of Zisha, and Manka Balsam of blessed memory. They were so happy at the occasion: "See Etka how far we have come. We Jews are permitted to march with our national flag together with the Poles.". They added: "How good would it be if we could make aliya and be like them in our own homeland".

Indeed! This was the dream of each one of us. This was the prayer of each one of us. Thus did we dream, struggle, join together in pioneering work, go out for hachsharah (aliya preparations), and educate the young generation in the spirit of Zionism.

In my group, there were some girls whose names I still remember: Sala Chaim, Nyusha Siedlisker, Ruchcha Kokok, Chaitza Bronheim, Gusta Schuldenfrei, as well as others whose names have escaped my memory. All of them were three years younger than I was, but quite mature spiritually. How great was their suffering with respect to their poisoned relations with their Christian peers! As they were still attending school, they would come to me to pour out their bitterness before me and to find comfort in our activities. On Sabbath mornings, we would go out far from the city, in order to shake off our depression in the bosom of nature. We would longingly discuss the far away, beloved homeland. The hearts of the Jewish children beat in the sea of evil. I, their counselor, would try to describe for them, as well as my imagination could, images of the different, better world of the pioneers of our nation working with song flowing from their mouths. These discussions ended with singing and an enthusiastic dance of the hora. With great difficulty, we would leave the forest or the field, and return slowly, without any desire, to the gray reality.

We had times of happiness and peace on Saturday nights in the winter, when we would gather at the headquarters of our group for celebrations around the burning fireplace, as we sang song of the Land and told stories about the lives of the pioneers. We would forget about the world around us.

The atmosphere was one of unity and friendship. These celebrations would last until late in the night. Sometimes, Shulek Taffet would bring along his violin and play it, and Rivka Taub would accompany him in song. This was wonderful.

On Sabbath evenings, in particular during the winter when the snow would crunch under the feet of the pedestrians, we would leave the tables of our parents and hurry to our Tarbut School. There, all the participants of the courses would gather together, listen to the reading of chapters of Bible. Someone would then explain the passages, or we would enter into a lively discussion about one of the questions. Such a debate would go on for many hours. Thus did we become accustomed to using the Hebrew language. I remember the meaningful lectures of Pinchas Lander, who is now with us in Israel. I enjoyed them very much. I also recall the feelings that I had as I prepared my first lecture in Hebrew. How fortunate was I that I was able to express my thoughts in the language of my people.

Then the war of the Nazis came, which was terrible for all humankind. The cruel hand cut down a rich harvest from among our ranks, which had been filled with the joy of life and sublime goals. How many were burned in the furnaces of the death camps, how many were rounded up into concentration camps and died! Only a small number, including myself, were miraculously saved.

We merited to witness the establishment of the State of Israel. However those that died had no such reward. Let us at least remember them with love and appropriate respect.

Translator's Footnotes:
1. I.e. he did not wear the skullcap or hat worn by Orthodox Jews.
2. Various letters of the Hebrew alphabet along with their vowel sounds.
3. The musical cantillation of the scriptures.
4. Shlep meant to pull or tug, and when used as a nickname for a person, it meanssomeone who just drags along.
5. A derogatory Jewish term for the church.
6. This is a derivation from a verse in the book of Psalms (Psalm 119) – "Itistime to do something for G-d, for they have negated Your Torah". TheTalmudicinterpretation changes the ordering of the phrases to mean that "if it is atime to do something for G-d, you should negate the Torah" i.e. that therearetimes of extreme societal urgency that make it incumbent to temporarily negateparts of the Torah. In Jewish law, this

interpretation is to be used verycautiously, as it is fraught with obvious dangers.

7. Oy Vey (literally Oh! Woe!) is a well-known Yiddish expression of anguish. Lard, being from pig fat, is not kosher.

8. Rebbi here is the term used for the teacher.

9. The Hebrew word here is "Chad Gadya", a reference to the final songof theSeder ceremony, which lists a chain reaction of events, starting with a father purchasing a young goat, and progressing to the cat eating the goat, etc. (muchlike the nursery rhyme "This is the House that Jack built").

10. There is a custom of administering symbolic whippings on the afternoon of theeve of Yom Kippur, as a form of penance. This whipping would take place on theback – which explains the reference below that in the cheder, the whipping tookplace both above and below

11. The four cornered fringed garment worn as an undergarment.

12. Various exegetical quotes from the Torah portion of Vayechi, the last portionof Bereshit (Genesis), which is generally read in the middle of the winter.

13. A section of the Avinu Malkeinu prayer recited on fast days and during the tendays between Rosh Hashanah and Yom Kippur.

14. Asentirung has the connotation of 'military conscription' obviously referring to the difficulty of the exam

15. The Song of Songs is read in the synagogue during Passover.

16. The Seder ceremony is divided into fifteen sections, the first two being Kadesh (reciting the Kiddush – the prayer over wine inaugurating the festival), and Urchatz (washing the hands). Kittel is a white cloak worn during the Seder andon the High Holy Days. Matzo shmurah (literally 'guarded matzo') is baked with special halachic stringencies, and is meant to be used specifically for the Seder, although extremely pious people will   use it throughout Passover.

17. Matzo shmura is baked with "mayim shelanu", which literally means "water that has remained (overnight)". The water is drawn the previous day, and remains overnight so that it will be at an optimal temperature the next morning for thebaking of matzo. This is prescribed in the Code of Jewish Law.

18. Yoreh Deah is one of the four sections of the Code of Jewish Law. A large partof it deals with the laws of kashrut, including the technicalities of

ritual slaughter, and the various conditions and lesions that can render an animal not kosher.

19. A reference to the section in Genesis where Isaac was about to bless Jacob (dressed up as Esau), and he said "the voice is the voice of Jacob, and the hands are the hands of Esau". Exegetically, the "voice of Jacob" refers to the study of Torah, and the "hands of Esau" refer to involvement inworldlyaffairs.

20. A verse from the book of Proverbs.

21. I am not sure as to what the bow stands for. Pitum Haktoret is a prayer that lists the components of the incense offering that was offered in the Temple. I do not understand the innuendo intended here – although the Pitum Haktoret prayer does make mention that one does not bring urine into the temple due to the honor of the temple. It is possible that there is a hint here to urinating off the bridge.

22. This sentence is a mixture of Hebrew, Yiddish and Polish, obviously proving that the Rebbi was not fluent in Polish.

23. A statement from the Passover Haggadah, describing that one who spends moretime telling the story of the Exodus of Egypt is praiseworthy.

24. I am not sure what this means.

25. Nach (Neviim and Ketuvim), the Prophets and Writings, are the latter two of the three sections of the Bible. The first part is the Torah itself. The Early Prophets include the historical books of Joshua, Judges, Samuel, and Kings.

26. A verse from Deuteronomy commanding the abhorrence of anything connected to idol worship.

27. One of the principal commentaries that appears on a Talmud folio, the other main commentary being Rashi. Tosafot (literally, additions), is a compendium of commentaries written by a variety of commentators, several of whom were Rashi's grandchildren.

28. A quote from the book of Psalms.

29. The Malbim is one of the latter commentators on the bible. Ein Yaakov is acompendium of the homiletic (aggadaic) material of the Talmud.

30. It is a custom, considered meritorious for the soul of the departed, to serveas the prayer leader on the anniversary of a parent's death (yahrzeit).

31. Literally expectoration.

32. This sentence uses two derogatory terms "tumah" (impure place) for a church, and "shkotzim" (literally disgusting ones) for gentiles.

33. Desecration of the name of G-d refers to any act of a Jew that brings disrepute upon the Jewish people and the Jewish religion. A Jew is expected to conduct himself in a manner that brings honor to his people and religion.

34. This cannot be translated literally, but it closely resembled "To hell with you, damn it!". I notice that the word cholera is in the Polish.

35. A Sabbath hymn.

36. Yossel or Yoshke is often used as a pejorative term for Jesus. Aunt Miriam obviously refers to Mary.

37. These two words (pronounced eit) are homonyms in Hebrew.

38. Perek refers to Pirke Avot, the Mishnaic tractate "Ethics of the Fathers", which is customarily recited on summer Sabbath afternoons.

39. Tisha Beov (The Ninth of Av), is the dreariest fast day of the Jewish year, occurring in the summer. It commemorates the destruction of the two temples and many other tragedies that befell the Jewish people over the centuries. The Tisha Beov service includes the public reading of the Book of Lamentations. The Sabbath preceding Tisha Beov is known as Shabbat Chazon (The Sabbath of the Vision), in reference to the prophetic reading for that Sabbath from the first Chapter of Isaiah ("The Vision of Isaiah...") which is replete with warnings of the dire consequences awaiting the Jewish people for abandoning the word of G-d. On some years, such as the one mentioned here, Tisha Beov itself falls on the Sabbath. If that happens, the observance of the fast is postponed to the following day, and that day is Shabbat Chazon. The period leading up to Tisha Beov is considered a particularly inauspicious occasion to start a new endeavor.

{Hebrew text – pp 141-147; Yiddish text – 148-155}

The Holocaust

The Murder of the Jews of Dembitz

Reuven Siedlisker-Sarid

Translated by Jerrold Landau

Forced labor before the outbreak of war.

No caption – five men at forced labor

Aleph.

On Friday, September 1, 1939, Hitler declared a state of war between Germany and Poland, and already by 11:00 a.m. the first German warplanes appeared over the skies of Dembitz. For the time being, they satisfied themselves with merely shooting. A day later, on the Sabbath afternoon, the German airplanes conducted their first bombardment. Several building were destroyed, including the house of Aharon Bar in the old city, as well as the Polish students' dormitory (the Bursa). A few bombs also fell near the train station.

A few residents of the city were killed in the bombardment, and immediately a disorderly flight to the villages took place. Most of the Jews of the old city fled to the villages of Wolka and Wiewiorka. The Jews of the new city fled in the direction of Lisa Gora, Stobierna, Stasiowka, and Niedzwiada. When they returned to their homes the following day in order to fetch some of their belongings, it became evident that most of the moveable property had been pillaged by the gentiles from the villages near and far. Their neighbors in the city also participated in the pillage.

Families were separated in the great confusion, and family members were searching for each other. It took a few days until we reunited. The bridge over the Wislok was destroyed by the bombardment, and it was necessary to cross in a raft. The bombardments continued.

The civic authorities disbanded, and there was no policing until the entry of the German army on Friday September 8.

While the refugees from Dembitz were still searching for shelter in the villages, the rumor spread among them that the Germans were murdering any Jewish male who they find. Immediately, the flight eastward began. A portion of the refugees succeeded in crossing the San River, which had been conquered in the interim by the German army. Others, whom the Germans intercepted along the route, gave up on the flight and returned from whence they came. At first, only the women were brave enough to return to the city, and later the men began to return as well. They found their homes pillaged and destroyed. Nevertheless, there was some degree of respite. For the time being, it seemed as if the mortal danger that was looking down upon them was lifted. The Germans did not pillage or murder. They sufficed themselves in snatching Jews from the streets and the houses in order to conscript them for cleaning their institutions. They were assisted by the gentiles, who showed them where to find the Jews.

Approximately two weeks after the conquest, Staron, the former mayor, was called to return to his post as head of the civic government.

One Sabbath eve, Tovia Zucker and a few other Jews were called to the building of the former regional governor (Starosta). They were received by German S. S. men from the Rzeszow command who informed them that they must provide a set number of sheets and bedding items to the Germans by morning, and woe would be unto the Jews if they did not fulfill this order. That night, they sent collectors around to the Jewish houses, and everything requested was given over the Germans in accordance with the order.

At this meeting, the beginning of the "Jewish government" over the Jews was established, which later on consolidated into the Judenrat. In accordance with the advice of Staron, Tuvia Zucker was chosen for this position, as he was the most honorable Jew who remained in the city, since the head of the community Reb Avraham Goldman fled to Russia.

Immediately after the entry of the Germans to Dembitz, the public schools were forbidden to teach Jewish children. The Polish gymnasia, the only one in Dembitz, was closed. The cheders were closed and the children studied in a private manner in the houses of the teachers, or were taught by their parents to the best of their ability. People who could afford it purchased some books for their homes. The Torah scrolls were removed from the synagogues and divided up among the Jewish residents.

Beit.

The German authorities in the city served at first as a regional government. The Gestapo did not get involved except in special circumstances. The government was headed by the district authorities (Kreiz Hauptmanschaft). Dembitz was regarded as its own "Kreiz" (district), along with a large surrounding area. The borders of the district were the towns of Rozwadow, Sedziszow, Pilzno, and Wielopole. The district head (Kreiz Hauptman) was Dr. Auswald, a reasonably easygoing German. His second in command was a young man from Vienna with the title of doctor. It later on became evident that he suffered the pain of the Jews and wished to help. Jewish matters were placed in his hands.

At the beginning of the occupation, the Jews of Tarnobrzeg (Dzikow) and Rozwadow were expelled to the other side of the San. Most of them remained in the Russian district. Some of them returned and obtained permission to settle in their former cities, through the intercession of the Judenrat of Dembitz and the aforementioned vice district head. The lot of the Jews of Mielec was worse. They were expelled under German provocation immediately after the conquest, at a time when several dozen of them were murdered when they were together in the Jewish bathhouse.

During the early period of the Nazi occupation of Dembitz, the Germans did not place any special restrictions upon Jewish business. The Jews were permitted to move around freely, even by train, until the middle of 1940. The Jews of Dembitz would travel to Tarnow to purchase merchandise from the wholesalers without being disturbed. They were also suppliers of the German army institutions, and received fair and customary payment.

The Germans apparently were not overly interested in the businesses of Dembitz, for there was only one privately owned German store, owned by the German Haze, which sold only iron merchandise.

In General, there were no incidents of pillage and murder in Dembitz, whether from the Nazis or the Poles.

The only decree placed specially on the Jews at that time was the "work obligation" through the Judenrat. This was set up on the advice of Staron, the mayor before the war, whom the Nazis put in charge of the city for a short time after the conquest. From that time, the Judenrat would send Jews to work for the Germans according to their needs, rather than having them being snatched up by the soldiers as happened in the early days of the occupation. They worked in offices and barracks, cleaned the streets, cleared the ruins of the bombardments, etc. The Germans accepted Staron's suggestion willingly.

The situation came to the point where the young Jews would attempt to find work in the official places, on account of the humane way that they were treated in those places. They also received work permits so that they would not be snatched up by the soldiers for work in other places.

During the winter months of 1939-1940, an unorganized escape movement was established from the area of the German district to the Russian district. Several dozen young people from occupied Dembitz moved over to the Russian district in this manner. The Germans knew about this and did not pay attention. However, the Russians would capture the escapees, imprison them, interrogate them, and accuse them of being German spies.

Nevertheless, when the refugees of Western Galicia found out about business in the west, and the proper relations that were established after the initial confusion – a reverse movement began among the refugees in the summer of 1940: they returned to their former places even though they were under Nazi rule. The Russian authorities noticed this and could not understand why anyone would want to return to the Nazi areas. They set up a registration for all those who wished to return, and then they deported all of those who were registered to areas in the interior of Soviet Russia – and thanks to this, many were able to survive.

Gimel.

At the beginning of 1940, the German authorities, by means of the city hall, organized a general registration of the entire population. Every adult received an identification card (ken karte) that was required to be carried at all times. Here, the first differentiation between Jews and non-Jews took place. The identification card of the Poles was gray, and that of the Jews was yellow.

In those days, a command was issued by the General Gubernator Frank whose seat was in Krakow, that all Jewish men and women were required to tie a white band with a green or blue Star of David on their right arms. The Jews of Dembitz began to feel that they were caught in a trap that had no exit.

At the time of the registration, a work office was established whose job was to employ any person who was able. Some of the Polish young men were sent to work in Germany. Not so with the Jews, who were only employed locally, in coordination with the Judenrat. A member of the National Socialist party from Germany headed the office. Anshel Taub, the son of Nathan, was the intermediary between the Judenrat and the work office. During the early period, this work was paid work, even for the Jews. It is obvious that there were some Jews of poor means who went to this work willingly. According to the law, every Jew was required to work a certain number of days per week. The Judenrat set up a possibility of exchange: if someone were to pay the Judenrat in return for the daily work assignment, they would be freed for that day, and someone else would go to work in order to receive the payment.

When it became known that there was monetary value attached to the go between function of the Judenrat, conflicts over the head position broke out. Tovia Zucker was pushed aside, or stepped aside, and Yossel Taub, the son of Nathan, became the head.

The main work that the Germans required was the expansion of communication networks and the building of giant factories for the railway industry. Later, it became clear that this was in preparation for the invasion of the Soviet Union. Dembitz had already become an important communication center from the time of Polish rule, and the Germans enlarged it significantly. All of the buildings that were erected by the "Central Manufacturing District" ("Czentralny Okreg Przemyslowy") were taken over by the Germans for storehouses for military supplies and ammunition.

Daled.

In the months of April and May 1940, a decisive change took place with the establishment of the "military training camp of the Waffen S. S." in the Postikow Forest near Dembitz. Tens of thousands of inductees from Germany and from the "Volks Deutsche" (descendents of German settlers who kept their connection to their German roots to some degree) were trained there. The Central Manufacturing District in its time had set up one of its largest munitions workshops in the forest of Postikow. Now, the buildings served as a training camp for the Nazi army. Various work camps, for Poles and for Jews, were very quickly set up surrounding the German camp. The Poles were organized into conscripted work groups (Junaki), while the Jews lived in closed work camps. The Poles were given time off from time to time, but the Jews were treated as prisoners.

In June 1940, the first round up (Eblawe) for the Postikow work camp took place. Anyone who could not prove that he was working in a government or military institution was sent off to be imprisoned in the Postikow camp. Jews from other cities of Galicia as well as from Congress Poland were also brought to Postikow.

The Judenrat of Dembitz had a great deal of work. People turned to it with requests to take action to free those imprisoned, obviously by bribing the head of the camp. The head of the Jewish camp of Postikow was Uber Schar Fuehrer Kopps, and the Judenrat knew how to "deal" with him. In accordance with his orders, and with the assistance of the soldiers who helped him, Jews were taken out of the camp and returned to Dembitz, from where they returned to their places of residence.

Due to the proximity of Postikow to Dembitz, a distance of only approximately ten kilometers, the contact with the S. S. soldiers who ran the camp took place in Dembitz itself. At first it was decided that the supplies and the kitchen of the Jewish camp in Postikow should be run by the Judenrat. A new organization was set up for the Jewish forced laborers, called "Zelbst Helfe" ("Self Help"). This organization was centered in Krakow and Dembitz, and was headed by Izak Shachner, the son-in-law of Getzel Laufbahn. It would receive shipments of sugar and pork from time to time for distribution to the

Jews of the camp and the city council. Since Jews had no need for the pork, exchanges were made between the Jewish institution and the city council: the city council would receive the pork for the Polish population, and in exchange, the Jews would receive an amount of sugar. Obviously, the Polish population had the better part of the deal. The first public kitchen in Dembitz, located in the basement of the Talmud Torah building, was established by Zelbst Helfe.

He.

The German authorities did not become involved in matters of living arrangements in Dembitz until the beginning of 1941. The Jews lived where they wanted without being disturbed. Suddenly, the matter of the establishment of the ghetto came to the fore. As soon as the Germans informed the Jews of their decision to establish a ghetto as a special residential quarter for the Jews, discussions began on this matter. The Judenrat advised that various districts in the city where Jews lived should be set aside for this purpose. On the other hand, the head of the city council under the direction of Staron, advised the setting aside of the Tepper Gesel (Potters' Lane) for this purpose. This was one of the most neglected areas of the city, located in a valley behind the Market Square in the new city. That suggestion was the one accepted. Staron stood his ground.

The Jews of Dembitz had to leave their dwellings, homes, stores, and workshops that had been set up through the course of centuries, and concentrate themselves into the designated place, which included only one alley out of all the roads in the city, the Potters' Lane (Tepper Gesel) and the lots that extended to the infantry barracks, where the S. S. resided.

The Jews left their homes, stores and workshops, and their gentile neighbors took them over, in accordance with the order that was set by the city hall.

At the time of the transfer to the ghetto, the Jews attempted to sell whatever property they could. All of the rest was left to the new residents, without payment. Since the buildings in the alley could not accommodate such a large population, bunks were built that could accommodate twenty people each. The dwellings in the ghetto were distributed by the Judenrat in accordance with each person's needs, but there was a set number of square meters allotted to each person. The crowding was great. However, it is important to point out that epidemics did not break out in the ghetto until much later. Dr. Mantzer of Andrichow and Dr. Idek (Yehuda) Tau of Dembitz, the son of Simcha Tau, served as doctors in the ghetto. They established and directed a sick room.

The transfer to the ghetto cut off the contact of the Jews of Dembitz with the outside world. From that time on, it was forbidden for a Jew to appear outside the ghetto without a special permit. Business and even postal contact were cut off.

The vast majority of the Jews of Dembitz were employed in public works, especially in the expansion of the train station, as well in German firms as paid employees. Of course, the means of conducting business changed. There were no more business dealings and requests for advice, so to speak. From that time, the Jews were treated as the private property of the Gestapo.

With the establishment of the ghetto in Dembitz, as well as throughout the cities of Galicia, the responsibility for governing the Jews was removed from the local authorities and transferred to the Gestapo. The head of the Gestapo in Dembitz, from the time of the beginning of Nazi rule until the time of the liquidation of the Jewish ghetto, was a German from Vienna named Gabler.

The first activity of the Gestapo in the ghettos was the separation of those who were fit for work from those who were not fit for work. The latter were the first to be sent off to the death camps.

Until 1943, the death camp to which the Jews of Galicia and Silesia were sent was Belzec.

In Dembitz as in other places, the Gestapo speedily changed the composition of the Judenrat, so that it would be fit for its new role. The former members of the Judenrat were replaced for the most part with members of the Jewish "Ordinungs Dienst" who were already used to accepting German orders.

Gabler, the Gestapo chief of Dembitz, behaved like all the other Germans in his first contacts with the Jews, that is to say that he attempted to derive the maximum personal benefit from them. He would often ask of the Jews all sorts of things, under the pressure of threats, and they did not refuse him. At first, he did not behave rudely toward them, and he himself did not shoot at his victims until the first aktion. Dembitz had a policeman of the Schupo (the German police) by the name of Urban, one of the Volkes Deutsche, who tormented the Jews for a variety of reasons: for example, if one was caught outside the ghetto without a permit or travelling on the train. Urban would capture the offenders, take them to the Jewish cemetery and shoot them dead. It was impossible for this to take place without the knowledge of Gabler, who behaved as a polite man and protected the law and order. It was only at the time of the first "ausziedlung", which he personally conducted, that Gabler removed the mask from his face. At that time, he displayed all characteristics of an experienced Gestapo man.

The Germans employed the Jews of the ghetto as they did previously in all sorts of work outside of the ghetto, primarily in the expansion of the railway lines and the building of shelters for the locomotives, which were known to be among the largest in all of Galicia.

Vav.

At first, from the time when the Nazis invaded the Soviet Union, the Jews held out the hope that their time of salvation was at hand. All eyes were looking toward a speedy redemption. When the Red Army was defeated, a greater oppression descended upon them.

From the time of the establishment of the ghetto, rumors began to circulate from various places regarding the deportation of Jews eastward by train. Nobody knew the reason for the deportations. The first transport that was known to the Jews of Dembitz not only by hearsay was of the Jews from Wolbrom, in Poland. Jews from the Dembitz ghetto who worked on the railway spoke with the deportees through the windows of the wagons, as the train rested for a few minutes near the station. These rumors augmented the fear and confusion. The Jews of Dembitz began to suspect that their turn would also come. A day or two before June 29, 1942, Jews from Sediszow, Ropszyce, Wielopole, Pilzno, Radomysl, and all of the villages of the region, including also apostates, were brought into the Dembitz ghetto.

A dark fear fell upon the Jews of the ghetto. The Jews began to search for hiding places with gentiles outside of the ghetto; some of these arrangements were through friendship and others through payment of money. Indeed, there were numerous cases of slander by the Poles. Those who were captured were taken to the cemetery and shot.

On the night of June 29 th, the ghetto was surrounded by S. S. men from a special commando unit that was responsible for the murder of Jews (Juden Farnichtungs Kommando) along with the Polish police. In the early hours of the morning, Gabler appeared in the ghetto along with his assistants and non-local Gestapo men, including Heinrich Wakunda, the head of the murder effort of the Jews of Galicia, and the official of the Judenrat in order to collect the work certificates (arbeits karte) that had been previously distributed by the work office (arbeit amt). This collection took place until the afternoon.

The next day, Yosef Taub, the head of the Judenrat, was called to the Gestapo and told to gather all of the Jews together for a selection to see who would remain in the place and who would be sent away (according to their words, to work in the east). The work permits, signed by the Gestapo, would be returned only to those who would be remaining.

The Judenrat fulfilled this decree in an exacting fashion. When Yosef Taub left the Gestapo office, he informed everyone that they must gather in the street between the house of Wolf Ader and the house of Shlomo Herschlag the baker. This took place. At the set time, most of the residents of the ghetto, as well as those who had recently come in from outside, gathered in the designated place.

In the hours of the afternoon, the Gestapo men sat at a table that was set up in the place next to the "Lunka", and the residents of the ghetto passed before them, every person with his family, as young sheep[1]41. All of those who had their work permits returned to them by the Judenrat held their permits in their hands and returned to a designated gathering place in the ghetto along with their families after the permit was signed by the Gestapo. Those whose permits were not returned to them (those who were older than age forty or fifty, as well as those whose work places were not recognized by the Gestapo committee) were brought to a second gathering place, directly below the Kaszanza Lunka.

After this selection, the Gestapo men, assisted by the Polish police and members of the Jewish "Ordinungs Dienst", went through the bunks and houses in order to search for anyone who was hiding. They found several dozen Jews who were brazen enough to hide. They were brought directly to the cemetery and shot on the spot.

That day, a large transport arrived by train. This transport included all of the Jews of Tarnobrzeg and Rozwadow. They were brought to the lower gathering place, and only four or five men from among them were brought to the upper gathering place, in accordance with the whim of the Gestapo man who was responsible for bringing the arrivals to the lower gathering place.

The rain was pouring down, and the ground of the Lunka turned into mud. The Jews of Dembitz, Sediszow, Ropszyce, Wielopole, Pilzno, Tarnobrzeg and Rozwadow waited in fear and trembling for the command. The angels of destruction of the S. S. kept the crowds orderly, dividing them into various groups. Suddenly the command was issued: "Kneel down!". The entire large crowd of men, women and children knelt down in the mud.

The Gestapo men approached the rows of kneeling people, and removed about 180 or 200 men. Those were placed on transport trucks and driven by the S. S. men to the edge of the Wilicka Forest at Lisa Gora. They were brought into the forest, and shot into a communal grave that had previously been prepared by the Polish Junaks. The Junaks were then called to cover over the grave at the conclusion of the dreadful murder.

This took place on the 7th of Av, 5702 (1942).

Zayin.

That same day toward evening, the rest of the people, approximately 4,000 Jews, including 2,000 Jews of Dembitz, were brought to the train station and sent eastward in covered train wagons. They were transported to the Belzec death camp. Several of them jumped off the moving train.

One group of those gathered in the lower gathering place was sent to Rzeszow to work in the Messerschmidt airplane parts factory. Some of them survived. Similarly, a few people from the group of young people who were sent to work in the "Flugzweig Werk Mielec" remained alive. A third group of young people was sent to work in Postikow, to the labor camp (Zwanges Lager) that was founded at the time of the liquidation of the Jews of Mielec. Only one person of this group, Yisrael Reiner, survived.

At the conclusion of these events, the Gestapo decreed that anyone caught without a signed document would be shot. The S. S. left the ghetto. The Polish police guarded the ghetto from the outside, and the Ordinungs Dienst from the inside.

Chet.

The study of Torah did not stop in Dembitz even in the days of the Nazi conquest. Not only this, but scholars conducted in depth study sessions as in earlier days. There were those who concerned themselves with learning even in the underground.

Yisrael Leib Frankel, the son-in-law of Reuven (Reuveli) Kluger, conducted an underground Yeshiva. He was a young man in his early thirties, born in Rozodol. He was a Hassid of Belz, and learned most of his Torah, including the hidden Torah[2] in the Beis Midrashes of Tarnow.

Reb Yisrael Leib opened up a Yeshiva in Dembitz a few years prior to the Nazi invasion, and this Yeshiva functioned until the outbreak of the war. When the Nazi army entered the city, the former students disbanded, and Reb Yisrael Leib gathered a different group of young people around him, aged between 14 and 16, primarily the children of lay householders. The studies were conducted in the attic of Yosef Rosh in the vicinity of the rabbi's house. The functioning of this Yeshiva under the conditions that prevailed at that time was literally a sanctification of the name of G-d.

The studies continued in this manner from the spring of 1940 until the autumn of 1941, that is to say until the beginning of the roundups for the Postikow camp. At first, Reb Yisrael Leib himself was sent off to Postikow, but he was later freed in return for a bribe.

Each morning at 8:30 a.m. the studies would begin with a class in Gemara, tractate Shabbat with the commentaries of Tosafot, Rambam (Maimonides) and Rashba. At noontime and in the afternoon, they would review the class. In the evenings, the students, either on their own or in groups, would study general studies. Some prepared for the Polish matriculation exams. The rabbi saw no contradiction between the holy and secular studies. He himself was secularly educated – they said of him that he was an expert in world literature. He had a general orientation toward worldly matters.

Reb Yisrael Leib did not only teach practical Jewish law (halachah) to his students. He also lectured to them on homiletic material (aggadah) and character improvement (mussar). He also touched on mystical matters. On one occasion, after the outbreak of the war between Hitler and Russia, several of his students and other youths came before Reb Yisrael Leib to hear his opinion on the victories of Hitler on the eastern front, which were announced by proclamations on the main streets of the city. This news instilled great trepidation in the hearts of the Jews, particularly in the youth, for everyone hoped that the battle with the Soviet Union would result in the imminent defeat of the Nazi army. Reb Yisrael Leib said: "On a practical level, these victories are only passing episodes, and from a mystical, religious level, they are actually signs of the redemption." Those gathered together left the discussion encouraged and full of hope. In general, he was always filled with joy and faith.

On Passover of 1942, the Judenrat sent Reb Yisrael Leib and his family to greater Radomysl along with dozens of other families. The purpose of the transport was, so to speak, to relieve the crowding in the Dembitz ghetto. However, on the fifth of Av, Reb Yisrael Leib, along with all the Jews of Radomysl, returned to the Dembitz ghetto. In the first Ausziedlung, he was sent along with 200 Jews of Dembitz to the S. S. punishment camp in Postikow, where he died.

His students included the two sons of Reb Yechezkel Shochet, the son of the baker Aharon Yaakov (the three of them are now in America), Tzvi Lisha, Menachem Ofan (living in Israel), Yitzchak Salomon, the two sons of Yosef Roth, Yitzchak Epstein (all of whom were murdered in Dembitz), as well as others.

In the summer of 1940, a refugee from Krakow, Reb Moshe Schmid, came to Dembitz. He was approximately sixty years old, one of the Torah giants of his city, one of those who was licensed to examine students who were applying to enter the Yeshiva of Chachmei Lublin. From the time he came to Dembitz, he would give the students a weekly class in Talmudic didactics (pilpul) on the topic that they had learned that week. His classes continued until the winter of 1941. He also was sent with the transport to greater Radomysl, however he never returned from there. He did not wish to return. He went out to the street with a Torah scroll and declared that he did not wish to return. The Nazis shot him, and he gave up his pure soul as he was reciting Shema, on that Sunday, the fifth of Av.

Tet.

It is hard to describe the feelings of trepidation among those who remained. A final sign was received from one of those sent away – a postcard with the postal cancellation of Przemysl, from Reb Naftalki Eisen. It is not known how this card came to the mail in Dembitz, since it had already been some time since mail were received in the ghetto.

A day or two after the aktion, those who had succeeded in hiding outside and had not been revealed started to sneak back into the ghetto, either under the cover of the darkness of night or along with groups of Jews returning from work.

In the meantime, the Germans issued a decree to the Polish population outside the ghetto that whomever would be found sheltering a Jew, or whomever would offer assistance to a Jew in any manner, would be shot.

Negotiations began again with the heads of the local German authorities in order to receive documents and certificates for those who returned. The negotiators of the Judenrat were Anshel Taub and Immerglick (from lesser Radomysl, the son-in-law of the butcher Mordechai Goldfarb). Documents were sold for money, despite the warnings of the Gestapo, for whoever would be found without a document would be shot. (Yosef Taub would say: "It's only money! It's only money!".) This was conducted without keeping records: for in this manner, the Germans would have exact knowledge of the number of Jews who remained.

In this period of time, until the days of the 7th and 8th of Tevet 5703 (December 15-16, 1943), the remaining people, mainly men but also some women, were employed in railway work and in various secret endeavors. A few worked in well-known places. The life in the ghetto was conducted in accordance with the workday: in the morning, groups would leave the gates, and after the workday of ten hours, they would return.

The Dembitz ghetto was considered to be an "arbeit lager" (work camp). The barbed wire fences surrounding the ghetto were shrunk, since there were only about 600 officially there. There were also people residing in the ghetto illegally, and on occasion, some additional people arrived, who were no longer able to hide outside.

It is worthy to point out that in this period between the first aktion and the second aktion, there was no incidence of reporting on Jews who were in hiding.

In this period, the Gestapo turned over to the Judenrat a Jew from Mielec named Kaplan, on the condition that he would make boots for the Gestapo men.

Since there was no word heard from those who were sent eastward, and rumors began to circulate about the death camp of Belzec, those that remained began to realize that their own end was approaching, and the fear was great that nobody would survive.

The Germans provided the ghetto residents with small food rations. Other food was brought into the ghetto by those who went out to work, as well as gentiles who brought various provisions to the gates of the ghetto, and received utensils, clothes, etc. in return.

On the 7th or 8th of Tevet 5703, a day before the second aktion, it became evident that the Germans were on the verge of liquidating the entire ghetto. At this time, the danger stared into the faces of the Judenrat members as well, and they looked for means to save themselves.

Yod.

On the final night, at 10:00p.m. Munek Schuss, one of the heads of the Ordinungs Dienst, came to ReuvenSiedlisker and told him that if he would agree to take some of the families of the Judenrat along with him to the bunker that he prepared for himself in the barn of the architect Krawczik in Grazilow – he would inform him of the situation regarding the liquidation of the ghetto that was to take place the next day. After Reuven consulted with his older brother Avraham, Reuven agreed to the condition and brought the head of the Judenrat, Yossel Taub, to his house. Yossel Taub lived in the house of Hirsch Lisha, behind the row of houses in the Market Square.

At that time, all of the family members of the Taub, Schuldenfrei, and Schuss families were present. Anshel Taub informed those present about the notification that he received from the head of the work office (arbeit amt), that as of tomorrow, the only people who would remain in the ghetto would be those employed by the railway and other limited services that would be needed for the forced labor camp that would be established instead of the work camp. This camp would be headed by Immerglick, with Witkower as the secretary and Kaplan as the advisor.

Reuven Siedlisker was already under the supervision of Munek Schuss, and only after urging did he permit him to go to his friends and inform them who could remain in the ghetto and who should flee. Any of those who heard the information and had any chance at all of finding refuge fled the ghetto in the middle of the night.

This time, the aktion was very brief. The ghetto was surrounded by the Ukrainian Zunder Dienst (Special service) who was responsible for the black work. They again rounded up Jews, in the same manner of the first aktion. All of those designated by Immerglick (a haughty, irresponsible, and prattlesome character, who did not even have family feelings) and his associates as workers in the railway and necessary services, received new certificates and were returned to the gathering place – this time the workers alone, without their families. The rest were brought to the lower area near the bogs, and from there were loaded on the train that was waiting for them. They were sent to Belzec.

Yod Aleph.

Along with the new police directors of the forced labor camp, Immerglick ruled with cruelty, by means of terror and threats upon those that remained. The searches for those in hiding in the ghetto were not conducted only by the Germans or their Ukrainian assistants, but also with the active participation of the Jewish members of the Ordinungs Dienst, who uncovered a large number of Jews hiding in bunkers. Those found were taken out to the Jewish cemetery and shot there.

At the conclusion of the aktion, those that were no longer able to remain in their hiding places, as well as a few who succeeded in jumping off the train, returned. A few people even returned from Lancut. They made their return journey at night next to the road or the railway tracks. Immerglick informed them that they would have to leave the camp, for otherwise he would turn them over to the Gestapo. The only place left to flee was the Bochnia ghetto, which still existed, and there were rumors that it was still possible to live there.

Word was spread by the Nazis, with a reliable basis, that from this time on, ghettos would remain in only five places: Krakow, Tarnow, Bochnia, Przemysl and Rzeszow. The Nazis intended to concentrate the Jews in only a few places. The Jews of Dembitz fled primarily to Bochnia, by train, on foot or in any other manner that was possible, with the help of gentiles who received a fee for their efforts.

The Gestapo relied on Immerglick and his assistants, who were primarily members of the Ordinungs Dienst, to bring the illegal residents of the camp, old people, sick people and children (approximately 52 people) to a room in the Talmud Torah, as if a hospital was being set up for them. However that night, he arrived along with the members of the Ordinungs Dienst and Gabler, and they murdered them one by one. The members of the Ordinungs Dienst held the victims in their arms, and Gabler shot. One of the Jewish assistants was shot about two weeks later for no apparent reason by that same Gabler, as he stood next to the gate at the entrance to the camp.

Yod Beit.

Those who came to Bochnia shared the same bitter fate of the Jews of Bochnia – most of them were sent to Auschwitz to be murdered at the beginning of September 1943. Some of them were sent to the Szewnia work camp near Jaslow, and from there, a few Dembitz natives returned to Postikow as volunteers. The largest portion of the workers of Szewnia, who were the remnants of the Jews of Galicia that were brought there from Tarnow, Rzeszow, Bochnia, and Przemysl, were brought to Auschwitz on November 29, 1943. They passed through the selection, and some of them were sent to the various work camps in the area, and from there, further on.

The forced labor camp of Dembitz existed until near Passover 5704 (1944). The camp was liquidated on the eve of Passover. The Jewish workers were transferred to the Jerozolimska-Krakow camp. The Jewish leadership of the camp remained in place for another two weeks, along with their closest relatives. From there, they were brought to the Flugzweig Werke camp in Mielec, and a few days later they were taken out to be murdered by the Gestapo men, apparently upon the advice of Gabler.

The Polish "Bahn Polizei" (Railway Police), which included young Poles from Dembitz and the surrounding area, played an important role in their murder. Even before this, they would shoot Jews, based on recognition alone, who were found on the train or in the area around it.

After the liquidation of the camp, the Polish police conducted a search and shot anyone who was found hiding. Those shot included the entire Schuss and Taub families, who were hiding in the forests of Wielopole and Staszowka. The Polish police conducted most of the searches for those hiding. Nevertheless, a few people survived, including one family – Faust and Yechezkel Shochet.

Yod Gimel[3].

At the time of the ausziedlung, the Nazis concentrated about 5,000 Jews in the designated square. These were from Dembitz, Pilzno, Baranow, Tarnobrzeg-Dzikow, and greater and lesser Radomysl. They were placed in groups of ten lines, with ten people in each line, including women and children.

Prior to the entry of the groups into the train wagons – one group per wagon – about 150 people were separated from them, mostly young people, to be sent to work in the P. Z. L. aircraft factory of Rzeszow, about 200 were sent to the S. S. punishment camp in Postikow, and a small group of 40 young people were sent to some place near Dembitz. The rest were loaded onto the trains and transported eastward, apparently to the Belzec death camp.

There were forty Dembitz natives among the 150 that were sent to Rzeszow. This group founded the Flugzweigs-Fabrik Reichschauf camp (Reichschauf was the German term for Rzeszow). The head of the camp was a man by the name of Alfred, a Dembitz native who had settled in Germany and was returned to Poland via Zbaszyn[4]. His assistants were Walter from Dembitz, and Jurek, a refugee from Lodz who lived in Dembitz during the war. Their behavior was extremely bad, and they were responsible for numerous murders in the camp.

This camp existed until the Russians approached Rzeszow in June 1944. It had a population of 500 people who were skilled in engraving, and were worked at a greater pace than normal, at 120%. The owner of the enterprise was the Heinkel firm.

At the last minute prior to transfer of the work camp westward, there was an escape attempt that was foiled through the efforts of the Jewish Zunder Dienst (Special Service). Seventeen people managed to escape.

Of the forty Dembitz natives in this camp, almost all remained alive until the time of the transfer. For the most part, they survived after the transfer to other camps, continuing in their engraving work for the Heinkel firm. They were spread out into thirteen places: Plaszow, Wilicka (the airplane factory), Flossenberg (in Bavaria), Kolmar (in France), the Oranienburg tunnel, Raunesweig (one of the enterprises of Herman Goering), Neugamma near Hamburg (a central camp), Bremen, and Bergen-Belsen. The latter was liberated on April 15, 1945, however no soldiers of the British army came to take care of the survivors until the next day. The English only appeared on Monday evening, and brought each person a quarter of a loaf of bread and a box of lard. The survivors had not eaten for several days. They ate and became ill with severe cases of dysentery, and thousands died. The ill were left in bunks along with the dead without anyone to help them, until a delegation was sent from block 12 (the Jewish block) to the Jewish army chaplain of the British army to describe the situation to him. He sent several girls of the first aid corps to take care of them, and the situation improved. They remained there for two weeks until they were taken away from there.

A Dembitz native in the camp after the liberation.

{Page 163}

Thus were they murdered

by P.F.[107]

Translated by Roberta Newman

When the Hitlerists began their occupation of Dembitz, the Kehillah[108] stopped its work, and as a result, the Rabbi, R. Hersh Melekh, a son of the Dembitz Rabbi Shmuel Horowitz, was left without a way to make a living. He and the *rebbetsin*[109]-- a daughter of the Blozhever Rebbe[110] (of whom it was said, that he sat on a golden chair, and in truth, he was indeed a great miracle worker)--along with their four daughters, sheer beauties, who she had miraculously given birth to eighteen years after their wedding, suffered from hunger, cold, and squalor. Sometimes, there wasn't any money to buy a bar of soap for washing.

In cold water, in the worst cold, the *Rebbetsin* herself would wash the shirts of her children. In their home, there was not one stick of wood for heating a little water and for giving the children something warm to drink.

Before the Hitler era, Rabbi R. Hersh Melekh was very wealthy and had money in the bank. There was a servant for each child. And now their troubles were even worse because no one would look in on them. People were afraid to be out on the street.

I was their nearby neighbor and so I did go and see them. Every time I visited, it was a big celebration for them, because I didn't come with empty hands. I would also go to the wife of the head of the ghetto[111] and she would give me a little bit of sugar, a little bit of fat[112] for the children, and so forth.

There were many days when the Rabbi and *Rebbetsin* would fast because they needed to reserve the bit of black bread they had for the children. Such an ordeal cannot be described. Someone should have had compassion and remembered that the Rabbi and his four children--one 5-year-old twin, and two others, 2 years, four months old; and 3 years, 3 months old--were suffering this way. It was a curse of the *tokhekha lo aleynu*[113].

The *Rebbetsin* managed to keep things going with all four children until the first Aktion[114]. But when they emerged from their hiding place, they ran into a Hitlerist and that was it... He ripped the children from the *Rebbetsin's* arms and shot them all before her eyes. She begged him to shoot her, too, and so he did.

The Rabbi, R. Hersh Melekh, was burned by the Nazis in Mielec.

Beyltshe, the *Rebbetsin's*--this is what we called the daughter of Rabbi R. Shmuel-- hid with her girl Miriam with a non-Jew. He turned them over to the Germans. They were led out to the cemetery and shot.

R. Khayim Yokele, Rabbi R. Shmuel's son, and his wife and brother-in-law and three or four girls were shot by the Germans. Mikhle--her husband was the Rabbi of Radomyśl--was shot with her five children. First the children, then her, Mikhle. The Rabbi survived in a camp and is now in America.

Nekhametshen, a daughter of R. Shmuel and the a daughter-in-law of the Rabbi of Sandz, was taken away by the Nazis to be burned along with her husband, R. Moyshele Halbershtam, and their five children.

Etele, the daughter of the Rabbi of Dembitz, and her husband, who was a rabbi in Siedlice, and their six children, who were also married to rabbis, died the death of martyrs.

Two sons of the saintly rabbi R. Alter Pechter along with R. Zindel Glantz, a son-in-law of R. Ruvele Kluger, and R. Yisroel Feigenbaum died in a terrible way. During the deportation, they hid in a cellar and allowed themselves to be locked in from the outside. Yes, they were saved from the Nazis, but after the deportation, no one from their families were left to get them out of the cellar, and so they starved to death down there in the dark.

R. Yoysek Loy's went dancing and singing to his death. His entire family was sent to the gas chamber: Mendel Brener and five children, Rachel Brener and her husband and child. The youngest were taken naked from the hospital and sent off to Belzec.

With song and singing did R. Dovid Shoykhet go the slaughter. He sang to the S.S. men who were dragging him: You can take my body, but you have no dominion over my soul!

{Page 165}

R. Israel Leib Frankel

by Moyshe Unger (Yaakov)

Translated by Roberta Newman

Behind the *Prostn besmedresh*[115] and the study hall of the Hasidim, over where the bath house and the slaughterhouse were, lived the elite Jews of Dembitz --two pillars of *Torah v'avodah*[116]--R. Alter (Pechter) and R. Ruvele (Kliger): R. Alter with Khine and their sons R. Shmuel and R. Yudl, who were busy studying day and night; and R. Ruvele with his four daughters, who were considered by men to be the most attractive young women in Galicia. For his youngest, Esther, a groom was brought from Tarnow, a young fellow, all of twenty years old at his wedding--R. Israel Leib Frankel.

In 1931 when R. Ruvele died and his body was brought to the Hasidic study hall for his eulogy, all the stores in Dembitz closed, and the same went for the *kheyders*[117] and Talmud Torahs[118]. Both the old and new city came to pay him last respects. Women wept loudly and filled the women's section of the synagogue, and the men, boys, and children were in the study hall and milling around outside near the open windows. The trustee, Shmuel Hekht, said a few words in honor of the departed, and then immediately afterwards, R. Ruvele's youngest son-in-law, R. Israel Leib, arose to give the eulogy. He was tall and thin with a short, black beard, and big, black eyes that looked penetratingly at a person, piercing him through and through. Almost as soon as he opened his mouth and began his wonderful speech, it became completely quiet. Everyone was deeply moved by his sorrowful and loving speech. It seemed at the time that he was bringing them to heights seldom attained by human beings.

Refined Jews from the old city, upon hearing R. Israel Leib for the first time, made their case to Shloyme Yaakov, his closest friend, that, for the sake of God, such an exceptional person should be put to good use. Shloyme Yaakov's heart swelled with pride at the thought that his closest friend, R. Israel Leib, had been discovered. Both of them were Belzer Hasidim who considered the Belzer *tsadik*[119] one of the pillars of the world. But as time went by, Shloyme increasingly began to hope that R. Israel Leib himself would be able to found a generation of Jews upon whom the light of the Torah would shine.

And Shloyme Yaakov did not keep quiet about it. He told Leyzer Oling and Hershl Faust about the Sabbath sermons that R. Israel Leib delivered in the new city, sermons that were infused with Torah, wisdom, and erudition. And so? The devil got into the act. It so happened that someone found in one of R. Israel Leib's sermons a word with roots in the Haskalah[120] or that had been drawn from an alien source, and he began to pour out fire and brimstone because maybe R. Israel Leib had taken a bit from that story, and such a person should not be listened to and obeyed. When the great, modest and God-fearing R. Israel Leib heard about it, he said, quietly: "Probably, I am guilty of the sin, my mouth is not pure and not worthy of preaching before such dear Jews, each one of whom is worth a thousand times more than I am. Probably, I had alien thoughts. I will *neyder*[121] not preach anymore." And that's the way it stayed.

Shloyme himself was a young man with a sharp intellect, as pious as can be, and an influential person. He sucked two hairs from his beard into his mouth and said, "I have an idea. Dembitz has everything except for a yeshiva. We'll establish a yeshiva with R. Israel Leib at its head. He will instruct the boys and an entire generation will grow--an example for Galicia, for Poland, for the world! And indeed, your Zalmen, R. Leyzer, and your Ruvele, R. Hershl, will have somewhere to go to school." And the two agreed to it and householders helped make the idea a reality, and in 1935, the Yeshiva Lomdey-Torah[122] opened, right over where the Bar Kochba sports club, the Poale Zion club, the Beys Yankev girls' school were. There, the voice of the Torah began to be heard. There, they studied twenty hours a day, held passionate discussions about Hasidism, dissected every nuance and detail, and immersed themselves in *gemore*[123], and thirstily drank in the Torah. The proudest young men were R. Israel Leib's students.

Building on the success of the first phase, a junior yeshiva was opened, where R. Israel Leib taught one class and Yose Frankel the other. There was no fighting, no cursing, no shouting, and you knew one's way around the page of *gemore* that you learned every week. you began praying with devotion. After the morning class, there were fine prayers, and after the fine prayers, you began to eat; after an uplifting meal, you passionately studied and once again committed yourself to spending the entire day in devotion to the Holy One, blessed be He.

Meantime, the Beys Yankev school, established in 1930 by Arn Yankev, Hersh Faust, Avrom Frankel, Hersh Taub, Alter Buxbaum, and Moshe Salomon, had developed quite nicely. At first, the Kolatshitsher Hasidim[124] looked with disfavor on the idea of education for Jewish girls. However, when they realized that the two hundred Jewish girls were preparing themselves for a modest, pious Jewish life, they smiled with pleasure.

And then World War II broke out and interrupted everything. On Friday, the first day of the war, German airplanes were already seen in the skies over

Dembitz. On Saturday, Dembitz was bombed heavily and everyone fled to the village. When the Germans marched in on September 13, they encountered almost no one, and couldn't shoot Jews in the marketplace like they did in other towns. The Jews weren't there. They hung up notices which said that nothing would happen to anyone and that everyone should return to the city. Gradually, first the non-Jews, and then the Jews, returned to Dembitz. By Rosh Hashanah, they already had someone to sweep in the marketplace: the Rabbi, R. Alter, his sons, and other Jews with beards, which, however, they immediately cut off. A few quiet days passed, and towards Sukkoth the town was already full. But the houses were completely barren. The non-Jews had looted everything during the bombardment. Almost every non-Jew became a thief and grew rich with Jewish property.

Jews starved, couldn't get any bread. The bakeries had their bread requisitioned by the Germans, may their names be blotted out. But the Germans hadn't shot any Jews. If they had, it is certain that most Jews would have saved themselves by fleeing to the Russian side of the border, where it was easy to sneak across. But since they let you live and some could still conduct business, instead of fewer Jews in town, there were more. Dembitz Jews who had fled returned to their families. And so gradually, the Germans began to persecute the Jews and drag them off to forced labor. Jews swept the streets, loaded wagons with coal, stones, etc. The salary for a week's work sufficed for one loaf of bread, bought on the black market. For the normal price, one got a pound of bread a week for each person. The refined wife of Aaron Taub, the great philanthropist, used to hide bread from her bakery from the Germans and give it out to dozens of poor people every week. The poor people were former elite householders, who now suffered from hunger.

This is how formerly beautiful Dembitz looked. The cultural life died out. Every attempt to initiate something that would give a little bit of encouragement to the people, was, from the first, impossible.

In only one house, in the small, ruined house of R. Ruvele, where the 29-year-old R. Israel Leib , Esther, and their three children, Efraim, Elozer, and Ruvn Yeshue Heshl were now living, were the hardships of starvation, the extraordinary despair, fear and sorrow not felt. There, R. Yisroel sat teaching his young students, Shmuel Reich, Moyshe Unger, Osher and Shaul Yoshes, Mendl Ofen, Efroym Reich, Yitskhak Salomon, and others. They did not feel any cold or hunger, they were not frightened by any shots fired from the rifle of an enemy. Their faces glowed, especially when R. Israel Leib began to explain to them the special significance of the times, the special role of the Jews, who were, God forbid, forbidden to commit any sin described in the Torah, particularly now when Satan ruled, when the angels of hell were bewitching and wanted to take over the world, wanted to murder everything that is spiritual, everything that is refined, everything that is the foundation of Judaism and the foundation of the world.

When you entered R. Israel Leib's house, you would encounter dozens of people listening attentively to his sacred utterances. Many who had, before the war, distanced themselves from Judaism, returned to their roots after seeing R. Israel Leib only one time. Yosef Faust and Hershl Altman became God-fearing Jews, standing amid their former comrades, the Zionists, like pillars of Judaism.

I myself, Moyshe Unger, a son of Arele Yaakov, had the privilege of spending an entire night with R. Israel Leib, at the bedside of the ailing Yerucham Kriger. This was in March 1940. That night I will never forget. It gave me the fortitude to withstand every terrible trouble-- all the struggles, all the wars of my soul-- and to pull through and remain a student of R. Israel Leib, which I hope to remain until the Messiah, the redeemer of righteousness, arrives.

When Moyshele Gewirtz came into R. Israel Leib's class and requested two students to stay over the night at Yerucham Kriger's, I spoke up and said that I would go. I hoped that no other student would do it, and that then the head of the yeshiva himself would go. I had waited for this for a long time already: to be able to be with R. Israel Leib and to learn something from him that couldn't be imparted to a crowd---and this is indeed what happened.

R. Israel Leib sat down and paged through a book that he had taken from the bookcase, but was soon overcome with a powerful sleepiness, and unwillingly, I had to agree that he could take a little nap while sitting at the table. R. Israel Leib assured me that he didn't need to sleep for long and that he would wake up soon.

With a tremble in my heart, I listened to the ticking of the clock. The rabbi dozed for exactly a quarter hour and awoke with a smile. He apologized for being such a sleepyhead and not being able to control himself. Remember, great saints don't need to sleep, they are above the laws of the natural world. Afterwards, he washed his hands and sat down at the table, opening up an old book by Ari Hakodesh[125] and explained to me a sacred essay, "*Ot brit kodesh.*"[126] I, the fifteen-year-old boy, felt his heart pounding. I was thrilled that the rabbi had hit upon just the right subject. It was 8:25 when he went into his explanation of the secrets of the words "foundation of the universe," "foundation of creation," and "beginning of creation," and how to attain the goal; how, in order to be consecrated and purified, one can attain different levels, rise above natural law, can take command of one's body, feelings and emotions, in order not be tempted. In the house, from time to time was heard a groan from the sick man. But I forgot where I was. Together with R. Israel Leib, I was elevated into a realm of truth, friendship, cleanliness, holiness, purity, and eternity. When the rabbi looked, it was six in the morning, time to recite the morning prayer. R. Israel Leib began to describe the greatness of the creator with such devotion, with such passion, with such wisdom and greatness that it is hard for someone who was merely his student to describe it on paper. One would need his power to do it, and he is no more, gone with all the martyrs.

In 1941, a typhus epidemic broke out among the poor in Dembitz. Dozens of families fell victim to this terrible illness, which is brought on by starvation. R. Israel Leib and his family were among those who were brought to the hospital. The students ran around full of self-doubt, blaming themselves about not having done enough to alleviate the hunger of their teacher. But by now, they had done everything that they could. Two weeks passed before I saw his holy face once again. Of course, there was no book in the world (except for the Shas[127]) that he didn't know by heart, as well as theory, ethics, and kabbalah. When he was fourteen years old, he was in the Amsterdam Library, where he sat reading for eight months...

It was with fear that I opened the door of Zindel Glantz's house, where R. Israel Leib was that first Sabbath. My heart gave a pang when I saw how much the Rabbi had outwardly changed, without his beard -- but he had the same eyes. I stood by the door, paralyzed, until a voice summoned me: "Moyshele, why are you standing so far away? Is there, God forbid, something that keeps you away from me?" I rejoiced to see that the rabbi hadn't changed, and with pleasure I demonstrated that no, nothing, God forbid, had changed. That despite the fact that the Sitra Ahra[128] was so rampant, all of his students stood there like fortresses of holiness.

And once more the voice of the Torah was heard in the house of R. Israel Leib. The rabbi fed all those who were hungry with a dear taste of Torah. There, it was like being on an island, far away from the dangerous reality of mass executions, fear, and despair. There, we lived in another world.

But not for long. During the intermediary days of Passover 1942, he and his family were deported to Radomyśl, along with other poor, "unemployable" families. Our hearts dripped pain like blood, feeling that there was no way to help, and that it might be the last time that we would see him--a terrible thought. R. Israel Leib smiled: "We will always be together, Moyshele."

Right after Passover, I got a letter from him in which he told me that I should, if possible, assemble the classes, and that I shouldn't, God forbid, succumb to despair. The letters came every day. With such letters, you can live years without food.

The most terrible time was approaching. On July 17, 1942, the Dembitz ghetto was established and entire towns of Jews were brought in there. Among them were also Jews from Radomyśl. All of them were assembled in the priest's field. They stood there for three days until most of the Jews of Dembitz were also forcibly driven there. My mother, five sisters, Brokhe, Rukhame, Breyndl, Gitl, and Blimele; were there, and I was, too. My brother Shumel was shot by those-whose-names-should-be-blotted-out, and Shloyme remained in the city until November 15. Afterwards, he too was sent to where his entire family was.

A day before the deportation, R. Israel snuck away from the field and came to us at home, and I once again had the privilege of speaking with him. He told me: "One must be strong. Redemption is near. The Jewish people will soon be redeemed. The fact that so many people are being murdered is only to fulfill the quota. The world stands before total redemption. In the last battle between holiness and purity with evil and sinfulness, many innocents are falling, but what does it matter? We will all meet again when the Messiah comes."

Translator's Footnotes:

1. The phrase used here, of passing before the men as young sheep, is borrowed from the Unetane Tokef prayer of Rosh Hashanah and Yom Kippur, which describes all the members of the human race passing before G-d on Rosh Hashanah and Yom Kippur, as sheep pass before their shepherd who is counting his flock.
2. A euphemism for Kabbalah and mystical studies.
3. The footnote on page 146 reads: "This chapter was written by Menachem Ofan".
4. Zbaszyn is a town on the former Polish / German border. This refers to the expulsion of Polish Jews who lived in Germany in the late 1930s back into Poland via this border crossing.

107. Perel Faust?
108. Jewish community council.
109. Wife of a rabbi.
110. Hasidic leader from Blazowa.
111. Yiddish: lager-firer's.
112. Yiddish:: gris.
113. A reference to Deuteronomy 28:47: "Because you did not serve the Adonai your God joyfully and gladly in the time of prosperity..." and the curses brought upon one who is disloyal to God.
114. Round-up of Jews.
115. The study hall of the common, unlearned Jews.
116. Religious commitment/study and work on the land of Israel, an axiom of the Mizrahi religious Zionist movement.
117. Traditional Jewish elementary schools.
118. Community-run, traditional Jewish elementary schools.
119. Saintly rabbi.

120. The Jewish Enlightenment.
121. "Without making a vow," phrase used by very pious Jews whenever speaking of a future action, to avoid the risk of unavoidably breaking one's word.
122. Torah Scholars Yeshiva.
123. Talmud, espeially the part that comments on the Mishnah.
124. Hasidic dynasty originating in Kolaczyce.
125. Isaac Luria (1534 –1572), a founder of Kabbalism.
126. Sign of the convenant.
127. Acronym for Shisha Sidrei Mishna - Six parts of the Mishna together with Talmudic commentaries.
128. A Kabbalistic concept reflecting the idea of a dualistic God, with an "other side," from whence all evil emanates.

{Hebrew text – pp 168-169.}

A Bitter Lamentation

Yehuda Gruenspan

Translated by Jerrold Landau

From speeches at the yearly memorial gathering

If we come to fulfill the edict of the great author of Lamentations [1] : "Make a private mourning for yourselves, a bitter Lament!", it would be fitting for each of us to be alone with our pain and sorrow, and to weep from our soul for our martyred relatives. However if it is incumbent upon us to mourn for the community in particular, it would perhaps be more appropriate for us to sit together in silence and devastation, the most fitting manner to express our mourning. Nevertheless, apparently we are not able to be silent; it has been decreed upon to speak, to fulfil the adage: "I will speak, so I will find relief." [2] .

Certainly this overview will not cover all the aspects of life in the town. No! It will be deliberately a one sided description, concentrating on the light alone and covering up the shadows, remembering the high points and forgetting the low points, exposing good deeds and hiding bad ones. For otherwise, it would be fitting that the ravens of the river should pluck out our eyes – in accordance with the words of the wise man [3]. Therefore, we will relate about those people who were lacking in their interpersonal relationships, who were overbearing in their business dealings, parochial in their politics, who spread controversy in the synagogues, Beis Midrashes and shtiebels on account of the challenges of the conditions of the bitter exile. Heaven forbid that we should be objective at this time. Let the accuser be silent!

This overview covers a short time of approximately fourteen years [4] , more or less the time between the two world wars. At that time, approximately 500 Jewish families lived in our city – the city that was situated between the pine and spruce forests on the west and the large meadows of pastureland (Lunka) on the east, between the Wislok River on the north and the Lisa Gora mountain range on the south. That is equivalent to approximately 2,500 people, and it is possible to say that we knew of them all. Therefore, it is possible for us to say, even at this point, that nothing made them stand out and they had no unique characteristics. As the poet says, "Man is nothing but a product of his birthplace", and the corner of the land where we were born and lived was not distinguished by anything. There were no tall mountains and no deep forests, no outstanding landscape and no physical characteristics that stand out in the heart. It was a simple and pure section of nature, green and pleasant in the summer, clear and frozen in the winter, rainy and muddy in the autumn, and bright and blossoming in the spring. Its people were similar – not great Torah scholars, but not without the aroma of Torah. Among them were a small number of scholars. The people were not full of outstanding ideas, but there was also not a dearth of ideas; they were not the wise men of the country, but also not without the wisdom of life; they were not zealots, but also not evildoers. For the most part, they were simple people, pure and of even temperament. They were average people – in accordance with the positive meaning of that term.

There was also the social component. We will describe for ourselves a body consisting of two pyramids whose bases touched each other, as a sort of octahedron. At the two extreme edges, the farthest apart, numbering only a small number each – were the group of wealthy people and extremely poor people, the well-connected on one side, and the unfortunates on the other side. The remainder were all middle class, not rich and not poor; proper, simple and modest people; good people who feared G-d and loved their fellow Jew.

The situation was similar with respect to their professions: On one side there was a small group of people involved in religious service (rabbis, rebbes, the city judge, shochtim 'ritual slaughterers', chazzanim 'cantors', teachers and shamashim 'sextons'). Adjacent to them was a group involved in the free professions (doctors, dentists, lawyers, officials, the pharmacist, and engineers). One the other side there was a small group of artisans: tailors, shoemakers, carpenters, smiths, scribes, musicians, porters, bath attendants, bakers, innkeepers, milkmen, etc.; people involved in various trades who earned their living from the work of their hands.

It is fitting to point out the small number of people in the city – in addition to the local villagers who would come to worship with us on the High Holy Days and the days that they observed yahrzeit – who did not sever their connection to the land. These included people who owned fields, who ploughed, harvested and filled up their silos, who planted trees and harvested fruit; as well as the few people who loved and tended to animals and provided us in our youth with the warm milk of cows and goats, and who transported us on horses and foals in their wagons, in particular in their winter wagons.

All of these groups were very small. Near the bases of the pyramids were the large groups of businessmen – the absolute majority of the population of our city. Of them there were a few who excelled in their efforts in their various endeavors as manufacturers, exporters, middlemen, builders and contractors; they established factories, flourmills, built dwellings and other buildings, and participated in the paving of roads and the taming of rivers. This was all without formal training in business, without political savvy, and without a diploma. Others, also a small group, opened branches and represented firms, cementing the connections that connected the local market with merchandise from the large cities; the forest merchants would cut down trees and market their products inside the state and outside; or they would be owners of lumberyards, filled with various boards and beams and sticks that would be used for fuel or building materials, while at the same time they would often be engaged in the production of wooden tiles. After them was the main group of large scale, intermediate and small scale merchants – the merchants of grain and fruits; the sellers of coal, pitch and fuel; the owners of stores selling textiles, fancy goods, metal implements, building materials; small scale general store owners; haberdasheries and stores selling sewing materials; merchants of fowl, feathers, duck fat, and all types of produce of the coop and the barn; owners of inns, guest houses, delicatessens, confectioneries, restaurants, and taverns; providers of provisions for the cafeterias at the train stations and other terminals for connection between the town and the larger cities, which provided for the busy and hurried passengers who possessed monthly train passes; and all the others who carried burdens upon their necks (in many cases, they were aided by their wives, diligent and valiant women), people bore a constant burden from the early hours of the morning until late at night, in the heat of the summer and the cold of the winter, whether in stores housed in stone buildings or wooden huts, whether at a booth in the civic market or in the fairs of the nearby towns. The people would perform charitable deeds at all times as they sustained their families. Some did so in a scanty fashion and others in an abundant fashion. All of them would be dependent on the mercies of Heaven and the goodwill of the nations. And with all this they lived with their faith, happy in their lot and filled with trust regarding what would come in the near or distant future, a faith that that was accompanied by some doubts ingrained at least in the subconscious of our ancestors. As testimony to this we only need to look at their weeping and tears during their prayers. One could notice their constant sighs or heartrending cries during the festival prayers or during the times of joy. What other explanation can we give other than the feeling of the unrest and holocaust that was approaching? From where was the sorrowful overtones mixed in with the recitation of the Hallel on the night of the festival of our freedom and the other festivals [5] ? From where were the cries of "Oy, Master of the World!" during the recitation of the Hakkafot on Simchat Torah, during the prayers for rain and dew directed to the land, during the wavings on Sukkot, and especially on Hoshanah Rabba [6] ? What other explanation would there be for all this groaning, other than a premonition of destruction and downfall?

That was all subconscious. However consciously, on all other days of the years, the world would run in its normal fashion; life would be conducted in a righteous and upright fashion, with "trust". The communal affairs were also conducted in this spirit. The administrative positions in the community were occupied by those upright and pious in their ways, who were concerned in a trustworthy fashion for the benefit of the entire community. The opposition was often fierce, setting out in crooked paths, particularly in nationalistic matters and in matters regarding relations between us and the government; however in general there was a united opinion in finding solutions to the problems that arose during that time. For our community was like this: there were very few strong parnassim (communal administrators) who would step over the heads of the holy people, taking revenge or bearing grudges, whose behavior would cause strife and bitterness. There were a few parnassim whose entire lives were literally dedicated to the needs of the community; who abandoned their private endeavors and family matters and were always available to bring forth redemption and minimize evil (on occasion by intervening with the mayor or the local commander, the "bormistasz" and the "kommandat"; on occasion with the district and regional governors, the "starosta" and the "woyewoda"; as well as to the tax representatives, the police chief, and all sorts of major or minor officials...). These communal activists were ready at all times to help anyone in need. Here is a story regarding the dedication of the head of our community, who was also one of the head trustees of the Chevra Kadisha (burial society), and one of the chief speakers on any topic, one of the doers: It was a Sabbath eve, and a rumor circulated in the Beis Midrash that a certain person was desperately ill and was in need of great mercy... and on the morning of the Sabbath, when the fathers came back from the mikveh (ritual bath) and the mothers returned from the bakery with their flasks of coffee [7] and from the houses, the voices of those who were reviewing "twice the text and once the translation" [8] rose out from the houses, suddenly to the surprise of all, the sounds of a wagon hitched to a horse could be heard from one of the alleys, upon which there was a person covered in blankets. A Jewish horse driver was holding the reins, and beside him walked the head of the community, dressed in his weekday clothing, with a fur hat upon his head. To the surprised questions, he answered briefly: "We are taking him to Krakow". [9] It was clear that this removal of the Sabbath clothing, the forgoing of public prayer, the Sabbath meals and Sabbath rest with the family, the arduous travel for many hours in a train, and the difficulties involved in caring for the sick person, etc... etc... the head of the community and the city notables accepted this upon themselves with love. These were your parnassim, oh Dembitz!

We must especially make note of the representatives of the community on the city council, in particular those who represented the Hatechiya movement (members of Poale Zion, the General Zionists, Mizrachi, etc.) They conducted a difficult and constant struggle against the Jew haters, with unforgettable resolve, uncovering plots that were seething with hateful venom. They would refute decrees and protect Jewish honor in that mixed forum. With pain and sorrow we must remember these members who supported our public life – and those of the intelligentsia circles who assisted them – with their lectures at gatherings and meetings, or with their articles in pamphlets and newspapers. They often sanctified the name of Israel in public.

All of the other communal activists in our town should also be remembered positively – the gabaiim (trustees) of the two synagogues (in the new city and the old city), of the two Beis Midrashes (the Proste and Hassidic), of the two prayer houses (of the rabbi of the city and the rabbi of Jadlowa), and of the three shtibels; the trustees of the Chevra Kadisha, Talmud Torah, the Mishna study group and the organization for purchase of books; and the trustees of the charitable funds and benevolent societies. The female workers of the Chevra Kadisha should be remembered for a blessing, those righteous women, our good mothers, who occupied themselves in doing good deeds toward the deceased and the living, who cooked soup for the sick people and the post-partum women, and who hurried to the Beis Midrashes to arouse mercy and to the cemeteries to measure out graves [10]. Once again, I will relate an incident that took place: One market day, a the time of one of the large fairs prior to the days of the non-Jewish festivals, when the profits were great, the wholesale general store was filled with gentiles. Thirteen sets of hands served the customers, but they could not keep up. The owner of the store, one of the head female workers of the Chevra Kadisha, had her hands full with work. Then suddenly a few women covered in black came to the door and called out inside: "We have to go out! There is someone seriously ill!" The owner of the store flailed her hands and began to lament with a voice filled with agony: "Oh woe! What a dark world!" She immediately left everything, and covered herself up and went out. Pandemonium broke out in the store. The uncircumcised ones [11] were left open mouthed and in wonderment. Only the worshippers of the synagogues and the Beis Midrashes knew the explanation for the situation, when the doors of the holy ark were suddenly opened, and the cries of "Oh such a dear soul! Such a pure soul! Please oh holy Torah scrolls, intercede! Beg for mercy and pray!" were heard.

Who would have spoke, and who would have imagined that such dear, pure souls as these would have nobody to pray or wail over them?

Finally, we should remember for blessing all of the activists and the hundreds of members of the various movements in our town, covering all ends of the spectrum and all fields of endeavor: the founders, leaders, and members of the General Zionist Organization, and of each group – Dvora, Akiva, Hanoar Hatzioni, Mizrachi, Young Mizrachi, Hashomer Hadati, Poale Zion, Jugent, Freiheit, Gordonia, Boslia, the Revisionist, Betar, Trumpelder, Hashomer Hatzair, the left leaning Poale Zion, and others. the heads of the committees and activists of the Hebrew school and kindergarten (Prablowka) should be remembered for blessing, along with the teachers – those who instilled the Hebrew language to our lips, the parents' committees of the youth groups, the committees of the two Jewish libraries and the sports clubs, along with many many more... Hundreds of dear members, male and female, young and old, who dedicated a great deal of their energy and time for Zionist activities and national revival activities.

It would be fitting to tell of all of this holy work in minute detail, telling about the effort expended, for example, in the distribution of the Zionist Shekel, and in the diverse branch activity for the benefit of the various funds; the great effort that was expended with love in the preparation of various plays and performances, and the income of these presentations that was collected for the benefit of the funds and cultural organizations. I will again relate a characteristic story, which is not known by very many of the natives of our city. After one of the residents of the suburbs died, quite a distance from the center of town, word spread that it was possible to receive a significant sum for the benefit of the nationalistic activities in return for the transporting of the deceased to the bounds of the city, where he would be received by the members of the Chevra Kadisha. A group of organized young people volunteered for this. Anyone who happened to be located in the suburbs of the city at that time could witness this strange funeral procession, where the coffin was born on the shoulders of four young people, followed by a group of young people accompanied by only one member of the Chevra Kadisha. On behalf of Zion, there was no shortage of people to carry the coffin.

The lot of these enthusiastic people, those who were enthused with the Zionistic ideal, for the most part did not merit them to see the fruits of their labor, the realization of their dreams and desires, to be with us here in Zion... If only they would have merited – along with all the residents of the town – to a normal human death. What happened to them cannot even be called by the term "death" [12] . We remember what death in Dembitz meant from our youth – as we heard the workers of the Chevra Kadisha say: "My good friend, we ask your forgiveness! The entire city begs your forgiveness!" [13] . An omen, so to speak, from the heavens.

As we returned from the cheder on clear winter nights, with the crisp snow under our feet and the sky filled with twinkling stars above our heads, we would often wonder about the twinkling heavenly hosts, and what deep secrets they were hinting to us. We thought at that time that they were the souls of the good and the righteous. If a star were to "fall", we would see this as a sign that someone had just given up his life. This celestial host that looked down onto the city – these were the souls of the good and the righteous who left their earthly lives and took up residence in the heavens above the city.

Years later, this legend was refined again: There is a story of the Besht [14] who worshiped his Creator in the darkness of night. Suddenly, the sound of a cry reached his ears, seemingly the sound of a child wandering in the darkness and sobbing. The Besht felt sorry for the wandering child, and ran out side to take him into his house. However, outside, he did not see any living soul. This was a star in the heavens that burst out crying because a small cloud covered it. The star wept and begged that its light would be able to be revealed in the world. The Besht immediately recited a brief prayer, the cloud scattered, and the light of that star again shone forth. The weeping ceased.

The smoke clouds of the crematoria covered the light of millions of stars – among them thousand of stars from the skies of Dembitz. The stars weep at night in those skies. We have no "prayer" in our power to return them to the light of the living. Let us remember them always. And when they remember us – these star-souls wink to us – we are alive".

Translator's Footnotes :

1. A reference to the prophet Jeremiah, who is considered, according to Jewish tradition, to be the author of the book of Lamentations. The quoted verse is from Jeremiah 6, 26. _

2. This verse segment is from Job 32, 20. _

3. The adage is based on Proverbs 30, 17, indicating that the ravens should pluck out the eyes of he who mocks his father and mother. The 'wise man' referred to here is King Solomon, who was the author of the book of Proverbs. _

4. The term used here for fourteen is 'two sabbatical year cycles', the biblical sabbatical year falling once every seven years. _

5. Hallel is the term given to the Psalms of praise (Psalms 113-118) recited on the various festivals.

6. Simchat Torah is the last day of the Sukkot festival, when joyous processions (Hakkafot) are made around the synagogue with the Torah scrolls, accompanied by singing and dancing. The prayer for dew is recited on the first day of Passover, and the prayer for rain on Shemini Atzeret (the eighth day of Sukkot, prior to Simchat Torah), marking the times of the change of seasons in the Holy Land. The 'wavings' refer to the waving of the lulav and etrog (palm frond and citron) that take place during the first seven days of the Sukkot festival. Hoshanah Rabba is the seventh day of Sukkot, when there are seven processions made with the lulav and etrog, and when prayers are recited to mark the end of the season of judgement that started prior to Rosh Hashanah.

7. On Sabbaths, cooking is forbidden. People would often store their coffee thermoses or other hot victuals in the oven in the bakery from before the Sabbath, and then go to bring them home during the Sabbath. This was because not everyone was able to leave an appropriate oven burning for the duration of the Sabbath.

8.   A reference to the custom of reviewing the weekly Torah portion twice, and the Aramaic translation (known as Targum Onkelus") once each week.

9.   Violation of the sanctity of the Sabbath is permitted, even mandated, when it comes to saving a life.

10.   The Chevra Kadisha (burial society) was not only involved in the burial of the dead, but also in the tending to the ill. This was common in Europe, but has not carried over in North America. _

11.   Here a term for gentiles.

12.   Death here referring to a natural death in the course of human life.

13.   After preparation of the body for burial, it is customary for the members of the Chevra Kadisha to ask forgiveness of the deceased for any embarrassment caused during the preparations.

14.   The acronym of Rabbi Yisrael Baal Shem Tov, the founder of Hassidism.

{Hebrew text – pp 170-172; Yiddish text – 156-159.}

Jumping off the Train

Bronia Oling Burg

Translated by Jerrold Landau

On the eve of the Sabbath, November 13, the evil tidings spread in the ghetto that in two more days, on Sunday December 15, the expulsion would take place. My two brothers had good places of work, and they were certain that they would be able to remain in the ghetto. I myself worked in the hospital, and we hid father in the bunker.

Such a pleasant Sabbath did we have!

Already at the time of the conclusion of the Sabbath, the Polish and German police surrounded the ghetto. At daybreak, when I went out to work to the hospital, my two brothers comforted me that they would also remain in the ghetto.

Suddenly, the sound of a loud noise was heard. People scampered about, as if they went mad: the head of the Gestapo was standing outside and reading a list of 540 people who worked in the railway industry – only they would remain. Only they would merit to remain alive. The rest of the Jews would be exterminated.

Shortly thereafter, the thieves came to the hospital with an order: everyone, healthy or ill, must leave the hospital. How bitter were these words in my ears, for I must also go to death. I will never see my father and my brothers.

Those ill with typhus, with temperatures above forty degrees, were evacuated from the hospital. The cold outside was very severe, and the sick people, wearing only their tunics, were prepared to be sent off. We, the healthy young people, were chased with threats, whips and guard dogs to the field from where the shipment was to be sent off. Thousands of people from various cities and towns were being prepared to be sent off!

I stood and watched to see lest they bring here, Heaven forbid, my father and my two brothers. We walked to the train station in rows of five. The order was repeated over and over: "To the left, to the left". Thus did we go out as sheep, to die in the furnace of Belzec.

One hundred people entered each train car. My turn came to enter the death train. There would certainly be no way to flee from this train. It is clear that we were travelling to our deaths.

There were sixty cars, sixty train cars to Belzec. Old and young, men, women and children. Our lot was the lot of all the Jews – to travel to our deaths.

The Jews would arrive at the machine of poisonous gases [1] , they would get out, and become contorted until they would choke to death through the torture.

The train only started to move at 8:00 p.m. There were many who thought that they would be able to save their lives, that they would not arrive to where the train was taking them. The night was dark, however a small amount of light shone into the cars from the flashlights of the S. S. men who were standing on guard.

The people in the cars were crowded together like sacks. This was a long journey of torture, a cramped journey where everyone was standing. Death awaited.

Who would die here? Who would die due to the tribulations of the journey? What difference would it make if they survived the journey?

Where were we going? We were like sheep to the slaughter, sacrifices to the crematoria.

Nevertheless, any moment that one is still alive is a found moment. Who knows what would take place? Perhaps some people would be saved.

There was no bench upon which to sit down. People sat where they stood.

The wild beasts were prepared to administer beatings whenever they heard a sound breaking forth, even for the crime of a loud sigh. People moaned inside, as they bit their lips and swallowed their tears. One could only wave their hands, beat their head, or pull out their hair. A silent cry to the Master of the World, a call to mother and father in the world of truth [2] .

As soon as we heard that we were moving, the weeping broke out with greater strength. We wept until there were no more tears: heavy sighs broke forth from weary hearts. Many were silent, for they had no strength. However, nobody could see those that fainted in the darkness of the night; the glazed eyes when the lips became silent and a heart ceased beating.

There were many children in the car, who were not separated from their mothers.

Suddenly, the voice of an old Jew was heard. It was Feivel Wilner. "Jews, let us recite Psalms! Let us recite the confession, we must be prepared".

The weeping of the women grew greater, and the men started to move. Yosef Taub called out that he would remove a piece of the wooden floor in order to be able to escape outside, and others would be able to be saved. Whoever had the desire and the strength would be able to jump out of the moving train. However, what could he do with his small pocketknife? He did not give himself any respite: "Jews", he said, "we can yet merit to see the end of the war, in a few weeks. We must save ourselves. We must find some way to jump out.".

Not far from me sat his wife with his two beautiful children. The girl burst out crying, for something hurt her.

The mother comforted her daughter, stroked her beautiful hair and said to her: "This will not last much longer. We will arrive at your aunt's house, and there you will receive nice toys." A groan passed over everybody.

However, to us, the distraught mother was saying something entirely different, quietly, very silently: "When I arrive at the dreadful place, I will give the children a bit of the poison that I took with me. I know that it is forbidden for a mother to do that. However, where are we going? We are going to Belzec." Suddenly she cried out from her broken heart: "Why have You given me children, that I may kill them? Therefore I am giving them poison, so that they will have an easier death."

The husband again groaned quietly: "My dear, we are all required to say to ourselves that we are eighty year old people. We have all finished living in this beautiful world, and there is nothing left for us but death."

The men cried out: "If only we could die, but not have to wait for such a terrible death as this."

Everyone in the car was suffering from terrible thirst. The children were begging their mothers: "Mother, my throat is burning, give me water."

Before we entered the car, the Germans spread plaster dust in it. That was what was choking the people's throats. Everyone was prepared to give everything that they had for a sip of water.

The S. S. men threw a bottle of water into the car when they heard the screams, one bottle for one hundred people. We would give them silver and gold, but who would merit to drink from the water? People grabbed the bottle from one another. These were no longer humans; they no longer had a sense of life. Quarrels broke out, if only to assuage the terrible thirst.

Then the S. S. men came to us with a suggestion. If we would give them everything that we still had, they would open the locked door for five seconds, and anyone who was able to jump out could do so, and would certainly survive.

Everyone gave to them what they had. They took everything, and they no longer looked through the small window. They cheated us. This was only mockery on their part.

The men continued to think of how they could, with all this, save themselves from death. Yosef Taub got up from his place, went to the small holes in the windowpane, and retrieved his small "weapon", his penknife, once more. With it, he began to cut the metal wires. Suddenly, he called out: "I cut the wires. Now, people, you can save yourselves!" From the side, the old Jew issued forth his complaints: "I can no longer save myself. I am already too old. I am sick and weak. If I jump, I won't get up again, and it will have taken my life with my own hands. I will die by the death that the Master of the World chose for me. If it is to be by burning, it is to be by burning".

He said further: "I no longer know what is appropriate, and what is not appropriate, however whoever has enough strength to do so should do so and save himself. Whoever wishes to jump out should jump with all his might, remain complete of body, not fall into the hands of the Germans, and should merit to see the salvation."

The old man jumped out of the window to see if any S. S. men were standing on guard. The men strengthened themselves. Mendele Siedlisker was the first to jump. He was ill with typhus, and had a temperature of forty degrees. We did not hear them shooting after him. We prayed to G-d that he would return in peace to the ghetto.

I stood next to my relative Feivel Wilner. Brachale, he said to me – why are you not together with your two brothers? They are also in this transport, in the first car."

I could not listen to his words – I was certain that that they had remained in the ghetto. I broke out in a cold sweat. I had no energy to answer him.

I broke forth with strength to the small window in order to jump. Perhaps I would die under the wheels of the train – so long as I do not see their bitter death in Belzec. Before me, a few men jumped out. I also wanted to be among them. However, they pushed me aside. They did not permit me to jump. However, my will was greater than their opposition. Nevertheless, they did not wish to be responsible for my life.

I placed myself next to the window. Yosef Taub was looking to see if they could see a German guard or not. He suddenly told me: "You can jump now."

My heart was beating like a hammer. I gave over my piece of bread that I had with me, and prepared to jump. I was first in line.

The train was travelling too fast. The young men helped me, and I jumped. I disappeared. I fell onto the white, beautiful snow that was on the tracks. I was injured, as would be expected, on my right side. I heard very well that they were screaming that I jumped. This was a distance of ninety kilometers from Dembitz.

I wished to remain dead under the wheels of the train, but G-d willed that I live.

The train continued along its way, not fast. It was a very dark night. It was 4:00 a.m.

I looked at the passing cars that were transporting the people, both those close to me and those more distant to me, to their deaths, and I could not help them at all. The train disappeared. I turned back to return to Dembitz, to return to the ghetto. I followed the lanterns until I arrived at the Lancut train station. I concealed myself among the Germans, and arrived to the outside of the city. Various thoughts were going through my mind: would not everyone who saw me realize that I jumped off the train.

I arrived at a Christian house at 6:00 a.m. The Tracanski family lived there. I opened the door, requested a bit of water, and asked what time it was. The woman answered that she realized that I am a Jewish girl. She told me to enter into her room, and that she had already hid a few Jews with her. Therefore, she told me that I should not Heaven forbid be afraid, but rather that I should enter. The Christian woman gave me my own room and spoke to me like a mother. She immediately gave me breakfast and prepared me for my journey. I wished to give her everything that I had, if she would only give me a kerchief for my head so that I would be able to hide my Jewish eyes somewhat. She took out a new green kerchief from her closet and told me: "Green is a symbol of hope. That is an omen that you will return home." She wished me much success on my journey and asked me that I should write to her.

It was very cold outside. I walked quickly. It seemed to me that behind me, the shadows were after my life. I saw only fields and forests. The ground was covered with snow. The wind blew me from side to side. At night, I arrived at Rzeszow. I stood before the ghetto. One gentile woman said to me: "You are a Jewess. I can tell that immediately. You want to enter the ghetto now? Do you know what is going on in the ghetto right now? They are searching for Jews who are still hiding after the deportation in order to shoot them, and you are liable to be one of them. Go to the village, rest there for the night, and come to the ghetto in the morning." I wanted to, indeed had no choice but to, listen to her and I set out for the village.

I entered one of the houses and asked the Christian homeowner to permit me to spend the night. He requested my documents, for it was forbidden to allow strange people to stay over. I entered a second and third home, and was answered with the same answer. I was forced to sleep outside. I ran to an area between the trees. I plucked a branch of the tree from the thickness of the thicket and lay down to sleep in the snow, with the branch under my head. I tried to sleep, and a deep sleep overtook me until the morning.

Day had already broken. I was completely frozen. I wished to drink something warm, but from where? There was only plenty of snow for me to eat. I could not even buy a piece of bread with the money that I had with me. I ate up the frozen bread that I had with me with a great appetite.

I continued walking through the fields and forests. I had to still walk a great distance until I arrived home. Night fell again. I was again outside. I looked for a covered barn or coop to spend the night in, but all the doors were closed and locked.

I found a small chamber in front of me. I hid in it. I quietly hid myself under some straw and burst out weeping. The tears choked me. Were my sins so great? Was I deserving of such great tribulations? G-d, have mercy upon an orphan girl, perhaps I would still find my father alive. I swallowed my tears and fell into a fitful sleep until the morning.

I left the chamber at 6:00 a.m. The owners of the house had already woken up and had started their day's work. I went into their room and asked for some water. I had no strength to continue. The people looked at me as if I was mentally disturbed. They had pity on me and gave me some milk and a slice of bread. However they quickly realized that I was a Jewess, and ordered me to leave the room immediately.

I gave their daughter twenty guilder and asked her to lead me along a sure path, so that I would know how to continue my journey. Children were going to school, and they called out: "Here is a Jidowica (Jewish girl) walking. She certainly escaped from the ghetto."

My blood froze in me. It seemed that I would not be able to make it to the Dembitz ghetto. However, the more that people placed stumbling blocks before me, the greater my determination grew.

On Wednesday evening, I saw a gentile woman standing in a field with her young daughter, harvesting turnips from the ground. I requested from her that she might perhaps take me with her, and let me sleep in the barn that night. The young daughter had great pity for me, and requested that her mother do so. However the mother answered that she must ask her husband. When we came to him, he realized that I was a Jewess... how difficult it was to be a Jew, I thought at that time. The farmer asked me for money, and showed me a place to rest in the attic.

Late at night, he called me to come down to the house. He gave me a bit of potato soup and a piece of bread. Immediately thereafter, I hurried back to the attic.

They woke me up from my sleep at 5:00 a.m. The husband instilled great fear in me by telling me that there were S. S. men in the village, and they were checking the papers of anyone who passed through. I asked him to help me. I would give him 50 guilder if his wife would take me along the way. He agreed for the price of 200 guilder, however his wife only took me from the house outside, remained standing in the door, and did not move. She closed the door and called out after me: "there are no Germans here at all."

The farmer only wanted to cheat me out of my money, and he succeeded. He was lucky. But I also had my luck.

I arrived at the Dembitz ghetto on Thursday night. However, I did not want to enter until I would receive the news that father was still there. I asked several gentiles whom I knew, and it became clear that they had recently spoken to father. He was in the ghetto.

I had to wait until it became completely dark. In the dark, I cut a few wires in the gate and entered.

Young and old people shouted: "Bronia has returned from the death train". I made my way through the people and finally came to father.

Before I arrived, people had already come to tell father that I had come. Father waited for me in front of the house. I fell on his neck with great weeping. I could not stop. Father kissed me and stroked me as one would stroke a young girl.

I did not recognize my beloved father. During the course of a few days, he had aged several years.

The neighbors were comforting father the whole time that I would certainly return from the journey. Now their words had been fulfilled.

I told him the entire story in great detail, about the train car and the difficult journey. I went to sleep only very late at night, and I thought: Oh would it be that the better times for the Jews would already come.

Translator's Footnotes :

1. The gas for the gas chamber of Belzec was produced by a diesel engine.
2. The 'world of truth' is a reference to those who have passed on.

{Hebrew text – pp 173-174; Yiddish text – pp 159-161.}

Twenty-two Months in Hiding with Gentiles

Translated by Jerrold Landau

The Shamash Reb Yisrael and his wife, parents of the author of this article.

Reltche Taub and her son remained in the ghetto. At first, they lived in a storehouse of eggs. The egg storehouse very quickly filled with people, mostly from the old city. Dozens of families lodged there. Their belongings, bedding and clothing were hidden away in the attic, and they hoped that they would be able to be salvaged in this manner. In the end, after the aktion, the Nazis uncovered the hiding place, chose the best of the bedding and linens for themselves, and sold the rest in a public sale. Announcements were posted that there would be a sale of linens, bedding, clothing and furniture that had belonged to Jews. Gentiles gathered from all of the neighboring villages and purchased the property of the Jews for a very cheap price.

This event took place at a time when my husband and myself were already in hiding with a gentile in our home. He told us about this. He himself also purchased many items from that sale.

There were already people lying one on top of another in the egg storehouse of the Taub family, and it was difficult to move. Reltche was good to them all. I was also in her house at the time of the final aktion. About fifty people stayed there in the dark for two nights and one day. There were many children there. They were given sleeping potions so that they would sleep, would not have to eat, and would not cry. People fainted from the cramped conditions and from the bad odor in the air that came from the nearby toilet.

I was the first to leave there. I lost my voice from the dryness in my throat. I looked around me, and I saw nobody on the streets. I entered into one of the houses – it was empty and abandoned. There were no people there. Everything was open and ownerless. Everyone had been murdered or sent to the gas chambers.

A few days later, a few more people were discovered, but they were afraid to go out on the street and they lived in an attic. At that time, even the members of the Judenrat and their families had been sent away. Yosef Taub, the head of the Judenrat, had succeeded in jumping off the train. He made it to a village, where a gentile acquaintance hid him until the liberation. He is now in Paris. I met him after the liberation, and he told me that his wife advised him to jump and she and their two children would swallow poison. Thus it was.

But now I want to describe how we were saved.

In the days of the ghetto, my son worked in forced labor on the railway track. He talked with a person, a railway worker who was one of our tenants, and told him that my husband and I would register our house in his name if in return he would take us in for a short time until we would find somewhere to go to, for example to Hungary. The tenant did not answer. He said that he had to ask his wife. The next day he declined, for his wife did not agree.

About two weeks later the gentile met my son and told him that now he was able to take us in with him, for his daughter had taken suddenly ill and died. Therefore his wife had to travel to where their daughter had lived in order to care for the five young children, and he was now alone in the dwelling.

We slipped out of the ghetto and went to the gentile. However the wife returned home a few weeks later. What happened? She had an argument with her son-in-law and now she found us in her dwelling. The gentile woman pulled out the hair of her head, for her husband had taken us in, and in addition she brought with her two granddaughters, little girls aged seven and five. Indeed, the crowding was a great danger. Adding to the danger, one of the Gestapo men lived in the dwelling that we had vacated, which was on the other side of the wall. It was dangerous to utter even a word, for everything could be heard from there.

The gentile asked that we leave the room immediately, for she did not want Jews in her dwelling.

I begged her to let us stay until night. Thus did we sit, with out bags in our hands – for we would leave shortly. Then the young girl entered and asked why we were sitting that way. The gentile women told her that she was expelling us. The young girl clapped her hands together and said in Polish: "Grandmother, if they leave, they will shoot us, for they will certainly reveal that they were with us!" She immediately offered a suggestion: they would take the closet that was near the door and put it in a corner, and we would stay there until it was possible to leave. Thus did we sit, my husband and myself, on two low wooden stumps, for twenty-two months.

As long as we had money we lived on bread alone, for we thought that our son would soon come to take us out, and we would need our money. On occasion, our son would send us some items of food via the gentile railway worker. However after three months, someone reported that my son was talking with a gentile through the wire fence of the ghetto. They immediately brought him to the cemetery with his spade over his shoulder. He himself was required to dig a pit and enter it, and they shot him. Thus was his tragic end at the hands of the Hitlerist murderers.

As long as our son was alive and sending food for us, the gentile also benefited from this, and his relation to us was still quite good. However, from the time that our son was no longer alive, the gentiles began to afflict us by saying that they had to kill us! They did not want to keep us any more, but they could not let us go, for then they would be in danger. Indeed, they were in great danger, for every conversation was heard through the door. They asked us what type of death we preferred: poisoning, cutting of our heads, or burial alive. We did not answer. We hoped that the all-powerful L-rd would be able to assist us. Indeed, the gentile tried twice to poison us, but the Master of the Universe saved us.

On one occasion, they told us that the next day, people would be going around to search for Jews among the Christians. In the room there was a pit that he had dug, one meter wide and one meter long. We were forced to enter it, and he placed the closet on top of us. He covered the pit and left. We would soon have been asphyxiated there. We could not continue on. My husband tried to lift the covering with his feet, until the closet moved from its place. When the gentile heard the sound, he was afraid that we would scream out. He came and moved the closet. My husband got out, and I remained lying down, half dead. They pulled me out from the pit and poured water on me until I revived.

We again sat behind the closet, but soon other afflictions began. They beat us, and did not give us food to eat or even water to drink. We even had to attend to our bodily needs behind the closet. A small box of jam preserve had to sustain two adults for 24 hours. There was no place to urinate. We were in a nicely furnished room, and when the gentiles were not home, I would urinate in a vase; but this was not always possible. There was an open toilet in the garden, which was used also by the Gestapo man. The gentile worried that the

Gestapo man would notice that it filled up too quickly. Therefore he did not give us anything to eat, so that we would not have to excrete. Indeed, the gentile was correct. Thus did we sit for 22 months, starving, being fed with morsels of bread four finger breadths in width and a bit of black coffee in the morning and evening.

On one occasion the gentile told me to take out the vessel myself. I was willing to do so, for it would be an honor to do it myself. In the morning, he called me to take the vessel outside. I took it and started to go. When I arrived in the lobby, he ordered me to put down the vessel. He pushed me onto the bundle of straw and began to strangle me. At first I thought that he was joking. However, it became evident that he indeed intended to strangle me. I pleaded with him to back off, until I no longer had a voice. I realized that my last moments were coming. I gathered all my strength and shouted out Shema Yisrael [1] in a voice that sounded like an ox being slaughtered. The gentile became afraid lest the Gestapo man who lived in the house hear, and then he backed off.

Now he began to try poison again. He twice tried to serve us poison, but he did not succeed. The second time, I tasted a bite of moldy, dry bread, and I swallowed it. Until this day I have a burn in my esophagus. He tortured us so that we would lose our strength. When my husband lay down on the floor at night and the gentile entered, for he always guarded us, he kicked my husband with his foot. We were forced to sit the entire night on low wooden stumps. During the day we would stand up to stretch our limbs.

It is difficult to describe how we survived for these 22 months. Once we heard the gentile telling his wife that tomorrow he would finish us off, therefore she must leave the house with the children. For four days previously he had not given us anything to eat, or even a glass of water to drink. They tried to weaken us so that it would be easier to kill us.

We did not know that the Russians were already behind Dembitz. We had no idea about how the war was progressing. Morning arrived, and we did not hear anybody in the dwelling. The Gestapo man had already removed his belongings from the house. There was a great silence around. We moved the closet slightly and I approached the door and peered through the keyhole. I saw that there was nobody there. I returned to my husband and said to him: "Chaim, listen to me, perhaps now a miracle from heaven will occur, and the Creator will have mercy on us. Let us flee outside." My husband did not wait for another word and we both went outside quickly. Indeed, four weeks previously, my husband had dreamed that the holy rabbi Reb Shmuel of holy blessed memory said to him: "You should know that you will only have to stay here for four more weeks."

The gentile saw as we fled outside and tried to run after us, but Hitler's army stood on the street. Nevertheless, we continued on our journey. I was on one side, and my husband on the other. Our feet were shrunken, and we fell a few times as we walked. The soldiers saw us, but the Master of the World confounded them. They thought that we were certainly vagabonds, for we were so black since we had not washed ourselves for 22 months.

We went on our way dirty, wearing torn clothing and covered with hair. They went after us and laughed each time we fell. We approached the river and continued to walk until the bank until we came to an area between two hills that hid us. There, we first drank some water, which we had not tasted for several days. Then we took off all of our clothes, even our shirts, and washed everything in the river. On them there were more vermin than threads, for we had not changed shirts in four months. The vermin gnawed at us and were everywhere, even in our shoes and socks – each insect was the size of a pea. Thus did we sit by the river and dig up potatoes from the field. It was the month of Elul [2] and it was pleasant outside. Now it was good for us. We drank river water to our satiation, and satisfied our hunger with live potatoes. We could no longer sit by the river after it got dark. As soon as we got out of the water a shegetz [3] noticed us. He put his hands to his mouth and whistled, and then about ten shkotzim came running and turned us in to the command headquarters, which was now the village, for the Russians had already entered the city. When we were brought to the police, the German guard did not do any check upon us, but he immediately summoned a guard with a gun and told us to take us to a specific place to shoot us. What choice did we have? We had to go. As we were going along the way, the screamed after us: "Halu! Halu!" The soldier with the gun told us to stand and said to us: "They are calling us to return! We must return."

The commander told us that we must thank the old couple who stood there, for they requested that they not shoot us. They must have been two angels from heaven. After that, he ordered us to leave the village immediately, and pointed us where to go. However, it was already 8:00 p.m., and it was dangerous to walk alone in the fields. We lay down among the potatoes and slept there.

First thing in the morning, as we set out on our journey, some shkotzim met us and turned us again over to the police. We told the Hitlerists that we had already been there and were freed, but they did not want to listen. They brought us to another commander, and we told him how the commander freed us yesterday. He did not wish to believe us, and he sent us, accompanied by armed guards, to the head commander. As we arrived he came down to us, since we did not have the strength to go up the stairs. He said to us: "Aber haben sie die Leute gut verpflegt!" (Indeed, the people fed you well!) He told us to stand, and he brought us from inside two nice pieces of bread and gave them to us. I refused to take them: "Zum Tod brauch ich kein brot" (for death I do not need any bread). He caressed my hand and said: "Nein, sie werden nicht erschossen, nur gehen sie mit diesen weg in den wald, dort aben sind Bauern, dort werden se getotet." (No, no you will not be shot. Just go along this way in the forest. There, there are homes of farmers, and there you will be killed.)

This was what happened. We slept in different forests for eight days and eight nights, for we were afraid lest someone find us. Then a Russian patrol from the Red Army, searching for Germans, found us.

We showed them the way. Then they brought us to a Jewish captain from the Russian army. We were free.

Translator's Footnotes :

1. Shema Yisrael (literally Hear Oh Israel), is a verse from Deuteronomy, which serves as the most important Jewish confession of faith, recited every morning and evening. It is also to be recited, if possible, during a person's last moments of life.
2. August or September.
3. A derogatory term for a non-Jew. Plural is shkotzim.

{Hebrew text – p 175; Yiddish text – p 162.}

One Was Saved

Ben Steinhauer

Translated by Jerrold Landau

In 1942, I was assigned along with 29 other friends to work in the Fuerst-Richter building enterprise. The work was difficult. I carried bricks in a trestle for twelve hours a day, thirty bricks at a time. The skin of my shoulders became chafed from this work, and blood dripped from me. I was forced to be quiet and work. In the winter, after my shoulders healed a bit, I got an abscess on my right foot and it became difficult for me to go out for work.

Only G-d knows how much I suffered. I visited the infirmary every day, where they poured a small bit of water [1] on me, and it did not help at all. This went on for three months, and when my right foot was healed, I got an abscess on my left foot. I cannot even describe my suffering, and in addition, I was forced to go out daily to work. Once I asked the doctor, who was the Dembitz native Y. Tau (now in America), that he grant me permission to remain for a day or two in the camp. However, I was not suffering from fever, and according to the orders of the Gestapo he did not have permission to free me from work.

Thus did I suffer until the end of 1942. When things got better for me again, I thought that I was already free from all of the tribulations. But in the beginning of 1943, the abscess in my left foot returned, this time in a different place. In my life I could not believe that I would be able to manage through this without receiving the proper medicine. I again went to the infirmary daily, where they bandaged up my leg and sent me home. This went on until February 23, 1943. That day, when I came to the infirmary after work, Dr. Tau bandaged my foot. Just as I was ready to leave, I was ordered to remain. He entered the other room, and a few minutes later returned with a permit for me to remain in the camp the next day. It was difficult for me to believe that, after having being refused this many times, he himself was now bringing me the permit without my having requested it.

The next day, February 24, when all of the groups went out to work as on all other days, I had no suspicion at all that a black cloud was hanging over the heads of all of my best friends who were now going out to work.

Only in the evening, when the first group was supposed to return but was now late, did I become uneasy. I asked the other groups, but they did not know what was happening. Only after a few minutes did I find out that the entire group was imprisoned by the Gestapo and the railway police as it was already on the route back to the camp. A fright fell upon me. In the meantime, the entire camp became agitated. Immediately, Immerglick the head of the camp and Bitkover the head of the police went out to find out why the people were imprisoned. They were answered with various pretexts, and until this day, it is not known why they were imprisoned. That evening, they were all shot in a field next to the camp along with other Jews.

I do not know what took place during the time that the shooting started, but when I woke up the next morning, I found myself in the room of my older brother who was also in the camp.

The rest of the people remaining in the camp went out to work as usual, as if nothing happened. But they had to hide me, since I was in the list of those who were liquidated.

The liquidation of the camp began in March. The director of the camp Immerglick smuggled me to the Offenbach group where my two brothers worked, and that same month, we were sent to the ghetto of Rzeszow.

I will now list the names of some of my friends who perished, as well as I remember their names: Chaim Herbst, Moshe Fertziger, Yosef Roschwald, Shlomo Reiner, Yosef Eizen, Yosef Roth, and Asher Wagschall.

These are some of the people who were murdered in sanctification of G-d's name. May their souls be bound in the bonds of eternal life.

<u>Translator's Footnotes :</u>

1. The term used here is 'mayim acharonim', literally 'final waters', the small amount of water that is traditionally used to wash one's fingers after a meal.

{Hebrew text – p 175.}

From Among the Righteous Gentiles

Translated by Jerrold Landau

The house was in Dembitz, near the Gestapo building. Thirteen people were hidden in that house. They spent most of the time in the attic and some of the time in the cellar under the garage. Indeed, during all the years of Nazi occupation, there were stories of human might, but only a few can equal the might of the young Polish doctor, Dr. Alexander Mikolikow and his wife Leokida. They endangered their lives and the lives of their young children to prove that decent people who value human life and humane values can still be found.

Dr. Mikolikow cannot speak for himself, for he was killed on the day of the liberation of Dembitz as he was assisting one of the wounded. But one of the thirteen who were saved, A. R. who today serves as a rabbi in Brooklyn, has published the story of the bravery of the doctor and his wife. For two years, he has tried to obtain an entry permit to the United States for Mrs. Mikolikow, who very much wants to see those that she saved, and not only for a short period. To his great dismay, he is frustrated by the refusal of the government of the United States. The young 33-year-old rabbi, married and the father of three children, cannot to this day speak without emotion about the tribulations that befell him. This is his story, as was told over to me.

The Nazis conquered Dembitz in 1939, and they immediately began to persecute the Jews and the Polish intelligentsia. One of their first activities was the establishment of a concentration camp, and later also a ghetto.

Dr. Mikolikow, who was a government physician, could not make peace with the restrictions and the persecutions that the Nazis conducted against the Jews. He felt that the injustice against a part of the population was an injustice against all.

The rabbi, who was a thirteen year old boy at the outbreak of the war and had been healed by the doctor prior to the war, requested that he provide him with some sort of work so that he could escape, for a short period at least, being sent to the camp. The doctor's position enabled him to employ the boy as a messenger boy for some period.

One Friday morning, Mrs. Mikolikow appeared in the ghetto and said that she knew that the Germans were preparing to liquidate the Jews within a few days. The news of the impending tragedy spread through the ghetto very quickly. Overcome with fear and trepidation, the Jews began to build shelters under their houses, or they decided to flee for their lives. Then the doctor told the messenger boy that he intended to save his entire family, even though this would be fraught with great danger.

On June 17, 1942, it became known, again from Mrs. Mikolikow, that the liquidation would take place in a few hours. Mrs. Mikolikow gave the messenger a key to her attic and told him: "Try to save whomever you can". During the course of a few hours, the boy succeeded in smuggling everyone from his family and his uncle's family into the attic, with the exception of one sister who was not at home.

The house was not large. It was two stories high. The doctor, his family and maid lived on the first floor. A tenant, a single bachelor, lived on the second floor. These two bothered the doctor greatly, for he saw in them a potential fifth column, and he had to be careful of them just as much as he had to be careful with the Gestapo.

One day the rabbi found out that there were signs posted outside the city that anyone who was hiding a Jew would be shot. He immediately turned to the doctor and told him that those who were hidden could not expect that he endanger his life and the life of his family on their behalf. Dr Mikolikow answered: "I am always willing to risk my life in order to save innocent people."

During the nights, when the tenant and maid were sleeping in their rooms, the doctor of his wife would bring those hidden something to eat. Since the attic had no sanitation facilities, there was a pot that served them for their bodily needs. The doctor would empty the pot every night, without ever complaining.

In the meantime, the Nazis began to concentrate a large number of Jews from the entire region, to the point where their number reached 12,000. 6,000 were sent to Belzec at the time of the first aktion. 3,000 old people and children were murdered locally. Thus, only 3,000 people remained. All of these were selected workers.

In order not to endanger the life of the doctor further, those in hiding left their shelter and moved into the ghetto under the cover of night. Despite his young age, the rabbi became responsible for two families. This was a natural state of affairs given the situation at the time, for children often matured beyond their years. "Once", the rabbi relates, "I heard an eight year old girl comforting her mother before being sent to the camp, telling her that from there, the road leads to the Garden of Eden."

Life in the ghetto was unbearable. We worked in backbreaking work in return for starvation rations of ¼ kilo of bread a day. Offering assistance to a Jewish family was fraught with mortal danger, but nevertheless, Mrs. Mikolikow would appear during the nights, bringing sacks of food with her.

One day, Dr. Mikolikow brought a note to the rabbi's family, informing him that the end of the Jews in the ghetto was quickly approaching, and that they should come to him as soon as possible. The thirteen people moved to the doctor's house one at a time in order not to arouse suspicion. They hid in a cellar behind the garage for nine months. By working for a few nights, they were able to dig a secret passageway from the cellar into the garage, through which the doctor would bring them food at night.

The conditions in the cellar were very difficult. It was completely dark inside. Not even a candle was lit for fear of the Nazis. The cellar would flood with water when it rained, sometimes up to the neck. However, there was one benefit to this: the dampness kept the lice away, for they could not tolerate this. Not so with the humans, they maintained themselves.

One day, the Gestapo suddenly appeared and requested that the doctor give them the keys to the garage. This was without any explanation. They simply requested that the garage be emptied within 24 hours. That night, all of those in hiding were transferred to the attic, where they remained until the liberation. It is a wonder in the eyes of the rabbi, as he thinks back now about that time, how they managed to survive in those conditions. Apparently, the deep desire to merit the redemption and witness the downfall of the enemy gave them the required strength. The cramped conditions in which they lived often caused controversy among them, but their learned and G-d fearing father always succeeded in calming them.

An additional source of support was drawn from the unusual dedication of this noble couple. In order to understand the magnitude of the sacrifice of the Mikolikow family, it is important to point out that if they were to have been exposed as hiding people, both of them would certainly have been taken out to be killed.

On June 6, 1944, the Poles, encouraged by the advance of the Russian army, attempted to rise up against the Nazis, and killed one of them. Thirsty for revenge, the Germans began to comb through house after house to search for those that rebelled. They arrived at the home of the doctor. At that time (in the words of the rabbi), something occurred that can be termed a modern day miracle. The Nazis erected a ladder from the entrance to the hiding place, and one of them started ascending the rungs. It is impossible to describe in words the state of those above. Overcome by fear, they began to whisper the confessional, believing that their end was near. It was already possible to see the murderous face of the Nazi captain when something fell down. He descended to see what happened, and he did not ascend again.

A few days prior to the liberation, those in hiding heard the sound of bombing and shooting. This was close to the homes, and as a result there was no possibility of bringing food to those in hiding. The thirteen remained for a few days without food at all.

The rabbi cannot remember the exact time when the news of liberation reached them. He remembers one thing: how they broke outside. It is impossible to describe the appearance of the faces of the survivors. They were filthy, bloated from hunger, and half-blind from their long sojourn in darkness. They did not bear the appearance of humans.

After the liberation of the city by the Russians, they were all taken to a hospital for an extended period of convalescence. Despite their serious condition, they regained to their strength, and they merited witnessing the victory that they had dreamed about during all their years of suffering. However the noble doctor, who suffered so greatly in order to see them to freedom, did not merit seeing the victory. He was killed on the day of the liberation of the city as he was administering first aid to an injured person. The rabbi relates: "I remember the anniversary of his death every year". I believe in life after death, and I believe that Dr. Mikolikow occupies a place that is fitting to him.

After his death, the widow remained without any means of livelihood. The survivors transferred ownership of their house in Dembitz to her, and when they moved to the Displaced Person's Camp in Austria, they immediately began sending packages of food to her from the rations that they received for themselves.

When they arrived in the United States, they immediately began to send packages of food, clothing and medication, which helped her raise her two sons. One of them is today a doctor and the other is an engineer.

(Translated from an English Newspaper in the United States by Fruma Grossman-Salomon.)

{Hebrew text – p 177-182.}

The Cradle of our Youth

Ruchama Bornstein

Translated by Jerrold Landau

Dembitz, our Dembitz, is no longer. Even the "good land", upon which we so used to enjoy taking a walk around, is no longer. More than 45 years have passed from the time I left my home, the house and the factory opposite the synagogue. It was not easy to leave everything – father, mother, sisters, brothers, grandfather and grandmother, good friends and neighbors, and indeed the town itself in which I had grown up, became active in the movements, and perhaps also helped others to find their way to a better and nicer life.

We fought numerous battles with many righteous, pious Jews, and not a few with dark fanatics who viewed us, Zionists and members of Poale Zion, as the devil incarnate [1].

And indeed, how wonderful were the Sabbaths and festivals in the town! The synagogues and Beis Midrashes were full with people. The prayers would tear down walls [2]. The broken hearts of Jewish mothers, dissolving in sighs and tears, would find comfort and consolation there. Who can forget the High Holy Day services conducted by the rabbi! The prayers of my grandfather, Reb Mendel Mahler of blessed memory, are unforgettable to me. His voice and melodies remain in my ears to this day.

Who in Dembitz never heard the 'chatzot' observances of pious Jews in the middle of the night [3]? Who in the old city did not hear the call of the shamash at night: "Arise Jews to the worship of the Creator"? Who has not witnessed on a Friday afternoon, close to the Sabbath, the hurrying of people to the bath, so that they would be able to come to the synagogue or Beis Midrash refreshed, cleaned from their weekday concerns?

Subconsciously, the Dembitz of that time is cast before the eyes in a new light. The one-time battles are repressed deeper into the memory, and the warm home of yesteryear, the cradle of our youth, is what remains.

The gravestone of Reb Yitzchak the son of Shimon Shrage Gruenspan, of
blessed memory, died 17 Elul 5632 (corresponds to September 18, 1932)

Page 178}

Memorial-stone for Nathan and Debora Grenspan, and their children, murdered by Germans: Dr. Israel Sandhaus and his wife Reha with their children Ruth and Zeev Menachem; Shimon and his wife Rahel with their children Menahem and Josef; Yitzchak and his wife Hana with their daughters Ruth and Judith. Translator's note: The stone indicates that Nathan died in 1942 and Debora died in 1940.

Memorial-stone for Zilla Ascheim nee Goldfarb, her son Hersch with his wife
Ita, Leizer son of Samuel Feilbogen and his stister Helena, victims of German
massacres in 1943.

{Page 179}

Memorial stone in Lisa Gora for 500 Jews, murdered on the 10th of Av, 5702 (corresponds to September 18, 1942). Translator's note: the inscription is in Polish. It includes the note that it was funded by Bar-Natan Gurenspan, Tel Aviv.

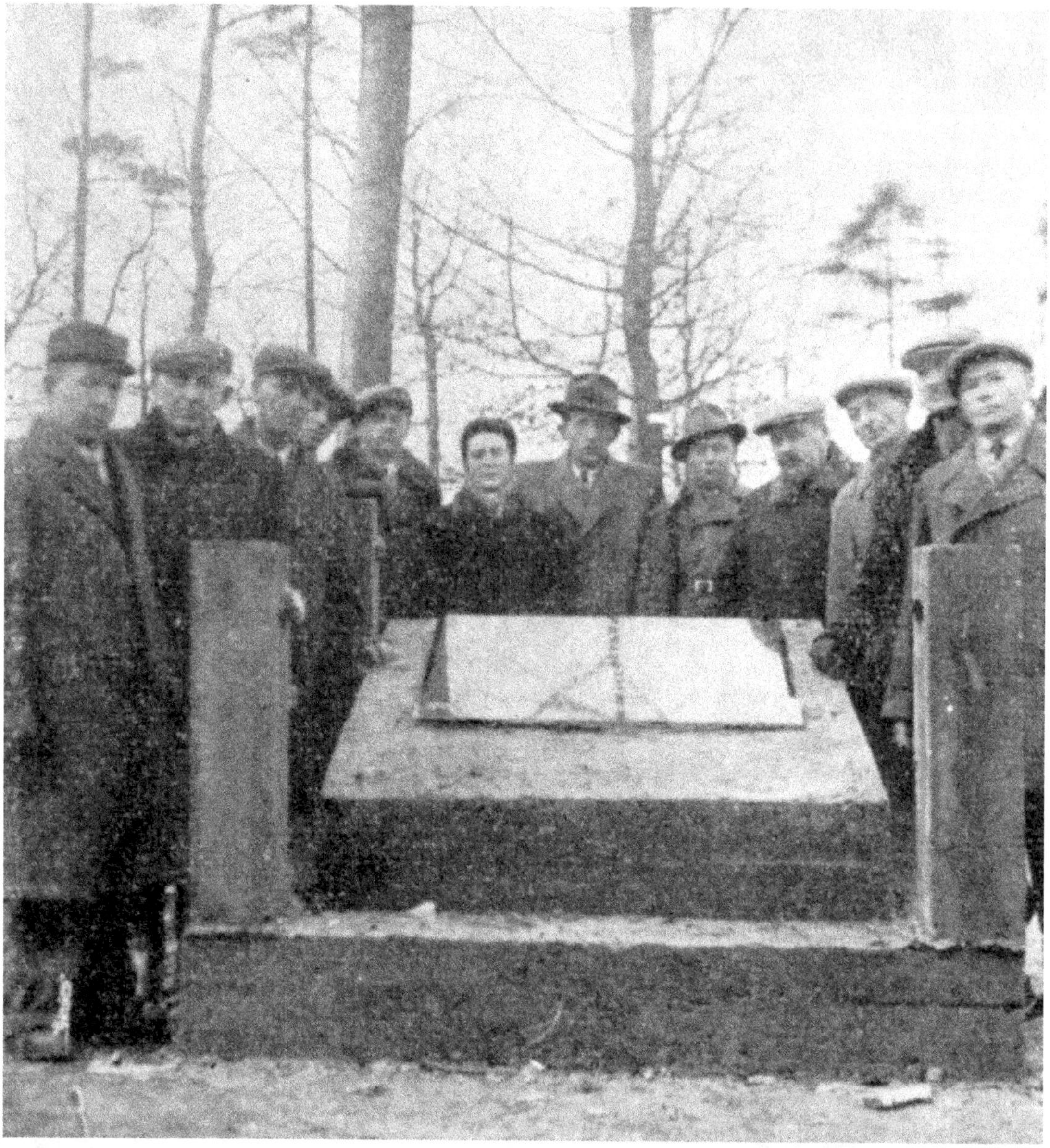

No caption. A group of people in front of a memorial stone

{Page 180}

At the Dembitz cemetery.

{Page 181}

Memorial stone at the Pustkow Labor camp for the 25,000 Jews martyred by
the German murderers from June 11, 1942 until Stepmber 5, 1943 (4 Elul
5703). [4]]}

{Page 182}

Memorial stone at Puskow Camp.

{Hebrew text – p 183.}

The Terebinth of Weeping[5]

Translated by Jerrold Landau

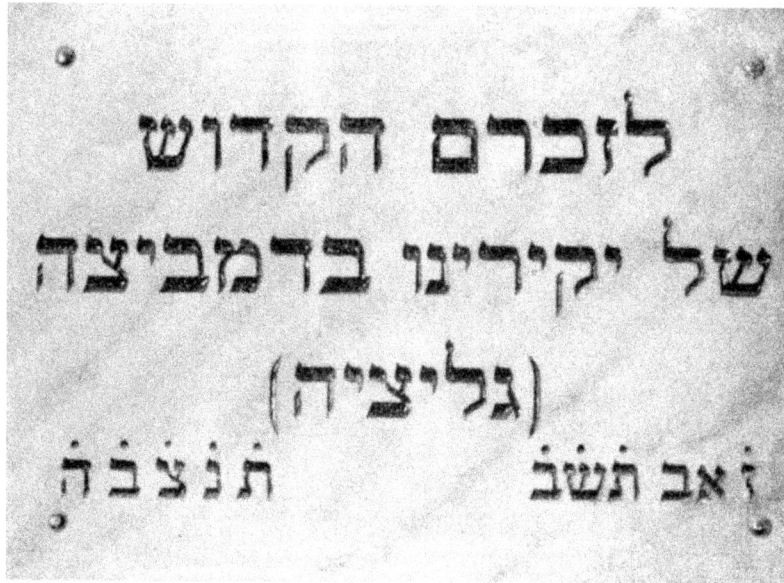

Memorial stone for Dembitz martyrs at Mount Zion, Jerusalem.

Translator's note: The memorial stone reads: In holy memory of our beloved ones of Dembitz (Galicia), 16 Av 5702. May their souls be bound in the bonds of eternal life.}

Translator's Footnotes :

1. The term used here is 'sitra achara', which means 'the other side' in Aramaic. It is a Talmudic term used for Satan or for dark forces in the world. _
2. Most likely a reference to the 'walls' between humanity and the divine. This is a common metaphor in Jewish religious thought. _
3. A reference to Tikkun Chatzot, a set of prayers and laments recited in the middle of the night, marking the destruction of the temple and the low state of the Jewish people. This service is not obligatory, and is generally only recited by unusually pious individuals. It is not commonly practiced today. _

4. The English translation provided on the page is incorrect here, as it indicates that the martyrdom was until June 11th, 1942. From the Hebrew and Yiddish, it is evident that this date was the starting date. _

5. A biblical reference to a memorial monument (in the biblical case, a tree) to Rebecca's nursemaid who accompanied the patriarch Jacob on his travels.

List of Martyrs of Dembitz

{Page 185}

    This list of the martyrs of Dembitz, who perished in the Holocaust, which is presented down in this section, was gathered from natives of our city and the neighboring villages under very difficult circumstances. We have attempted not to omit anyone – relatives reported about their families, neighbors about their neighbors and acquaintances, but nevertheless, we could not always obtain complete information, especially with respect to children and elderly parents. In some cases we were unable to determine the relationships between those mentioned in this list, and it is possible that, aside from the omissions, there are also errors. With this in mind, we beg forgiveness from the relatives and friends who perhaps will be upset. May the souls of the forgotten ones be bound up for eternity alongside all those mentioned.

{Page 186}

The family tree of the Rabbis of Dembitz of the Horowitz family.

Translated by Jerrold Landau

[1] Until the time of the outbreak of the terrible war and the extinguishing of the lights, when the days froze and the holy legacy of generations drowned in the sea of blood at the hands of the cruel Germans may their names and memories be blotted out, at the time of the liquidation of the ghetto and work camp of Dembitz in the months of Nissan 5703. May G-d avenge their blood and may their memories be a blessing to intercede for good upon the Jewish people, so that they may merit to wreak vengeance upon their enemies and witness the comfort of Zion and Jerusalem a the time of the advent of the righteous redeemer, may it be soon, Amen.

The first Admor and head of the rabbinical court of Dembitz was the holy Rabbi Reuven Horowitz the son of the holy Rabbi Eliezer, the head of the rabbinical court of Dzikow, who was the son of Rabbi Naftali of Ropczyce of holy blessed memory, who was the son of the holy Gaon Rabbi Menachem Rubin, the head of the rabbinical court of Lisko, who was the son of the holy Gaon Reb Yaakov of holy blessed memory, the head of the rabbinical court of Lisko.

The above mentioned holy Rabbi Menachem (Rubin) Lisker was the son-in-law of the holy Gaon Rabbi Yitzchak HaLevi Ish Horowitz of holy blessed memory, the head of the rabbinical court of the three holy communities known as Ahe [2] (Hamburg, Altona, and Essenbach). He was the son of the holy Gaon Rabbi Yaakov Halevi Ish Horowitz of holy blessed memory, known as Reb Yokel, the head of the rabbinical court of Glogow. He was the son of the holy Gaon Reb Meir HaLevi, the head of the rabbinical court of Tyktin. He was the son of the holy Gaon Rabbi Shemlke HaLevi Ish Horowitz of holy blessed memory, the head of the rabbinical court of Tarnow. He was the son of the holy Gaon Rabbi Yehoshua Aroch, the head of the rabbinical court of Premisla, and who can trace his holy roots back to the holy Rashal and Rashi, and all the way back until King David, may peace be upon him.

After the death of the holy Gaon Rabbi Reuven of holy blessed memory, his eldest son the holy Gaon Rabbi Alter was appointed as the head of the rabbinical court of Dembitz. He died, may Heaven protect us, after a short time without leaving any children. His younger brother, the Gaon Rabbi Shmuel Horowitz of holy blessed memory, was accepted as the rabbi and head of the rabbinical court.

Rabbi Shmuel was the son-in-law of the Gaon and Tzadik of Przytiki, who was a descendent of holy stock, of Rabbi Elimelech of Lizhensk of holy blessed memory and of Rabbi Kopel of Lukow. He died in his fifty-fourth year, and his son the holy Gaon Rabbi Tzvi Elimelech, may G-d avenge his blood, was appointed in his stead. He conducted the rabbinate until the end of the city, which was destroyed by the cruel ones, may their names and memories be blotted out.

The following are the holy sons of the Gaon and Tzadik Rabbi Shmuel of holy blessed memory, who were killed by unnatural deaths by the enemies until the year 5703, may G-d avenge their blood.

a) His son the Gaon and Rabbi Tzvi Elimelech, the last head of the rabbinical court of Dembitz of the Horowitz family. His wife was Hinda the daughter of the holy Gaon and Tzadik, the Admor of Ropszyce, of the Shapira family, descended from the Blazowa and Dinowa dynasties. They were killed with their four daughters, may G-d avenge their deaths.

b) The holy Tzadik Rabbi Chaim Yaakov, who was killed in Dembitz along with his wife Sara of an important family from Przytiki, along with their four children.

c) His daughter Nechama along with her husband the Tzadik Rabbi Moshe Halberstam of Tzanz, who was a son and grandson of holy rabbis and Admorim, along with five children, may G-d avenge their blood.

d) His daughter Etel and her husband the Tzadik and Gaon Rabbi Shlomo Eichenstein, who was the rabbi and head of the rabbinical court of the communities of Chodorow and Siedliska, a descendent of the Zidichov and other dynasties, along with their seven children, may G-d avenge their deaths.

e) His daughter Mirl along with her six children, may G-d avenge their blood. Her husband the Gaon Rabbi A. Wagschal of Radomysl was saved with the help of G-d, and lives with his new family in the United States.

f) His daughter Beila along with her three children, and their father the Gaon and Tzadik Rabbi Avrahamile Horowitz, may G-d avenge their blood. He was the son of the holy rabbi and Gaon Rabbi Eliahu Horowitz of holy blessed memory of Zwolen, the son of the holy Gaon Rabbi Naftali Chaim of holy blessed memory, who set up his home in the Land of Israel and died there. He was the descendent of the holy Admorim of Dzikow, Ropszyce, Tzanz, may their merit protect us.

A lone daughter of the Tzadik Rabbi Avrahamile and his wife Beila of Dembitz, the Rebbetzin Rechil, may she live long, was saved with Divine mercy after suffering great tribulations. She was hidden in the Dembitz ghetto in the attic of a gentile house for more than 24 months along with members of her first husband's family – the Wolf and Reich families of Dembitz.. Her first husband was murdered in the Plaszow Concentration Camp, may G-d avenge his blood. After the liberation she married her relative Rabbi Yoel Halperin, who was the rabbi of Jaslow and the chief rabbi of Bergen-Belsen after the liberation. Today, they live in the United States, and he is the rabbi of the Jaslow and Dembitz communities of New York.

The fourth daughter of the holy rabbi and Gaon, Rabbi Shmuel Horowitz of blessed memory, Rebetzin Chava Perel, may she live long, along with her husband the Tzadik and Gaon Rabbi Yitzchak Horowitz, the Admor of Mielec may he live long, and their five children live in the United States, having arrived before the war.

By Rabbi Yoel Halperin, the head of the Rabbinic court of Jaslow and Bergen-Belsen from the Ropczyce-Tsanz-Premishlan-Zolochow lines. Author of "Asuf Takanot Agunot". Currently residing in Brooklyn. May G-d protect him, Amen.

In Memory of the Rabbinical Family of Jadlowa

By Rabbi Yehuda Leib Frankel, Rabbi of the "Or Emet" Synagogue, Tel Aviv.

Translated by Jerrold Landau

In memory of my righteous parents, my brothers and sisters and their sons and daughters who died in sanctification of the Divine name during the terrible Holocaust at the hands of the Nazis, may their names and memories be blotted out. These are as follows:

The holy Gaon Rabbi Shlomo Zalman Frankel of holy blessed memory, the son of the Tzadik and Admor Rabbi Avrahamele of holy blessed memory of Wielopole.

My mother the righteous Rebbetzin Gitel the daughter of the Rabbi and Gaon Efraim Frankel who perished in sanctification of the name of God in Dembitz on the 7th of Av.

Their son Rabbi Avraham Frankel and his wife Chava, their children Tirza, Naftali Chaim, Tzipora and three other children.

Their daughter Shifrale with her only son Avrahamele, and her husband Rabbi Asher Anshel Zeltanreich.

Their son Efraim of holy blessed memory, of the city of Mielec, Galicia.

Their daughter Etel Frankel, the wife of Rabbi Meir and their four children of the city of Dambrowa.

Their daughter Breindel Frankel the wife of Rabbi Chaim Yosef of holy blessed memory, the son of the holy rabbi and Tzadik, the head of the rabbinical court of Makowa, with their three young children, may G-d avenge their deaths.

Their son the rabbi and Tzadik Meir and his family, may G-d avenge their deaths.

Their daughter Freidel, with her family and children, may G-d avenge their deaths.

Their son Rabbi Yaakov Menachem, may G-d avenge his death.

Translator's Footnotes:

1. This first paragraph appears to be a continuation of a sentence started by the title line.
2. A mnemonic acronym.

Families of the Martyrs of Dembitz, may their memories be a blessing.

{p 187}

Alef	א	Beit	ב	Gimel	ג	Daled	ד	He	ה
Vav	ו	Zayin	ז	Chet	ח	Tet	ט	Yod	י
Lamed	ל	Mem	מ	Nun	נ	Samech	ס	Ayin	ע
Pe	פ	Tzadik	צ	Kof	ק	Resh	ר	Shin	ש

Family Name	Given Name	Remarks

Alef   א

Family Name	Given Name	Remarks
Ader	Liba	her husband and their daughter
Ader	Wolf	and his family
Ader	Roiza	the daughter of Yochanan Sommer
	Moshe	her son
	Miriam	her daughter
Ulman	Naftali	
	Hinda	his wife
	Elimelech	their son and his wife
Unger	Asher	the son-in-law of Reb Yoel Gritzman
	Henia	his wife
	Izrael	(the boiler-maker) and his family
Eisen	Naftali	
	Gittel (nee Mahler)	his wife
	Yaakov	their son and his family
	Yosef	their son and his family
	Tauba	their daughter

	Sommer	
	Beila Guter	their daughter
	Sala Steiner	their daughter
	Hinda Cymbler	their daughter and their families
Eisen	Yosef	the son-in-law of Yoel Gritzman
	Chaya Sara	his wife
Eyal	Michel	and his family
Eisler	Aaron	from Zasov
	Chaya	his wife
	Yehoshua	their son
	Adla	their daughter
Altman	Yaakov	
	Chaya	his wife
	Mina	their daughter
	Tzvi	their son
	Yehoshua	their son
	Moshe	their son
Oling	Eliezer	
	Chayale	his wife
	Hershel	their son
	Bluma	their daughter
	Zalman	their son
Oling	Reizel-Zigman	their daughter
	Zeev	her husband
	Gittel	their daughter
	Mirl	their daughter
	Esther	their daughter
Oling	Gittel - Wasserstrum	her husband
	Yehoshua	
	Sara	their daughter
	Shmuel	their son
Oling	Moshe	
	Sara	his wife
	Tova	their daughter
	Alter	their son
Oling	Serel-Bier	her husband
	Shlomo	
Oling	Yechezkel	and his wife
Alster	Elimelech	and his wife
	Lula	their daughter
	Nechama	their daughter
Alster	Bracha	
	Bina	

	Miriam	
Ostern		the engineer and his wife
	Kuba	their son
	Yanke	their daughter
	Hela	their daughter
	Frania	their daughter
	Alec	their son
Ofen	Yechiel Meir	
	Chana	his wife
	Chaim	their son
Ofen	Shalom	their son
	Freda	his wife
Appel	Yaakov	the son-in-law of Efraim Hakeh
	Natalia	his wife
Appel	Hersh Nissan	
	Gittel	his wife
	Yaakov	their son and his family
	Yosef	their son and his family
	Keila Hachheizer	their daughter
	Yechezkel Hachheizer	her husband
April	Yaakov	from Pustkow
	Reizel (nee Hollander)	his wife
Ardover	Feivish	
	Bracha	his wife
	Leib	their son
	Avraham	their son
	Yitzchak	their son
	Sara	their daughter
Ascheim	Hersh	
	Rachel	his wife
	Wolf	their son
	Asher	their son
Ascheim	Shimshon	and his wife
Ascheim	Meir	
	Tzvia (nee Goldfarb)	his wife
	Hersh	their son
	Guta	his wife

Beit ב

Badner	Avigdor	his wife

	Chana	their daughter
	Beila	
	Moshe	their son
Balsam	Shmuel	
	Miriam	his wife
	Moshe	their son
	Yitzchak	their son
	Reizel	their daughter
	Rivka	their daughter
	Rachel	their daughter
Balsam	Chaim	
	Tzila	his wife
	Hentshe	their daughter
	Bluma	their daughter
Balsam	Shlomo Mordechai	their son
	Gittel Rachel	his daughter
	Avraham	his son
Balsam	Moshe	
	Sara Golda	his wife
	Miriam	his daughter
	Shlomo Mordechai	his son
Balsam	Yechiel Michel	his son
	Gittel Rachel	his wife
	Freidel	their daughter
	Dvora	their daughter
	Reicha	their daughter
	Shmuel	their son
Balsam	Riva Basha	her daughter
	Chava	
Bornstein	Shlomo	
	Sara	his wife
	Shabtai	their son and his family
Bornstein	Malka-Tefler	
Bornstein	Fela-Slepter	
Bornstein	Anna-Segal	
Bornstein	Yehuda	
	Miriam (nee Rosenbaum)	his wife and their children
Borer	Avraham	and his family
	Isser	and his family
Buchbaum	Berl	
	Hinda	
Buchner	Hershel	the son-in-law of Zisha Precker

	Lea	his wife
Buxbaum	Alter	
Buxbaum	Golda	the daughter of Reb Shmuel Fishlerhis wife and their children
Beier	Sara Lea	
	Miriam	her daughter
	Beila	her daughter
Blaustein	Dov Aryeh	
	Sheindel Rivka	his wife
	Nechama Dershowitz	their daughter
	Dov Aryeh Dershowitz	her son
Blumenkel	Yosef	and his wife
Blevis	Hersh David	and his wife
	Fania	their daughter
Becher		(with Dr. Hertzig)
Bek	Reuven	
	Chava	his wife
	Gittel	their daughter
	Tzila	their daughter
Bek	Yaakov	the son of Reuven
	Chana	his wife
	Moshe	their son
	Liba	their daughter
	Feiga	their daughter
Ber	Aaron	
	Freidel	his wife
Ber	Sima Bina-Horowitz	their daughter
	Yitzchak Elimelech	her husband
Ber	Rivka	the daughter of Aaron
	Bronka	the daughter of Aaron
	Sala	the daughter of Aaron
Ber	Elimelech	the son of Aaron
	Tauba	his wife
	Alter	their son
Ber	Pinchas	
	Chentsha	his wife
	Bronka Mingelgrin	their daughter
	Rumek	her husband
	Moshe	their son
	Lea	their daughter

	Etke	and her family
	Dvora	the daughter of Pinchas
	Miriam	the daughter of Pinchas
Ber	Shmuel	
	Yaakov	
	Sara	his wife
	Zisha	their son
	Nachum	their son
	Miriam	their daughter
	Rivka	their daughter
	Leib	their son
	Berta (nee Kazshenik)	his wife
	Dvora	their daughter
	Abba	their son
Bernstein	Ezra	
	Sara (nee Derfler)	and their children
Berel	Nechemia	and his wife
	Leibish	their son
	Netta	their daughter
	Esther	their daughter
Berel	Shlomo	his wife and their children
Bernstein	Alter	and his wife
Bronheim	David	
	Reizel	his wife
	Naftali	their son
Bronheim	Hersh	
	Malka	his wife
	Rhoda	their daughter
	Hodes	their daughter
	Sima	their daughter
	Hela	their daughter
Bronheim	Naftali	their son
	Esther	his wife
	Savka	their son
Bras	Yehuda	
	Sabina	his wife
	Zigmond	their son
Bras	Mauricy	their son
	Ronia	his wife
	Tashke	their daughter
	Yosef	their son
Bras	Anda - Hauser	the daughter of Yehuda
	Alla	her daughter

Bras	Fela - Grünspan	the daughter of Yehuda
	Zigmond Grünspan	her husband
Brik	Chaim	and his wife
Brik	Aaron	and his wife
Brener	Yosef	
	his wife (nee Eyal)	
	Mendel	their son and their family
	Aaron	their son
	Nechama	their daughter
	Tzipora	their daughter
	Rachel	their daughter
	Freda	their daughter

Gimel ג

Goldblatt	Yaakov	
	Pesel	his wife
	Elisheva	their daughter
	Chava	their daughter
	Miriam-Rachel	their daughter
	Moshe	their son
	Rachel	their daughter
	Shlomo Leib	their son

{page 189}

Goldblatt	Michael	
	Chana	his wife
	Rachel	their daughter
	Yitzchak	their son
	Chava	their daughter
Goldblatt	Moshe	and his wife
Goldblatt	Baruch	the son-in-law of Rosenblatt and his family
Goldblum	Kalman	
	Rivka	his wife
	Yosef	their son
	Shmuel	their son
	Abba	their son
	Moshe	their son
	Bracha	their daughter
	Tzila	their daughter
Goldblit	Mordechai	

	Chana, Sara	and other sisters
Goldberg	Yechezkel	
Goldberg	Chaim	his son
	Esther	his wife
	Yechiel	their son
	Dvora	their daughter
	Nachman	their son
	Doba Zisel	their daughter
Goldberg	Moshe	the son of Yechezkel
	Fela	his wife
	Hersh	their son
	Dvora	their daughter
Goldberg	Mendel	
	Hodes	his daughter
Goldberg	Yitzchak	(the teacher)
	Nicha	his wife
	Miriam	their daughter
	Sara	their daughter
Goldberg	Sheindel	
	Yitzchak	her son
Goldman	Chana	
Goldman	Moshe	the son of Avraham
	Hinda	the daughter of Avraham
	Esther	the daughter of Avraham her husband
	Freiberger	and daughter
Goldfarb	Zelig	
	Sara Zlata	his wife
	Beila Feilbogen	their daughter
	Eliezer	her son
	Hinda	her daughter
Goldfarb	Eliezer	the son of Zelig
	Sheindel	his wife
Goldfarb	Gittel	
	Feiga	
	Freda	
Goldfarb	Aaron	
	Sortshe	his wife
	Feiga	their daughter and her husband
Goldflus		the pharmacist and his wife
Goldflus		the lawyer
	Gitta	his sister
Ganz	Yitzchak	and his wife
Ganz	Mendel	and his family
Ganz	Aaron David	and his family
Garn	Lea	

	Beila	
Gorlitzer	Pinchas	
	Paula	his wife
	Lotti	their daughter
Gezshiv	Feivel	and his wife
Glantz	Zindel	
	Hinda	his wife
	Rivtsha	his daughterand other family members
Gleicher	Moshe	his wife and their children
Glickman	Mordechai	and his wife
	Avraham	their son
	Tova	their daughter
	David	their son
Glickman	Nathan	
	Miriam (nee Ofen)	his wife
	Moshe Yaakov	their son
Gewirtz	Moshe	
	Rivka	his wife
	Pinia	their daughter
	Bina	their daughter
	Sara	their daughter
	Miriam	their daughter
	Rachel	their daughter
	Shmuel	their son
Gelb	Shimon	and his wife and their daughter
Gelb	Bunim	
Gelb	Shmuel	
Gembitziner	Glickl	
	Yisrael Meir	and his family
	Leib	and his family
Gembitziner	Chaim	
	Chana	his wife
	Mirl	their daughter
	Yosef	their son
	Avraham	their son
Gembitziner	Menashe	and his family
Gembitziner	Hershel	and his family
Gembitziner	Meir	and his family
Geminder	Leib	
	Beila	his wife
	Nicha Kurtz	his daughter
	Moshe Kurtz	her husband
	Aryeh Kurtz	their son
Geminder	Mina	

	Aryeh	her son
Geshvind	Philip	
	Tanka	his wife
Groder	Avraham	
	Liftsha	his wife
	Levi	their son
	Wolf	their son
	Shlomo	their son
Grin	Eliahu	
	Malka	his wife
	Feiga	their daughter
	Lea	their daughter
	Sara	their daughter
	Yaakov	their son
Grin	Leib	
	Serel	his wife
	Menieh	their son
Greenberg	Yerucham	
	Dvora (nee Kanner)	his wife
	Rivka	their daughter
	Yosef	their son
Grünspan	Yitzchak	
	China	his wife
	Sara	their daughter

{page 190}

Grünspan	Nathan	
	Dvora (nee Mahler)	his wife
Grünspan	Shimon	their son
	Rachel (nee Sapir)	his wife
	Mendel	their son
	Yosef	their son
Grünspan	Yitzchak	the son of Nathan
	Chana (nee Faust)	his wife
	Ruth	their daughter
	Yehudit	their daughter
Gritzman	Yoel	
	Feiga (nee Peper)	his wife
Gritzman	Shmuel	the son of Moshe Peper may he live long

Daled ד

Dar	Pinchas	
	Rachel	his wife
	Gittel	their daughter
	Miriam	their daughter
Dar	Feiga	
Dar	Feivel	and his family
Dar	Reuven	and his wife
	Eidek	their son, and another son
Dar	Baruch	
	Reizel	his wife
	Eliezer	their son
Diller	Yaakov	
	Yitzchak	and his wife and daughters
	Shaul	their son
	Yosef	their son
Desser	Moshe	
	Breindel	
	Strum	his daughter
	Asher	her son
Dereshowitz	Chaya	
Dereshowitz	Beinish	and his family
Dershowitz	Asher	the son of Shlomo may he live long
	Gittel	the daughter of Shlomo
	Leib	the daughter of Shlomo
Dereshowitz	Leib	
	Gittel	his wife
	Asher	their grandson
Derfler	Feivel	and his wife
	Yechiel	his son
	Shmuel	his son
	Rivka	their daughter
	Avraham	their son
	Pinchas	their son
Dreisiger	David	
Dreilich	Israel	and his wife

He ה

Haber	Dora
Haber	Yoel
Haber	Karl

Haber	Paul	
Haber	Chaim Leib	from Bzizinitz
	Reizel	his wife
	Chanoch	their son
	Golda	their daughter
	Pepka	their daughter
	Sara	their daughter
	Yosef	the son of Sara
	Chaim	the son of Sara
	Reuven	the son of Sara
Hauser	Hinda	
	Leibish	her son
	Mala	his wife
	Israel Yehoshua	their son
	Rachel	their daughter
	Tzila	their daughter
	Feiga	their daughter
Hollander	Berish	
	Lea	his wife
	Leibish	their son
	Moshe	their son
Hollander	Moshe	from Pustkow
	Chana	his wife
	Avraham	their son
	Feivel	their son
	Tova	their daughter
	Menachem Israel	their son
	Rivka	their daughter
Hand	Avraham	
	Golda	his wife
Handelsman	Yosef	
	Gitta (nee Kanner)	his wife
	Emil	their son
Honig	Reuven	
	Mindel	his wife
Hakeh	Refael	
	Liba	his wife
Hakeh	Efraim	
	Gusti	his wife
	Norbert	their son
Hakeh	Yitzchak	the lawyer their son
	Gusti	his wife
Hakeh	Shimon	the son of Efraim
	Henia	his wife
Horowitz	Tzvi Elimelech	the Rabbi
	Hinda	his wife the Rebbetzin and three daughters
Horowitz	Naftali	the Rabbi
	Bracha	his daughter and her husband

	Beila	his daughter and her husband
Horowitz	Chaim Yaakov	and his family
Horowitz	Baltshe	
	Yehuda	her son
	Avraham	
Horowitz	Mirile	
	Wagschal	
	Yudel Meir	
Horowitz	Naftali Chaim	his wife
	Ethel	
	Feiga Bluma	their daughter
	Yocheved	their daughter
	Chaya	their daughter
	Dvora	their daughter
Hartman	Zalman Reuven	and his wife
	Dina	their daughter
	Bina	their daughter
	Aaron David	their son
	Beila	their daughter
	Rivka	their daughter
Hutner	Eliezer	
	Rachel	his wife
	Yeshayahu	their son
	Shmuel	their son
Henig	Bracha	the daughter of Shmuel Hezl
	Hentshe	her daughter
	Israel	her son
Herbst	Chanina	
	Sara	his wife and their children
Hertzberg	Moshe	his wife
	Sara	
	Bluma Strum	their daughter and her husband
	Chana	the daughter of Moshe
	Shmuel	the son of Moshe
	David	the son of Moshe

{page 191}

Hertzig	Dr.	and his wife
	Lonek	their son
Hershlag	Shlomo	and his family
Hershlag	Yechezkel	and his family
Hershlag	Shalom	and his family
Hershlag		(the wife of Getzel may he live long) and their children
	Hershele	the banker
	Yehudit	his wife
	Zlate	their son

Vav ו

Wagschal	Beila	the daughter of Moshe Yosef Sommer
	Meir	her husband
Wagschal	Pinchas	
	Rivka	his wife
	Israel	their son
	Leib	their son
Walner	Israel Yitzchak	
	Shlomo	his son
Walner	Beila	
Wallach	Mordechai	
	Sara Rivka	his wife
Wolf	Pinchas	the son of Yaakov
Wolf	Moshe	the son of Yaakov
	Rachel (nee Horowitz)	
Wolf	Yaakov	
Wolfgang	Moshe	the judge and teacher
	Tshek	his wife
	Rachel	his daughter and her family
Warech	Reuven	
	Freidel	his wife
	Chana Miriam	their daughter wife of Yitzchak
	Dina Lauterhaus	daughter of Reuven
	Gittel	daughter of Reuven
Wurtzel	Regina Budjik	his wife
Wurtzel	Arnold	and his wife
Wulvick	Perele Lishe	his wife
	Chaitshe	their daughter
Wulvick	Chaim	
Widerspan	Shemaya	his wife
	Manya	their daughter
Widerspan	Ben-Zion	
	Pesel	his wife
Widerspan	Efraim	
	Malvina	his wife
	Aaron	their son
Veizer	Moshe	
	Rivka	his wife
	Meir David	their son and his family
Veizer	Chaim	
	Perel	his wife and their children
Weidenbaum	Hendel	
	Malka	her daughter
	Feiga	her daughter
	Tzila	her daughter

Weingarten	Israel	
	Tzipora	his wife
	Zushka	their daughter
	Manya	their daughter
	Rozka	their daughter
	Manes	their son
Weintraub	David	
	Miriam	his wife
	Beila	their daughter
	Henek	their son
Weiss	Moshe	
	Reizel	his wife
	Mina	their daughter
	Sara	their daughter
	Chava	their daughter
Weisler	Shlomo Yosef	
	Feiga	his wife
	Chana	their daughter
	Kalman	their son
Weisman	Eliahu	
	Sara	his wife
Wilner	Avraham	
	Chaim	
	Sheindel	his wife
	Simcha	their son
	Sara	his wife
	Aaron	their son
	Bluma	their daughter
Wilner	Feivel	
	Taube	his wife
	Rivka	their daughter
	Binyamin	their son
Wilner	Mendel	their son
	Sara (nee Taub)	his wife
	Rachel	their daughter
Wilner	Shmuel	
	Breindel	his wife
	Tsharna	their daughter
	Chantshe	their daughter
	Elchanan	their son
Vind	Shmuel	
	Hinda	his wife
	Aaron	their son
	Hersh	their son
Weiner	Aaron	and his wife
	Simcha	their son
	Sara	their daughter
	Rozshka	their daughter
Weiner	Shlomo Yona	
Weiner	Chaya Miriam	

Weiner	Israel	
Weiner	Yehuda Meir	
Weiner	Nechama	

Zayin ז

Sommer	Yochanan	
	Sara	his wife
	Shmuel	the son of Yochanan
	Tashke	his wife
	Simcha	the son of Yochanan
Sommer	Yaakov	(son-in-law of Yoel Gritzman)
	Frimet	his wife
Sommer	Reuven	and his wife
	Moshe	their son
	Mina	their daughter
	Bronka	their daughter
Zolderling	Akiva	
	Tzila (nee Widerspan)	his wife
	Elza	their daughter
	Benno	their son
Zeigfried	Chaim	
Zeigfried	Mendel	
Zeigfried	Binyamin	
Zeigfried	Shalom	
Zeigfried	Avraham	
Zeigfried	Fishel	
Zeigfried	Yitzchak	
Zeigfried	Rivka	
Zeigfried	Yente	
Zeigfried	Chana	
Zeigfried	Chava	
Zeigfried	Reizel	
Zeinwald	Avraham	
	Chaya	the daughter of Hersh Nissan his wife, two married daughters
Zilberman	Shmuel Hezel	
	Ruchama	his wife
	Sara	their daughter
	Avraham	their son
	Moshe	their son
Zinger	Leib	
	Bluma	his wife
	Avigdor	their son
	Israel	their son
	Reuven	their son
	Pinchas	their son

{page 192}

	Pesel	their daughter
	Gittel	their daughter
	Avraham Yaakov	their son
Zinger	Asher	his wife
	Rachel	their daughter
	Rivka	their daughter
	Yechezkel	their son
Zinger	Gittel	from Zavade and her family
Zisman	David Leib	
	Tashe	his wife
Zisman	Yosef Matityahu	
	Tzartel	his wife
Zisman	Moshe	
	Steffa	his wife
	Yaakov	their son
	Akiva	their son
	Yoel	their son
Zisman	Chaim	
Zisfeld	Libe	
Zshavner	Zelig	and his wife
	Yosef	their son
	Wolf	their son
	Leizer	their son
	Lea	his wife
	Yaakov	the son of Zelig
	Moshe	the son of Zelig and his wife
	Shmuel	the son of Zelig
	Moshe	and his wife
	Feiga	

Chet ח

Chaim	Moshe	
	Rivka	his wife
	Eliezer	their son
	Yaakov	their son
	Zeev	their son
	Lea	their daughter
	Salka	their daughter
Chaim	Littman Avraham	
	Rivka	his wife
	Elazar	their son
	Rafael	their son
	Lea	their daughter
	Mina	married to Lauterhaus
	Chana	their daughter

Chaim	Shmuel	
	Rivka	his wife
	Chaitshe Libe	
	Elchanan	her son

Tet ט

Tager	Mordechai	
	Yosef	
	Serel	his wife
	Dache	their daughter and her husband
	Peretz	their son
	Feiga	their daughter
	Yaakov	their son
Taub	Yaakov	
	Chaya	his wife
	Chava	their daughter
	Sara	their daughter
Taub	Eidel	married name Reimer
	Yitzchak Reimer	her husband
	Sara Reimer	their daughter
	Yehudit	their daughter
Taub	Nathan	
	Eidel	his wife
Taub	Moshe	
	Malka	the son of Nathan, his wife
	Meir	their son
	Esther	their daughter
Taub	Anshel	the son of Nathan
Taub	Aaron	the son of Nathan
	Feiga	his wife
	Aryeh	their son
	Chaya	their daughter
Taub	Yitzchak	the son of Nathan and his wife
	Rina	their daughter
Taub	Miriam	
Taub	Shimon	
Taub	Rina	
Taub	Asher	
	Chuma	his wife
	Shalom David	their son
	Ethel	their daughter
Taub	Feivel	
	Reizel	his wife
Taub	Hadassah	
	David Katz	her husband and their children
Taub	Mendel	
	Gittel	his wife

	Feiga	Rozka
Taub	Sara	
	David Nirenberg	her husband and their daughter
Taub	Shmuel	
	Reltshe	his wife
	Moshe Tovia	their son
Taub	Anshel	the son of Feivel
	Chaya (nee Eisen)	his wife
	David	their son
Taub	Hersh	
	Itta	his wife
	Moshe	their son
	Chana	their daughter
	Feiga	their daughter
	Rachel	their daughter
	David	their son

{page 193}

Taffet	Efraim	
	Dvora	his wife
	Shmuel	their son
	Chana	their daughter
	Pinchas	their son
Taffet	Yeshayahu	
	Anka	his wife and their family
Taffel	Avraham	
	Kreindel	his wife and their daughter
Taffel	Yosef	
	Treina	his wife
	Naftali	their son
	Menashe	their son and their daughter
Taffel	Sara (Mantel)	
	Basha	her daughter
	Yocheved	her daughter
	Frumka	her daughter
Taffer	Hershel	and his family
Tahoi	Simcha	
	Sara	his wife
	David Aaron	their son
	Shmuel	their son
	Chaika	their daughter
Tahoi	Chava	with her husband Max Ber and their children
Tuchman	Yehoshua	
	Tzipora	his wife
	Yechezkel	their son
	Fruma	their daughter
Tintenfas	Yechezkel	and his wife
	Yehuda	their son

	Yeshayahu	their son
Tewel	Yehuda	
	Pesia	his wife
	Hersh	their son and his family
	Reizel	their daughter
	Manya	their daughter and her family
	Bronka	their daughter
	Salka	their daughter
	Gita	their daughter
	Wolf	their son
	Shmuel	the son of Yehuda
	Eidel (nee Sapir)	his wife
Tennenbaum	Eliahu	
	Gittel	his wife
	Chaim	his son
	Yaakov	his son
	Moshe	his son
Trachtenberg	Eliakim	
	Sheindel	his wife
	Leizer	his son and other children
Trotiner	David	
	Sala (nee Kornreich)	his wife
	Rozka	their daughter
Treiman	Yosef	and his wife
	Bluma	their daughter
	Manya	their daughter

Yod י

Jachimovitz	Yechezkel	
	Beila	his wife
	Avraham	their son
	Chaya	their daughter
Jachimovitz	Meir	
	Tema	his wife
	Yehoshua	their son
	Chaim	their son
	Nathan	their son
	Miriam	their daughter
	Chaya	their daughter
	Bluma	their daughter
	Golda	their daughter
Yam	Rivka	
	Yechezkel	her son
	Yehudit Kornreich	her daughter
	Leila Kornreich her daughter	

	Yehuda Kornreich	her son
Jakob	Aaron	
	Chana	his wife
	Shmuel	their son
	Shlomo Zalman	their son
	Esther Bracha	their daughter
	Ruchama	their daughter
	Gittel	their daughter
	Breindel	their daughter
	Blumka	their daughter

Lamed ל

Labin	Leib	the son-in-law of Reb Naftalchi
	Rikel Horowitz	his wife
	Moshe	their son
Laob	Moshe	
	Chana	his wife
	Shmuel	their son
	Yehoshua	their son
	Chava	their daughter
Laob		family from the old city
Lauterstein	Yehoshua	
	Beila	his wife
	Avraham	their son
	Yocheved	their daughter
Langer	Baruch	
	Esther (nee Kanner)	his wife
	Tzipora	their daughter
	Gizla	their daughter
Lauterhaus	Beila (nee Precker)	his wife
Lauterhaus	Avraham	the son of Moshe and his family
Landau	Gershon	and his family
Last	Shmuel	
	Shimon	his son
Laufbahn	Elyakim (Getzel)	
	Rachel	his wife
	Pinchas, Dr.	their son
	Israel	their son
Laufbahn	Mordechai Yoel	and his wife
	Yehuda	their son
	Lea	their daughter
	Yehudit	their daughter
Lustman	Tzipora	the daughter of Moshe Asher Padauer

Lustgarten	Yehoshua	
	Dvora	his wife
	Beila	their daughter
	Nachum	their son
	Itta	their daughter
	Sala	their daughter
Libenheimer	Leib	
	Idzshe	his wife
	Sidshe	their daughter and her family
	Paula	their daughter and her family
	Chaika	their daughter and her family
	Gusta	their daughter and her husband
	Shifra	their daughter
	Aaron	their son
	Roza	his wife

{page 194}

Licht	Nachman	his wife
	Rachel	
	Chava	their daughter
	Esther	their daughter
	Hinda	their daughter
	Baruch	their son
Lichter	Berl	
Lichter	Rivka	
Lilienfeld	Rachel	
	Eizik	her son
	Israel Mendel	her son
	Asher	her son
	Shifra	her daughter
	Aaron	her son
Lishe	Meshulam (Zishe)	
	Yocheved	his wife
	Yeshaya David	their son and his family
	Yaakov	their son
	Shmuel Nachum	their son
	Mina	their daughter
	Duba	their daughter
	Chaya	their daughter
Lishe	Malka	her husband and their children
Lishe	Dreizel	
Lishe	Wolf	
	Feiga	his wife
	Serl	their daughter
	Liba	their daughter
	Dache	their daughter
	Rachel	their daughter
	Shalom	their son

	Israel	their son
Lishe	Reizel (nee Diller)	
	Yocheved	her daughter
	Shalom	her son
	Shaul Eliezer	her son
Lishner	Yitzchak	
	Itta (nee Kanner)	his wife
Lederberg	Maan	and his family
Lezer	Pinchas	
	Tzila (nee Kehat)	his wife
	Yechiel	their son
Lempel	Shlomo	
	Feiga	his daughter
Lefler	Hinda	
Lefler	Chaim	

Mem מ

Mahler	Chaim	the watchmaker
	Rivka	his wife
Mahler	Rachel married name Auerbuch	
	Chaim Auerbuch	her husband
	Fela Auerbuch	their daughter
Mahler	Esther	the daughter of Chaim
Mahler	Yehuda	the son of Chaim
Mahler	Dina	the daughter of Chaim
Mahler	Malka	
	Hersh	her son
Mahler	Shmuel	her son
Mahler	Salka	her daughter
Mahler	Avraham	his wife and their children
Mahler	Avraham	and his family
Mahler	Chaim	
Mahler	Reuven	the son of Chaim
	Rozsha	his wife
	Hinda	their daughter
	Chaika	their daughter
	Dushka	their daughter
	David Dr.	their son
	Chanina	the son of Chaim
	Tiltshe	his wife
	Chaya	their daughter
	Sala	their daughter
	Chava	their daughter
	Rachel	their daughter

Mahler	Israel Dr.	the son of Chaim
	Hinda (nee Rosenberg)	his wife
Mazel	Wolf	his wife and their children
Mazel	Israel	and his wife
Meir	David	and his wife, his brothers
Manderer	Mendel	
	Henia (nee Farster)	his wife
	Henek	their son
	Avraham	their son
Mantel	Zisman	
Millet	Avraham Dr.	
	Gusta	his wife
	Zigmond	their son
	Leon	their son
Miller	Pesach	and his wife and children
Mintz	Michael	
	Beila	his wife
	Fela	their daughter
	Ronia	their daughter
	Shmuel	their son
Metzger	Moshe	
	Malka	his wife
Metzger	Feivel	the son of Moshe
Metzger	Yitzchak	and his wife

Nun   נ

Natt	Michel	
Natt	Pinia	
Natt	Bashe	her husband Eliahu
	Lea	their daughter
Natt	Reizsha	Baruch her husband
	Yehuda Leib	her son
Natt	Nachman	
	Regina	his wife
Nusbaum	Yitzchak	
	Mala	his wife
	Wolf	his son
	Sheindel	their daughter
Neimark	Shlomo	
	Taube	his wife
Neishtat	Alter	
	Bluma	his wife
	Nachum	their son and his family
	Yitzchak	their son and his family
Nichthauser	Krola	
Nichthauser	Kuba	

Maurice
Bernard
Bronka
Malva
Malia
Giza

Samech ס

{page 195}

Salomon	Leibish	
	Zelda (nee Eyal)	his wife
Salomon	Moshe	
	Bina	his wife
	Yaakov	their son
	Yehoshua	
	Chava Mattel	their daughter
	Yitzchak	their son
	Miriam	their daughter
Salpeter	Paula (nee Bornstein)	
	Ziga	her son
	Samuel	Yechezkel
	Roiza	
	Yaakov	
	Henna	
Samselik	Hodes (nee Shneps)	
	Lea	her daughter
Sandhaus	Israel Dr.	
Sandhaus	Recha (nee Grünspan)	his wife
	Ruth	their daughter
	Fredek	their son
Sandhaus	Chanoch	
	Minda	his wife
	Shmuel	their son
Sapir	Yehoshua	
	Roza	his wife
	Aaron	and his wife
Socher	Avraham (Rosenberg) Yehoshua	
	Gittel	his wife
	Yaakov	their son
	Israel	their son
Sroka	Zalman	
Sroka	Esther	his wife

Ayin ע

Ebert	Shmuel	
	Berta	his wife
	Reiza	
	Eidek	
	Reuven	
Etinger	Rabbi Yitzchak	
	Chana	
	Hilda	
Elster	Leib	
	Itta	his wife
	Shimon	their son
	Sala	their daughter
	Elster Bluma	and her family
Elster	Alter	
	Rachel	his wife
Elster	Akiva Leib	
	Esther	his wife and their children
Elster	Shalom	and his wife and children
Elster	Michael	
	Feiga (nee Green)	his wife
Elster	Avraham	
Epstein	Israel Meir	the son-in-law of Nathan Taub
	Chana	his wife
Epstein	Israel	
	Adla	his wife
	Yitzchak	their son
	Lusha	their daughter
	Avraham	their son
Erlich	Yosef	the son-in-law of Leib Leiner
	Basha	his wife and their children

Pe פ

Padauer	Eliezer	
	Sara	his wife
	Koppel	their son
	Feiga	their daughter
Padauer	Yosef	
	Akiva	his son
	Hinda	his daughter
Padauer	Avraham	
	Sara	his wife
	Kresel	their daughter

Faust	Gedaliahu	and his wife
	Avraham	their son
	Dov Berish	their son
Faust	Avraham	and his wife
	Yechiel	their son
	Rafael	their son
Faust	Hersh	
	Baltshe (nee Siedlisker)	his wife
	Feivel	their son
	Chaya	their daughter
	Hinda	their daughter
	Pesel	their daughter
Faust	Wolf	
	Lea	his wife and their three children
Faust	Yosef Avigdor	the son of Chaim Faust
Polaner	Zalman	
	Sara	his wife
	Rachel	their daughter
Polaner	Israel	
	Maltshe	his wife
	Reizel	their daughter
Fallik	Aaron	
	Bluma	his wife
	Golda	and another daughter
Fas	Pinchas	his wife and three children
Fas	Avraham	and his wife
	Yosef	their son
Pardes	Avraham	the lawyer
Fortgang	Anshel	
	Tova	his wife
Forster	Aaron	
	Shlomo	his son
Puter	Mendel	
	Tauba	his wife
	Wolf	their son
	Esther	their daughter and her family
	Moshe	their son
Puter	Wolf	
	Miriam	his wife
	Levi Yitzchak	his son and other children
Fus	Sender	
	Sara (nee Gewirtz)	his wife
	Yehoshua	their son
	Yehuda	their son
	Feiga	their daughter
		{page 196}
Fuchs	Sara Rivka	
Feigenbaum	Israel	

	Alte	his wife
Fink	Avraham	
	Zelda	his wife
Fink	the teacher in the Gymnasia and his family	
	Netta	his wife
Fink	Yitzchak	
	Rachel	his wife
	David	their son
	Mirl	their daughter
Fink	Avraham	
	Esther	his wife
	Reizel	their daughter
	Sala	their daughter
	Chava	their daughter
Fish	Shlomo	
	Roza	his wife
	Hela	their daughter
	Yudel	their son
Fishler	Zigmond Dr.	and his wife
Fishler	Shmuel	
	Mirl	his wife
Fishler	Moshe	and his family
	Shlomo	their son
	Liba	their daughter
	Chana	their daughter
Fishel	Yitzchak	and his wife
	Yaakov	their son
	Berl	their daughter
	Flam Leib	
Flam	Avraham	and his wife
	Yosef	their son
	Beila	their daughter
Flank	Rachel (nee Koss)	
	Yosef	her son
	Ben-Zion	her son
	Avraham	her son
Feigenbaum	Tzvi	
	Tonia (nee Eisler)	his wife
Feder	Avraham	
	Chaitshe (nee Shneps)	his wife
	Shmuel Leib	their son
Fett	Bendet	
	Chanale	his wife
Fett	Michael	
	Hela	his wife
	Dorka	their daughter

	Wolf	their son
Pechter	Reb Alter	
	Miriam	his wife
	Shmuel	their son and his family
	Yehuda	their son and his family
	Sheindel	their daughter
Pechter	Pinie	
Pechter	Israel Meir	
Pechter	Elchanan	and his family
Feld	Rachel	
	Chana Tzirel	her daughter
	Dvora Rivka	her daughter
Ferber	Avish	
	Golda	his wife
	Yechezkel	their son
Ferber	Mendel	
	Gittel	his wife
	Esther	their daughter
	Nechama	their daughter
	Shmuel	their son
	Rivka	their daughter
Perl	Yeshayahu	
	Bracha (nee Grünspan)	his wife
	Chaya	their daughter
	Breindel	their daughter
	Shimon	their son and his family
	Esther	their daughter
	Rivka	their daughter
	Moshe	their son
Perlmuter	Elimelech	
	Sheindel	his wife
Perchinger	Aaron Yosef	
	Hendel	his wife
	Yaakov	his son and another son
Perchinger	Chaim David	
	Shifra	his wife
Perchinger	Leibish	and his wife
Perchinger	Moshe	and his wife
Freiman	Yechiel Michel	
	Sara (nee Laufbahn)	his wife
	Bat-Sheva	their daughter
	Lea	their daughter
Freiman	Hersh	and his family
Perchinger	Mendel	and his family
Freidman	Pinchas	and his wife (nee Strauss)
	Leibish	their son
	Moshe	their son
	Rivka	their daughter
Freidman	Chanale	

Freidman	Berl	and his wife
Freidman	Yaakov	and his family
Freidman	Yosef	
Frankel	Rabbi Shlomo Zalman	and his family
	Yaakov	his son
Frankel	Israel Leib	
	Esther	the daughter of Reuven Kluger, his wife
	Efraim	and other sons
Frankel	Yosef	
	Henia (nee Bruk)	his wife and their children
Precker	Yechezkel	
	Lea	his wife
	Dvora	their daughter
Precker	Shlomo	
	Lea	his wife
	Yaakov	their son
Precker	Petachia	and his family
Precker	Zisha	
Precker	Yisachar	and his family
Precker	Yosef	
	Malka	his wife
	Chaya	their daughter
	Gittel	their daughter
Precker	Hertzl	
	Sheindel	his wife
	Malka	their daughter

Tzadik צ

{page 197}

Zanger	Wolf	the son-in-law of Leib Reiner
	Feiga	his wife and their children
Tzugehaft	Moshe	
	Sheindel	his wife
	Leibish	their son
Zweig	Meir	and his wife
	Yechezkel	their son
	Anda	their daughter
	Hersh	their son
Zucker	Tovia	
	Feiga	his wife
Zucker	Berta (Einhorn)	and her daughter
Zucker	Elimelech	the son of Tovia
Zucker	Moshe	the son of Tovia
Zuckerbrot-Litman	Lea	

Zeiger	Shalom	
	Chava	his wife
	Gella	their daughter
	Avraham	their son
	Rachel	their daughter
	Miriam	their daughter
	Chana	their daughter
	Yaakov	their son
Zeiger	Yosef	
	Rivka	his wife
	Zelda	their daughter
	Shmuel	their son
	Yaakov	their son
Zeizler	Tzipora	
	Ada	her daughter
	Avraham	her son
	Zeizler-Mash	Hilda
	Israel Mash	her son

Kof ק

Kozshenik	Hersh	
	Sabina	his wife
Kozshenik	Frania	
	Yaakov	her husband
	Miriam	their daughter
	Michael	their son
Kozshenik	Yaakov	
	Berta	his wife
	Renia	their daughter
Kozshenik	Renia	the daughter of Michael and Reiza may she live long
Kochan	Yaakov	the teacher and his wife
	Tzadok	their son
	Nachman	their son
	Yosef	their son
Kalb	Manele	
Kalb	Reiner Rachel	his wife
Kalb	Leibish	and his wife
	Yaakov	their son
	Menachem	their son
Kamf	Eidel	and her children
Kanarefogel	Eizik	
	Menucha	his wife
Kandzshezsher	Hershel	and his family
Kanieh	Yeshayahu	
	Itta	his wife

Kanner	Hersh	
	Sara	his wife
Kanner	Mendel	
Kanner	Leibish	and his family
Kanner	Avraham	and his family
Kanner	Shalom	
	Feiga (nee Ulman)	his wife
Kanner	Yitzchak Leib	
	Chaya	his wife
	Chana	their daughter
	Yaakov	their son
Kanner	Refael	and his wife
	Israel	their son
	Sender	their son
	Sala	their daughter
	Beila	their daughter
	Nechama	their daughter
	Esther	their daughter
Kanner	Gimpel	
	Gila	his wife
Kanner	Moshe	
	Rachel	his wife
	Gusta	their daughter
	Sara	their daughter
Kanner	Aaron	their son
	Chanale (nee Grinheit)	his wife
Kanner	Yitzchak	
	Dvora	his wife
	Fela	their daughter
Kanner	Mordechai	
	Manya (nee Reich)	his wife
Korngott	Shlomo	
	Yehudit (nee Fishler)	his wife and their children
Kornreich	Mordechai	
	Yaakov	his son
	Rozshka	his daughter
	Henech	his son
Kornreich	Avish	and his family
Kornreich	Yitzchak	
Kornreich	Yosef	and his family
Kornreich	Moshe	
	Fela	his wife and their children
Karpiol	Mendel	and his wife
Karpiol	Bunim	and his wife
Kupfer	Rachel	
Kupfer	Aaron	
Kupfer	Rivka	

Kehat	Pinchas	
	Freidel	his wife
	David	their son
	Feiga	their daughter
	Sheva	their daughter
Kehat	Moshe	
	Chana (nee Taub)	his wife
	Freidel	their daughter
	Avraham	their son
Kupferman	Mechtshe	
Kupferman	Zalman	
	Esther	his wife
Kupferman	Ezriel	
	Sara	his wife
	Avraham	their son
	Yitzchak	their son
	Yosef	their son
Kukuk	Lipa	
	Mindel	his wife
	Eidel	their daughter
	Esther	their daughter
	Rachel	their daughter
	Bina	their daughter
Kurtz	Malka	

{page 198}

	Yaakov	her son
Kurtz	Hersh Leib	and his family
Kurtz	Malka	
	Yehoshua	her son
Kurtz	Yaakov	
Kirshenbaum	Malka (nee Zilberman)	
Klagsbrun	Dov	
	Sara Rivka (nee Kanner)	his wife
Kluger	Reb Reuven	
	Alte	the wife of Reb Reuven
Kleinman	Simcha	
	Esther	his wife
	Rachel	their daughter
	David	their son
Kleinmintz	Pinchas	
	Freda	his wife
	Reizele	and her family
	Rechke	
	Eidek	
	Moshe	
Kerner	Shaul	
	Zelig	his son and his family

	Chanoch	his son and his family
	Yona	his son and his family
	Serl	his wife
	Daniel	the son of Shaul and his family
	Eliahu	the son of Shaul and his family
	Sara	his wife
	Chana	their daughter
Kerner	Moshe	the son of Shaul
	Henia	his wife
	David	their son
Kerner	Yitzchak	
	Bluma	his wife
Krantz	Yaakov	the dentist
	Dora	his wife
	Ruthi	their daughter
	Yosef	their son
Krantz	Israel	and his wife
Krantz	Sima	
Krantz	Yaakov (Kuba)	
Krantz	Yehuda	
Kriger	Aaron Naftali	
	Maltshe	his wife
Kriger	Gedaliahu	
	Serke	his wife
	Miriam	their daughter
Kriger	Beila	married name Wilner
	Betzalel Wilner	her husband
Kriger	Yerucham	
	Bracha	his wife
Kreiswerth	Chaim	
	Chana	
	Papka	
	Koppel	
	Feiga	
Kreiswerth	Yechezkel	
	Esther	his wife from the house of Yitzchak
	Dvora Grünspan	their daughter
	David	their son
	Ruth	their daughter
Kreinik	Shmuel	
	Chaya	his wife
	Yitzchak	their son
	Avraham	their son

Resh ר

Rosen	Yosef	
	Itta	his wife
	Moshe	their son

	Leibish	their son
	Feiga	their daughter
Rosen	Avraham (Shneps)	
	Rechtshe	his wife
	Yitzchak	their son
	Sala	their daughter
	Feiga	their daughter
Rosenbaum	Chaim (Chaimish)	and his wife
	Pinchas	his son
	Shalom	his son
Rosenberg	Shlomo Chaim	
	Sashe	his wife
	Rosa	their daughter
Rosenberg	Ben-Zion	and his family
Rosenberg	Ozer	and his family
Rosenberg	Moshe	
	Freidel	his wife
	Chaika	their daughter
	Avraham	their son
	Yosef	their son
Roth	Yosef	
	Botshe (nee Alster)	his wife and their son
Roth	Yosef	and his wife
	Asher	their son
	Shaul	their son
	Keila	their daughter
	Rand Sara (Levis)	her son
	Shmuel	
Roshwald	Herman	
	Meir	
	Yosef	
Rubenstein	Israel	the son-in-law of Leibtshe Reiner and his family
Reich	Reuven	and his wife
	Eliahu	their son
	Dina	their daughter
	Yehoshua	their son and his family
Reich	Meir	
	Gitta (nee Goldman)	his wife
	Yaakov	their son
	Aaron	their son and their daughter
Reich	David	the ritual slaughterer
	Mamele	his wife
Reich	Mendel	the son-in-law of Moshe Chazan
	Rivka	his wife
	Feiga	their daughter

	Esther	their daughter
	Moshe	their son
	Leibish	their son
Reiner	Nechama	
Reiner	Meir	
	Feiga	his wife
	Shmuel	their son, his wife and their children
Reiner	Matityahu	and his wife
	Moshe	their son
Reiner	Reuven Ber	his wife and their children

{page 199}

Reiner	Leibcha	
	Nechama	the daughter of Mendel Mahler his wife
	Yaakov	their son
	Sara	his wife
	Nechama Chaya	their daughter
Reiner	Shlomo	
	Esther	his wife
	Sheindel	their daughter
	Bashe	their daughter
	Shmuel	their son
Reiner	Yechiel	
	Chana	his wife
	Wolf	their son
	Bina	their daughter
	Rivka	their daughter
	Esther	their daughter
	Sara	their daughter
	Shlomo	their son
	Pia	their daughter
	Sheindel	their daughter
Reiner	Rachel	
Reiner	Shlomo	the son of Israel may he live long
Reiner	Nechama Esther	the daughter of Israel may he live long
Reiner	Moshe	and his family
Reiner	Yitzchak	
	Tzina	his wife and three children
Reiner	Mendel	the watchmaker
	Roiza	his wife
	Chaika	their daughter
	Moshe	their son and other children
Reiner	Yechiel	the son of Israel (the synagogue trustee)
	Roiza	his wife
	Chaya Sara	his daughter
Reiner	Chaim	the son of Israel (the synagogue trustee)
Reiner	Bluma	his wife
Reiner	Wolf	their son
Reiner	Chaya Sara	their daughter
Reis	Alter	

	Salka	his wife
Ringer	Shmuel	
	Lea	his wife
Ringer	Chaya Chava	their daughter
Ringer	Yitzchak	their son
Ringer	Rachel	their daughter
Rik	Moshe	the sexton of the synagogue in the old city
	Beila	his wife
Reder	Chaim	
	Feiga Rosa	his wife
	Asher	their son
	Chana	their daughter
	Mindel	their daughter
Reder	Avraham	and his family
Recht	Shalom	
	Sara	his wife
	Leibel	their son
	David	their son
	Bracha	their daughter
Recht	Moshe	and his family
Recht	Nathan	and his family
Remer	Mordechai	
Remer	Sheindel	
Remer	Aryeh	
Remer	Lea	
Remer	Shimon	
Reck	Moshe	
	Reizel	his wife and their children

Shin ש

Shachner	Eizak	
	Chaya (nee Laufbahn)	his wife
	Menachem	their son
	Henia	their daughter
Schwartz	Meir	
	Tzirel	his wife
	Israel	their son
	Betzalel	their son
	Avraham	their son
	Yehoshua	their son
	Pesach	their son
	Malka	their daughter
	Pesel	their daughter
	Frimet	their daughter
	Miriam	their daughter
Schuldenfrei	Aaron David	
	Chenia	his wife

	Roiza Anisfeld	their daughter, her husband and their children
	Sima	their daughter and her husband
	Yitzchak	their son
	Mirl	their daughter
	Chaya	their daughter
	Simcha	their daughter
	Tzila	their daughter
Schuldenfrei	Yoel	
	Esther	his wife
	Mina	their daughter
	Efraim	their son
	Gusta	their daughter
Schuldenfrei	Leibish	his wife and children
Schuldenfrei	Avraham	
	Reizel	his wife
	Mina	and her family
	Yaakov	their son
	Baltshe	their daughter
Schuldenfrei	Sima	the daughter of Hersh
Shum	Mordechai	
	Chaya	his wife
	Freda	their daughter
Shum	Hertzka	
	Beila	his wife
	Moshe	their son
	Chana	their daughter
	Rachel	their daughter
Shum	Avraham Leib	
	Lea	his wife
	Mordechai	their son
	Freidel	their daughter
Shum-Lanker	Breindel	
	Shlomo Lanker	her husband
	Miriam	their daughter
	Reizel	their daughter
Shum	Yaakov	
	Yehudit	his wife
	Mordechai	their son
	Rivka	their daughter
	Moshe	their son
Shum	Elimelech	
	Salka (nee Precker)	his wife
	Rozka	their daughter
Schtortz	Avraham	
	Rodzha	his wife
	Chaya	their daughter
	Moshe	their son
	Aaron	their son
	Yaakov	their son and his family

Shtarch	Shimon Shtarch Yehoshua	and his family
Shtarch	Rachel	her husband and their children
Shtarch	(Kerner) Malka	{page 200}
	Naftali	her son
Shtof	Shimon	
	Shoshana (nee Kanner)	his wife
	Roni	their daughter
	Maltshe	their daughter
Shtortz	Yaakov	their son and his family
	Yaakov	their son and his family
	Yosef	their son and his family
	Hershel	their son and his family
	Shtortz Rivka	married name Roth and her husband
Shturm	Avraham	
	Tema	his wife
	Rivka	their daughter
	Hinda	their daughter
	Yosef	their son
Shturm	Moshe	his sister and their family
Steiglitz	Meir	
	Hela	his wife
Steinhauer	Wolf	and his wife
	Shmuel	their son
	Asher	their son
	Mali	their daughter
	Moshe	their son
	Chaim	their son
Steinhauer	Nachum	
Steinhauer	Chana	
Steinhauer	Peretz	
Steinhauer	Chaya	and their children
Steinhauer	Leibish	
	Zissel	his wife
	Mala	their daughter
	Yitzchak	their son
	Efraim	their son
	Avraham Chaim	their son
	Ethel	their daughter
Shteier	Hersh	and his wife
	Moshe	their son
	Elimelech	their son
	Freda	their daughter and her family
	Sala	their daughter
Shtimler	Tovia	the ritual slaughterer and his wife
	Yehoshua	their son

	Mordechai	their son
	Moshe	their son
	Yaakov Yitzchak	the ritual slaughterer son-in-law of Reb Tovia
Stern	Yehuda	
	Pesel	his wife
	Teresa	their daughter
	Yechiel Michel	their son
Strum	Leila (Mendelson)	
Strum	Shimon	
	Dina	his wife
Strasburg	Shlomo	
Strasburg	Breindel (nee Taub)	his wife
	Yitzchak	their son
	Rozka	their daughter
Stern	Eliahu	and his family
Sheinfeld	Feiga (Yosles)	Mottel her son-in-law and his family
Sheinfeld	Avraham	
Sheinfeld	Yocheved (Yechet)	
Shilai	Reb Berish	the judge
	Freda	his wife
Schild	Chaim Yoskes	and his family
Shlesinger	Chaim	
	Yocheved	his wife
Shlesinger	Finia	their daughter married name Roth and her children
Shlesinger	Freda Ethel	
Shlesinger	Yona	
	Leitshe	his wife and their children
Shlesinger	Reuven	their son-in-law
	Chaitsha	his wife
Shlesinger	Chaim	
Shnur	Yitzchak	
	Chaya	his wife
	Dvora	their daughter and three other daughters
Shneeweis	Hershel	and his family
Shneeweis	Shmuel	and his family
Shnier	Getzel	and his wife
	Dolek	their son
	Yoel	their son
Shnier	Henek	and his family
	Rechke	
	Henke	
Shneps	Avish	
	Zelda	his wife
	Asher Chaim	their son
	Sara	their wife
	Yitzchak	their son
	Naftali	their son

Shneps	Moshe	the son of Avish
Shneps	Baruch	
	Sara Eidel	his wife
	Shmuel Reuven	their son
	Miriam	his wife
	Hela	their daughter
	Rachel	their daughter
Shneps	Ester Hershkowitz	and their son
	Moshe Hershkowitz	her husband
Shneps	Rechtsha, married name Maneh	
	Hersh Maneh	her husband
	Dvora Maneh	her wife
	Henech Maneh	their daughter
Shneps-Zilberman	Feiga	
	Yitzchak Zilberman	her son
	Moshe Zilberman	her son
Shneps	Hena	the son of Baruch
Shneps	Rivka	the daughter of Baruch
Shneps	Rachel	nee Kerner
Shneps	Feiga	her daughter, the children of Chaim may he live long
Shneps	Shaul	her son
Siedlisker	Leib	
Siedlisker	Sara Itta (Suzi)	his wife
	Mendel	their son
Siedlisker	Avraham	the son of Leib
	Duba	his wife
	Esther	their daughter
	Shmuel	their son
	Chana	their daughter

{page 201}

Siedlisker	Israel Aaron	
	Chanale	his wife
	Avraham	their son
	Tonka	their daughter
	Belka Shiowitz	their daughter
	Yosef	her husband
Siedlisker	Gedaliahu	
	Sara	his wife
	Hersh	their son
	Belka	their daughter
	Rivka	their daughter and another daughter
Shechter	Moshe	

	Golda	his wife
	Fela	their daughter
Shek	Avraham	
	Dvora (nee Taffet)	his wife
	Israel	their son
Sher	Yehuda	
	Esther	his wife
	Refael	their son
	Naftali	their daughter
Shrank	Miriam	
	Eidel	their daughter
	Golda	their daughter
	Beila	their daughter
	Chaya	their daughter
Shrank	Hersh	from Zaowade, his wife
	Berish	their son
	Henech	their son
	Shlomo Neimark	(the blind) the teacher and his wife
	Toive	their daughter

{p 203}

Addendum

Holocaust Righteous Gentiles Recognized by Debica

Jacek Dymitrowski

English Translation by Ireneusz Socha

Acting upon a motion by Towarzystwo Przyjaciol Ziemi Debickiej (Society of Friends of the Debica Region), The City Council of Debica has given the name of Aleksander and Leokadia Mikolajkow to a square located between the Gawrzylowski Brook and the City Public Library complex. The square is near the house in which the couple had saved the lives of 13 Jews during the World War II.

Aleksander and Leokadia Mikolajkow settled in Debica as a married couple in 1930. They had acquired the ownership of the house at 248, Kosciuszki Street. It was in there where their two sons – Leszek and Andrzej – were born. Both had been professionally engaged in the health care. He was a social insurance doctor; and she was a hygienist working for children and youth. Apart from the professional duties they were active in the Polish Red Cross. They did carry on like that until the outbreak of the WW2. The cruel wartime was to bring an eternal glory to them.

As soon as the German occupants had entered Debica, they immediately began to persecute both the Jews and the Polish intelligentsia. After a ghetto had been established in 1941, doctor Aleksander Mikolajkow employed a young boy named Efraim Reich as an office assistant and a messenger. As a result the boy was able to keep away – for some time at least – from imprisonment in the Debica ghetto. In July 1942, when the Germans began the first ghetto liquidation action, the doctor and his wife took Efraim's entire family in – upon his request.

That was contrary to the then occupation law. The Poles who kept Jews in hiding and the hidden Jews – as well as their entire families – were all subject to the death penalty on the Generalgouvernement territory. Despite the clear evidence, there are some people today defying the fact that 1/3 of all persons recognized as Righteous Among the Nations are Poles, and claiming that Poles could have saved much more Jews. I can answer the claims by reminding of the German regulation that provided that anyone who would hide Jews in the occupied Poland was subject to the death penalty – while, let us say, in the occupied France that was a fine totaling one-day salary. It is really hard for a normal individual to convert human life to a relatively small amount of money. Please bear in mind that the German occupants had encouraged Poles to denounce their Jewish neighbors by offering a high compensation, e.g. a one-kilo bag of sugar or a bottle of vodka, in exchange for a human life. Subsequently, there in fact were some mean individuals who out of greed, jealousy, envy or an ordinary human wickedness would denounce Jews and Poles to the Gestapo. The people, called "szmalcownicy", were later uncovered by proper units of the Home Army and judged severely by the Polish Underground State's tribunal that not infrequently would adjudicate the death penalty.

After the first liquidation action, the Germans posted up announcements saying, "Those who do not turn in the hidden Jews will be shot dead". Consequently, the Reichs had decided they would not endanger the Mikolajkows' lives and would go back to the ghetto immediately. But Dr. Mikolajkow said, "I am always willing to risk my life to save respectable and innocent people", and continued to keep them hidden for the next few days. After a few days, when the things had calmed down a little in the ghetto, the Reichs went back to it. In the meantime, Ms. Leokadia would bring some food to the Jews in the ghetto despite the fact that any Christian caught near the ghetto fence would also be shot dead.

The Jewish family was re-evacuated in November 1942, when the Germans began to prepare themselves to the second liquidation action. The Reichs had found a shelter in the Mikolajkow house again. After a few days they had returned to the ghetto once more. Happily, they were not to stay there long. Thanks to the nature of his profession and his interpersonal contacts, Dr. Mikolajkow had learned that yet another liquidation action was due towards the year's end. So it had to be the final evacuation. In a few days, the 13 members of the Reich family sneaked across the ghetto fence to the Mikolajkow house. Since that time, between December 1942 and the end of August 1944, the Reichs' shelter would in turn be an attic, a garage, a cellar and the attic again. Without access to light, running water and fresh air, they would stay hidden in complete darkness – sometimes up to the neck in rainwater that flooded the garage – under the immediate and permanent threat of uncovering, until the Red Army liberated Debica. To make things even more dreadful, all that time the Gestapo had its headquarters in a building next to the Mikolajkow house. After nine months, the Gestapo commandeered the doctor's garage to use it for their needs and consequently they did not give him much room for maneuver in his fugitive relocation efforts.

Evidently, Aleksander and Leokadia Mikolajkow were not able to bear the cost of supporting a group as large as that all by themselves. Nevertheless, they had never taken or demanded any money from the fugitives. Everything the Mikolajkows were doing for them, they were doing out of the goodness of their hearts. Happily, the Mikolajkows' efforts had been secretly supported by activists of the county branch of the nationwide charity organization called Central Welfare Council – headed by Princess Helena Jablonowska and Mr. Franciszek Sadowski – the principal of the local high school.

Moreover, Aleksander and Leokadia Mikolajkow were regularly helping the Jewish children who had survived the liquidation actions and were placing them in Polish orphanages. They were also engaged in some underground activity. When the Red Army was liberating Debica, the Home Army was in the middle of its nationwide military action called "The Storm". The height of the action's progress in our region was a battle the Home Army soldiers fought with the Germans in the Kaluzowka clearing. During the battle the Mikolajkows had been medically supporting the area.

It may be deemed a historical paradox that on the very same day that the 13 members of the Reich family were saved, their benefactor was killed. Aleksander Mikolajkow's body was allegedly found by his son Leszek first and then by his wife Leokadia. It still cannot be resolved today, who had fired the bullet that actually hit him: a Soviet or a German soldier? Anyway, please bear in mind that it was a time when everyone was shooting at everything that moved. Dr. Mikolajkow was buried in the Old Cemetery in Debica. An inscription on his tombstone says, "He lived and died serving his neighbors". Yet the most beautiful epitaph was written and published in the New York Post by the saved young Efraim Reich in 1960, "I remember the anniversary of his death every year. I believe in life after death, and I believe that Dr. Mikolajkow is one of the greats there. If there are still people like him around, the world will have to become a better place at last."

After his death, the widow had to obtain a livelihood all by herself and her life was full of humbling experiences. Actually, she had suffered the worst humiliation of all when the government of the United States turned her visa application down despite a special invitation sent in by the New York Jews. In the meantime, the same government would keenly welcome some ex-Nazi experts. Upon several petitions, when Ms. Mikolajkow had finally been allowed to the U.S., the ultimate tribute was paid to the great woman. The Jews had stopped the traffic to greet her, then they put her into a limo and pulled it by tow ropes along the main street by hand among the cheering crowds. Israel had also remembered the heroic couple. The Israeli parliament had awarded the state's supreme decoration for non-Jews, that is the "Righteous Among the Nations" medal, to her and her husband posthumously. Two trees had been planted in their honor around the Yad Vashem Institute site.

The young Efraim Reich had undergone a spiritual metamorphosis in the occupation hell. A happy-go-lucky young man had turned into a man of immense faith. He had become a rabbi in New York and then he left for Israel where he lives and teaches to this day.

On January 31, 2006, at its 35th session, the City Council of Debica did approve the petition submitted by the Society of Friends of the Debica Region and it gave the name of Aleksander and Leokadia Mikolajkow to the square located between Kazimierz Wielki Square, Rzeszowska Street, Gawrzylowski Brook (earlier known as Debica Brook) and Solidarity Square. This is a great news that will help rescue the eminent individuals from oblivion among Debica residents today. It is all the more so since the historic building, that once was the scene of the events described above, has recently been designated for demolition. It must be added that the building is located in the immediate neighborhood of the aforementioned square. One must certainly recognize the road communication needs of our fellow residents but nevertheless one must also bear in mind that it was just the communication needs that once persuaded the authorities of the city of Krakow to demolish the old city walls. Not infrequently, the present day descendants of the councilmen kick themselves when foreign tourists (Poles are not as naïve as this) happen to ask, "What's the name of the invaders who have wreaked such havoc in the cultural heritage of the city?"

Perhaps a cheaper way (note that one has to provide substitute accommodation for all of the current residents) would be to move the building and lay it on new foundations 5-6 meters away? That manner of operation would help save the nearly 100-year-old building that surely may not be considered an outstanding architectural relic but admittedly is one of the town's existing monuments of the tragic history of the 20th century. Some proper promotional activities may make the house known globally as a symbol of our town as well as of its residents' dedication. It is already the most recognizable Debica building among visitors from the U.S. and Israel.

However, if Debica residents – by the agency of their City Council representatives – choose to demolish the house anyway, one should place a memorial plaque with a proper description of the dramatic events in there.

Memory of the likes of Aleksander and Leokadia Mikolajkow should be retained for ever. Thanks to people like them we may still pass the tale of goodness and humanity on to next generations. And we are thankful to them for this.

The author is a historian and the president of the TPZD.

The article was published in the Obserwator Lokalny Weekly No. 6 (287) in Debica, Poland on February 11, 2006

Reprinted here with permission of Jacek Dymitrowski.

Introduction to the Polish Translation
Debica Yizkor Book

We are indeed fortunate to be able to present a Polish translation of selected chapters of this yizkor book. There are many people to thank for this collaboration: Ireneusz Socha, who proposed the translation and who translated from the English to Polish; Jacek Dymitrowski, President, TPZD; Marc Seidenfeld, Project Manager of the Debica Yizkor Book Translation, and Mr. Meir Goldman, of the Dembica Landsmannschaft in Israel. All agreed that this was a worthwhile project and cooperated in its implementation.

TPZD, Towarzystwo Przyjaciół Ziemi Dębickiej, is translated into English as Friends of Debica Region Society. Its membership consists of historians, artists, and journalists who are preparing a book on the history and culture of Jews from Debica. This bi-lingual book will include some chapters from the Debica yizkor book. It was agreed that permission to use chapters from Sefer Dembitz would be given to TPZD and that the Polish translation would be donated to JewishGen so that it can appear alongside the English translation.

We wish the TPZD success with their book. The group is eager to correspond with former Dembitzers who would like to share their reminiscences.

Joyce Field, Emerita Yizkor Book Project Manager, May 2005

{Page 202}

Translation from English to Polish

Translated by Ireneusz Socha

Introduction to the Polish Translation

Debica Yizkor Book

I am very pleased to announce that the Scientific Publishing House of the Society of Friends of Sciences in Przemysl is releasing the first Polish edition of "The Book of Dembitz" in 2014. The Polish edition's full title reads "The Book of Dembitz. The Cradle of our Youth – Memories of the Jewish Residents of Debica". I prepared this edition together with Arkadiusz S. Wiech – a professional historian. We worked two years to complete the book. The volume includes all chapters from the original edition in my translation and a historical essay by Arkadiusz. The book comes with a selection of some rare and highly interesting prewar photographs and a dictionary of Jewish religion and culture.

It was not until 1999 that I found out that the Sefer Dembitz had existed. I simply discovered it when researching the Internet on the history of the Jewish community in Debica, Poland. At first, a few chapters from the book were translated to English and made available by JewishGen, Inc. online. Those were texts completely unknown in Poland: so revealing and captivating in their own right. I kept reading them, looking forward to each new chapter over the years. I had made a decision to translate that book into Polish one day. All the more so none of Polish historians had cared for commemorating Dembitzer Jews back then.

In the beginning, I contacted Joyce Field – the then coordinator of the Yizkor Books Project – and told her I wanted to translate the book. She agreed and was very helpful and cooperative. I began my work in 2004 by translating two texts: "The City and its rabbis" and "The Baking of Matza Shmura". I never received or asked for any remuneration. I did it pro bono, in accordance with the principles JewishGen adheres to.

Later that year I met Jacek Dymitrowski, the chairman of Society of Friends of the Land of Debica (TPZD), whom I tried to convince that Dembitzer Jews were a great topic for a book. I informed him about the Sefer Dembitz and gave him my first two translations, suggesting he might use them in the book. Also, thanks to my initiative and help, an agreement was signed based on which JewishGen granted TPZD permission to use those two chapters in the forthcoming book. The plan was even mentioned in the American edition of the Time Magazine in the article by Marjorie Backman entitled "Books of Life" (May 5, 2004). Unfortunately, TPZD's book has not been published yet. However, I did continue to work on the translation. Chapter by chapter, Polish language versions began to appear online on this website. I did it in my free time, so it took a very long time – ten years. But I finally made it.

I would like to express special thanks to the people who offered their precious comments and knowledge and encouraged me to complete my work over the past ten years: Joyce Field – Emerita Yizkor Book Project Manager, Lance Ackerfeld – Yizkor Book Project Manager, Marc Seidenfeld and Aviva Weintraub – The Book of Dembitz Project Coordinators and last but not least Oded Golan and Israel Salmon from Irgun Yotsey Debica be-Yisrael.

Ireneusz Socha, July 2014

Note: Those of you interested in purchasing a copy of "Księga Dębicy" may contact the publisher at: tpntpn@wp.pl

Wstęp do tłumaczenia na język polski
Księga Dębicy

Z radością informuję, że w 2014 r. Wydawnictwo Naukowe Towarzystwa Przyjaciół Nauk w Przemyślu opublikuje „Księgę Dębicy". Jest to pierwsze wydanie w języku polskim. Pełny tytuł książki brzmi: „Księga Dębicy. Kolebka naszej młodości – wspomnienia żydowskich mieszkańców Dębicy". Przygotowałem ją wespół z zawodowym historykiem – Arkadiuszem S. Więchem. Prace redakcyjne zabrały nam dwa lata. Tom zawiera wszystkie rozdziały oryginału (w moim tłumaczeniu) oraz esej historyczny pióra Arkadiusza. W książce znalazły się również niezwykle rzadkie i interesujące fotografie sprzed II wojny światowej oraz słowniczek terminów związanych z religią i kulturą żydowską.

O tym, że taka książka, jak „Sefer Dembitz", istnieje, dowiedziałem się w roku 1999, przeczesując zasoby internetu w poszukiwaniu materiałów na temat historii gminy żydowskiej w Dębicy. Organizacja JewishGen opublikowała wówczas na swoich stronach internetowych kilka jej rozdziałów przetłumaczonych na angielski. Były to teksty w polskiej historiografii nieznane i niezwykłe – ich lektura wciągnęła mnie bez reszty. Czytałem je, czekając na każdy kolejny rozdział nieraz przez cały rok. Postanowiłem, że przetłumaczę tę książkę na język polski, gdyż wówczas żaden z historyków nie zajmował się zachowaniem i popularyzacją pamięci o dębickich Żydach.

W tym celu skontaktowałem się z Joyce Field – ówczesną koordynatorką „Yizkor Books Project". Pracę nad przekładem rozpocząłem w roku 2004. Wówczas powstały polskie wersje dwóch tekstów: „The City and its rabbis" („Dębiccy rabini") oraz „The Baking of Matza Shmura" („Pieczenie strzeżonej macy"). Za pracę tłumacza – i na początku, i później, aż do samego końca – nie pobierałem żadnego wynagrodzenia: robiłem to bezinteresownie, pro publico bono, zgodnie z pryncypiami, którym hołduje JewishGen.

W owym czasie zacząłem rozmawiać z prezesem Towarzystwa Przyjaciół Ziemi Dębickiej (TPZD), Jackiem Dymitrowskim, o potrzebie napisania pierwszej monografii o Żydach dębickich. Przekazałem mu również informację o istnieniu strony, gdzie można przeczytać angielskie tłumaczenie kilku rozdziałów „Sefer Dembitz" i dałem mu moje pierwsze przekłady z tej księgi. Towarzystwo podjęło decyzję, aby rozpocząć pracę nad wspomnianą monografią. W tomie miały się znaleźć dwa, wymienione wyżej rozdziały z „Sefer Dembitz" w moim tłumaczeniu. Dzięki mojej inicjatywie i pośrednictwu, na mocy umowy, JewishGen udzieliło TPZD pozwolenia na wykorzystanie tych rozdziałów w przygotowywanej książce. O planowanej książce wspomniano nawet w amerykańskim wydaniu tygodnika „Time" z 5 maja 2004 r., w artykule Marjorie Backman „Books of Life". Niestety, planowana przez TPZD książka nie powstała. Ja jednak nie poprzestałem na dwóch rozdziałach i kontynuowałem pracę nad przekładem. Tłumaczyłem w wolnych chwilach, dlatego trwało to bardzo długo, bo aż 10 lat. Ale dokończyłem dzieła

Pragnę gorąco podziękować osobom, które w ciągu ostatnich dziesięciu lat dzieliły się ze mną swoimi cennymi uwagami i wiedzą oraz zachęcały mnie do ukończenia pracy nad przekładem: Joyce Field, Lance'owi Ackerfeldowi, Markowi Seidenfeldowi, Avivie Weintraub, Odedowi Golanowi oraz Israelowi Salmonowi.

Ireneusz Socha, lipiec 2014

Księga Dębicy

Translated by Ireneusz Socha

Niniejsza księga została opublikowana dzięki staraniom organizacji byłych mieszkańców Dębicy, którzy wyemigrowali do Izraela. Organizacja ta została założona w roku 5711 (1950-1951). Jej członkami są: Ruchama Bornstein, Jehuda Grünspan, Fruma Grosman (Salomon), Pinchas Sommer, Aka (Rywka) Zilbershatz, Aszer Salomon, Jicchak Freiman, Rywka Shenker, Matylda Siedlisker, Ruben Siedlisker oraz Chaim Shneps, a zorganizował ją Daniel Leibel.

„ Księga Dębicy" jest próbą odmalowania miasta takim, jakim naprawdę było – bez jakiejkolwiek cenzury wynikającej z pobudek ideologicznych. Księga nie ma ambicji wyczerpania tematu. Wystarczy, jeśli będzie pamiątką miejscowości, w której się urodziliśmy oraz pomnikiem żydowskiego życia, które zostało przecięte przez wroga.

Eseje i zestawienia są po hebrajsku lub w jidysz, czyli w językach, w jakich zostały oryginalnie napisane, z wyjątkiem otwierającego księgę rozdziału nt. historii gminy oraz końcowego rozdziału o Holocauście – oba są i po hebrajsku, i w jidysz.

Wydano nakładem oficyny „Achdut", Tel Awiw

Spis treści
Translated by Ireneusz Socha

INDEX

T

www.ingramcontent.com/pod-product-compliance
Lightning Source LLC
Chambersburg PA
CBHW050407110426

42812CB00006BA/1826

9 781939 561350